CREATING AMERICAN CIVILIZATION

A M E R I C A N C U L T U R E

Cutting across traditional boundaries between the human and social sciences, volumes in the American Culture series study the multiplicity of cultural practices from theoretical, historical, and ethnographic perspectives by examining culture's production, circulation, and consumption.

Edited by Stanley Aronowitz, Nancy Fraser, and George Lipsitz

CREATING AMERICAN CIVILIZATION

A Genealogy of American Literature as an Academic Discipline

DAVID R. SHUMWAY

American Culture, volume 11

University of Minnesota Press

Minneapolis London

Published by the University of Minnesota Press
2037 University Avenue Southeast, Minneapolis, MN 55455-3092
Printed in the United States of America on acid-free paper

Library of Congress Cataloging-in-Publication Data

Shumway, David R.
   Creating American civilization : a genealogy of American literature as an academic discipline / David R. Shumway.
      p.   cm. — (American culture ; v. 11)
   Includes bibliographical references (p.) and index.
   ISBN 0-8166-2188-8 (alk. paper). — ISBN 0-8166-2189-6 (pbk. : alk. paper)
   1. American literature—Study and teaching—United States—History.   2. American literature—History and criticism—Theory, etc.   3. United States—Civilization—Study and teaching.   4. Canon (Literature)   I. Title.   II. Series: American culture (Minneapolis, Minn.) ; 11.
   PS41.S48   1994
   810'.7'073—dc20   93-27477
                                                                             CIP

For Robert C. Shumway and Harriet Melcher Shumway

Before we have an American literature,
we must have an American criticism.
James Russell Lowell

Contents

Acknowledgments

I've been working on the scholarship discussed in this book off and on since I was an undergraduate, so my debts go back a long way. I first read Matthiessen, Lewis, and Lawrence's *Studies* while studying under C. Roland Wagner, and conversations with him started me in the direction of this project. In the American Studies Program at Indiana University when I did graduate work there in the 1970s, the discipline I describe in chapter 9 was very much the dominant practice. Christoph Lohmann helped enable me to evade that practice and to pursue work that got me further down the road.

In the early 1980s, when I was teaching at Miami University, Jim Sosnoski encouraged several of us interested in the institution of literary studies to form a collaborative research group that soon became known as the GRIP Project. Sosnoski's idea has blossomed into an international circle concerned with knowledge production in general. But it was during those first few years in Oxford, Ohio, that I figured out that there was something interesting to be said about the history of American studies. It is safe to say that were it not for GRIP I would not have written *Creating American Civilization*. Many who have participated in GRIP are acknowledged below, but there are many others to whom I can only thank as a group.

My obligations to people who have written about the history of American literature studies begin with Richard Ruland, whose book *The Rediscovery of American Literature* showed me as a graduate student that the history of criticism had a cultural context. Kermit Vanderbilt's research provided me with much information that I would not have been able to discover on my own. I wrote the first outline of this book after having read a draft of Gerald Graff's *Professing Literature*, a book I admired all the more for leaving me an opening. My disagreements with each of these scholars do not diminish my debts. My thinking about the history of the disciplines of American literature and English has benefited from the work of Nina Baym, Paul Lauter, Richard Ohmann, Russell Reising, and Jane Tompkins.

Among those who took the time to discuss or argue with me about this project or who were willing to share their knowledge, I want to thank Jim Berlin, Louis Budd, Tim Conley, Arthur Geffin, Giles Gunn, Greg Jay, Ronald Judy, Geraldine Murphy, Lee Quinby, Amos St. Germain, Alan Trachtenberg, and Evan Watkins. Students in seminars I have offered on English as a discipline have contributed to this project, especially Craig Dionne, Sally Magargee, and Karen O'Kane.

I am lucky to have had the support and encouragement of friends and colleagues Ellen Messer-Davidow, Peter Copek, Alan Kennedy, Khachig Tololyan, and Ellen Rooney. I am profoundly grateful to those who took the time to read this book in earlier stages. Liahna Babener, Brian McHale, and Dana Polan read and commented on most of the manuscript, and it is immeasurably better for their efforts. Jim Creech, Gerald Graff, Peggy Knapp, Judith Modell, and Khachig Tololyan offered helpful comments on shorter sections. Series editors Stanley Aronowitz and George Lipsitz and press reader Donald Pease offered important criticism and advice.

Thanks for research assistance at various stages go to Craig Dionne and Shea Wilson. I am grateful to the librarians at the Jay B. Hubbell Center, William R. Perkins Library, Duke University for their assistance. Thanks also to John Stuhr, Molly Hite, and Douglas Lanier who invited me to present some of this material at their institutions.

The Center for the Humanities, Oregon State University, offered me a fellowship that enabled me to begin writing and to

Acknowledgments

complete about a third of the manuscript. A Faculty Development
Grant from Carnegie Mellon University helped to defray the costs
of travel and research.

The usual disclaimers apply.

Pittsburgh
February 1993

Introduction:
The History of a Discipline

Why? Simply because I am interested in the past? No, if one means by that writing a history of the past in terms of the present. Yes, if one means writing the history of the present.

Michel Foucault

We usually think of academic disciplines as associated with particular subject matters, defined worlds of objects that academic fields more or less successfully seek to represent as knowledge. Members of the profession and the public at large normally think about "American literature" as the novels, poems, plays, and some special works of nonfiction prose written by Americans, things to be investigated, studied, interpreted, like other things. We are most of the time convinced that American literature has as much an independent existence as a rock or tree. It is the premise of this book that although it is possible to think of all of the writing in certain genres produced in the United States as "American literature," the term in critical or scholarly practice has never meant that. Rather, "American literature" has always meant a small selection of writings produced in this country. When we think of American literature we are unlikely to think of *Ben Hur* or *Deadwood Dick in Leadville*, but we are likely to think of *The Great Gatsby* or *Moby-Dick*. Moreover, what has counted as American literature has changed. In 1900, *Moby-Dick* would not have been recognized by many as American literature; those who

1

did recognize it as such would not have accorded it a privileged position. Not only are different works and authors included or excluded at different historical moments, but the entire category has shifted its meaning. American literature is not in any meaningful sense an independent object to be investigated, but something dependent for its identity on the institutions that deal with it.

In many respects, literature differs from other potential objects of research in that it implies a prior evaluation. Imagine a discipline devoted to the study not of all rocks and minerals, as is geology, but of only pretty rocks.[1] Still, even disciplines like geology don't deal with natural objects. Plain old objects, things that simply exist in the world, do not lend themselves to organized research programs. They are always too complicated, not necessarily in themselves, but in their very embeddedness in human experience. The modern organization of knowledge removes things from this experience. For example, the significant difference between the prescientific books about nature of the fifteenth and sixteenth centuries and the first natural history of the seventeenth century is what the latter leaves out: categories such as legends, medicinal uses, and biblical mention.[2] What we today think of as "literature" is also the product of a systematic reduction from all that is written to works of a certain value, especially fiction, poetry, and drama. But a disciplinary object is not defined merely by what it excludes. It also has a positive set of characteristics on which research is focused.

The academic field of American literature, like all other academic disciplines, constituted its own object of investigation. The object that disciplinary inquiry addresses is not available independently of disciplinary language and practice. At one level, this means that physical things—rocks or muscle fibers or literary texts—are understood differently by practitioners in different disciplines. In a larger sense, each discipline constitutes an idealized object that is the domain of its investigation. A discipline's object has only the properties and attributes that fit the discipline's assumptions. The object of history, for example, has traditionally included war and politics, but excluded much of the rest of what happened in the past. While historians work most often with texts as their sources of evidence, the texts themselves are not the object of the discipline. The assumptions of the discipline of history render the text a mere medium for facts or information. If interpretations of historical documents became the preoccupation of historians, interpretations of historical events might well be permanently deferred. The object constituted by the discipline embodies the assumptions of the discipline, without those assumptions being made available for reflection. The disciplinary object appears to members of a discipline engaged in their normal practice as entirely natural and independent.[3] It is only by stepping back from such normal practice that we can begin to become aware of what the discipline takes for granted. A historical perspective is one way to get a purchase on the disciplinary practice in which one is normally engaged in the present. Traditionally, however, histories of scientific disciplines have most often focused on ideas that paved the way for major discoveries or on the *men* who made these discoveries. These histories have usually been offered as explanations of a field's success at discovering truth or as justifications for its claims to such discovery. Histories of disciplines, whether of sciences or humanities, usually tell stories of progress in ideas. One theory is held to replace another in the sciences because it is a more accurate representation of the world and in the humanities because it is aesthetically, epistemologically, or morally better.

While traditional histories of the natural sciences sometimes acknowledge the influence of institutional or cultural events, in these histories such external forces can only speed up or slow down the process of change within the discipline and can never be determining factors in such change. In this conception, cultural and institutional history can have no significant relationship to disciplinary history. Disciplinary history itself is essentially irrelevant to the conduct of the discipline. Its only purpose is to justify current activity in the field. Thus the natural sciences have tended to swallow their own histories. History was least interesting here because there was less need for such justification. In the humanities, competing schools of theory and practice could use history to legitimate their positions. Such histories have rarely claimed to be histories of disciplines, but histories of ideas. The histories of literary criticism produced in the twentieth century have usually treated in chronological order the work of major

3

critics. Most such histories have until recently ignored the cultural and institutional setting of criticism, as well as the massive enterprise of literary education. As in the histories of other disciplines, the professions and institutions producing and disseminating knowledge have been regarded as entirely external to the knowledge itself. History tends to disappear in these works because criticism is treated as a timeless essence, essentially the same for Aristotle as for Roland Barthes.

In the past few years, however, the marginality of disciplinary history has begun to lessen. The history of the formations of knowledge has become more important as a result of theorists such as Thomas Kuhn, Michel Foucault, and others, who have argued that knowledge is socially produced and historically contingent. Starting from these assumptions, an investigation into the formation of a body of knowledge cannot remain internal to the content of that discipline, but must take into account cultural, institutional, and professional influences. In literary studies, several recent histories, including Kermit Vanderbilt's *American Literature and the Academy: The Roots, Growth, and Maturity of a Profession* and Gerald Graff's *Professing Literature: An Institutional History*, have proclaimed themselves histories of professions—meaning that they will not only devote attention to the ideas or intellectual contributions of the fields they discuss, but will try to understand those fields in the context of institutional conditions.[4] Vanderbilt's history remains largely internal to the discipline while Graff's is more or less external to it.[5] In spite of Vanderbilt's concern for the professional side of academic life, his book is in the tradition of the histories of sciences that have as their goal the demonstration of the field's success. Vanderbilt has not set out to justify any particular set of ideas about American literature, but rather to show how the field became a significant academic enterprise. He uses the metaphor of organic development to frame his story of a profession's rise to "maturity," suggesting that there is a natural growth pattern common to academic enterprises. Although Vanderbilt is not a historian of ideas, and discusses in great detail the ways in which scholars worked together to write collaborative histories, to start academic journals, and to build learned societies, he does not draw more than incidental connections between these activities and the knowledge they produced. Thus, while Vanderbilt presents an immense amount of useful information, much of which is highly revealing of the political dynamics of the discipline, his determination to see the story as one of progressive development prevents him from even entertaining differing conclusions that might be drawn from the facts. Graff avoids the pitfalls of such progressive accounts by shifting the focus to unresolved conflicts rather than an emergent consensus. His book is focused on a series of debates that have occurred throughout the history of literary studies in America (he devotes only one chapter to American literature studies) over the proper nature and mission of such studies. Graff notes that these debates sometimes occur in response to larger cultural or social conditions. His main point, however, is that these conflicts have been relegated to the margins of the profession's teaching and publication, even though they represent what is most vital within the field. Thus, although Graff is often concerned with the political dimensions of the conflicts he recounts, his analysis tends to stress their bearing on professional questions rather than their larger social context. And in focusing on what might be called the profession's self-reflexive writing, Graff quite properly takes for granted the "literature" that English professors studied and taught. Moreover, in spite of their focus on professionalism, neither Graff nor Vanderbilt (nor anyone else) has studied American literature as a *discipline.*

There is a need for a history that confronts rather than marginalizes the impact of the institutional formation and cultural context of the discipline on the knowledge that it produces, a history that puts into question the naturalness of its object of study and attempts to assess the work the discipline performs within American society. I have tried to show how American literature as a discipline (or, properly speaking, a subdiscipline) of English has adapted to changing macro- and microsocial arrangements. To use Fuller's terms, my history is not Panglossian, and it is therefore noncanonical (309). I don't believe that there is an epistemological condition, an essential subject matter, or a transcendental mission upon which the discipline is founded—or that it has failed to recognize. My goal is neither to justify nor to reform the field, but to understand how its history has shaped it. It is in this sense that *Creating American Civilization* is a history of the

5

present. The current field of American literature—which is not itself my subject—can only be understood in relation to its history.
That is because the knowledge itself, the field at its most fundamental level, is historically contingent. This knowledge has a
history that cannot be subsumed under a narrative of progress or
of failed progress. Though the knowledge the field is currently
producing is partially determined by its present temporal context,
it is also both restricted and made possible by its history.

A discipline is not a passive receptacle for outside influences,
but is itself an active force in the culture. One of my main tasks,
then, is to explain the cultural work the academic field of American literature has performed. My argument is that the discipline's
most significant achievement was to secure for Americans a belief
in their success as a culture. I call this achievement the "creation
of American civilization." The discipline, in other words, produced a widely accepted representation of American civilization
that not only defined its character but "verified" its existence.
This ideological project doubtless began to be pursued from the
first days of the discipline's establishment, but a great variety of
other forces and motives would shape its history. *Creating
American Civilization* will offer no single, all-encompassing explanation for the development of the discipline. Neither the Marxist conception of historical materialism nor the Foucaul-
dian/Nietzschean notion of genealogy as the "endlessly repeated
play of dominations" is adequate as a totalizing principle.[6] Still
less adequate are the usual inductive assumptions of historians
that lead them to believe that documenting the words and deeds
of leading or representative individuals in enough detail will produce the truth. The shape American literature took as an academic
field cannot be explained solely on the basis of nationalism in the
larger culture, for example, nor, to mention a different extreme,
solely in terms of arguments over whether the romance has a special importance in American literary history. American literature
was shaped by conflicts at all levels on the scale from microcosm
to macrocosm. In order to reveal that range of forces, I have focused on different ones in different chapters. I thus make no claim
to tell a complete history, whatever that could be.

It is partly in recognition of this incompleteness that I have
called *Creating American Civilization* a "genealogy." It recog-

nizes also that history is not continuous development that can be charted as events. The study of American literature has neither an origin nor a telos. It may seem at points that I treat the creation of American civilization or the "discovery" of the unity and distinctiveness of American literature as a telos for the field. But I do not claim that there is any ahistorical or essential nature of literary study that drives its development. Rather, the particular conception of literature and its relation to culture that emerges in the nineteenth century made the project of inventing a tradition necessary. American writing could have been constituted in an infinite number of other forms, but it would not then have looked like literature. Literature was valuable, while mere writing was not.

The chapters that follow trace the constitution and reconstitution of the object of American literature by examining the discipline's practices and techniques, discourses and structures, paradigms and unstated assumptions. My focus is on research practices as revealed in publications of scholarly articles and books. I have also been concerned with pedagogic and curricular practices, but I have not treated these in as much detail, because a discipline, as I understand it, is dedicated to the production of knowledge, so that under the disciplinary model, transmission of knowledge becomes a mere means to further production.[7] If I were dealing with one of the disciplines of the natural sciences, such an approach would be uncontested. Indeed, it is only recently that science studies has begun to consider transmission in a serious way. On the other hand, the humanities have often been understood as being in the business of preserving and transmitting works and the values supposedly contained in them. Such an understanding of the humanities has served since the 1880s to explain to the academy and to the public the importance of teaching and research in literature, but it was never sufficient to the task. This was especially true within the university, where the disciplinary model was hegemonic. For literary studies to be recognized there, it would have to produce knowledge. Early scholars in English, however, did not regard this as an onerous burden imposed on them from the outside. On the contrary, they made the study of literature a discipline out of their own commitment to science and research.

Even critical students of the humanities are likely to assume that the history of a discipline means mainly the story of changing ideas, theories, paradigms, or discourses. Each of these terms, were it to become central, might produce a different history. My own focus on the constitution of the disciplinary object can be more illuminating because it does not entail the conscious awareness of practitioners usually implicit in discussions of ideas or theories, nor the particulars of Kuhn's conception of science, nor the restriction to surface meanings sometimes implied in uses of the term "discourse." Moreover, the disciplinary object is not assumed to be produced merely in the heads or in the writings of scholars.

This book is nevertheless to some extent a history of ideas. Ideas do change, do have influence, do perform work in the world and, hence, ideas about American literature are very much my concern. It would be unsatisfactory to deal exclusively with the metadiscourse of the discipline, because its ideological work is often accomplished by explicitly enunciated ideas. On the other hand, I have tried to avoid writing the kind of cultural history that would itself serve to create or recreate American civilization. I have therefore not sought to explain the creation of American civilization in terms of longterm cultural continuities or exceptional American conditions. While such a conception of culture has been widely criticized in recent years, it has remained operative even in the work of some of its critics. For example, "pragmatism" has become in many studies a new way to name what distinguishes American culture, a conception that seems to reproduce American exceptionalism.[8] Even as critical a student of American culture as Cornel West seems to succumb to this temptation when he creates a tradition of "pragmatists" running from Emerson to Lionel Trilling, all of whom evade epistemology.[9] Pragmatism is doubtless an important American contribution to knowledge, but I believe that it is best understood as a movement proper to (and to some extent subversive of) the discipline of philosophy, a discipline that neither Emerson nor Trilling practiced. In any event, most academic Americanists had little use for John Dewey and his ilk. The most important systems of ideas in the constitution of American literature were those such as the new humanism, which arose out of literary study in the university, and

8

those such as positivism, which were underlying assumptions of the research university itself.

The formation and mutation of the field does need to be understood as responding to forces in the larger culture. But the most important of those forces are not conscious ideas but economic and political interests and the ideologies that served them. The constitution of American literature as a field served the interests of particular factions within the profession and those of the dominant class, race, and gender within American society. As a result, race, class, and gender bias were structural to the object the discipline constituted in the 1920s, and remained so as the object was reconstituted after World War II. Disciplines are by their specific historical constitution exclusionary. They use the power to exclude to punish those who violate their discursive limits, but they also use their institutionally sanctioned power to exclude in advance those who do not seem "normal." Historically, those Others of academic disciplines have included, to one degree or another, Jews, women, African Americans, and the working class. I hope that my own study will not be read as continuing this exclusion in its focus on the dominant. I have acknowledged emergent forces where I have discovered them, but the simple fact is that before the late 1960s the academic study of literature was not rife with emergent forces. Not only did WASP males dominate membership in the discipline, but most of the authors it studied were white men as well. Even more than literary criticism outside of the academy, the discipline excluded most female authors and virtually all African-American, non-English-speaking, or other minority authors. The Harlem renaissance flourished during the 1920s, but academic Americanists took no note of it until perhaps the 1960s. Of course, they took little note of any contemporary literature until after World War II, but a few leading white poets and novelists were discussed earlier. The point here is that the exclusion of women, African Americans, or other minorities was not done in the face of any pressure to include them. The virtual absence of black scholars and the general marginalization of women Ph.D.s into teaching institutions or composition slots meant that there was no organized opposition to white male hegemony. Even outside of the academy, feminists did not seem to regard literary criticism as a high priority. Gertrude Stein, Amy Lowell, and Mary Austin all contributed some work that might be regarded as feminist criticism, but it hardly represents a movement and it had no impact on the discipline. There were African-American literary critics, including W. E. B. Du Bois, but as far as I have been able to discern, they were completely ignored by white academics. It is wishful thinking to assume that there was significant opposition to the racism and sexism structural to the discipline during the entire period of this study.

But the effects of larger social conditions and political interests do not explain everything about the discipline. In order to understand how the object of American literature gets formed and reformed, it is necessary to consider the institutional conditions under which disciplinary practice occurred. I am therefore interested in aspects of academic life that we usually name "professional" rather than strictly disciplinary, though in my view they are integral to the modern academic discipline. The "discipline" is a historically specific form of knowledge production that is made possible by the strategies and techniques of power Michel Foucault describes in *Discipline and Punish*.[10] The departmental form of organization, the modern learned society, and the academic journal all serve to make individual professors subject to the normalizing power of the academic discipline. They also enable the discipline to resist the control of the university and to produce vastly increased quantities of knowledge.

The modern academic disciplines are the product of the nineteenth century; in the United States, they developed simultaneously with the research university. For this reason, it would be incorrect for one to speak of a discipline of English existing prior to the 1880s, though certain elements of what became English were taught and studied earlier. Prior to this, literature as it came to be understood within English was not normally taught or studied in American colleges. Students were instructed in classical languages and in rhetoric, but not in the reading or history of literature. Such teaching was aimed neither at the production of knowledge nor at that new knowledge producers.

Even after English became a discipline, however, American literature was far more often discussed outside the university. Such criticism or histories of American literature were also non-disciplinary. The genealogy of American literature as an academic field cannot deal merely with what goes on in the academy, however, for the field is produced by relations between disciplinary practitioners and various nondisciplinary groups. Because important nondisciplinary critics continued to publish throughout the period I am discussing here, the field was shaped by the need for academic Americanists to assert authority over their field. They thus sought to establish disciplinary boundaries to protect their turf against other disciplines and against nonacademic literary criticism. Like other forms of professionalism, the academic discipline must compete for control of work: "Control of knowledge and its application means dominating outsiders who attack that control. Control without competition is trivial."[11] My interest in the men of letters, the literary radicals, the Nashville and New York intellectuals, and other critics who worked outside the academy is not merely a matter of their intellectual influence. Their very presence shaped the discipline by forcing academic Americanists to compete.

As a study of a discipline, however, *Creating American Civilization* is not a history of criticism. It could not be, because criticism was not the standard practice of the discipline throughout most of the period it covers. While the modern practice of criticism can be traced well back into the nineteenth century, criticism did not become a standard academic practice until after World War II. On the other hand, the history of criticism of American literature is relevant to my subject, and bits of it are told here. But I have made no effort to tell the complete story. Thus some publicly influential nonacademic critics—Edmund Wilson and Malcolm Cowley are two—have been given little or no mention because in my view their criticism was not a significant influence on the way American literature got constituted in the academy. Because I am interested less in opinions about individual authors than in conceptions of American literature as a whole, I have not discussed the many critics whose major contributions to the field are studies of single authors.

The history of a discipline must be a history of the various practices conducted in its name. Such practices do change and different ones may coexist at a given moment, but they all tend to be shaped by the disciplinary environment. One characteristic of disciplinary knowledge formations is that, although such formations restrict what may count as knowledge, the production of that knowledge is in principle an unending task. Moreover (and as a result), such knowledge does not result in unified beliefs or theories but in increasingly disparate statements of fact or hypothesis. Thus the knowledge that the discipline of American literature produced was not unified but dispersed. Although it constituted an object to be investigated, in neither of its two forms did its investigations lead to a unified body of knowledge; rather, what resulted was dispersed statements of historical fact or textual interpretation. In order to get at that dispersion, one is forced to look at the routine and ordinary practice of scholarship. This does not mean the neglect of works of major figures but a concentration on the contents of professional journals, text-books, anthologies, and forgotten histories. While I have told a story of conflict, I have focused on dominant products and prac-tices. The works of the brilliant but marginal are not my concern. Certain "monuments" do emerge: the major collective literary histories, for example, and disciplinary exemplars such as Mat-thiessen's *American Renaissance*. In dealing with this material, my object is not to describe the meetings and the plans that led to its being written, as Kermit Vanderbilt, for example, has done, but to discover the conditions of its possibility. The focus is not mainly on the ideas proclaimed and disputed, but on apparently insignificant truths taken for granted by virtually all participants. The point is to show that such truths are not the natural condi-tions they appear to be, but rather are culturally produced under the particular conditions of the period.

Perhaps the most taken-for-granted "truth" of the discipline of American literature was literature itself, a timeless category con-sidered the natural outgrowth of language under the conditions of advanced human civilizations. Today, on the other hand, the argument that literature is a relatively recent invention is well known.[12] The basic claim is that only during the nineteenth cen-tury did "literature" come to mean imaginative writing—mainly fiction, poetry, and drama—of enduring value. According to Ray-mond Williams, when "literature" was first used in English in the fourteenth century, it was "a condition of reading: of being able to read and of having read. It was often close to the sense of the modern "literacy," which was not in the language until the late nineteenth century." "Literature" differed from "poetry" as a general term for imaginative writing in that it designated something to be read, rather than something one made. "*Literature*, that is to say, was a category of use and condition rather than of production. It was a particular specialization of what had hitherto been seen as an activity or practice, and a specialization, in the circumstances, which was inevitably made in terms of social class. In its first extended sense, beyond the base sense of 'literacy,' it was a definition of 'polite' or 'humane' learning, and thus specified a particular social distinction" (46–47).

Williams observes three ways in which the scope of "literature" becomes restricted. First, literature had meant something in principle available to all classes, "learning," but it came to be more strongly associated with "taste" and "sensibility" (48). The qualities of taste and sensibility cannot be acquired as one might have acquired learning. They are in fact the habits of the dominant class rendered as inherent qualities. As Williams describes their function, " 'taste' and 'sensibility' were essentially unifying concepts, in class terms, and could be applied over a very wide range of public and private behavior to (as Wordsworth complained) either wine or poetry." Criticism developed together with literature as a means by which its distinction was promoted and defended. Its own development reflects the increasing specialization of "literature" (49). A new term in the seventeenth century, "criticism" shifted from the practice of commentary on learning to the "conscious exercise of 'taste,' 'sensibility,' and 'discrimination.' " In the nineteenth it becomes "the only way of validating [a] specialized and selective category. It was at once a *discrimination* of the authentic 'great' or 'major' works, with a consequent grading of 'minor' works and an effective exclusion of 'bad' or 'negligible' works, and a practical realization and communication of the 'major' values" (49–51).

In the second restrictive tendency, literature became specialized to imaginative works. This was undoubtedly in part a ratification of the reality that science had taken over as the principal source of knowledge. Poetry, which since Sidney had been supposed to instruct and delight, was always assumed nonetheless to be truthful. The dominance of scientific discourse led to the association of poetry with the increasing quantity and popularity of

13

fiction. Furthermore, taste and sensibility were obviously not quite the appropriate standards with which to judge works that seemed to have some clear utilitarian function, and hence most nonfiction prose was not regarded as literature.

While this restricted conception of literature was well developed and widely disseminated in late-nineteenth-century America, it was not uncontested. Journalism and other "subliterary" genres remained widely understood as literature, although that identification was in part perpetuated in order to borrow value from the narrowly literary. Literature in the restricted sense was regarded as an important source of cultural and economic value, and by the late nineteenth century a variety of institutions were already in competition for control of that value. The institutions in society that held the power, at a given historical moment, to confer the value of literariness and the meaning that such value has when conferred are what I call "the literary." The value that literature comes to have in the late nineteenth century is a function of its historically persistent association with learning and its new, narrower identification with the class-specific quality of taste. Furthermore, literature was also regarded as having the utilitarian value of producing social cohesion around the dominant culture. It ideologically reinforced the class, gender, and racial hierarchies that structured society. As a bearer of these values as well as others—as entertainment, for example—literature is a source of cultural capital, as well as a marketable commodity. These historically contingent values go a long way toward explaining why literature came to be studied in the university.

Lest the reader think I denigrate literature by according it only contingent value, it is perhaps necessary to say that I assume with Barbara Herrnstein Smith that all value is historically contingent and culturally produced.[13] As Smith shows, such a position does not entail most of the consequences that believers in objective value think that it does. It does not, for example, open the gates to intellectual or cultural chaos; that values change does not mean that there are not always values. Nor does it rule out the existence of common human needs or interests, but rather recognizes that such needs and interests are experienced differently in different cultures and therefore do not produce uniform values or tastes. Finally, the position does not render evaluation and canon formation arbitrary or capricious; critics do not, for example, simply make up the canon out of their whims. On the contrary, the claim is that history, culture, and society all limit the range of evaluations that can be made. One of the most powerful of these limits is the history of evaluation and canonization itself. As Smith puts it, "the canonical work begins increasingly not merely to *survive within* but to *shape and create* the culture in which its value is produced and transmitted and, for that very reason, to perpetuate the conditions of its own flourishing. Nothing endures like endurance" (50, italics in original). But even works that endure do not remain the same, since readers and critics of different eras constitute works differently; in new cultural contexts enduring works come to serve new needs or desires, and different features of such works come to be valued (48). As a result, even the persistent high evaluation of a few American authors does not demonstrate their universality nor the continuity of American culture; the Emerson or the Hawthorne valued in 1900 is not the same as the one valued in the 1950s.[14]

In 1900, however, American writing had not yet attained a clear evaluation as literature, in part because it did not seem to meet all of the requirements for literature in the dominant sense. For example, American literature, even that most highly regarded, did not seem to embody unambiguously the taste and sensibility that was understood to be embodied in Shakespeare and Milton. And even the nationality of American literature was ambiguous, since it was written in the English language. This last difficulty is related to the third way that Williams describes "literature" as becoming more restricted in its meaning. This restriction was the concept of tradition, which entailed an increased association of literature and nation. The national literature came to be constituted as the embodiment of class-specific values by which criticism distinguished literature from nonliterature. The national literature "ceased to be a history and became a tradition. It was not even theoretically all that had been written or all kinds of writing. It was a selection which culminated in, and in a circular way defined, the 'literary values' which 'criticism' was asserting" (Williams, 51–52).

The development of "literature" and of literary traditions is thus connected to the rise of nationalism. Moreover, the new conception of literature cannot be separated from the concurrent development of the related notions of "civilization" and "culture." The term "civilization" emerged during the Enlightenment when it meant "an achieved state, which could be contrasted with 'barbarism,' but now also an achieved state *of development*, which implied historical process and progress. This was the new historical rationality of the Enlightenment, in fact combined with a self-referring celebration of an achieved condition of refinement and order" (Williams, 13). "Civilization" served to distinguish the rationality and progress of Europe from the irrationality and stagnation of the rest of the world. In the Enlightenment conception, civilization was a single process. Only in the nineteenth century does it become possible to speak of plural civilizations. In the meantime, the related term "culture" emerged from Germany to designate an inner or spiritual process, often contrasted with civilization, characterized as merely outward, artificial, or even superficial. "Culture" in this sense was picked up by the romantics and was eventually made into a program by Matthew Arnold. Though Johann Gottfried Herder is often cited as the point of emergence of cultural relativism, his conception also made possible the hierarchical ranking of civilizations, and thus can be seen as the emergence of cultural nationalism as well.[15] Aesthetic achievement was one significant measure for such ranking. "Culture," far from coming to stand unambiguously for relativism, became in the Arnoldian sense an absolute, "the best that has been thought and said," and thus a standard by which civilizations were judged. By the late nineteenth century, however, both "civilization" and "culture" have become highly ambiguous. Civilization no longer seems secure, "denoting on the one hand enlightened and progressive development and on the other hand an achieved and threatened state, becoming increasingly retrospective and often in practice identified with the received glories of the past. In the latter sense, 'civilization' and 'culture' again overlapped, as received states rather than as continuing processes" (Williams, 15). Only during the twentieth century does "culture" come also to mean a social process, or the "whole way of life," of different peoples, and thus to be common to all humanity. In this relativist or anthropological definition, culture implied none of the specifically European conditions that characterized the older conception of "civilization" as a process.[16]

The terms "culture" and "civilization" have not during the twentieth century been sharply distinguished except perhaps in anthropology. Early in the century, "civilization" was by far the more significant term in the United States. While Arnold was influential, his American disciples, such as Horace Scudder, did not emphasize his key term, often preferring "literature" instead. "Culture" perhaps seemed insubstantial or precious or elitist. "Civilization," given its associations with material progress and historical achievement, was precisely what Americans wanted. And yet, as we have seen, the term itself also conveyed a sense of threat from material progress. American literature was a possible source of relief from this threat. At the turn of the century, Americans' conception of the writing produced in the United States had not yet begun to undergo the final and most restrictive transformation into a tradition. At that time, the tradition that embodied the values of the bourgeoisie was English, not American. English or Anglo-Saxon civilization was understood by many to account for what was good or successful in America. The history of American literature was just beginning to be widely disseminated, in textbooks where it was often explicitly told as part of the English tradition. America was thus rendered an outpost of English civilization.

The idea of American civilization was a problem. On the one hand, the elite did not wish to exclude themselves from the civilized, but on the other, much of what they associated with American history or contemporary American society seemed opposed to civilization. Insofar as America was civilized, it was like Europe; its differences from Europe seemed to render it uncivilized. Arguments for a distinctively American civilization remained not entirely convincing or acceptable. For example, Turner's frontier thesis (1892) seemed to make American civilization the product of a lack of civilization or at least the encounter with the uncivilized: Indians, who were regarded as "savages," i.e., those without civilization. The importance of the term "civilization" is revealed in this same encounter, however. The concept allowed white Americans to assert their superiority over the racial others whom they dominated internally, while at the same time justifying imperialism abroad. While Americans never were entirely sanguine about the imperialism entailed in Kipling's conception of the white race's "burden" of civilizing the world, the popularity of Kipling in the United States suggests that his view was not repugnant either.

Thus the term "civilization" was central to American ideology. But was America really a civilization? In terms of material progress, that status could not be disputed, but the question arose on at least two counts. One was the lack of connection of America to the glories of the past, and the other the very dominance of industrialism, materialism, and democracy, all of which were thought to threaten civilization. The claim to membership in British civilization might answer the first problem, but it would not in the long run satisfy the demands of nationalism. But both obstacles could be alleviated if American literary tradition could be discovered. Such a tradition would contain its own past glories and aesthetic achievements, and its very existence would refute the charge that civilization had been inhibited or destroyed by American conditions.

The quest to create an American civilization would be spurred by the nationalism arising in connection with the world wars, though the lack of civilization was felt much earlier. At least some American writers of the nineteenth century lamented the lack of history or tradition out of which to make literature. While this lack would later become a defining trait of the American tradition, it would first help spawn the search for that tradition. But if Americans believed that they were somehow deprived of an authentic, deeply historical tradition that other nations had by virtue of their longevity, we now know that they were mistaken. All national traditions were invented, most no earlier than the late eighteenth century.[17] Benedict Anderson has suggested that the medium of print enabled the development of national consciousness and that the novel and the newspaper in particular provided "the technical means for 're-presenting' the *kind* of imagined community that is the nation."[18] The United States, which is sometimes thought not to be a typical nation-state, emerged precisely at the moment when nationalism was being born. The emphasis in the narrative of the United States on its newness, its creation *ex nihilo*, did restrict the appeal American nationalists could make to the past. Unless Americans wanted to identify themselves with aboriginal peoples they had displaced or exterminated—a problematic alternative that was nevertheless not altogether rejected—they could not construct a unique historical tradition. Thus a literary tradition became all the more important, but not much easier to maintain. While American literary nationalism has a history that dates virtually from the revolution, it failed to become dominant until the twentieth century.

The major reason for this failure may have been the changing meaning and political valence of "nation." Eric Hobsbawm argues that "The primary meaning of 'nation,' and the one most frequently ventilated in the literature, was political. It equated 'the people' and the state in the manner of the American and French Revolutions. . . . The 'nation' so considered, was the body of citizens whose collective sovereignty constituted them a state which was their political expression. For, whatever else a nation was, the element of citizenship and mass participation or choice was never absent from it."[19] "Nation" in early nineteenth-century America was a term that conveyed a democratic theory of the state. "Indeed, if 'the nation' had anything in common from the popular-revolutionary point of view, it was not, in any fundamental sense, ethnicity, language and the like. . . . As Pierre Vilar has pointed out, what characterized the nation-people as seen from below was precisely that it prerepresented the common interests against privilege" (Hobsbawm, *Nations*, 20). This democratic sense of nationhood helps to explain why literary nationalism was the program mainly of the non-elite, and why it remained disreputable among the men of letters of the late nineteenth century.

From about 1870 on, however, nationalism became increasingly identified with language and ethnicity, philology having helped pave the way for the former while Spencer, Darwin, and other contributors to evolutionism gave what passed for scientific support for the latter. It is during this period in America that historians first proposed the Teutonic-origins theory of American civilization, that Anglo-Saxonism and Anglophilia reached its peak among the American cultural elite, and that concerted efforts were made to Americanize immigrants. Such events show the impact of nationalism in general and the increasing importance of American nationalism in particular. But there remained a cultural standoff between those who wished to identify America with a single ethnic group, whether named Anglo-Saxons or Teutons, and those who wanted to identify it with all of those who were citizens. It is only after World War I that American nationalism comes to replace Anglo-Saxonism as the dominant ethnocentrism within the literary. The war and the Wilsonian propaganda that had accompanied it had the effect of forging an identity between "America" and "democracy." Instead of being a form of solidarity among the people, nationalism now becomes much more an ideology aligned with government and the ruling class. It is perhaps not surprising that the idea of a distinct American literature began to be deployed by the cultural elite immediately after the war.[20]

The project of creating American civilization served this end. To understand its function it is good to remember that a particular nationalism is not constructed on the basis of a coherent theory or a single narrative. "The cultural shreds and patches used by nationalism are often arbitrary historical inventions. Any old shred would have served as well."[21] Literature itself is of course merely a shred of culture, and other shreds might have done as well. There are historically contingent explanations, however, for why literature did serve American nationalism in a more significant way than music, painting, or even sports. But a literary tradition is itself a matter of shreds and patches, and the story of this volume is of how they got stitched or glued together differently at different times. Even during the 1950s, when the tradition was the most coherently conceived and the least diverse, however, it never added up to a "national narrative."[22] As a whole, the tradition came to consist of a group of related narratives told by critics rather than by novelists or poets. As Jonathan Arac has argued, writers such as Cooper, whose work does retell larger stretches of American history, have not been accorded a central place in the canon.[23] A similar point could be made about the marginal role of Vernon Parrington's *Main Currents of American Thought*, the closest thing to a coherent narrative of American literary history yet produced. There has never been a single work or story that served as a synecdoche for the American nation, the way the flag and ideas such as freedom have served. Even the "American dream" remains too nebulous to be regarded as a single story. The works that have been held central to American literature have been those that demonstrated its aesthetic success. American literature was not needed primarily to give Americans a sense of identity or purpose, but to certify their achievement of a national civilization.

The disciplinary form of American literature studies thus ultimately came to serve American nationalism quite effectively. The dispersed shreds produced by disciplinary research were perfectly suited to be the raw materials of a new cultural nationalism. It did not matter that the tradition Americanists created consisted of myths and symbols rather than actual history. What was important is that these myths were uniquely American and that they had produced great literary works. The importance of the "American Adam" or the "pastoral myth" was not mainly what they told us about America, but that they guaranteed the cultural significance of its literature. Myths and symbols were the patches of the American literary tradition. A tradition so constructed is relatively easy to patch again, but it is very hard to discard.

Part I
Beginnings

1

The Literary in America, 1890–1920

At the turn of the century, American literature was taught only sporadically in universities and colleges (literature itself being a relatively recent addition to the curriculum). The literary culture of the early part of this century was dominated by men of letters, who tended to be not only critics and writers but editors as well. There were stronger connections between journalism and the literary world than between that world and the university. Even within the university, many of the leading figures were men of letters rather than researchers. Thus literary research in the university was a minor aspect of the literary environment. American literature in particular was defined outside of the university and was thus a very different object during this period. While the validity of the term "American literature" was still very much contested, it had also become common usage. Its meaning was also contested, however, and its dominant meaning differed significantly from the one we now assume. Rather than being understood mainly as a historical tradition or canon, it was, at least as much the contemporary practice of writing, a practice that could be held or captured, defended or transformed. Many involved in literary culture would have agreed with Randolph Bourne that "our American cultural tradition lies in the future."[1] It is true that Emerson, Hawthorne, Longfellow, and some of their Boston colleagues were recognized as "standard authors," but they did not constitute a canon, since they were too recent for their immortality to be proclaimed. Nor were they regarded as identical with American literature. A better sense of that concept may be gained from anthologies, such as the eleven-volume *Library of American Literature* or *An American Anthology*, which by their inclusiveness suggest that American literature is the product of many writers and that it is still very much in production.[2] *An American Anthology* covers the years 1787–1900, includes more than 500 poets, and runs to 773 pages, excluding biographical notes and indexes. The standard poets—Bryant, Emerson, Holmes, Whittier, Longfellow, and Lowell—account for a mere 93 of those pages. Well over half of the *Anthology* (465 pages) is devoted to the period 1861–1900, which includes no standard authors.

During the period between the turn of the century and the institutionalization of American literature in university English departments, American literature became increasingly understood as a historical object and thus the sense of it as a current practice, the writing of fiction and poetry, receded. That occurred because of changes in the cultural construction of the literary. Literature by this time had largely emerged in the form Williams outlines, and as such it had already come to serve the ideology of turn-of-the-century America. Literature was thus a source of cultural and symbolic capital—as well as a valuable commodity—and control of these sources of value was contested. The men of letters, who exercised critical and editorial authority at the turn of the century, lost their place in the new mode of literary production that brought with it new literary institutions, a new function for literature, and new conditions of literary work. The changed conditions produced a crisis of succession in literary—and especially critical—authority. As editorial control was assumed by entrepreneurial publishers and the professionalized staffs they hired, public discussion of literary values became less important. As a result, the exercise of critical judgment could be captured by such groups as the "literary radicals" and the New Humanists. These groups explicitly contested previous conceptions of American literature, but none succeeded in establishing its own as dominant.

Literature and the Literary

By the late nineteenth century, literature had become a significant source of cultural value in the United States and other Western societies, and literariness an important form of cultural capital, which was contested by different groups within these societies.[3] But it had not always been this way; as Williams has shown, the specific character of literature was a nineteenth-century development. Undoubtedly, for a long time in the history of written language, the mere ability to read and write was a powerful enough distinction. In certain cultures, all writing was regarded as sacred, and in most, writing was more valuable than words merely spoken. As long as the dissemination of written words was difficult, the value of writing was assured. Having experience in reading documents worthy of preservation, "having literature," distinguished one as having knowledge, since knowledge was contained in those documents. With the invention of the press, and especially the steam-powered presses of the nineteenth century, writing itself became cheap and also more and more essential for everyday life. As education became available to larger portions of the population, the mere ability to read lost its status, as did readable objects. While it is clear that not all writing was accorded equal value prior to Gutenberg, afterwards the problem of making distinctions among written works became considerably greater. "Literature" in the modern sense is the ultimate product of this need for distinction. But if "literature" comes to mean only superior works in certain genres of writing, its specification is also partially a cultural demotion, for "literature" by the nineteenth century is no longer the equivalent of "knowledge."

It would be misleading to assume that literature loses entirely its earlier association with knowledge. But where it once was synonomous with knowledge in general, literature, along with the other fine arts, was now understood as a bearer of moral truth and therefore as being a means of social melioration. At one time, of course, literature had been assumed to represent and convey religious truths. In the nineteenth century, literature had established a certain autonomy from religion, but literature and other elements of culture were believed to contribute to "the moral education of the people."[4] Like Matthew Arnold, American critics such as Horace Scudder understood this education as a way to prevent the "anarchy" that the antagonism of the lower classes could produce. Like Arnold also, these critics increasingly saw literature and culture as alternatives to religion rather than as vehicles for it. The old ideal of "having literature" was replaced with "having culture," meaning to have experience and appreciation of literature and other elite categories of art. Having culture distinguished one as socially and morally superior.

When Arnold argued that poetry was the criticism of life, he was articulating the role literature played in the nineteenth century. Yet even this reduced role was under attack. Literature found itself in competition with the emerging social sciences, which sought a scientific basis for moral instruction, for the role of criticism of life. Arnold's work makes explicit the functions literature had been performing; he had to make them explicit because literature was threatened with losing them. Literature and science were in competition, not only over authority for moral instruction, but also over which would define knowledge itself. The famous "two cultures" debate, which C. P. Snow named in the 1950s but which was actually inaugurated by Arnold and T. H. Huxley, is a manifestation of this competition. When the natural and social sciences began to perform functions for the culture that literature had previously performed, the character of those functions changed as a result. The emerging social sciences substituted science for the wisdom of the ages, and they succeeded because science had established itself as the dominant form of truth. The possibility of modern academic literary criticism emerged when literature lost to social science its function of social guide and became defined primarily as an aesthetic enterprise. Even today, however, the literary continues to be partially identified with the moral or intellectual content literature is supposed to convey.

By narrowing the purview of "literature," the value of texts that had been previously understood as the substance of learning could continue to be asserted. The cultural construction of the literary results from this narrowing, which I described in the introduction. The term "literary" first meant reading ability or experience in reading.[5] Its original value undoubtedly derived from the earlier rarity of reading. As literacy increased after the invention of printing and the decline of Latin, concepts such as sensibility doubtless allowed for distinctions among texts. The modern term "literature" that emerges in the nineteenth century is a function of the "reading revolution" at the end of the eighteenth.[6]

Reading patterns had been formed by the scarcity of books, so that a few books were typically reread often, usually aloud and in groups. After 1800, readers encountered new kinds of books and other printed matter at prices low enough that reading material came to be consumed as much as it was preserved.[7] The greatly expanded number of books led to the need for more rigorous distinctions.

Those texts distinguished as "literary" become class-identity markers, invested with the class-defined value of taste. But the literary was not valued simply as a means of class distinction. Literature, despite the heavy burden it was made to bear by the doctrine of culture, continued to be regarded as a source of pleasure. In the nineteenth century, however, the "literary" conveyed creativity, imagination, and other qualities that were more than mere occasions for delight. Under the influence of romanticism, these qualities were held to be essentially human. The need to affirm them was a response to industrial capitalism. The value of the literary partially resided in its difference from the mechanical and repressive experience of work under this regime. Reading itself was respite from the factory or office routine, but only certain kinds of reading material could be certified genuinely imaginative or creative. Such values were in practice not freely available to all who read imaginative writing. Rather, the authority of institutions and individuals determined which works would carry these values and which would not. Thus not all writing, or even all imaginative writing, counted as literature under this definition. "Literature" and "literary" are honorific terms that assign high value to the objects they describe.[8]

What was for a time merely an adjective becomes a cultural sector and a way of life. But what I am concerned with in this volume is not mainly the culture of "the literary" nor the way of life associated with it. Rather, my focus is on the institutions in American society at a given historical moment that were most identified with literature, and which therefore held the power to confer the value of literariness; and the meaning that such value has when conferred under that power. The book as a whole will trace the capture and transformation of "the literary" by the university.

In order to explain what I mean by the literary, let me propose a comparison to the ideal of nationhood. Nationality and literariness are similar in their functioning as symbolic capital.[9] A thing that can be understood as in some way essentially American will for many Americans be more valuable than it would be without such an association. If a piece of writing is judged to be literary— or better yet, is simply assumed to be so—it is invested with symbolic capital that nonliterary writing does not carry. The power to assign and define the value of literariness is the control of a certain measure of symbolic capital. But neither nationality nor literariness are easily objectifiable. As a result, they are always potentially redefinable. What it means to be an American, a Pole, or a German is not a blank space that can simply be filled in at will by whatever new regime happens to take power, but neither is it fixed in stone, or, as is sometimes claimed, in genes. Similarly, what it means for something to be described as literature or as literary has a historical dimension that prevents an absolute reassignment of the term, but it cannot prevent its mutation. It is the historical persistence of literary and nationalist discourses that enable them to have cultural value, but it is their malleability that causes the struggle for control of that value to take the form of a debate over definition.

As a form of symbolic capital, literariness could be used to enhance the value of other objects. The control of the literary was valuable not only for the power and money that accrued directly from it, but also as a value that could be invested elsewhere. For example, an important form of this investment is the association of literariness with the nation, and thus with the state. Literature —especially poetry and drama—had long served to glorify England, "the land of poets" and home of Shakespeare. But literariness could also be claimed by those opposing the current regime, as indeed could nationality itself. As cultural capital, the literary could enhance or secure the status of individuals or institutions. Like all sources of value, the literary was something worth fighting over; such conflict meant that the character of the literary would depend upon who controlled it and by what means such control was gained. At its most basic level, the struggle was economic: ownership of the means of production and distribution of books and magazines was one way that such control was exercised. And changes in production and distribution do account for the shift in literary power from Boston to New York that occurs at the end of the nineteenth century. But the cultural value of literariness is not produced by presses nor distributed through the mails; nor, for that matter, does it simply flow from the pens of authors and poets. Literariness is the product of institutional authority that not only assumes the resources of presses and mails for its exercise, but enables in addition the marshaling of intellectual consent. My claim is that the authority of the men of letters was not a product of their own voices or genius but of the roles they filled in the literary system.

The struggle for control of the literary was sometimes waged between opposing schools of thought within the same cultural sector, but it is just as often waged between different cultural sectors and among different institutions within those sectors. For example, at the turn of the century in the United States there was a contest between, on the one hand, the men of letters and the traditional magazines and publishing houses they represented and, on the other hand, the new, mass-market periodicals and their publishing houses. It was not necessary for this contest to be centered on the term "literary." The mass-market publishers often used the term pejoratively to designate what they considered the effete products and practices of their opponents. But this did not stop the mass-market magazines from seeking to publish the most important men of letters. John Brisben Walker went so far as to hire William Dean Howells to be the editor of *Cosmopolitan*, although he lasted only a few months. Another kind of struggle occurred between the men of letters and a new generation of "intellectuals." In the first decade of the twentieth century, the dominant conception of the literary came under attack by both right-wing New Humanists and mostly left-wing literary radicals. While both the new publishers and the intellectuals gained some measure of influence over the literary, they did not succeed in completely overturning the old institutions. A third group of aspirants, the professors, would eventually establish their dominance over the literary, but that would not occur until after World War II.

The Ideological Work of the Literary

The literary served three different but related ideological functions at the turn of the century: its "aesthetic" character provided

31

an alternative to and relief from the increasingly rationalized realm of work; it encouraged solidarity among the dominant class in terms of racist and patriarchal identities, as well as those of class; it was one element in the construction of a national identity meant to bind the largely immigrant working class to the bourgeois state. All of these functions were ideological in the sense that they were not beliefs that literary works explicitly urged on their readers. By "ideological," I mean more or less what Althusser meant when he used the term to name that part of experience which we take so completely for granted that it becomes "nature." Ideology so defined is a " 'lived' relation to the real" that has a powerful hold on the subject because it is largely unconscious.[10] Thus, to quote James Kavanagh, "at stake in [ideological conflicts] are not different *opinions*, but different *realities*. The ideological . . . is not some mental sphere of dogma or doctrine that one can embrace or reject at will (and that afflicts only *others*, who try to 'impose' it on reality), but an unavoidable terrain of social practice."[11]

If ideology does not normally appear as such, that does not mean that it remains unarticulated. On the contrary, it is expressed everywhere, including in literary works where it may be explicit or implicit. In turn-of-the-century literary culture, the level of explicitness of major ideologies differed greatly. Racism was openly embraced, while the existence of classes was often denied. Thus dominant or bourgeois American reality assumed racial hierarchy but no permanent or oppressive class distinctions. Sexism fell somewhere in between. While maleness was sometimes regarded as one of the distinguishing characteristics of the Anglo-Saxons, literature is also valued for its expression of the feminine—but in this literature affirms the dominant construction, or "reality," of gender.

Though I do not use the term "ideology" to mean dogma, almost all critics of this era assumed that literature had a didactic function. They agreed that it was supposed to convey moral truths even if they differed on what those truths were. American critics continued to assume that literature should instruct and delight, but they tended to dwell on instruction. Both realists and their opponents believed that literature should tell the truth and that such truth telling would serve the purpose of improving the nation and humanity. The literary was thus a repository of a particular kind of knowledge, whether that knowledge was real or ideal.

One of the dominant functions ascribed to literature in the nineteenth century was to reflect the ideal, to represent the world as it should be rather than as it is. Howells had opposed this position in his war for realism, and he illustrated it as a preference for a "wire and cardboard" grasshopper over a grasshopper found "out there in the grass." The former is "very prettily painted in a conventional tint, and it's perfectly indestructible. It isn't very much like a real grasshopper, but it's a great deal nicer, and it's served to represent the notion of a grasshopper ever since man emerged from barbarism." To pay attention to the real grasshopper is to "sin against culture."[12] This metaphor calls attention to two aspects of the dominant position. Besides the preference for the ideal over the real, it also suggests that received conventions are valued by virtue of their longevity. These conventions serve to distinguish civilized peoples from the barbarous. Thus the literary was presumed not only to show us the truth behind all of the accidents of time and experience, but in so doing to confirm our triumph over those accidents.

While there was disagreement among the idealists about the relative importance of the aesthetic and the didactic functions of literature, the idealist position entailed no inherent conflict between them. In fact, the identity of truth and beauty was often asserted. Realist writing, however, threatened to deprive literature of its aesthetic character. Simply put, if the world from which literature was supposed to be a respite became the subject of literature, literature could no longer play that role. Howells solved this problem in theory and in his own practice by excluding the worst conditions of modern life from his definition of the real that literature should depict. Yet in his defense of Zola and in his support for Crane and Norris, Howells admitted a place for these conditions in realist literature. The contradiction is dramatized in Howells's novel *A Hazard of New Fortunes*, where literature is represented as a higher and more spiritual calling than mere commercial endeavors such as the insurance business. Literature was for the book's protagonist, Basil March, "a high privilege, a sacred refuge. . . . [He] was satisfied to read. He was proud of reading critically, and he kept in the current of literary interests and controversies. It all seemed to him, and to his wife at secondhand, very meritorious; he could not help contrasting his life . . . and its inner elegance with that of other men who had no such resources."[13] Literature proves to be insufficient to protect March from the realities of poverty and the violent struggle between labor and capital in New York, but bringing such realities into the novel affirmed all the more the need for such refuge.

Howells's novel is unusual in that it takes the class struggle as its subject. Even though the late nineteenth century had spawned record numbers of strikes, most literature of the period simply ignored what was perhaps the major social conflict of the age. The issue was so touchy that the *Century* insisted that Howells remove a reference to dynamite from *The Rise of Silas Lapham*, which it was serializing. While readers of the most prestigious magazines were hardly restricted to the true bourgeois, many of them were members of the growing professional-managerial class. The magazine's audiences did not include the most important oppositional force of their day, the working class. It was not just magazines that ignored class conflict; there is an almost complete absence of literature sympathetic to the labor movement. Even fiction critical of social conditions did not usually take laborers as its subject. Rather, such fiction focuses on sympathetic but nonthreatening girls, as in *Maggie* and *Sister Carrie*, or on small farmers or businessmen threatened by the trusts, as in *The Octopus*. As Howells put it, "the American public does not like to read about the life of toil. . . . What we like to read about is the life of noblemen or millionaires."[14] Doubtless Howells was accusing the public of romanticism, of preferring the ideal to the real, but given who the reading public was he also calls our attention to its identification with the rulers rather than the ruled.

When most men of letters discussed the role of literature in the modern world, they certainly did not see it as a force for social change. Some took the Arnoldian position that literature could be a force for social stability, a way to control the working classes. Horace Scudder, who has been called "the most widely quoted American spokesman for an Arnoldian view of cultural education," argued that the schools were the nation's line of defense against "hands that are nervously pulling at the stones of our political edifice. . . . Therefore in this hour of its coming struggle the nation looks to its schools, and says: Here shall we make our stand, cast up our entrenchments, and be ready to meet the enemy."[15] Literature is the main weapon Scudder offers in this struggle, for American literature can teach Americanism.[16] The function of literature, however, is not mainly the teaching of political ideas, but "spiritual training."[17] Like Arnold, Scudder lamented the diminished ability of religion to provide such training and he offered literature as an alternative. The problem of "inflamed Labor . . . the peril which springs from an anarchic force outside the true democratic order is accompanied by the peril which arises from the more insidious, disintegrating force of disbelief resident in every part of the body politic" ("Place of Literature," 11). Literature can disarm both these perils by offering to labor an alternative to the materialist vision of the good life that made workers so desperate, but also by giving the nation as a whole faith in its ideals.

The notion of literature as a means of spiritual training and an antidote to the nation's materialism is closely related to the view that literature was the expression of creativity and imagination, for "literature of spirit . . . finds a response in the imagination and fancy" ("Place of Literature," 16). These qualities were regarded as especially vital here because American literati perceived themselves to be living in the midst of a particularly mechanical and unspiritual civilization. Among the men of letters at the turn of the century, E. C. Stedman's "rank as a critic of poetry [was] beyond dispute; for his three published volumes in this department of literature constitute the most important body of systematic and serious criticism thus far produced by any American writer."[18] Stedman illustrates the influence of romanticism among late-nineteenth-century American critics. His theory of poetry explains the connection between the spiritual and the creative, the latter being a microcosm of the former. The beauty of the poets' "imaginings coming from within, just as the beauty of nature is the efflux of the universal spirit."[19] "Poetic expression," Stedman asserts, "is that of light from a star, our straightest message from the inaccessible human soul" (259). In attributing poetic ability to genius, Stedman opposes poetry and industry or work. It is not labor that makes poetry, but "imaginative and emotional endowments" together with "the special gifts which . . . come only at birth—'the vision and faculty divine' " (277). Poetry represents the absolute other of profane human experience. The value of literary pursuits was frequently stated in terms of their distance from science and the material. Thus there is found "a fundamental sympathy between [Dante] and the spirit of our age," which is a reaction against science and the unspiritual character of the nineteenth century.[20] The literary was valued for its place seemingly outside of what were perceived as increasingly confining conditions of work and thought.

If Basil March finds literature a refuge from the commercial world in which he earned his living, he also recognizes that it is not available to everyone. He contrasted his life "and its inner elegance with that of other men who had no such resources." The literary is valued here not only for actual benefits it provides but for the distinction it gives March over other men. Literature, however, seems for March more a source of individual identity than of class identity, since it is from other members of his class that his literary interests distinguish him. The literary built class unity not as a special interest—which indeed was regarded as suspect by its similarity to bohemianism—but insofar as it defined and was identified with good taste. Such taste was founded on common formal and informal education. College education had long been a significant class marker, with knowledge of Latin and Greek the most telling distinction. But the late nineteenth century saw a shift from classical languages to English as college increasingly was understood to contribute to direct occupational training. Technocratic considerations became more significant than those of cultural distinction. This accounts for the growing importance of the teaching of English composition, but English literature was also an important subject by 1890. Knowledge of it remained a significant form of class distinction, and by teaching it the project of unifying the professional-managerial class with the bourgeoisie could be furthered as the appropriate sense of taste and cultural decorum were inculcated. The point was not to create literati such as Basil March, but rather individuals who identified with the culture of the elite.

It is not for nothing that we know these tastes today as the "genteel tradition." It is true that later generations exaggerated the narrowness of these tastes. Almost all of the leading men of letters were less "Victorian" than their successors have depicted them. Howells defended Zola, while Stedman found value in Poe and Whitman. But it is precisely because Zola, Poe, and Whitman were beyond the pale of accepted standards of taste that they needed to be defended. Such taste is well represented by the leading older magazines, including the *Atlantic*, *Harper's Monthly*, *Scribner's*, and *Century*. These magazines protected the bourgeois family by refusing to publish material that could not comfortably be read in its circle. They refused to publish work that could offend on any of a number of grounds: religious, linguistic (e.g., slang), political, or even temperamental (as in unrelieved pessimism). But these magazines also presumed some positive qualities in their audiences. They published articles reflecting "the ideal of the educated man, the philosopher, who is at home not merely in his own land and his own age, but in all lands and all ages."[21] This ideal is, of course, perfectly ethnocentric and not at all at odds with the agenda of imperialism. Yet even those who were anti-imperialist would share the assumptions of the common education of their class, that they could know man. On the other hand, they seemed reluctant to know contemporary America too well: "Concerned as they were with editorial fare for the genteel, the magazines in retrospect seem curiously remote from the dramatic changes then taking place in American life. Literature, art, manners, travel, and history got their attention, and their editors often seemed to have had their eyes more closely on Europe than on America" (Peterson, 3).

The magazines didn't ignore America only to hide disturbing news, however. Another reason for their interest in Europe was certainly the continued belief that America had not achieved the same level of culture as had European civilizations. This sense of cultural inferiority actually contributed to the cultural distinction of the elite and working classes. The latter were often chauvinistic and egalitarian, and regarded things European, and especially British, as aristocratic.[22] While elite American attitudes toward Britain shifted with political events, the exponents of culture understood America as sharing the heritage of Britain. They identified America with Anglo-Saxon or English civilization, and did not speak of an independent American culture. The belief that the

American and English peoples were a common race was hegemonic at the turn of the century, and what were called Anglo-
Saxon qualities were often cited as responsible for whatever was
best about America. Race was a fundamental category of explanation in American culture in general. Even those who were skepti-
cal of much that was asserted on the basis of race nonetheless did
not reject this role for race. For example, Josiah Royce said, "We
do not scientifically know what the true racial varieties of mental
type really are. No doubt there are such varieties."[23] The presumption of Anglo-Saxon superiority gave Americans a sense of
their own place atop the evolutionary hierarchy, but it also defined who was really an American and the character of the idea
of America. Clearly race was a significant basis for bourgeois unity
in a nation experiencing what seemed an inundation of foreign
immigrants who arrived to join a growing industrial proletariat.

Literature was more than peripherally related to this racism
since it was widely held that literature expresses the essential
character of a race. This was true because language, the substance
of literature, "is an expression or function of race."[24] Thus the
persistence of defining American literature as a branch of English
literature can be understood as having been motivated by more
than cultural humility. Much was made of the common Anglo-
Saxon origins of the two nations, but it was not necessary for
Anglo-Saxon to be identified as the common root. When the notion of an American literature was dismissed with the assertion
"we are English" the same exclusive identification of America
with one "nationality," or "race," is assumed.[25] Nor was racism
restricted to Anglophiles. Bliss Perry, editor of the *Atlantic* from
1899 to 1909, spends much of the first chapter of *The American
Mind* expressing his doubts about explanations based on race, but
he concludes the chapter by asserting that "our task is to exhibit
the essential Americanism of these spokesmen of ours . . . to
find . . . among the books which are recognized as constituting
our American literature, some vital and illuminating illustrations
of our national characteristics."[26] Whether America's ancestry
was described as Anglo-Saxon or English or even to have spontaneously generated from New World conditions, Americanness
was defined so as to exclude most other ethnicities.

Literature could serve not only to unite the rulers but to marshal the consent of the ruled. Ethnic diversity had been regarded as a threat as early as the 1830s. One response to this threat was the Whig project of unifying the diverse American people under the aegis of New England by locating the nation's origins in that region.[27] This was part of a continuing deployment of American nationalism, the most significant element of which was the public education system, of which Hobsbawm says, "Until the triumph of television, there was no medium of secular propaganda to compare with the classroom."[28] Public education helped to create a nation not only by directly inculcating patriotic ideas but also by creating linguistic and cultural homogeneity. In primary schools, the McGuffey readers and others like them used literature to convey nationalist content as children were taught to read. By teaching English, American schools helped to create Americans out of the children of immigrant parents. The importance of the language itself is signaled by the requirement of English for citizenship. As immigration exploded, developing American nationalism became a much more explicit goal of public education: "from the end of the 1880s on [the USA] began to introduce actual worship under the new civic religion . . . in the form of a daily ritual of homage to the flag in every American school" (Hobsbawm, 150). This deployment of nationalism corresponds to a growing interest in American literature as a school subject. Scudder urged the teaching of American classics as "the one essential and most serviceable means for keeping alive the smouldering coals of patriotism" ("American Classics," 47). That Scudder's view proved influential is demonstrated by the fact that "a new reader could hardly be in the running without selections from Longfellow, Whittier, Holmes, and the rest" and by the large number of textbook editions of standard American authors sold in the early years of this century.[29] As a result, the New England poets came to be known as the schoolroom poets. The large number of textbook histories of American literature produced in the nineteenth century were part of this effort. But it was not necessary for these histories to reject Anglo-Saxonism to promote American nationalism. As Baym argues of the textbooks, "the histories rather emphasized than played down the English origins of the American nation, thereby instructing classrooms of children of non-English ancestry to defer to the Anglo-Saxonism of their new country's heritage" (463). Thus the teaching of English literature can be understood to have served the ends of American nationalism.

The value of literariness was assured by its ideological functions. I want to insist that literature was far more important ideologically than it was as a medium of explicit moral or political ideas. In spite of the repeated Arnoldian claims about the moral values literature expressed, even at this stage there is little elucidation of what those values were. Rather than teaching a set of moral truths, literature came to represent imagination, creativity, and spirituality. It symbolized—rather than explained—the character and success of European and especially Anglo-Saxon civilization. Those functions allowed the claim that literature would civilize the barbarians. When we add to these functions class-defining markers such as taste, we can understand why the literary would become enshrined in universities and protected from the market when it was no longer profitable.

Literary Products, Literary Work

The qualities ascribed to the literary by nineteenth-century critics and other custodians of bourgeois culture did not provide a clear set of criteria for distinguishing literature from nonliterature. The continual contestation of the literary meant that there would be no fixed definitions of key terms. Thus while the increasing specialization of the term "literature" is certainly evident in nineteenth-century America, the pattern Williams describes did not yield a unitary meaning. At the turn of the century, there remained a productive overlap of literature in the most specialized sense and literature as the product of a particular industry or profession. Occupations we would now describe as journalism or commercial publishing were regarded as literary. The literary named a sector of culture that produced writing not as a means to some other end but as an end product. The shift in the meaning of "literature" from experience to product is predicated on the commodification of writing. Previously, relatively little literature was produced; literature rather was something to be conserved. By the late nineteenth century in the United States, however, the economic value of literature had come to rival its cultural value.

In the 1890s a new breed of cheaply priced magazines, supported by advertising, fueled a spiraling demand for writing. Publishers of all kinds did not hesitate to use symbolic capital to increase sales, which meant that there was an alliance of sorts between the dominant men of letters and the dominant producers of written commodities.

Indeed, even in the late nineteenth century, literature was not always distinguished from journalism. In *A Hazard of New Fortunes*, which describes the launching of a magazine in New York, literature seems to include all of what we would now call journalism but also to retain the sense of a higher or more spiritual calling. March is called "a natural-born literary man"—but he is neither a novelist, a dramatist, nor a poet but an insurance man recruited by Fulkerson, an entrepreneur, to edit his new magazine (*HNF*, 7). What March writes are realistic sketches of New York life. Both "literature" and "literary" are applied to newspapers. For example, when March discovered Fulkerson was "in that newspaper-syndicate business, [he] told him about [his] early literary ambitions" (*HNF*, 16). Fulkerson, whose business is based on S. S. McClure's first enterprise, was "supplying literature to newspapers for simultaneous publication" (*HNF*, 17). McClure's syndicate supplied fiction for Sunday supplements—imaginative writing, but without special claims to taste or sensibility.

One way to read these sentences of Howells is to assume that "literature" has two distinct definitions, one designating any written matter and the other high art. But it is my contention that while these do indeed represent two poles in the use of the term, the "literature" Fulkerson supplies to newspapers is not radically distinguished from the "literature" in which Howells himself dwelt. The reason that a radical distinction cannot be maintained is that the literary was identified with institutions such as magazines and publishing houses, which produced literature of all kinds. They were the only literary institutions when they first emerged in the early nineteenth century. The existence of such institutions in all regions of the country gives the lie to the claim that literary culture existed only in New England. What was different about New England, however, is the greater power and significance of the literary in that region, and especially in Boston. There are complex reasons for this, including the greater impor-

41

tance of literature as learning in Puritan culture and the resulting social influence of Harvard College. The theological trajectory of New England made it the place where literature would first begin to serve as a substitute for religion. It is Emerson who most clearly embodies this transition from religion to literature, both in his "problem of vocation," which took him from the ministry and into the literary, and in the character of his writings, which openly seek to substitute themselves for Christianity. Emerson is not a genius who invented a literary culture, but the product of the same social conditions that gave rise to the literary culture that would nurture him. If the transcendentalists, and Hawthorne from his very different perspective, address the intellectual problems of the waning of religion, men of letters such as Holmes and Lowell who did not take up such issues also attained prominence because of it.[30]

It was thus the relative dominance of the literary in New England that enabled New England's literary dominance of America from the 1850s through the 1880s. Such dominance has been recognized at least since Tyler's *A History of American Literature* (1878), but it has usually been misunderstood. New England's dominance did not result from its having produced the best literary works, but from its having established the strongest and most influential institutions. These institutions shared the goal of civilizing, that is, of spreading a particular morality for purposes of maintaining social order. New Englanders established a "vast invisible empire" of public school systems, private colleges, and state universities from coast to coast, and the "intellectual focuses of [this] empire were Boston and Concord."[31] Harvard provided the conditions for the development of literary culture in Boston. Public schools established by New England's example throughout the nation spread New England's literature.

It is important to specify, however, that literature as we know it was not a subject in public schools or in colleges. Literary works were taught in courses on rhetoric and oratory, language and grammar, but neither literary history nor interpretation were taught. But schools did expose students both to New England authors and to the Whig version of American history, and the *Atlantic* and the *North American Review* picked up where schooling left off. Their national readership enabled them to introduce

New England works and authors to the rest of the nation, to readers prepared by their schooling to approve of what the magazines offered. The Boston men of letters who produced the *Atlantic* "set it in authority over American literature."[32] The men of letters themselves, however, achieved their reputations as a result of institutional power: "The standardization of American authors . . . is the product of this New England empire, more specifically of Ticknor and Fields and their publishing successors," especially Houghton Mifflin, which published and republished their American literature list in editions designed for schools (Jones, 86). Houghton Mifflin also promoted their own list and the New England writers through the biographical studies published in the American Men of Letters Series, initiated in 1880. The dominance of New England institutions and authors depended upon the circular relationship they had with each other. The "greatness" of the New England men of letters was a product of their institutional affiliations; their reputations in turn caused their magazines and publishers to have the most influence.

The struggle over control of the literary was first felt in the nineteenth century as a regional conflict. That conflict is a subtext for *Literary Friends and Acquaintance*, where the dominance of New England and Boston in the nineteenth century is often remarked. Howells's rhetoric attempts to justify New England's dominance:

> The editors of the *Atlantic* had been eager from the beginning to discover any outlying literature; but, as I have said, there was in those days very little good writing done beyond the borders of New England. If the case is now different, and the best known among living American writers are no longer New Englanders, still I do not think the South and West have yet trimmed the balance; and though perhaps the new writers now more commonly appear in those quarters, I should not be so very sure that they are not still characterized by New England ideals and examples. On the other hand, I am very sure that in my early day we were characterized by them and wished to be so; we even felt that we failed in so far as we expressed something native quite in our own way. The literary theories we accepted were New England theories, the criticism we valued was New England criticism, or, more strictly speaking, Boston theories, Boston criticism. (*LFA*, 115)

43

As Howells recognized, however, New England was not in 1900 homogeneous either: "New England has ceased to be a nation in itself, and it will perhaps never again have anything like a national literature; and it will probably be centuries yet before the life of the whole country, the American life as distinguished from the New England life, shall have anything so like a national literature" (*LFA*, 116). Undoubtedly, Howells's notion of the older New England was romanticized, so that the literature of his Boston heroes seemed to him an organic expression of the whole people of New England, which it was not. Yet he was certainly right in his assessment of the end of regional isolation and in his sense that American life was far more diverse than New England had been. But Howells's remarks about the lack of an American national literature seem strange in light of recent historical reconstructions of the period. Indeed, one critic has gone so far as to assert that the literature administered by the men of letters may be "the closest thing to a coherent national literary culture that America has ever had."[33] But what Howells assumes about a national literature is that it must be the expression of the unified experience of the nation, and he recognizes that the America of 1900 lacks such unified experience. Perhaps more important, however, Howells assumes that a national literature is an expression of "life" rather than a selection of products that are taken to be representative of that life. This view is typical of most conceptions of national literatures, which assert an organic relation between literature and life and hold that the selection of works for the national literature was disinterested. Howells compares American literature at the turn of the century to this ideal and finds that the literature does not measure up. More recent critics, who assume that a national literature entails the dominance of a particular faction of literary producers over the others, note the recognition of Howells and his fellow men of letters beyond the literary world as grounds for their view that a national literature did exist. Neither Howells nor these critics, however, is willing to assert what the academic field of American literature assumed from the beginning: that the works of dominant writers are organic expressions of American life.

By the time of *Literary Friends and Acquaintance*, of course, Boston was no longer dominant in literature, even if its ideals and examples may still have been (as Howells's own move from the *Atlantic* in Boston to *Harper's Monthly* in New York symbolized). New York was not the same kind of literary center as Boston, however. Where the Boston writers were natives of the city or its environs, New York drew its talent from the country as a whole. This fact seems to have led Howells himself to misrecognize New York's centrality in favor of the idea that America had "no literary centre."[34] New York had become a genuinely national center, while Boston had remained a regional one in spite of its dominance. The development of a national literary center represents changes in the publishing industry rather than in the origins of authors. During most of nineteenth century, American publishing was highly regionalized owing to the difficulty of national distribution. Improved transportation, the development of rationalized methods of production for magazines, and more favorable copyright laws all helped New York publishers to assume national dominance.

The shift of literary power to New York at first produced few changes in literary products or ideas, because New York's publishing houses and magazines were still much influenced by New England. In 1890 the literary was "still characterized by New England ideals and examples," as Howells suggested a few years later, in spite of its New York center. Many of the leading men of letters in New York were raised and educated in New England. The influence of the "New England empire" outlasted the actual rule of Boston. The leading magazines of 1890, the *Century*, the *Atlantic*, the *North American Review*, *Harper's Monthly*, and *Scribner's*, continued to express the literary ideals of New England, but those published in New York had larger circulations. By today's standards, they were all literary magazines. Most published fiction and poetry. All of them devoted considerable space to discussion of books, and many included discussions that we would be inclined to classify as literary theory. This suggests that the literary was a cultural area of considerable prestige and influence.

But effects of New York's more commercial environment would begin to be felt during the decade of the 1890s, when the world of magazine publishing underwent a revolution. A group of new magazines appeared that soon had circulations of more than twice that of *Harper's*. Published by newcomers such as S. S. McClure, Frank Munsey, Cyrus Curtis, and John Brisben Walker, these magazines achieved the first mass audiences for any media. The fundamental change was neither ideological nor regional but material: the mode of literary production changed and with it the literary product. The stimulus for these changes was the invention of a new product, which magazine publishers began to sell as their chief source of income: "the *attention* of the *audience*."[35] Prior to the 1890s, magazines were chiefly financed by their purchasers: "The magazine's relatively high price and limited geographical range gave them the select audience they desired."[36] After magazines came to depend on advertising income, the publisher's role changed: "No longer was he interested in the reader just as a reader; he became interested in the reader as a consumer of the advertiser's goods and services" (Peterson, 26). The new magazines needed to appeal to an audience that would be worthy of their advertiser's interest: "National advertising did not simply generate increased revenue. It reoriented editors away from the cultivation of a select audience and toward attracting advertisers who could be sure of a stable, recurring mass readership. In sum, the mass market transition will be underestimated if it is seen as simply increased 'commercialization.' The new editors not only expanded the scale and finances of the American magazine; they altered the very *idea* of the magazine" (Wilson, 48–49).

It was not just the contents of the magazine that changed, but the process by which the magazine and its contents were produced. Any literary work is a product—and by the nineteenth century, at least minimally, a commodity—but when Hawthorne, Emerson, and their New England compatriots were making their renaissance, literary production was organized on something like the craft model. While it may be a bit of an exaggeration to say that the New Englanders constituted themselves as a guild, the relatively closed circle in which they functioned protected them from competition. While many of them certainly were professionals in the sense that they earned a living from their literary activity, unlike guild members (or still less, professionals), there was no formal training for or regulation of their work. The New England authors had a great deal of freedom to organize their work lives as they chose. All of this changed, however, when the labor of writing became rationalized, first in newspaper production and then in magazines. As Christopher Wilson has shown, the transformation of the publishing industry produced a new kind of author. Instead of an individual who wrote on his or her own schedule under conditions of a degree of leisure, now the author was often someone who learned the "trade" on the staff of a newspaper, where a production quota had to be met. Or like Jack London and the autobiographical hero of *Martin Eden*, the author might practice in what amounted to a personal sweatshop, turning out piece after piece to be sent to editors and to be rejected over and over again. The difference between, say, Henry Thoreau, taking the time to know beans and to rewrite *Walden* eight times, and Martin Eden, working himself to the point where his ultimate success is not worth the price he paid for it, is so great that it is hard to think of the two characters as having the same occupation, even though we call them both authors.[37]

The changes in literary work went beyond the work lives of individual writers. Throughout most of the nineteenth century, magazine editors selected among materials offered to them for publication. But the new magazines increasingly planned their contents and solicited articles from writers. Staff planning encouraged professionalization of writers as specialists in certain subject areas, and magazines maintained lists of freelance writers from whom they regularly commissioned articles. In the first decade of the twentieth century, magazines began to publish materials written by salaried staff. The result of these changes was that the unknown writer had an ever smaller chance of getting his or her contribution accepted.

The familiar distinctions between literary and popular writing, between high and low culture, come into being as a result of the mass market transition. But they do not spring into existence fully developed. Critics in the older magazines lamented the poor quality of the new ones. Journalism was frequently blamed for the degeneration of literature in America, and these magazines were understood (correctly) as products of journalism. But journalism was also seen as affecting the quality and character of the older magazines themselves.[38] By the standards of magazines after World War II, even the new mass market magazines of the 1890s could be called literary. All of them published short stories and

47

serialized novels. The work of Ida Tarbell and Lincoln Steffens that appeared in *McClure's* seems more scholarly than journalistic, although, to the new editors, "literary" already could have pejorative connotations. When S. S. McClure tried to get Hamlin Garland to write "on the topics of the day, or stories of big personalities" for *McClure's*, the editor urged the author to "drop your *literary* pose and come with us."[39] But the new editors did not reject the literary so much as attempt to take it over. According to Wilson, "by exploiting the basic rhetoric of the culture of professionalism, the new editorial elite attempted to reunite 'art' and 'industry' and thereby bring the literary enterprise back into the mainstream."[40] This meant directing editorial content toward a broader audience than the Northern elite, and meant also the reorganization of publishing to make it resemble other commercial enterprises.

It would be a mistake, then, to simply regard the older magazines such as *Harper's* and the *Atlantic* as literary and the new ones as subliterary. The authors whom the field of American literature would pick to represent the period from 1890 to 1920 include mainly those who worked under the new, rationalized system of literary production. Henry James and Howells himself are obviously exceptions, but Crane, Dreiser, Norris, London, and even Willa Cather all experienced the new system at first hand. Other products of the system, such as Upton Sinclair, were regarded as significant literary figures at the time, although their work is no longer regarded as canonical. What needs to be kept in mind is the enormous influence of all kinds of writing during this period. This may seem less surprising if we remember that the other media now dominating mass culture were then barely in existence. While sound recording and motion picture technology existed, neither in 1900 had become significant forms of mass communication. Radio and television were decades away. While it would ultimately be the power of images and sounds that dethroned the literary, the development of mass market publishing marked the beginning of the end of its hegemony. As soon as the product became the audience's attention rather than the writer's work, literary considerations no longer governed profitable magazines. As a result, the men of letters, who established criteria and applied them in judgment, lost the power they had held. Their fall resulted in a crisis of succession as various cultural factions sought control of the literary.

Men of Letters and Literary Radicals

By about 1890, literature had become established in the newly formed English departments of colleges and universities, but the university had not yet begun to be a serious rival of the world of publishing for literary influence. More important for our purposes, American literature was neither much taught nor studied in these English departments, and it was certainly not the distinct object of an academic discipline. In fact, English literature had just attained that status by the turn of the century. Even the history of American literature was not mainly the province of scholars. Rather, this history was an element of the general literary culture, the realm of the man of letters, with influential treatments of the history of American literature written by Howells, Barrett Wendell, E. C. Stedman, Thomas Wentworth Higginson, and George Woodberry. Howells was the most influential person in American literary culture at the turn of the century, and no university scholar came close to challenging him for this position.

But this is not to say that by 1900 professors were without influence. As I will argue, the attacks made on "the professors" in the early years of the twentieth century were a response to the growing influence of the universities. If the university did not become the dominant cultural location of the literary until much later, perhaps not until after World War II, it nevertheless was influential enough at the turn of the century to begin to pose a threat to professional men of letters. The separation between the university and the world of letters was not, of course, absolute. After all, the research university was still quite new, and there remained many individuals in universities such as Harvard—to say nothing of the colleges—whose careers were formed prior to this development. There were men of letters, including Wendell and Woodberry, who held positions in the major universities. Brander Matthews was identified mainly as a man of letters who happened to hold university appointments during a portion of his career. What distinguished men of letters in and out of the university from scholars was their radically different discursive practices. Scholar-

ship was philological and historical, while the men of letters practiced criticism. Even when both wrote history, their practices
differed. The men of letters sought mainly to make knowledge of
literature available to the public while at the same time exercising
critical judgment. The scholars practiced in the positivist spirit.
Their goal was to add to the accumulation of knowledge about
language and literature.

In 1900, the leading critics, poets, and novelists were likely to
be connected with one another by virtue of their association with
the same magazines. Often the leading poets and novelists were
the leading critics. The most important of these was undoubtedly
Howells, who not only never taught in a college or university but
never attended one either. Howells begins his personal history of
American literature with the assertion that "If there was any one
in the world who had his being more wholly in literature that I
had in 1860, I am sure I should not have known where to find
him, and I doubt he could have been found nearer the centres of
literary activity than I then was, or among those more purely
devoted to literature than myself" (*LFA*, 1). But what is the literature in which Howells's being dwelt? It was not literature defined
in Arnoldian terms, since Howells was principally interested in
contemporary literature and not in the best that had been written
since the dawn of time. What Howells himself had done up to that
point is publish some poetry, including a book shared with another author, and write sketches and criticism for the *Saturday
Press*, a New York literary magazine. It is this second role that is
the more important in Howells's definition of himself, and not
only because poetry would not be his metier. Writing reviews and
sketches put Howells in touch with the literary world in a way
that merely writing poetry probably would not. It was Howells's
roles as editor of the *Atlantic Monthly* and critic for *Harper's* that
gave him his place of influence in American letters. While it is
doubtless the case that his reputation as a novelist contributed to
this influence, merely writing novels would not have been sufficient. Literature in Howells's times included criticism; editing a
magazine was just as literary as writing poetry.

The historians have argued about who among the men of letters dominated this national literature. Ruland, for example, asserts that those with the real power—"the Band," E. C. Stedman,

Richard Stoddard, Bayard Taylor, George Henry Boker, and Thomas Baily Aldrich—regarded Howells as an enemy.[41] These "Victorians," as Ruland aptly describes them, disapproved of Howells's realist aesthetics and his politics, especially his urging of clemency for the Haymarket anarchists. These disagreements were real, but they were contained within the literary community; whatever difference of opinion these men might have, they derived authority from and thus owed allegiance to the same institutions. So even though members of the band had opposed realism in no uncertain terms, Howells remained one of them; by the turn of the century they seemed to have forgiven him his earlier transgressions. In 1912, Howells's seventy-fifth birthday was celebrated by a lavish dinner thrown by Colonel Harvey, the head of Harper's publishing house and attended by 400 notables, including President Taft. The dinner itself is significant because it demonstrates the value accorded literariness. It would be hard to imagine such a dinner any time much before—or since. Howells was aptly described as "a valuable national possession" and as a "a public symbol" that stood for "the dominance of a single, old, traditional set of doctrines over American life, politics, and art."[42] The importance of the meaning of Howells as a symbol is not the injustice it manifestly did to him, but in the ultimate irrelevance of his opinions to his construction as a cultural treasure. The literary was already a category of value that could invest an object regardless of what other values were attached to it.

It is tempting to look back longingly to a literary world that was as broadly influential as the one these men of letters inhabited. Unlike the philologists who were defining the field of English in the universities, men of letters did not see themselves as specialists. On the contrary, as one of their number, Barrett Wendell, described him, "It is the privilege of the man of letters that he may venture on occasion to discuss matters in which he makes no pretense to be expert."[43] They wrote for a public that they took to be informed but equally unspecialized. Their organs were not little magazines, but the most prestigious periodicals then being published. Yet it would be an overstatement to assert that the men of letters of 1900 addressed a general public or polis. Their audience may have been unspecialized, but it was most certainly an elite. "Seven percent of the fourteen-to-seventeen-year-olds attended secondary school in 1890; by 1900, the percentage had increased to 11.4."[44] Only a tiny fraction of Americans had graduated from college. While the audience for major magazines such as *Harper's* could not have been limited to college graduates, it is hard to imagine that many of its readers had not attended secondary school. It is reasonable to assume that the educated elite shared an ideology that many other Americans did not. These other Americans may or may not have been illiterate. Many of them were literate in languages other than English. But the most significant difference was doubtless one of class.

The loss of a public literary and intellectual culture has lately been lamented by critics who contend that domination of intellectual life by the university has spelled the end of a public realm of political opposition.[45] No one, however, would mistake the men of letters who ruled turn-of-the-century literary culture for oppositional intellectuals. Nevertheless, they were intellectuals in the broader sense of that term used by Gramsci.[46] Using this broader definition, Zygmunt Bauman argues that "the world of the intellectuals was politically divided. They threw in their lot with one or the other of the class opponents engaged in a bitter conflict for the power resources of the state. Each choice, however, was argued and legitimized in terms of the hope that the selected class would desire, and be able, to create or sustain a society comfortable for intellectual pursuits; a society that admits in practice the centrality of specifically intellectual domains (like culture and education) and the crucial role of ideas in the reproduction of communal life."[47] The men of letters clearly threw in their lot with the bourgeoisie. Even Howells, who by the 1880s had become, under the influence of Tolstoy, a socialist, could hardly be called a member of the opposition. This is not to deny that Howells often took unpopular positions on literary and political issues. His campaign for realism was unpopular with many of his closest friends and he was virtually alone in his plea for clemency for the Haymarket anarchists. But Howells believed in America and American democracy as the instruments that would lead the world to greater justice and equality. His attitudes as a critic were "strongly favorable to realism, democracy, and patriotism."[48] And Howells seems like the radical fringe compared to the other leading men of letters of his day. They saw themselves as conservators of culture and defenders of the established order.

Yet, as Bauman shows, intellectuals could be critical even if they were not oppositional, that is, even if they did not identify themselves with the oppressed class, and the men of letters were critics of American culture. Some of this criticism was rooted in explicit moral or political positions. Many New England intellectuals, for example, opposed the imperialism that manifested itself in the Spanish-American War and its aftermath on the grounds that it violated the principles of democracy. Most often, however, the men of letters criticized America for failing to sustain their chosen intellectual pursuit, the literary. There was pervasive criticism of what the men of letters perceived as a decline in American intellectual life and literary tastes, a decline they often blamed on journalism and its influence on the new, mass-market magazines. Such criticism was one expression of the cultural hierarchy that had become a significant fact of American life only in the last quarter of the nineteenth century.[49] In identifying the literary with the top of this hierarchy, the men of letters created a space for the generation of oppositional "intellectuals" that came into being beginning around 1910. It was not, however, the same space the men of letters themselves had held. The new intellectuals saw themselves as the antithesis of Howells and the older men of letters, but they shared with them the assumption that the literary was a cultural force and that literature was a matter not merely of taste but of truth. It was because of the power of the literary under the men of letters that the new generation would regard it as worthy of their attempt to capture it. Though they might, in Bourne's words, be "converted from an aspiration for the career of a cultivated 'man of letters' to a fiery zeal for artistic and literary propaganda in the service of radical ideas," the new intellectuals sought to occupy the same cultural place the older men held.[50] Yet in spite of their unquestionable significance in American cultural history, this group never succeeded in this quest. They could not succeed because the place held by the men of letters ceased to exist.

The group I am calling the new oppositional intellectuals included Van Wyck Brooks, John Macy, Randolph Bourne, and Waldo Frank, who were identified at the time as "literary radicals." On the right, we find the New Humanists, Irving Babbitt, Paul Elmer More, and Stuart Sherman, critical intellectuals identified perhaps less with the bourgeoisie than with a mythical aristocracy. In Williams's terms, these two groups may be understood as representing, respectively, emergent and residual ideologies. All of these critics have been claimed as originators of the criticism of American literature. The new intellectuals may be distinguished from the old by their relative marginality. While they were not "independent" of the publishing apparatus, they also did not have control of it. Both groups were critics of American culture and not merely of American literature.

Literature plays a central role in the work of each group, though for neither group is American literature a starting place. What it means to be a "literary radical" is explained by Bourne when he describes his fictional alter ego, Miro, as owing "all his later emancipation" to a lecture by the Yale professor of English William Lyon Phelps. What Phelps did was to discuss the modern novel: "Hardy, Tolstoy, Turgenev, Meredith, even Trollope. . . . Modern novels . . . started the rift that widened into modern ideas" ("History," 189). Miro and his friends are described as abandoning the narrow confines of "literary studies" for history and philosophy, which would give meaning to literary scholarship and make the world the object to be known. And yet most of the literary radicals in practice continued to focus on literature. Brooks, Macy, Bourne, and Frank all held some genuinely radical political views and explicitly identified themselves at times with oppressed groups including workers, women, and immigrants, but for the most part they lacked a political program. And since their politics developed out of their experience of literature and not the reverse, the literary radicals did not have the means to offer a political analysis of literature. The literary radicals agreed that a new American tradition must be carved out of history, a position most familiarly stated in Brooks's essay "On Creating a Usable Past." They rejected what they saw as the Puritanism of the cultural conservators, whom they typically called "the professors." Brooks argued, in another influential formulation, that the American character had been formed upon the distinction between highbrow, "the acquisition of culture," and lowbrow, "the acquisition of money."[51] The radicals thus complained about the materialism of capitalism and industry as well as about the moribund idealism and moral rigidity of the cultural conservators. But not all of the radicals' critique was new. One of their basic demands, that literature and life be more closely connected, recapitulates a doctrine of Howells's realism, yet none of the radicals recognized in realism a partial enactment of their program, which if anything seems to have been less conscious then Howells's of the social realities of the day.

The radicals' literary nationalism did constitute a break with the predominant Anglophilia among the men of letters. Bourne explicitly rejects the Anglo-Saxon theory of American culture, and he calls for a new American nationalism, "transnational America." But even Bourne continued to protest against America's "cultural humility," the repetition of a theme as old as Emerson. And Bourne's "new nationalism" is not articulated by the other radicals.[52] If Brooks could be accused of chauvinism by older critics, he shared with them a basic acceptance of the primacy of racial and national categories, which he, like them, confused rather than distinguished. Brooks's views on literature and race, for example, share a great deal with those of George Woodberry.

If the literary radicals wanted a culture that reflected the realities of modern life, the New Humanists looked to the past to find an antidote to those realities. Babbitt must be regarded as the founder of this more unified movement, many of the members of which had been his students at Harvard. Where the literary radicals sought to create a legitimate American tradition, the New Humanists sought to bring the classical tradition to America. The central philosophical tenet of the New Humanism was the dualism of the human and the natural. Since neither was inherently dominant within the species, self-discipline or the "inner check" was necessary to rein in instinct and allow reason to prevail. Reason to the New Humanists was not the logic of science but the rational truths that were preserved in the great works of culture and in institutions such as property. Given this position, it is not surprising that the New Humanists were in the habit of praising the "natural aristocracy," which in practice usually turned out to be the actual cultural, financial, and political elites. It was, however, the idea of an aristocracy that appealed to the New Humanists more than any current set of rulers. The New Humanists were genuine reactionaries, antimodernists who found little to like in any aspect of contemporary American life. While most of the leading New Humanists were at one time or another teachers of literature, Babbitt himself wrote relatively little literary criticism. His work could best be described as moral philosophy or social criticism. Paul Elmer More published a good deal more literary criticism, and a substantial amount of it dealt with American authors and works. Though More often found things to praise in American writers, he did not seek to construct an American tradition. For most of the New Humanists, the tradition began with the Greeks and ended in the Renaissance.

Both the New Humanists and the literary radicals were critical of the university and its relation to American culture. This criticism marks the historical point of emergence for what seems now to be an eternal opposition between the intellectuals and the academy. Why did this opposition emerge in the 1910s? One reason surely is the simple fact of the rising influence of the university and of literary instruction therein. All of the new intellectuals had studied literature in the university. While many of the men of letters had been to college, they had not studied literature there since literature was not part of curricula until the late nineteenth century. Literature for them was an extracurricular activity or an occupation. By the time the intellectuals attended college, literary instruction was common. Macy and Brooks took undergraduate degrees at Harvard, graduating in 1899 and 1907, respectively, while Stuart Sherman received a Harvard Ph.D. in English. Bourne studied at Columbia and Waldo Frank at Yale. Their experience of literature in the university partially explains why "the professors" are so often portrayed by these new intellectuals as the enemy. Of course, the rise of the university made such complaints plausible. Previously, professors had not been socially powerful enough to engender such attacks.

The literary radicals did not offer a blanket critique of specialization, and science was not an object of their attack; their scorn was directed specifically at professors in literature and the humanities. The literary radicals came to depict the professoriate as standing in the way of the growth of American civilization. This view grossly inflates the importance of the academy in the literary. Brooks, in his most influential essay, "On Creating a Usable

Past," writes as though the academy had already established a monopoly over the discussion of American literature, even though the subject accounted for less than 10 percent of the literature courses offered by English departments: "Our professors continue to pour out a stream of historical works repeating the same points of view to such an astonishing degree that they have placed a sort of Talmudic seal upon the American tradition. . . . I am aware, of course, that we have no cumulative culture, and that consequently the professors who guard the past and the writers who voice the present have less in common in this country than anywhere in the Old World. The professors of American literature can, after all, offer very little to the creators of it."[53] It may be that Brooks was responding to the *Cambridge History of American Literature*, the first major attempt to produce a scholarly history, but whatever the immediate provocation, his opposition to the professors is primarily a response to the academy's encroachment on territory previously held by writers or men of letters. Yet the discipline of American literature would not successfully respond to Brooks's challenge to "invent a usable past" until around 1940. Until at least that time, criticism of American literature remained largely outside of the university and almost entirely outside of American literature as a discipline.

Unlike the literary radicals, the New Humanists did not blame "the professors"; they were professors. Rather, the New Humanists blamed America's literary ills in part on the research university for abandoning the classical curriculum. Babbitt's first book, *Literature in the American College*, is an indictment of the entire culture of the new university. Research, the elective system, and the influence of science and romanticism join the absence of the classics as evidence of the decline of the American college.[54] Sherman, the only one of the new intellectuals with a Ph.D., complained that philologists like George Kittredge did not encourage their students in the "love of good literature" and warped the profession by their insistence on training graduate students in turning up meaningless facts about the Middle Ages.[55] Babbitt advocated a new degree that would place less emphasis on research and more on wide reading, good taste, and humanistic values (132–49). The problem with the American university, according to the New Humanists, is that it was all too much like modern American culture: materialist, romantic, scientific, humanitarian, industrial, and so on.

The literary radicals agreed that the university shared the culture's materialism or lack of spirituality, but they also found in the university the Puritanism of the men of letters. The radicals grouped the New Humanists with the men of letters and literary researchers and called them all "the professors." They not only failed to recognize the differences between conservatives in and outside of the university, but also lumped all professors inside of it together. It is perhaps not surprising that undergraduates would have failed to perceive the divisions that the professors themselves reported in the Harvard English Department, or that they would be unaware of the conflicts that already troubled MLA meetings in the first decade of this century.[56] Brooks was aware that "there were many mansions in the house of literature at Harvard, and Kittredge, Briggs, Baker, and Mr. Copeland, Bliss Perry and Irving Babbitt inhabited not mansions but worlds of their own," but he was not aware of any organized opposition between generalists and scholars. On the contrary, it struck him that "all the professors, whatever their specialties might be, seemed to be in addition men of letters."[57] The radicals addressed their attack mainly toward the professors' tastes and values. What both scholars and men of letters in the university shared was a preference for English literature and European culture. Furthermore, most of the courses offered, at least at Harvard, covered the period from the Middle Ages to the Renaissance. The intellectuals thus felt doubly estranged from the literature they learned at the university: it was remote both culturally and historically.

Yet Brooks's account of his years at Harvard doesn't suggest that he felt estranged then. He describes Harvard as "intensely literary," and that he went there because he "knew he was born a writer." The literariness of Harvard seems to have been as much a part of the atmosphere as of the curriculum. The elective system allowed Brooks to follow his literary interests "counterbalanced by little else." But the literary at Harvard was not what one would expect given the attacks on stodgy professors. In Brooks's circle, "the 'Harvard aesthete' was the type to which a majority of the members were more or less related." At its extreme, this type "liked to quote Baudelaire and Huysmans, Mallarmé and the Marquis de Sade" (*Autobiography*, 105–6). Rather than being the seat of moralizing idealism, Brooks's Harvard seems thoroughly aestheticized: "the cultivation of taste at Harvard was not only occasionally mistaken for talent but sometimes went far to stultify it" (107–8). The tastes prevalent at Harvard, far from being those of the last century, look forward to modernism: "When one added these tastes together, the royalism and the classicism, the Anglo-Catholicism, the cults of Donne and Dante, the Sanskrit, the Elizabethan dramatists and French symbolist poets, one arrived at T. S. Eliot, the quintessence of Harvard" (112). It was not, then, mainly the character of literature at the university that led the literary radicals to reject the academy. Rather, the radicals believed that the university stood for the mainstream of American culture. They wanted to position themselves outside of that mainstream and outside of its institutions. Although Brooks taught American literature briefly at Stanford, the radicals became writers rather than academics.

Finding themselves on the outside, however, the radicals became aware of their own marginality. The conditions that allowed them cultural significance without cultural power were to some extent recognized by Brooks in his discussion of the highbrow and the lowbrow. This distinction is the first recognition of the intellectual consequences of the development of mass culture. Brooks, of course, thought that he had discovered a permanent division in American culture since the Puritans, but he is reading back into history a distinction that is far more applicable to American culture since the 1890s. His complaint is that in America only two kinds of writing are recognized: literature, to which a writer may belong only after he is dead and which in conception is so "high and dry" as to be beyond the reach of the living, and the typical best-seller, the "immitigable trash" that is literature's opposite (*Coming-of-Age*, 5–6). What this opposition cannot accommodate is precisely the sort of living literature Howells describes in *Literary Friends and Acquaintance* and imagines in *A Hazard of New Fortunes*. Paradoxically, it is just this kind of living literature in which a "born writer" such as Brooks seeks to dwell. The protest of the literary radicals was, as much as anything else, against their own marginalization.

It is this marginalization, however, that would allow the emergence of an oppositional literary culture in the 1930s. When economic forces fracture the literary power represented by the men of letters, a literary opposition is allowed to develop, but also the university is allowed to establish literary dominance and to represent through literature the cultural dominant.

During much of the nineteenth century, "American literature" signified a project rather than a history. Critics repeatedly called for a literature that would live up to the democratic character of the new land; this call was best exemplified by Emerson in "The American Scholar." By the late nineteenth century, while those calls had not entirely ceased, it was generally accepted that there was literature in America. Such literature was the subject of numerous histories, most intended as primary and high school textbooks; those histories will be the subject of the next chapter. But history of literature was, for those outside of the academic research community, preparation for a literary career. It was not a career in itself. For the men of letters, American literature was not merely historical; it was also a current practice, something people were actively engaged in making. And if it was history, it was not yet a tradition. No real canon existed, and, although standard authors were recognized, nothing united these authors as distinctively American. The American literature over which the men of letters governed and the literary radicals sought influence was contemporary literature.

In the next chapter, we will look at the prehistory of American literature as a discipline, the early histories and their attempts to make an American tradition. Many of these histories were written by men of letters; a few were written by teachers. But none of them until the *Cambridge History of American Literature* was the product of literary researchers. Since these histories have an impact on the way the subdiscipline of American literature is constructed, they constitute the major way that the men of letters directly affected that field. The literary radicals also contributed criticism of historical figures in American literature, as did their right-wing counterparts More and Sherman. We will find that much of the debate will center not on the literature directly, but on questions of the existence and character of American civilization.

2

Preprofessional History and Criticism

In 1900, the American literary world was permeated by the sense that an era had recently come to a close. Certainly one of the major interests of *Literary Friends and Acquaintance* to its contemporary audience was the fact that Howells had managed to meet all of the then-departed literary lions of New England, and had been friends with many of them. The last of the major Boston writers, Oliver Wendell Holmes, died in 1894. A memoir of Brook Farm published in 1900 notes that of all of the "memorable company" of literary lights not one was then alive.[1] A second edition of a school history dated 1903 begins with a list of authors and men of letters who had died since the first appeared seven years earlier, including William Ellery Channing, John Fiske, Bret Harte, Edward Bellamy, and R. H. Stoddard. Some critics such as Barrett Wendell were already speaking of the era of Hawthorne and Emerson, which he named the "New England renaissance," as a peak from which contemporary literature was much fallen.[2] This American fin de siècle lacked, for the most part, the sense of decadence and extremity that characterized the period in many European cultures. The political and social situation—at least as the cultural elite saw it—did not support the conclusion that radical change was in the offing.

Nevertheless, many within the literary perceived American literature to be adrift, having been cut off from its moorings in Boston. The construction of an American literary tradition is the subject for this book as a whole, but in the America of 1900, such tradition-building was in its infancy. In fact, many commentators argue against the idea that there was an American literary tradition. Howells believed that the New England group had failed to found a tradition: "It may be ungracious to say that they have left no heirs to their peculiar greatness; but it would be foolish to say that they left an estate where they had none to bequeath."[3] Similarly, George Woodberry lamented that the complete failure of the literature that flowered before the Civil War "to establish an American tradition—none of its authors left any successor in the same line—indicates something parasitical in it, as if it were not self fed; a literature from European culture we have had, but it does not perpetuate itself in an American culture; and in the change of conditions, apparently, it is only from a new growth that literature may now be anticipated."[4] Rather than forming a national tradition, Woodberry concludes that "Our past literature is in the main sectional" (249).

It was not just continuity that was lacking. The previous era was not long enough past to assure one that those who seemed giants when compared to the current generation would in fact turn out to be giants when history compared them to Shakespeare or Milton. Thus Howells refused to deem the greatest of American poets canonical: "What Longfellow's place in literature will be, I shall not offer to say; that is Time's affair" (*LFA*, 211). Few critics were willing to go out on a limb, as Brownell did in believing that time had already enlarged Emerson's figure: "Emerson is of the company of Plato and Pascal, of Shakespeare and Goethe, emulating their cosmic inclusiveness."[5] But the problem was larger than the issue of individual rankings: it was as much a matter of what the term "American literature" designated. It could not refer unambiguously to a canon—a term much in use at the time—because only time could determine what writing was canonical. On the other hand, the idea of literature was so strongly dependent on the notion of a canon that most early histories are compilations of the biographies of more or less the same list of authors. These standard authors were a de facto canon, but it is important to understand the difference between them and the acknowledged canon of English literature. That canon was more or less beyond criticism. As we will see in the next chapter, the value of Chaucer, Spenser, Shakespeare, and Milton could only be reaffirmed. None of America's standard authors had reached that exalted level. Brownell finds that what Emerson's style "lacks is art in the larger sense" (184). Thus the highest ranking of American authors were typically subject to criticism, even in textbooks. Furthermore, while textbook histories typically did not discuss living writers, such books still portrayed American literature as in process, and thus did not identify it entirely with the standard authors.

The issue of defining American literature was not simply a matter of the status of its authors. The relationship of American to English literature was perhaps the most frequently discussed issue, but it reflects the larger question of the relationship of American to English civilization. As we saw in the previous chapter, many American critics wanted to understand America as a branch of English civilization and did not distinguish a unique American civilization. The first generation of professional American historians typically explained American history by reference to a Teutonic heritage. This theory held that American democracy resulted from the racial characteristics of Germanic peoples that had produced protodemocracies in prehistoric villages. Such explanations were in 1900 relatively recent in their popularity. Racist theories did appear in the works of the major historians of midcentury—George Bancroft, John Motley, William Prescott, and Francis Parkman—to a greater or lesser degree, but in general these historians did not explain American institutions in racial terms. From around 1870 until after 1895, however, when Turner's frontier thesis had begun to make itself felt, the Teutonic origins theory was the chief means by which the unique character of America's institutions was explained.

For some historians, Anglo-Saxon blood explained the existence of democratic institutions themselves, while others thought that race explained why rule of law prevailed in spite of these institutions.[6] This ambivalence about democracy among America's cultural leaders seems to have grown as the century progressed. As early as the 1850s, in the face of a rising tide of immigrants, Boston's elite began to abandon the democratic ideals of earlier generations. The Civil War brought a renewed outpouring of rhetoric in favor of democracy, but afterward, in response to increasing immigration, claims for Anglo-Saxon superiority become increasingly attractive.[7] In the early part of the century, anti-

British sentiment was common in American writing in all fields. A cult of literary nationalism from the 1830s through the 1850s demanded cultural independence from Britain.[8] While literary nationalism never disappeared, in the later part of the century the leading critics were far more likely to assert the connections between American and English literature. Nineteenth-century primary-school textbooks, including readers, histories, geographies, and even spellers, moved from depicting England as a "corrupt monster . . . fighting to maintain its tyranny" during the American Revolution to a vision of England as a beneficial parent: "by the end of the century American textbooks had fully reclaimed their British heritage. The English relationship had been fused into American nationalism, giving it a glorious past and an inherited soul of virtue and prestige, but purified in the American environment."[9]

Such dependence on England, however, made it harder to distinguish what was unique about American civilization. Both the skepticism about democracy and the affiliation with England contributed to the failure of American literature to be generally accepted as independent from English literature by the keepers of culture. While Emerson and Lowell in the 1830s and 1840s could readily identify America with the democratic spirit and look forward to its triumph, the cultural leaders of the later part of the century found whatever hope for the future they could in the influence of the Anglo-Saxon heritage and English culture. As I argued earlier, the assumption of the superiority of the Anglo-Saxon race and of English culture served the purpose of reinforcing the position of the dominant ethnic group, but it also restricted the development of an independent conception of American civilization and American literature. While the early histories of American literature express different points of view on the independence of American literature, they imply by their very existence that the subject is distinct enough to merit separate study. Nevertheless, even Fred Lewis Pattee, who makes the strongest statement on behalf of American literary independence, is unable to say in any certain terms what makes American literature distinct.[10]

Regardless of the position the histories took on the relations of English and American literature, all of them were expressions of nationalism. The wide production of these books, mainly for use in schools, cannot be explained by the recent perception that Americans had produced a significant body of literature, nor by the belief that an era had ended, nor even by the existence of a powerful literary sector of American culture. All of these factors doubtless contributed, but they did not provide a motive for the use of these textbooks in the schools and thus for the market that would spur production of even more titles. On the other hand, nationalism was a growing force in American society, and the schools were one place where this force was expressed. Horace Scudder was undoubtedly correct when he asserted that "nine out of ten educated Americans, if asked what is the chief end of the common schools, would answer, To make good American citizens."[11] They may not have agreed with Scudder's view of the importance of literature in this endeavor, but such agreement would explain why histories of American literature were produced in such numbers and why standard American authors came to be regarded as essential to any successful common-school reader. It is worth keeping in mind, however, a major point of the last chapter: American literature was identified as much if not more with contemporary writing than with a history of past authors and works. The whole enterprise of history writing represents only one part of the pre-World War I conception of American literature.

Early histories of American literature fall into four categories. The largest included textbooks designed for elementary or high school use. Since American literature was largely absent from the college curriculum, there could have been little market for such texts there. The textbooks may be subdivided into two groups: those focusing almost entirely on the standard authors and those describing a much broader range of American writers. The second major category of histories were critical statements of men of letters, and later, of a few literary radicals. These works contained more criticism and fewer bare facts than did the textbooks, and they were to some extent less focused on biography. The difference between the textbooks and the more critical histories is suggested in the preface to Wendell and Greenough's *A History of Literature in America*: "When it was proposed that Wendell's *Literary History of America* should be reprinted in a school edition, it was clear to us that for such use the book needed thorough revision. Many passages, which properly found place in a book intended for general reading, involved expressions of opinion obviously unsuitable for schools."[12] In practice, all of the textbooks were based on the history and criticism of the men of letters and on the books of the third category, those few that deserve to be called comprehensive histories and from which the professional study of American literature would most directly follow. These are Moses Coit Tyler's *A History of American Literature*, and Charles F. Richardson's *American Literature 1607–1885*. The books by Tyler and Richardson are cited by virtually every other historian, and are seminal to the project of American literature as a field of study. Finally, the most important early history is *The Cambridge History of American Literature*, which differs from the others in its scope and in the collaborative character of its production.

Comprehensive Histories

Moses Coit Tyler's *History of American Literature* (1878) is the first academic history of American literature, although Tyler was a professor of history rather than English, and his interests were very much influenced by this academic affiliation. This book covers the years 1607 to 1765, while another work, *The Literary History of the American Revolution*, deals with the later eighteenth century. What is striking about Tyler's work today is its inclusiveness—at least of writing by white men. While Tyler consistently offers evaluative comments unsupported by argument— a habit we will find in most works discussed in this chapter—he does not seem to use his aesthetic judgments to exclude authors or works from consideration. Tyler's comprehensiveness lies in the quantity of authors treated and the detail of the historical context he presents. He offers no frame to distinguish American literature, except the location of its production, and finds no patterns that are characteristic. Literature for Tyler is as much a record of intellectual history as it is of aesthetics. Rather than providing merely a history of belles-lettres, Tyler discusses at length sermons, theology, and political writing, and even includes brief mention of journalism and physical science. Thus Tyler accurately describes his book as a search for the record in written words that Americans have made of their minds.[13] His critical commentary on the stylistic or aesthetic qualities of the works he discusses is one part of the description of that record, but it is subordinate to his larger task, which is historical. Because of its exhaustiveness, *A History of American Literature* was used by other early historians as a reference work, but its role in carving out the field of American literature was limited to a very rough marking of its boundaries.

Even the latter, however, cannot safely be asserted of the second installment of Tyler's work, *The Literary History of the American Revolution*. While the earlier history covers more than a century and a half, the later one deals with a mere twenty years. Since the books are of roughly the same length, it is clear that the history of the revolution must assume a very broad notion of the literary. Tyler observes that the "period actually had a literary product very considerable in amount."[14] The literary product, however, includes writing of virtually any sort and, not surprisingly, a great deal of prose concerning the political issues of the revolution. Tyler is aware that "literature" may have a more restricted definition: "literature in the higher sense of that word,— literature as an expression of the aesthetic mood, literature apart from mere instruction, apart, also, from the aims of debate." But this sense of the word, which will be the dominant one in American literature as a discipline, is clearly subordinate in Tyler's literary history of the revolution. While he notes that new literary life was beginning before the revolution, "from about the year 1774, little trace of an aesthetic purpose in American letters is to be discovered until after the close of the revolution" (*LHAR*, 1:11). Tyler's history thus deals mainly with works that will not even be considered literature by most other writers of literary histories, before or after American literature is institutionalized. Tyler's concerns are far more typical of the historian than of the literary scholar, but his broader use of the term suggests that literary study was not in the late nineteenth century irrevocably bound to constitute the kind of object it did. The distinction between history and literature as disciplinary objects was only in Tyler's time becoming established, and Tyler himself is an example of its remaining blurred. As a result, Tyler's histories serve mainly as resources, rather than as models, for later literary histories.

Yet it has been asserted that in one respect, Tyler determined the future course of the field of American literature from his day to the present. In the earlier history, Tyler discusses mostly literature produced in New England, and the argument goes that in so doing Tyler attributes the origins of American literature to New England and thereby neglects the contributions of other colonies. The apparent result is a narrative of the development of American literature centered around the development of a literary culture in New England during the nineteenth century.[15] It is curious, however, to attribute this narrative to Tyler. The most glaring problem is that Tyler does not discuss nineteenth-century literature in any of his four volumes. Tyler does provide a comparatively detailed account of why much literature was produced in New England and little elsewhere, the facts of which have not, to my knowledge, been challenged. Not all of Tyler's account is persuasive, as, for example, when he asserts that New England was a thinking community rather than an agricultural or manufacturing one (*A History*, 1:98). But in pointing out the high level of education in New England and the early existence and use of a printing press there, as opposed to the lack of education and presses elsewhere, Tyler is engaged in social analysis that one will rarely find in other histories. By taking into account specific historical circumstances, Tyler avoids making race the all-determining factor in the development of American literature. How could race be determinate when Virginians were just as English as New Englanders, but failed to produce a literature of their own? Finally, while Tyler does claim that the people of seventeenth-century New England had the largest share in founding American literature, he makes no claims that attribute the characteristics of later American literature to colonial New England; on the contrary, he concludes *A History of American Literature* with the assertion that from the time of the revolution "American literature flows in one, great common stream, and not in petty rills of geographical discrimination" (2:318). In the later work, he names "two chief centers" of higher literary life, "one in New England, one in the Middle Colonies" (*LHAR*, 1:11).

Tyler's work remained an important body of historical research well into the twentieth century, but, contrary to the conventional wisdom, Richardson's book seems to have been the model for most other early histories. His *American Literature* (1886) is explicitly an attempt to define American literature, and he works at this from several different angles. Where Tyler's definition of American literature is no more than a tautology, Richardson uses the theory of Teutonic origins to define Americans and thus those who might produce American literature. To drive this point home, the first chapter opens with a brief discussion of Native American predecessors of the English who "left unimportant literary remains."[16] Richardson acknowledges that Native Americans have had an impact on American literature, but this has not been a result of their own literary productions. Rather, these are mentioned only as the other against which American literature will be defined. But the fact that Native literature is mentioned at all demonstrates that definition was still an issue. A second kind of definition involves critical discrimination among works by Americans. The book's stated goal is by "applying well-known laws of criticism" to answer questions such as "What have American writers thus far done, worthy to be mentioned beside . . . the great writers of this and previous centuries? What of our books are world's-books, and why? How and why have American writers succeeded and failed?" (ix, xx).

Richardson was a professor at Dartmouth College, where he had graduated in 1871 before going on to spend ten years in journalism. Before returning to Dartmouth in 1882, he published *A Primer of American Literature*, a small volume that contains commentaries on 100 writers. Although Richardson was a member of the MLA, there is no record of his attending any of its meetings, and he seems to have achieved a reputation as a great teacher of undergraduates rather than as a scholar.[17] *American Literature* comes too early to have been much influenced by the organized research program of the discipline of English, and the book's mission is clearly critical rather than philological. Yet his book is academic for more reasons than its having been produced by a professor. The book's goals of comprehensive history and definitive critical judgment are ones inspired by the ethos of the university rather than that of magazines. Richardson also shows the influence of the academy when he describes Anglo-Saxon as "the first English" which is so important that "without its study no intelligent knowledge of our language or literature can be attained" (401).

There is no indication that Richardson's knowledge of the Anglo-Saxon language had any impact on his understanding of American literature. On the other hand, his conception of that literature is thoroughly imbued with the racism of the Teutonic origins theory. Thus another guiding question is, "What have been the relations between cause and effect, between the Saxon mind in England and the Saxon mind in America?"(xx). Saxon racial characteristics include strength, courage, excess of gluttony and drunkenness, love of home and children, a stern and undemonstrative temper kindled most by patriotism and love of family, monotheism, individualism, and the capacity for adaptation to new environments and assimilation of foreigners. Three Teutonic nations share these traits—presumably, Germany, England, and the United States—which are thus "akin in race, in speech and in general attitude toward religion and social progress. Two of these three nations read each other's books and periodicals, have a constant interchange of material and intellectual goods, and are in essentials but a single folk" (9). Literature throughout America is thus English literature, since even those of different races are quickly assimilated by the Saxons (34–35).

Since the Saxon "race-type" is the same in England and America, what distinguishes Americans and American literature can only be the new environment in which the race finds itself. Richardson begins by asserting some positive impact of climate and other physical conditions on intellectual development, but later seems to back off from attributing any specific effects of these conditions on literature. The relevant conditions are mainly what we would call cultural. One of the most important of these is America's previous colonial status and its attendant provincialism, which caused American literature until the nineteenth century to remain imitative of British literature and dependent upon English institutions. Richardson asserts that the United States did become a nation, however, not a confederation of nations. Political and social events beginning with the revolution have produced national sovereignty and forged a national character, though one that remains essentially English. Richardson dismisses regional differences and asserts that there exists an "essentially united American people, with common hopes and a common destiny" (42–43). The homogeneity of America, on which Matthew Arnold remarked during his visit in 1885, is a result of the process of Americanization, which in turn is made possible by American institutions such as general education in addition to the remarkable assimilative powers of the Saxon race. Americanization, together with the isolation that has made the United States a peaceable nation, has prevented social and political instability: "Purely socialistic disorders can be quelled more easily in the great American cities than in European capitals, partly because of the peaceable habit of the citizens, rich and poor, and partly because property is more widely distributed. Even the denizens of 'shanty-town' in New York City own some property, and do not want a communistic distribution of their goats and geese" (45). Nevertheless, Richardson notes with alarm the existence of "ignoramuses," who, unlike intelligent women and youths, may vote, and the residuum of a "debased foreign society" in New York. Only a natural aristocracy that is "on top" keeps these potentially anarchic elements in check. "The town-meeting of the colonies has developed into no commune today" (46). It is thus elitism and inequality that are responsible for America's political and literary success. American authors for the most part have been "sons of aristocrats," though of a natural aristocracy of "righteousness, intelligence and good-breeding, handed down from father to son; but from this aristocracy the literature of our nation has sprung" (56). Richardson stresses his conception of literature as against one that would identify it with "deck-hands, longshoremen, and stage drivers, California miners, Chinese, highway robbers, buffaloes, and Indians" (xv). In his vision, "America literature is the literature of a cultured and genuine Democracy, a sort of Saxon-Greek renaissance in the New World" (61–62).

Richardson does celebrate religious freedom and finds advantages in the freedom America had from historical tradition. History and tradition are helpful for literature, but "it is the American mind, after all, which has made [American] literature possible." Isolation is thus, on the whole, beneficial: "High intellectual independence is sure to produce literature sooner or later, when it recognizes the real bounds of its freedom, and gathers schools and scholars about it. American isolation promoted active religious work; religion soon demanded political freedom as well as spiritual; and the free prayer and the free vote left the whole mind free. Cotton Mather, Samuel Adams, Ralph Waldo Emerson—the logical sequence is as clear as the chronological" (50–51). In another place he asserts that "Bradford and Winthrop were the intellectual ancestors of Emerson and Hawthorne" (xvii). Here we find the first suggestion of claims that will later be made for the historical continuity of American civilization and literature, and we see them firmly rooted in a racist conception of Americanism.

Yet Richardson's book does not use much of the framework he establishes to actually analyze American literary works or authors. He does not, for example, systematically attempt to answer the question, "What have been the cause and effect relations between the Saxon mind in America and the literature it produces?" He will occasionally assert something like "Emerson's philosophy . . . is an Anglo-Saxon philosophy" (348), but the book does not consistently show what works or elements of them are attributable to racial traits or environmental factors. Explicit criteria and demonstrable evidence, however, are not necessary to separate sheep from goats. Perhaps the most consistent expression of Richardson's racism is his selection of authors to be treated. As might be expected, given Richardson's racism and elitism, authors who are not white and from the middle or upper classes are mostly excluded. Women are also given little attention. Anne Bradstreet and Phillis Wheatley are dismissed in the same sentence as "mere curiosities" (40). Richardson's racism, sexism, and class bias are not merely expressed opinions unrelated to his aesthetic judgments. His theories inform those judgments in a fundamental way, even if they do so silently. In the school histories, we will find an even greater silence, since most of these fail to articulate their assumptions about race, gender, or class, but they represent American literature mainly as the product of male aristocrats of English descent.

If Richardson fails to offer a systematic historical analysis, his book is more consistent in its critical project. Even here, however, the book lacks argument and analysis. Richardson offers summary judgments of every writer he discusses, but, despite his reference to "laws of criticism," no criteria are articulated. While most later histories of the pre-World War I era generally imitate Richardson's pattern of exclusion and his rankings, he left them no coherent aesthetic by which these could be justified. The issue is not merely the absence of explanation for individual judgments, but the lack of an aesthetic that would explain the value of the standard authors. Thus, while white, male, elite New Englanders are virtually the only group eligible for discussion, Richardson finds much to disapprove of in their work. Emerson, for example, is treated as an important figure, perhaps the most important, since he is the only one who merits two chapters, one on prose, the other on poetry. Emerson's value lies in his truth or correctness; his faults are aesthetic or formal. Emerson is guilty of "vagueness of thought and utterance. . . . Emerson maunders along in well-balanced, terse sentences, which are not devoid of sense, separately, but are combined in no consistent or valuable whole" (367). Yet there are no comparable passages explaining why Emerson's prose is successful, even if it is asserted that his style is "original." For Richardson, Emerson and other leading American authors have enough aesthetic merit to qualify as producers of literature, but they remain valuable more for the truth they convey and the race and class character they embody.

The School Histories

Tyler and Richardson both construct their versions of American literature on a principle even more prominent in the school histories.[18] That principle is authorship, and it is more important in Richardson than in Tyler because of the latter's fuller presentation of history. But both texts make the author the major principle of organization after simple chronology (and, in Richardson's case, generic categories). Literary history is thus rendered less as a narrative than as a chronicle or sequence. Narrative is reserved for individual sections of Richardson's work, and these stories are most often authors' biographies. Biographies in greater or lesser detail are offered of all major and many minor figures.

In most of the school histories, the reliance on the author is even more pronounced. Given the lack of a narrative in most of the histories, it is hard to figure out how Baym could conclude that they were all telling the same story of the rise of American literature in New England culture. In fact, the majority of the school histories make no such claim, let alone tell such a story, and only a few, such as Pancoast's book, are genuinely narratives. The histories do uniformly regard the standard authors of mid-nineteenth-century Boston and vicinity as the high point of American literature. What they do not do is tell any more than the briefest narrative of the emergence of Boston as a literary center or its influence on later American authors. The form the school histories took was doubtless a reflection of the pedagogy typical of the era. Students were much more likely to be asked to memorize the material they were presented than to analyze or synthesize it. These books seemed designed to produce "mental discipline" in students, rather than to serve as the beginning of training in an academic discipline.

The school histories vary greatly in size and complexity, with somewhat less variation in manner of presentation. While some of them, such as Mary Fischer's, could be described as collections of biographies, others, such as Pancoast's, provide more in the way of framework for the successive biographies. Some of the histories stick exclusively to those authors who are considered major figures, while others devote considerable space to the mention of minor writers. Some books restrict themselves to a definition of literature that includes little other than poetry, fiction, and the essay, while others include political oratory, theology, and history as significant literary genres. All of the histories foreground the standard authors: Irving, Cooper, Hawthorne, Emerson, Bryant, Longfellow, Holmes, Whittier, and Lowell. Histories such as Fischer's and Burton's present American literature as if it were produced only by these and a few other writers, who might include Franklin, Poe, Whitman, and Thoreau. Yet as presented in these histories, these writers do not form a tradition. There is nothing that links them into a coherent group. More typical are histories that, while giving more space and prominence to the standard authors, mention numerous other figures. Pattee's book is an extreme example of this approach. After a brief introduction offering a justification for considering American literature as independent of English literature and mentioning four "agencies" that determine the character of a literature—race, environment, epoch, and personality—Pattee organizes his book as a chrono-logical progression of authors grouped into larger periods. The larger periods are introduced by brief descriptions, but these in no way mitigate the fragmentation of the book, which is only emphasized by the ubiquitous headings and subheadings. Perhaps because Pattee hoped his book would be used as a college text, he provides copious references to secondary materials such as biographies and lists of "required readings" in the works of the authors he discusses. Pattee casts a much wider net than usual, including even a chapter on "Woman in Literature"—in which, however, woman writers since the Civil War are dismissed in advance as monotonous because they are confined to a few genres and subjects.

Barrett Wendell

If Richardson set the agenda for most early histories of American literature, of these Barrett Wendell's seems to have had the most impact on later, professional treatments of American literature. As Vanderbilt effectively summarizes, Wendell's *History* contributed a number of concepts that have had lasting influence on the discipline of American literature:

> Wendell remains important for several pioneering theses: his notion of the renaissance of New England, accompanied by his speculations of the literary cycle; his suggested herding of most of his major writers in prewar America into the mode of romanticism; and his faithful pursuit of inexperience as the salient feature of American life and character. No doubt Wendell was strongly influenced in this last case by his friend Henry Adams's brilliant analysis in the *History of the United States* (which Wendell cited). But Wendell was more tenacious in tracking that potentially creative naïveté and can rightly be considered a chief forerunner of the spate of studies in the 1950s whose authors recognized (or believed they had discovered) the explanatory power of innocence in the various phases and subject areas of American history.[19]

Yet Wendell's innovations, of which this is only a partial list, do not tell the whole story. His book remains a recognizable product of the literary at the turn of the century. Wendell's critical judgments are based on the same criteria as founded criticism in the leading magazines; like Stedman and Howells, Wendell was a "custodian of culture,"[20] even though he expresses doubts about the idea of "culture" as a social force in Matthew Arnold's sense. Like his contemporaries, Wendell valued formal qualities such as "refinement," something he found in literature of both the middle states and New England. American literature in general was also characterized by its "decency," a trait that distinguished it from contemporary European literature. Virtually every major writer, even Poe—though not Whitman—is praised for his "purity" or avoidance of decadence. This Victorianism would seem to make Wendell himself an example of the sort of innocence Henry May describes as ending during the decade of the 1910s. The quality that most distinguishes New England literature for Wendell is its seriousness. Despite their formal successes, Irving, Cooper, Bryant, and Poe "never dealt with deeply significant matters" (*LHA*, 230). Like the other men of letters of his era, Wendell demanded of literature serious moral purpose.

Yet Wendell's *A Literary History of America* distinguishes itself from all other early histories by the fact that it presents a coherent argument about its subject. Where Richardson, Pattee, and others merely assert that race and environment determine the character of a literature, Wendell has a theory about how these factors might actually affect American literature. One element of the theory is a cyclical conception of literary growth and decline. Literary periods, according to Wendell, inevitably develop in a pattern of innovation, flowering, and decline. Thus seventeenth-century English literature is marked first by the "spontaneous, enthusiastic versatility" of the Elizabethan world, but by the time of Milton, "the creative impulse which had made Elizabethan literature so vital had subsided" (*LHA*, 23). Wendell's theory has something in common with the far more sophisticated one of the Russian formalists, for Wendell makes intellectual or artistic innovation the mechanism of literary vitality, while the triumph of those new forms must eventually produce stagnation and decay. Yet "the Renaissance of New England," as Wendell named it, was not an era of primary innovation. That occurred in Elizabethan England, which turns out to be the origin of the American character and of American literature: "The origin of both countries as we know them today, was the England of Queen Elizabeth, with all its spontaneity, all its enthusiasm, all its untried versatility. From this origin England has sped faster and further than America" (*LHA*, 522). The relative absence of "wars and tumults" allowed America to remain closer to Elizabethan vitality, while such problems forced a conservative reaction in England that destroyed Elizabethan qualities. The New England renaissance, then, is conceived by Wendell quite literally on the model of the Renaissance itself. Nineteenth-century Boston "produced the most remarkable literary expression which has yet declared itself in America. . . . [This] intellectual outburst . . . took, on the whole, a form which best may be described as renascent. In all sorts of intellectual life a new spirit declared itself; but this new spirit was more like that which aroused old Italy to a fresh sense of civilized antiquity than like a spontaneous manifestation of native thought or feeling" (*LHA*, 244–45). Just as the spirit of classical antiquity was reborn in early modern Italy, so the spirit of Elizabethan England is reborn in nineteenth-century New England.

The effect of such an argument is not merely to establish American literature as a part of English literature, but to claim for it a kind of superiority over literature produced in Britain. Wendell explicitly defined his subject as "what America has contributed to the literature of the English language," "literature" here being defined as "lasting expression in words of the meaning of life" (*LHA*, 6). In the strongest sense of this definition, Wendell finds little that he thinks will qualify: the work of Hawthorne and Emerson seems most likely, but Wendell refuses to make unequivocal judgments even of these. Nevertheless, by linking nineteenth-century New England writers more closely to the high point of English literature than many intervening generations of British writers, Wendell claims for American culture Elizabethan qualities lacking in contemporary British culture. Thus while America may have failed to produce as many successful artists, it has preserved elements of the character of the race that the mother country has not.

Wendell's conception of how such character is constituted and passed on is more sophisticated than the typical Teutonic origins story as told, for example, by Richardson. Wendell's view of history is rooted in the evolutionism that was a dominant element of turn-of-the-century intellectual life. Where others understand racial characteristics to be essential and therefore potentially eternal, passed down so long as the race remains "pure," Wendell assumes that such characteristics must change over time under the influence of environment and historical accident. Perhaps more important, Wendell conceives of language, rather than blood, as the means by which the distinguishing elements of a "race" are preserved. Unlike the visual or other arts, literature can only be understood by those who know the language in which it is written. Thus "literature is of all the fine arts the most ineradicably national." Nationality is a function of common language, something "more potent in binding men together than any physical tie. . . . For these languages which we speak grow more deeply than anything else to be a part of our mental habit who use them. . . . in terms of language . . . and in no others, we formulate the ideals which consciously, and perhaps still more unconsciously, guide our conduct and our aspirations. In a strange, subtle way each language grows to associate with itself the ideals and the aspirations and the fate of those peoples with whose life it is inextricably intermingled" (*LHA*, 3).

Given these assumptions, it is clear that Wendell must understand Americans as fundamentally connected to the English, but he also must explain their differences, since the fact of their disunity cannot be overlooked. Wendell's agenda, however, is to claim that America and England have reached a historical moment when they again have common political cause in asserting their common ideals over those of other nationalities. The political system those ideals have produced Wendell is pleased to call "imperial democracy." Wendell reads American literature as on the whole conservative, and in the early nineteenth century he finds it to be considerably less democratic than English literature. This early literature of the middle states demonstrates the common sense and prudence of the American character, as well as a sensitive artistic conscience. America's first literature was marked by "an almost timid loyalty to the traditions of excellence" (*LHA*, 528). The literature of the New England renaissance is both more creative and more radical. It was closer to the poetry of England during the previous generation, the romantics. Still, even our radicals are less radical than those of Europe. The New England writers remained "true Americans."

It is perhaps not surprising that Wendell should have produced the closest preprofessional approximation of a critical history of American literature. Wendell was both a man of letters and a college professor. According to the reports of his students, he affected the manner and dress of a man of letters.[21] In addition to American literature, he wrote books on Shakespeare, on American national ideals, and on France (*The France of Today*); he also published several novels and some plays. According to one student, he "talked as if writing books was a common occupation."[22] The literariness of Harvard carried over from its days as a liberal arts college, but it also was the seat of George Lyman Kittredge, philologist and perhaps the leading academic literary historian of his day. Although Wendell had only a B.A. and wrote for a general audience rather than a professional one, the "Authorities and References" listed at the end of his *History* demonstrate that he had acquired the habits of a scholar. Because of its speculative character and informal tone, the book could not be mistaken for an academic literary history, but Wendell is concerned with the same problems of historical framing, origins, and continuity that will preoccupy academic historians. These concerns, combined with Wendell's highly refined but utterly class-identified tastes, make his *History* both the most forward-looking of the early histories and the one most representative of the literary of its own era.

What is surprising is the failure of *A Literary History of America* to have a significant impact during its own time. Two often-quoted reviews—by Howells and Pattee—objected to Wendell's regional bias, but this bias is unremarkable if one considers that Wendell's focus on the standard authors is typical of other histories of the period. What differentiates Wendell is not the greater importance assigned to New England by the claim for a renaissance there, but the asides and comments that smack of boosterism and regional chauvinism. In the long run, however, it was not Wendell's bias in favor of New England writers that prevented his book's acceptance, but his explanation of their works in regional rather than national terms. Interestingly, the regional framing of American literature, which remained dominant until it was replaced in the 1920s by Foerster's "factors"

(Puritanism, Romanticism, Realism, and the frontier spirit), has something in common with the recent reframing in terms of race and gender: in both frameworks works and authors are chosen because they represent different elements of the nation. They are each a form of "ticket balancing" that attempts to satisfy competing interests. During the period in between, such interests are denied. Even though New England writers may hold the largest number of slots in the canon, they do so as Americans, not as New Englanders.

Although ultimately the regional frame itself would prohibit Wendell's history from definitive status, Wendell was more immediately disqualified because he is not ideological enough. Instead of presenting American literature as an expression of the most democratic nation on earth, Wendell presents it as the expression of a democracy quite properly qualified by class, race, and ethnicity. Wendell is most overt about his classism, and his honest statement of this position would by itself disqualify his *History* as a satisfactory representation of American civilization, the ideology of which is founded on the denial of class. One advantage of New England for the production of literature is the existence of a "Yankee aristocracy," which was disguised and not strictly hereditary, but which "provided every Yankee village with its principal people" (236). The persistence of this "recognized upper class, whose social eminence was sometimes described by the word 'quality' " in spite of the vicissitudes of various families assured that the "general social structure" would remain. "Names may have changed, but not traditions or ideals" (*LHA*, 235). It was thus New England's social rigidity that made it the cradle of American literature. Other more democratic sections failed to preserve traditions and ideals.

Wendell is not, strictly speaking, a racist, but rather a fierce ethnocentrist. He does not hold that other races are essentially inferior to whites, and he does not indulge in the myth of Anglo-Saxonism, since for him, as we have seen, language and not blood is the medium in which "racial" characteristics are preserved. But for Wendell, if blacks are not essentially inferior, they remain, by accident of history, inferior at present. Indeed, Wendell accounts for the character of the South in terms of the threat posed by the slaves, "the most dangerous lower class which had ever faced an

English-speaking government. . . . However human, native Africans are still savage; and although, long before the Civil War, the Southern slaves had shown such sensitiveness to comparatively civilized conditions as to have lost their superficial savagery, and indeed as still to warrant, in many hopeful minds, even the franchise which was ultimately granted them, the spectre of darkest Africa loomed behind them all" (482). The threat posed by the slaves made the South too conservative and unwilling to experiment. Thus, the literary efforts of this section remained derivative and stagnant. On the other hand, Wendell speculates that the South, unlike the New England and middle states, not having produced a significant literature, may be ripe to produce one in the future. Clearly, however, for Wendell, "still savage" blacks will have no part in this. How many more centuries of speaking English they will need to escape this condition, he does not say.

Given his conception of African Americans, it is perhaps not surprising that Wendell is not entirely sympathetic to the antislavery movement that flourished during the New England renaissance. Few Americans have been willing to admit what Wendell clearly understood, the intimate connection between American ideals and property; he sympathetically explains the opposition to abolitionism of conservative New Englanders who held "the conviction that slavery, whatever its evils, was really a form of property, and that an attack on slavery therefore involved a general attack on the whole basis of civilization" (344). Like his views on slavery, Wendell's belief in "imperial democracy" is perfectly consistent with his assumptions about class and ethnicity. Since English speakers represent the best traditions of culture and government, it makes sense for English speakers to govern the world. Wendell sees Britain and the United States doing just that, and urges them to cooperate with each other in order to do it better. Wendell's interpretation of the Monroe Doctrine as a "virtual declaration of imperial dominance" is refreshingly honest (150). Such honesty runs counter to American ideology, however, which denies imperial designs and claims that the Monroe Doctrine instead is a policy of protecting democracy from European imperialists. While it is true that some Americans were openly speaking of empire in 1900—just after the war with Spain and the conquest of the Philippines—such talk coexisted uneasily with the rhetoric of democracy. Few Americans were willing to yoke contradictory ideas together so openly as Wendell. American civilization could not be successfully created in the image of imperial democracy. Nor were Americans likely to begin to associate their civilization with property now, when they had refused to do so since the Declaration of Independence substituted "the pursuit of happiness" in Locke's formula "life, liberty, and property."

Wendell's book thus was not an acceptable narrative of the emergence of American literature because its conception of American civilization conflicted with the ideology that civilization would have to embody. His regionalism conflicted with the needs of nationalism. Even more than regionalism, however, Wendell's locating the spirit of American literature in Elizabethan England prevented his history from supporting a specifically American nationalism. Instead of a place in English civilization, what was needed was a conception of the uniqueness of American civilization.

Early Versions of Americanness

Many early studies, including Wendell's, are not without some sense of a unique Americanness, although most do not find it throughout American literature. Usually it was discovered in a few authors, and not surprisingly, it was most often discovered in Emerson. Wendell does not actually discover it there, but he does say of Emerson, "America produced him; and whether you like him or not, he is bound to live" (*LHA*, 315). Higginson and Boynton assert that "in coming to Emerson we arrive at the controlling influence, if not the creator, of modern American thought."[23] But the authors fail to express in what such influence consists. Brander Matthews finds special conditions in the United States: "For more than a century now, the American has grown up in a republic free from feudal influences, without caste and class distinctions." As a result, "there is such a thing as Americanism; . . . there have been Americans of a type impossible elsewhere in the world—impossible certainly in Great Britain. . . . Americanism has left its mark on the writings of the authors of the

82

United States."[24] Mentioned as examples of the American type are Washington, Franklin, Emerson, Lincoln, Farragut, and Lowell. Yet Matthews also fails to produce an argument that shows how Americanism has left its mark. Brownell makes the strongest claims for Emerson's Americanness: "He is ours—absolutely and altogether our own. If he is not typically, he is peculiarly, American. No other country could have produced him. And his own may take a legitimate satisfaction in the consciousness that its greatest is also one of its most characteristic minds."[25] Since Brownell's work is not a history, but a critical study of our "prose masters," he is able to discuss Emerson in considerably more detail than most of the others I've mentioned here. Nevertheless, Brownell is little more illuminating about Emerson's Americanness than the others, mentioning merely his individualism and democracy.

Several critics of the preprofessional era wrote books that apparently try to define what is characteristically American in our literature. One of these critics, Bliss Perry, was another product typical of the literary of his era. Like Wendell, Perry was both a man of letters—he edited the *Atlantic Monthly* between 1899 and 1909—and a professor of English at Williams, Princeton, and Harvard. He wrote two books of interest here, *The American Mind* (1912) and *The American Spirit in Literature* (1918).[26] Perry begins the former, like most of the early historians, with race. Unlike Richardson, Wendell, and many others, however, Perry is less certain that we know what characterizes the different races. I have noted earlier that he spends much of the first chapter of *The American Mind* expressing his doubts about explanations based on race. But Perry thus cannot escape the paradigm of heredity: "Blood will have its say sooner or later" (40). Since Perry recognizes that no single lineage exists for Americans, blood may pose a threat to America's powers of assimilation. So far, however, such assimilation and other factors have produced an essential Americanism that Perry sets out to understand. The problem, however, is that, unlike European nations, America lacks "racial unity and long lines of literary tradition. . . . our national literary tradition as to available material and methods is hardly formed . . . the very word 'American' has a less precise connotation than the word 'New Zealander' " (23). *The American Mind* might be seen as a first attempt at defining American civilization, but it is hampered by the author's belief that civilization is in fact lacking. Tellingly, Perry finds our most characteristic American writing to be "not the self-conscious literary performance of a Poe or Hawthorne," but "civic writing; a citizen literature, produced, like the *Federalist*, and Garrison's editorials and Grant's *Memoirs*, without any stylistic consciousness whatever" (43). Yet even this tradition is little illuminated. The traits that Perry discusses could have surprised no one: idealism, individualism, romance, radicalism, public spirit. Perry's later volume, *The American Spirit in Literature*, is a rather dated history for 1918; in general it does no better than those of twenty years earlier in defining American literature or its spirit.

Ten years earlier, John Macy had produced a refreshingly different handbook with the title *The Spirit of American Literature*. This book has a kind of critical life that we will not encounter again in the treatment of American literature until D. H. Lawrence in the 1920s. While Macy deals with mainly the standard authors, adding only Sidney Lanier, the James brothers, and Howells, his perspective on most of them is new. Reading it now, one is surprised by the case Macy is able to make for Longfellow, not as a great poet, but as an interesting one. Macy is clearly dissatisfied with both American literature and with the standard representation of it, but his book fails to score a direct hit on either. The standard histories are not attacked directly, but alluded to in occasional barbed comments. As for the standard authors, they are not in the main aesthetically successful, but they are not failures either. Although Macy would advance Thoreau, Whitman, and William James over Hawthorne, Longfellow, and Howells, he finds too much to like even in those he likes least to challenge the standard.

More important for our purposes, Macy's title turns out to be ironic. "The American spirit in literature is a myth, like American valor in war, which is precisely like the valor of Italians or Japanese. The American, deluded by a falsely idealized image which he calls America, can say that the purity of Longfellow represents the purity of American homelife. . . . Professor Van Dyke says that Poe was a maker of 'decidedly unAmerican cameos,' but I do not understand what that means."[27] Like most of his contem-

poraries, Macy considers American literature to be English literature, but unlike many of them, Macy claims that he knows of no
good account of its American characteristics (4). Macy thus does
not produce the tradition one might expect to find in a book titled
as his is. He is obviously suspicious of the project of tradition
building, and is content to recover what value he can, be it aesthetic or social. Still, there is a sense of the failure of American
literature that suggests the desire for a tradition. American literature has failed to represent American life. Instead of being provincial and crude, "our books are eminent for just those virtues
which America is supposed to lack. Their physique is feminine;
they are fanciful, dainty, reserved; they are literose, sophisticated
in craftsmanship, but innocently unaware of the profound agita-
tions of American life, of life everywhere. Those who strike the
deeper notes of reality, Whitman, Thoreau, Mark Twain, Mrs.
Stowe in her one great book, Whittier, Lowell and Emerson at
their best, are a powerful minority. The rest, beautiful and fine in
spirit, too seldom show that they are conscious of contemporane-
ous realities, too seldom vibrate with a tremendous sense of life"
(14–15). Macy regards literature as developing out of other literature, and he rejects cultural or environmental explanations. What
America lacks is genius (12).

Macy was looking for what Van Wyck Brooks would name,
several years later, "a usable past." Instead of a tradition, Macy
found a usable minority that stood out against the failure of the
rest. His standards might seem to anticipate those of Parrington
and the advocates of proletarian literature of the 1930s, but they
are more aesthetic and less political. Macy, who also wrote *Socialism in America*, clearly valued the "radical convictions" of "the
more powerful writers" (155), but *The Spirit of American Literature* does not provide a consistent way for us to discover or evaluate such convictions. Like the other literary radicals, Macy calls
for something he cannot produce. They were no better able than
their conservative opponents to create a conception of American
literature as a distinct entity.

Macy was the only one of the literary radicals to produce anything like a history of American literature, and this very attempt
may have made him less influential than Van Wyck Brooks or Randolph Bourne. These two critics made their reputations attacking

the literary dominant, which, as we saw in the last chapter, they personified as "the professors." Brooks would later go on to articulate his version of American literary history at some length in the *Makers and Finders* series, but in 1920, he was known mainly for his attacks on Puritanism and his still influential call for a "usable past."[28] Bourne was perhaps the most radical of the group; he was at least the most forward-looking in his conception of America as a multiethnic culture. His essay "Trans-National America" is in many respects a powerful critique of American nationalism that specifically opposed the assimilation of immigrants to Anglo-Saxon culture. These literary radicals had a significant impact on left-wing critics of the 1930s and on the New York Intellectuals, but ironically part of their legacy was a nationalist conception of American literature.

The literary radicals made their reputations in part by their attacks on American literature in its dominant conception, but expressions of American literary nationalism often have entailed an ambivalence about American literature. There has been a long history of this ambivalence, from Emerson's "The American Scholar" through the work of professional critics such as Lionel Trilling and Richard Chase in the 1950s. What we find in the jeremiads of radicals Brooks, Macy, Bourne, and Waldo Frank is a pattern in which the failure of American literature is measured against "the promise of a national culture" (Brooks, "On Creating a Usable Past," 341). The reality of the literature is a disappointment, but its prospects are unlimited. Again and again we find the demand that our literature express the true character of the American spirit. No one would deny that America long suffered from feelings of cultural inferiority vis-à-vis England and some European nations, but what needs to be made clear is that such feelings are a product of nationalism, not its antithesis. Bourne went so far as to argue that we needed "the cultivation of a new American nationalism" similar to the "cultural chauvinism" of the French.[29] Bourne testified to the dominance and character of nationalist ideology during this period when he complained that "vigorous nationalistic and cultural movements in this country among Germans, Scandinavians, Bohemians, and Poles" are attacked by the keepers of culture, "while in the same breath they insist that the alien shall be forcibly assimilated to that Anglo-

Saxon tradition which they unquestionably label 'American.' "[30]
While Bourne was forward-looking in his recognition of the value
of cultural diversity, his alternative to the Anglo-Saxon version of
American culture was to celebrate "the distinctively American
spirit—pioneer, as distinguished from the reminiscently English
—that appears in Whitman and Emerson and [William] James"
(272–73). What Bourne couldn't see—because nationalism is an
unquestioned assumption—is that the notion of a distinctively
American spirit requires the assimilation of other cultural traditions just as much as the genteel tradition requires it. If, as Kermit
Vanderbilt argues, this group of radicals helped bring about the
development of American literature in the academy, they did so
using nationalist arguments.

The Cambridge History of American Literature

The literary radicals and other critics positioned mainly outside
of the university are in most accounts given credit for originating
a new conception of American literature that came to fruition in
the 1930s and 1940s. Yet whatever these critics' later influence,
they need to be understood in the context of the literary of their
own era. In that context, *The Cambridge History of American
Literature* was far more representative of the dominant. As such,
its individual influence may ultimately be less than the marginal
but innovative utterances of a Brooks or Bourne, but much of the
conception of American literature it contains will be passed down
to future generations of academic Americanists.

Given this role, it may seem disingenuous to treat the *Cambridge History* as a "preprofessional history" since the majority
of its contributors did hold positions in English departments and,
more important, most of these held Ph.D.s in that discipline.[31] Indeed, Vanderbilt treats it as the beginning of the profession of
American literature. There is some justification for this treatment.
The *Cambridge History* was the first major cooperative project in
American literature to be undertaken within the academy, and so
it reasonably may be taken as a sign of the literature's increasing
acceptance in English departments. The production of the history
by professors of English also meant that the *Cambridge History*
would for the most part be literary-historical in approach. While

the scope of the project prohibited the inclusion of detailed influence and source studies typical of scholarly journals, like these articles, the chapters of the *Cambridge History* were devoted to fact rather than interpretation. Literary scholars in general neither received training in nor practiced criticism, a fact that in part explains the weakness of the criticism the volume does contain. A large-scale history such as the *Cambridge History* could not avoid critical judgments, but criticism is clearly a subordinate activity. In fact, beyond the bare judgments unsupported by argument or evidence, there is little we would be inclined to call criticism in this history. The *Cambridge History* is intended as a repository of factual knowledge, that is, as an "encyclopedic history."[32] Critical judgments were not considered merely subjective, but objective judgments could be arrived at only over time. There was no method for obtaining them, and thus all contributors could do was produce their best guesses. Close reading was not an option for these scholars; it had not been invented yet.

Yet to say that the *Cambridge History* is a product of the academy and, largely, of English, is not the same as saying that it is the work of a recognized subdiscipline. The *Cambridge History* was produced before such a subdiscipline had been formed. That most chapters are literary-historical in approach does not mean that they are much informed by academic literary-historical scholarship. In fact, the bibliographies show that almost no work on American literature had been published in professional journals. The last volume of the *Cambridge History* appeared about the same time that the American Literature Group was being established, and the history was produced during a period when American literature had little recognition within English departments. It was only after the formation of the ALG that scholarship in American literature came to be regularly produced. Nor did the ALG recognize the *Cambridge History* as a founding document. Rather, leading ALG members, such as Jay B. Hubbell and Robert Spiller, regarded it as fundamentally inadequate and almost from the beginning made plans to replace it with a history of their own. One of the major objections was the unevenness of the contributions, some of which came from nonacademics and did not reflect scholarly standards. This in itself reminds us that the *Cambridge History* represents a literary in which the man of letters continued to have considerable influence. Those who contributed included Paul Elmer More, George Putnam, Brander Matthews, William Payne, and one woman of letters, Mary Austin. Furthermore, a substantial number of the academic contributors were historians, philosophers, or others not trained as literary scholars.

The latter point is important because it suggests the most important reason for considering the *Cambridge History* a predecessor to, rather than the beginning of, American literature as a discipline. The boundaries it assumed for American literature failed to become the boundaries of the discipline. This is true not only in terms of who is authorized to write the history of American literature, but also regarding what shall be considered American literature. "Literature" is a broadly inclusive term in the *Cambridge History*, and no serious genre of writing on any subject falls outside of its purview. There are articles on philosophy, theology, and economics, on travel writing, political writing, and children's literature, on orators, publicists, historians, scholars, and humorists, on newspapers, magazines, annuals, and giftbooks, and, perhaps most tellingly, on "Non-English Writings." Of the 65 chapters, I count 30 that cover subjects falling outside of what would be defined as the object of American literature by the profession during the 1920s and 1930s. This division ignores entirely issues of the canon of fiction, poetry, and drama, since even minor writers of these forms would have been conceded some place in literary history. But since minor writers in practice were later accorded relatively little attention, one could easily support the assertion that less than half of the *Cambridge History* is devoted to writing that would later be regarded as significant in American literature.

It could be argued that the *Cambridge History* has much more in common with earlier representations of American literary history than with the disciplinary one that would develop later. Its inclusiveness was, however, atypical of both representations. Only Tyler, a historian, is similarly broad in his definition of literature. The inclusiveness of the *Cambridge History* doubtless contributed to the sense of amorphousness American literature has in its pages. Richardson, Wendell, and many of the authors of school histories present an American literature that has a more definite shape, and Wendell even managed a coherent theory explaining the development of that shape. But this problem may be as much a matter of genre as of breadth. Continuity in an encyclopedic history is usually a matter of the mere order in which disparate chapters are printed. Obviously, no narrative is possible under such circumstances, but explanation is also limited to individual essays; the form "precludes a total vision of its subject" (Perkins, 364). The school histories share the same problem, but not to the same degree. They may lack narrative or explanation, but American literary history still emerges as something more coherent: a procession of the lives of the standard poets and novelists, in most of them. In the *Cambridge History* it appears to be a hodgepodge.

On the other hand, the *Cambridge History* remains enough like these school texts to be more fairly grouped with them than, say, with Parrington's *Main Currents in American Thought*, the first major history to be published after American literature had been recognized by the MLA. For one thing, in spite of the enormous diversity of material and treatment, the standard authors retain their place. All of them, save Cooper and Holmes, have chapters to themselves, and even these two get enough pages that they could have separate chapters. In addition to Edwards, Franklin, Irving, Emerson, Thoreau, Lowell, Whittier, and Longfellow, the *Cambridge History* also gives separate chapters to Poe, Whitman, Mark Twain, and Henry James, but only the last two constitute distinctly new members of the standard list, Poe and Whitman having long been sometime members of it. These chapters on the standard authors read very much as they did in the earlier histories. They are dominated by biography and include many of the usual critical judgments usually uttered without even a bow toward textual support. Emerson remains "the outstanding figure of American letters" but he still is regarded as one "whose sentences may rattle ineffectually about our ears" (1:349, 352). And even when fresh judgments are offered, they are not based on criteria by which the majority of these authors can be aesthetically valued. While like most of the early histories, the *Cambridge History* specifically avoids the chauvinism of touting American authors because they are American, many of the contributors justify the importance of their subjects by citing their social or cultural significance. Whittier is called a "poet of the third rank," but is important for his expression of "the nation's passion during that period of heightened consciousness that preserved the Union" (2: 53).

Although its varied contributors represent a spectrum of literary and political positions, the *Cambridge History* generally shares the ideology of the earlier histories. Like most of them, it is overtly racist. The first sentence of the first chapter describes the "English folk who became Americans" as retaining "their share in the literary heritage of the race" (1: 1). And like its predecessors, the *Cambridge History* is, somewhat more covertly, sexist. It thus shares with earlier histories, and with the object of study the subdiscipline would constitute, the exclusion of blacks and women. The general inclusiveness of the volume makes it all the more clear that gender, race, and class are principles of exclusion, just as region remains a principle of inclusion. Of African-American writers, Booker T. Washington gets several pages in the chapter on "The New South," mostly in the "credit to his race" vein. Other black writers get exactly one paragraph located in the chapter "Dialect Writers," where the bulk of the discussion is on the use of black dialect and materials by white writers. The racism of the author of this chapter becomes apparent when he distinguishes Paul Lawrence Dunbar from Booker T. Washington and W. E. B. Du Bois by noting that Dunbar was of unmixed African descent. Dunbar is praised for his dialect poems, but his "command of correct English" is questioned (2: 351).

Women do a bit better. Emily Dickinson begins to emerge. She gets more than three pages in "Later Poets," but is still judged to have a "defective sense of form" and merely an "inconspicuous" place in American letters. Harriet Beecher Stowe gets five pages, and the other domestic-sentimental writers get some mention. Margaret Fuller gets two pages in "Transcendentalism," but is evaluated from a sexist standpoint. She is described as having suffered from overly demanding mental tasks imposed upon her by her father so that "she was overstimulated intellectually and emotionally." This in turn made her proud, imperious, overbearing, and sarcastic, and she was perceived to be vain and masculine, all of which caused her to be unpopular with the general public, although "she lived to master and in the main to outgrow her early defects" (1: 342). She is credited with being the transcendentalist literary critic, but little is said about her criticism. Later women writers like Sarah Orne Jewett and Mary E. Wilkins Freeman are named but not discussed. No black female writers are mentioned—even Phillis Wheatley is omitted—in spite of what we now know to be the large number of books written by black women in the late nineteenth and early twentieth centuries. The pervasive sexism of the volume is revealed in the preface, where the editors tell us that in going beyond the "purely aesthetic," they hope to "enlarge the spirit of American literary criticism and render it more energetic and masculine" (1: x).

Native American literature, however, is given a whole chapter. This is a remarkable inclusion, since American literature had been defined against aboriginal literature at the end of the nineteenth century, as the designation of American literature as a branch of English literature would seem to demand.[33] Mary Austin, on the other hand, wanted to find the roots of American culture in that of Native America. Relying on the Tainean assumption of environmental influence, as in "the power of the American landscape to influence form" (3: 633), Austin finds the same qualities in aboriginal literature that characterize the United States: "[early Amerinds] had become intensely democratic, deeply religious, idealistic, communistic in their control of public utilities, and with a strong bias toward representative government" (3: 610). Such a conception gives Native American literature an organic link to the culture of the United States. Austin offers little in support of these claims, although she does provide considerably more support for her assertions about the formal and thematic characteristics of particular texts. This is true in spite of the fact that she works with translations of an almost exclusively oral literature.

The importance of this chapter is not its influence, which seems to have been nil. While a few examples of Native American literature did find their way into anthologies published in the 1920s, that literature did not become part of the object of study the subdiscipline would constitute. Rather, Austin's chapter illustrates that the object was not the inevitable one. In fact, the very amorphousness of the whole volume demonstrates this. When the *Cambridge History* appeared it was still possible for the academy to have constituted American literature in many different ways. Obviously the ideological constraints that limited discussion of African-American and women writers would also work against the discussion of Native American literature, but the existence of Austin's chapter demonstrates that those constraints were not all-powerful. American literature could have been conceived as multilingual and multiethnic as early as 1920. There are other alternatives suggested by the *Cambridge History* as well. Clearly the vision of literary history that Arthur Schlesinger, Sr., would later advocate in *The Reinterpretation of American Literature*, in which the "super-excellent" does not completely displace the socially and politically significant, is strongly reflected in the *Cambridge History*. Another road not taken is reflected in Henry Cabot Lodge's chapter on Daniel Webster, in which Webster's oratory is given a genuinely *rhetorical* analysis. That Lodge's chapter was the editors' least favorite may suggest that they shared the antipathy to rhetoric and oratory that was already characteristic of English studies.[34] The *Cambridge History* reflects not just continuity, but also unrealized possibilities. American literature could have become something quite other than what it became.

This is not to say that the academic field that would develop hard on the heels of the *Cambridge History* would owe nothing to that work. Perhaps its most important effect was to establish the legitimacy of American literature as an academic subject. The much-praised bibliographies were doubtless a significant factor here, but more important was the fact of the successful completion of the project itself. It is hard to deny, in the face of four volumes of essays mostly by scholars holding the Ph.D., that there is something to be studied here. Furthermore, though the affiliation of American literature to English literature is nowhere denied, the former is not treated or presented as a mere branch of the latter. While earlier, Anglophilia was used in support of a certain conception of American nationalism, a close connection with English literature is much less often proclaimed by the end of World War I. The *Cambridge History* represents a declaration of the independence of American literary history, for in it American literature, however flawed and ill-defined, is treated as a separate national literature to be judged on its own merits. The *Cambridge History* also marks the beginnings of the capture of that national literature by the academy. American literature will henceforth have its primary reference to a history or tradition rather than to contemporary production.

In addition to legitimacy, the *Cambridge History* bequeathed the beginnings of the canon and the first inklings of a tradition. Little of this bequest was original to the *Cambridge History*. Furthermore, it cannot be credited even in a single instance with making a definitive case for or against an author. Yet of the authors given preeminent status by the MLA volume *Eight American Authors* in the 1950s, only Melville is not also presented in the *Cambridge History* as a major figure. Emily Dickinson is the only other later canonized nineteenth-century figure treated here as minor. More significantly, perhaps, Bryant, Holmes, Lowell, Longfellow, and Whittier are still treated as major figures, as is Howells, an aberration of this history. Still, the schoolroom poets' demotion is at least forecast, the gap between them and major figures such as Emerson and Hawthorne having grown. As for tradition, or what we might call the shape or connective tissue of the canon, the *Cambridge History*, for reasons of genre and conception, provides no clear representation. The hints of tradition it does convey are not original, but several of them will be significant later: the importance of the romance, as opposed to the realistic novel, the continuity between Edwards and Emerson, and the expression of democracy.

Perhaps the most important element of the tradition that we find in the *Cambridge History* is the centrality of Emerson. While this centrality is nowhere directly proclaimed, Emerson is ubiquitous in this history, being the most frequently mentioned author according to the indexes of three volumes. More's quite critical chapter on Emerson describes him not only as "the outstanding figure of American letters," but as "a steady force in the transmutation of life into ideas and as an authority in the direction of life itself [who] has obtained a recognition such as no other of his countrymen can claim. And he owes this pre-eminence not only to his personal endowment of genius, but to the fact also that, as the most perfect exponent of a transient experiment in civilization, he stands for something that the world is not likely to let die" (1: 349). Here More makes a historically grounded case for Emerson's importance, which should be contrasted to the elaborate transhistorical arguments of the numerous critics who will later make Emerson the center of the American literary tradition.

Whatever its bequests to the incipient discipline of American literature, the *Cambridge History*, like the other preprofessional histories, did not present aesthetic justification or a theory of the unity and uniqueness of its subject. Those will become major problems of the discipline, and theories of unity and uniqueness will continue to be proposed and debated through the 1960s. Since the early histories were not products of an academic discipline, they were not responses to the demand for the production of new knowledge. They did not assume a common object of study, and neither did they share a method or approach. The preprofessional histories of American literature, from Tyler's to the collective work of the *Cambridge History*, did pass on the embodiment of the dominant aspects of the literary during the first two decades of the twentieth century. The literary in this conception was defined as white, anglophone, masculine, and bourgeois. Exceptions to this definition were admitted, but they were precisely exceptions. To be sure, by the time of the *Cambridge History* Anglo-Saxonism was on the decline, and racism was less overtly expressed. But by going underground, the racism at the root of what would become the canon of American literature was largely forgotten. On the other hand, masculinism would become even more pronounced in the decades to come. Yet the most important factor in the reconstitution of American literature as the object of an academic discipline was the practice of literary historical scholarship in English departments, a practice that would contribute to the burying of the cultural conflicts forming its prehistory.

3

English as a Discursive Practice

If the literary was centered outside of the university in the early years of this century, literature was, nevertheless, a growing academic field. The spread of English literature as a subject of instruction at American colleges and universities was extremely rapid. Although Anglo-Saxon had long been taught at Virginia because of Thomas Jefferson's provision for it, English as a college subject was mainly a matter of rhetoric, composition, and oratory. In 1857, Francis A. March was named professor of English Language and Comparative Philology at Lafayette College, the first chair in English, according to his institution, but it was not until 1876 that Francis Child became Harvard's first professor of English literature.[1] When the Modern Language Association met for the first time in 1883, representatives from twenty major institutions could count only 39 teachers of English at their colleges, but by 1900 universities all over the country were offering graduate training in English literature, a subject that had become nearly universal at the undergraduate level.[2] Clearly the value that literature held in the culture in general contributed to its success in the university. Because of the belief that literature performed a useful social function, it came to be taught at all educational levels. In many respects the object that was taught as literature in the colleges and universities resembled the object that the men of letters venerated and hoped to conserve. There was little difference in the canon of English literature as it was constituted in and outside of universities. Furthermore, both university scholars and men of letters accounted for canonical works in terms of the genius of their authors. But what each group did with canonical authors differed radically, and as a result literature in the university came to differ from the literature of the critics.

At the turn of the century there was by no means general agreement about how college literature should be taught or studied. Yet, surprisingly, there seems to have developed a widely shared agreement about what research in the field should look like. A particular discursive practice had already become established as dominant in professional journals. My focus in this chapter is on this practice of literary scholarship within the academic field of English. By calling it a "discursive practice" I mean to indicate that my discussion will include not only the discourse itself, but the institutional and professional context in which it was produced. But it is important to emphasize that the difference between literary discourse in the university and outside of it is not a matter of professionalized versus unprofessionalized work. Both literary scholars and men of letters were products of the institutional environments in which they worked. There were special conditions in each environment that account for some of the differences in the two discourses. The most important of these was that, in the university, literature needed to be a *discipline* rather than merely a source of spirituality and moral uplift.

Disciplinarity

Disciplinarity is the form that the research university imposed on knowledge. The American research university emerged during the last quarter of the nineteenth century, and it replaced the college as the leading form of higher educational institution. The major goal of the college had been general education rather than specialized training or knowledge production. The chief argument offered for the emphasis on classical languages that characterized most college curricula was that learning such languages produced mental discipline. Early advocates of modern language study had to demonstrate that their subjects could be equally effective means of mental discipline, and the application of philological methods helped to achieve this end. Mental discipline was no doubt a "means of correct training," but it was not compatible with the disciplinary organization of knowledge production.[3] We might see it rather as a transitional phase in which disciplinary techniques have not yet produced disciplinary discourses.

Before the late nineteenth century, the disciplines that today structure knowledge did not exist.[4] What made such knowledge formations possible is the development of institutions in which disciplinary techniques are applied, not just to students, but to faculty. The most important of these institutions were the learned society and the university department. Both of these emerged in the late nineteenth century. The first learned societies in America—the American Oriental Society (1842), the American Association for the Advancement of Science (1848), and the American Social Science Association (1865)—were neither devoted to particular disciplines nor adequate to provide for the development of these disciplines. Roger Geiger remarks, in his history of research universities, "If there is a single crucial point in the process of academic professionalization, it would be the formation of a national association with its attendant central journal." Such associations established disciplinary authority over against that of university administrators or individual professors. The central journal served as an exemplar of research practice, but also made possible an accounting of a researcher's worth. Such journals made for the anonymous surveillance and judgment of practitioners, since the discipline, rather than individuals, was perceived to be the source of such judgments. Geiger concludes, "The collective authority to evaluate contributions to the field is what makes disciplines different from the myriad other voluntary associations."[5]

The new universities such as Johns Hopkins and the transformed colleges such as Harvard saw nurturing these new disciplines as coincident with the goal of knowledge production. The classical curriculum was replaced with curricula that would permit more specialized training and better use of specialized faculty. The now-familiar departmental form of organization allowed specialists control of appointments and advancement within their own fields. Research universities began to support learned journals and societies. Disciplinary organization decentralized authority within the university, but it allowed a more effective exercise of that authority. The result was vastly increased production of knowledge, and knowledge that was more valuable for being "scientific"—which is to say, disciplined, or deriving its authority from a discipline. The greater quantity and authority of disciplinary knowledge came at the price of much greater limitations on what could count as knowledge. In a nondisciplinary research environment, there are few formal restrictions on who may speak or what may be said. In practice, individual editors and publishers exercised control by deciding who and what would be published. Thus, in nondisciplinary environments, individual authority counted for a great deal. The power of men of letters like Lowell or Howells was dependent on institutions, but it was their literary personalities that these institutions produced, and these personalities were not available to all who might join the institutions. Furthermore, once the personality was produced, it attained a certain freedom from institutional restrictions because the "voice" of the individual was itself authoritative. Disciplines, on the other hand, entail an anonymous system of methods, of propositions considered to be true, of rules, definitions, techniques, and tools that may in principle be taken over by anyone who has been trained in them.[6] On the basis of such anonymous systems, academic disciplines are able to create formal restrictions on the discourse produced in their names and on who has the right to speak it. A discipline establishes its own standard form of training, which becomes a prerequisite for admission into the discipline, and it determines what forms of examination are to be administered to demonstrate the trainees' competence. The discipline also controls who will be given employment and advancement at a particular institution. Finally, the discipline controls its own process of publication, which sets the standard for discourse in that field. Each of these forms of control requires a process of formal evaluation, and each evaluation is another occasion for an individual's work to be declared beyond the boundaries of the discipline. But disciplinarity did not have the effect of reducing the overall quantity of discourse on a subject. On the contrary, while the demand for evaluation encouraged the repetition of previously successful work, it also required the continual production of such work. Thus disciplinarity requires the production of increasing amounts of similar work. As a result, disciplines can be conceived as Foucauldian

99

machines for the production of statements: "For a discipline to exist, there must be the possibility of formulating—and of doing so ad infinitum—fresh propositions" (Foucault, "Discourse," 223). A discipline is never the result of the need to answer questions or solve problems definitively. Rather, disciplines are structured by problems or questions that are in some way self-reproducing. If solutions to some become generally accepted, others are generated so that more work may be produced.

What I want to try to examine in this chapter is how the discourse of the discipline of English was organized in order both to limit what may be said and to assure that it might be said over and over again. The character of English as a discursive practice is relevant because American literature as a subdiscipline will take over much of its own discursive practice from English. My assumption is that the discourse of English is not a transparent window on a literature that exists apart from it. Rather, English, like other disciplines, constituted its own object of inquiry by means of the methods and assumptions with which it worked. In order to get a picture of that object, I will focus mainly on articles published in *PMLA* between 1900 and 1930. I take these articles to be not only typical of the research that scholars in English produced during the period, but also the most highly representative of the discipline's conception of itself, since *PMLA* was without rival as the leading journal. What an examination of articles published in *PMLA* will reveal is that English literature was constituted by the discipline as a very narrow canon of texts and authors, and that the canon was discussed in terms of a relatively few issues that arose out of a thoroughly positivist set of assumptions about knowledge and romantic assumptions about authorship.

English, I will argue, did become by the turn of the century as much a discipline as any other academic subject, but the labor that was performed under the name "English" was not exclusively disciplinary. Departments of American universities in all fields of knowledge have had typically to balance their disciplinary mission against demands for teaching that is not properly disciplinary. But English departments probably have been responsible for more of this extradisciplinary instruction than any of the others. From its earliest days, English has at most universities been charged with teaching elementary writing skills, and this task has doubtless constituted more of the labor of English than any other. In spite of the frequent practice of incorporating literature into such writing courses, they have not usually been understood as training in the discipline of English, but rather as preparation for university training in general. Nevertheless, since the majority of English instructors during the period I am discussing taught composition, one must acknowledge that English departments owe their relative size and importance and perhaps their very existence to the demand that college students be taught to write.[7] What Howard Mumford Jones observed in the early 1930s has been true more or less since the beginning of English departments: "the only course universally required by college life is Freshman English," a fact that has long assured jobs for English Ph.D.s.[8] The importance of composition in English departments has led some historians of the field to argue that this training reflects their most important mission: to train members of the professional-managerial class in necessary skills and the proper habits of work.[9]

Disciplinary research was only the most important of three programs of reform that helped shape the modern American university.[10] The teaching of composition fell within the mission of "utility"; in this conception, universities were understood as providers of useful training and practical knowledge both to individuals and to society as a whole. Within English departments, there were those who conceived of the field mainly in these terms. For them, teaching, and especially instruction in writing and rhetoric, were what was central to English. Yet this was distinctly a subordinate position. At research universities the bulk of composition courses were typically taught by individuals waiting for enough seniority to be assigned disciplinary courses; even at research universities, senior faculty might teach freshman English, and at other institutions, this was a regular assignment for most of the English faculty. Yet virtually all of them were trained in literary research and were devoted to literary study even if they had little time to practice it.

The third conception of the university's mission, the preservation and transmission of "liberal culture," was also reflected in English departments, which typically contained members whose view of literature resembled more that of the men of letters—

some of them were in fact men of letters—than it did that of the researchers. These exponents of liberal culture were particularly strong in liberal arts colleges where research was not demanded, but they existed in the departments of research universities as well. While writing teachers were not a very vocal group during this period, the liberal culturists were vociferous enough that some historians of the profession have regarded them as posing a serious challenge to researchers' hegemony.[11] In my view, the liberal culturists did not pose such a threat during the early years of the century. Because they wrote about literature, the liberal critics had more of a claim to disciplinary status than did the teachers of writing, but both the sort of discourse they produced and the positions they espoused kept them from attaining this status. Furthermore, the dogmas of liberal culture were accepted by virtually all members of English departments. Scholars did not reject, for example, the view that great literature transmitted essential human values. In fact, they also used this argument in support of their own work. Thus, while the practices of the liberal culturists and the researchers differed radically, there was a fundamental ideological agreement between them.

Insofar as English claimed to be a discipline, to be adding to the store of knowledge, it did so by its published research in literature. Of the three forms of practice that existed in English departments, only this one fit the model of disciplinarity that was developing in the university. Its practitioners claimed to be producing knowledge of the same epistemological status as researchers in chemistry or physics. Neither of the other groups claimed to be advancing knowledge. Insofar as the writing teachers had a discipline, it was rhetoric, but rhetoric was considered a discipline in the distinctly different sense of an ancient craft, the rules of which had been passed down with only slight modification since Aristotle. Doubtless the long opposition of rhetoric and philosophy made it more difficult to conceive of rhetoric as a field of investigation—that is, as a science. In any event, rhetoric became discredited in English departments, and those committed to it largely became part of the field of speech communication. Likewise, the critics and exponents of liberal culture saw themselves not as producing knowledge but as preserving truth and beauty. The liberal culturists saw no need to *advance* knowledge, for the most important forms of knowledge were already available. Their job was to protect truth and beauty from the numerous forces that opposed them, but the criticism that resulted from such a mission did not fit the disciplinary model: however much the fundamental values might be agreed upon, particular critical statements could not be distinguished from mere tastes or opinions. Furthermore, the liberal critics who did publish were more interested in reaching the general public and thus may have avoided purely professional venues such as *PMLA*. The liberal critics were forced by the logic of their own position to concede much of the territory of the discipline to the researchers.

As a result of the undisciplinary character of the other practices in English departments, the researchers quickly became the most powerful faction of the profession. They controlled the departments at leading universities; the leading professional association, the MLA; and the leading professional journals. In 1903 the MLA abolished its pedagogy section, indicating the complete victory of the researchers in that group. The teachers of language and writing in time formed their own associations, while the liberal culturists continued to make trouble on the margins, increasingly from positions outside the university. Because researchers shared many fundamental assumptions with the liberal culturists, the complaints of the latter could continue to command attention. Nevertheless, it was the researchers who dominated the profession in the 1920s, and it was their practice that was adopted by the new subdiscipline of American literature.

The Practice of English

Relying so heavily on *PMLA* as a representation of the standard practice in English may seem overly narrow, but as the journal of the discipline's primary professional association, it was the organ the discipline itself held up as representative. Furthermore, there were few other professional journals published until the 1930s, when subdisciplines began to be represented by their own organs. *American Literature* and *ELH*, for example, did not begin publication until 1929 and 1934, respectively. Earlier in the century, a few other professional journals, such as *Modern Language Notes*, *Studies in Philology*, and *Modern Philology*, appeared, while an occasional piece of literary scholarship was published in the *Nation* or, less frequently, the *Atlantic*. While significant articles were published in these other locations, even taken together they do not provide as clear a picture of what researchers in English were doing as does *PMLA*. In addition to writing articles, leading scholars in English did publish books. But books were not nearly so significant a medium for professional publication as they have since become. One of the most important kinds of books was the critical edition of a major author. Such work was highly valued, and it was dependent upon the kind of research that was published in the journals. A second typical kind of book publication was that aimed at students at various levels. This category included the handbook or guide to the work of a major author, or a textbook covering a period or periods of literary history. Relatively rare during the period are books containing the kind of historical research typically published in the journals. This may seem less surprising when we recall that this remains the pattern in the sciences, where a researcher's reputation is made by publication of professional articles and where book publication is regarded as a nice avocation for those who have already established themselves. This model seems to be the one English followed in the early part of this century. As Stuart Sherman observed, academic literary history "has not been very prolific in important books, [but] it should be remembered that one of its maxims is, 'Anyone can write a book; the difficult thing is to write an article.' "[12] That some articles published during the period are the size of monographs suggests the greater importance this venue had at the time.[13]

Books, on the other hand, seem to have been somewhat marginal to regular professional practice. Consider, for example, four major books on Chaucer published between 1906 and 1934. The first of them, R. K. Root's *The Poetry of Chaucer: A Guide to Its Study and Appreciation*, is precisely a guide. Its stated purpose is "to render accessible to readers of Chaucer the fruits of [scholarly] investigations."[14] As such it does not claim to be presenting original research or a fresh perspective of its own. The other three, G. L. Kittredge's *Chaucer and His Poetry*, John M. Manly's *Some New Light on Chaucer*, and John L. Lowes's *Geoffrey Chaucer and the Development of His Genius*, are all by scholars who ranked at the top of the profession during the period in question, each of them having been elected president of the MLA.[15] The book each publishes on Chaucer is composed of public lectures delivered at the invitation of an institution other than the scholar's own. As a result, the books are less strictly professional than are typical journal articles. The books omit footnotes and other formal citations and references, and they are characterized by relatively informal diction and rhetoric. What is most curious is that the scholars all waited until the occasion of a lecture invitation to produce a book on an author who was a major research subject for each of them. All of this suggests that a book covering the work of a major figure is a privilege earned by publishing significant research in scholarly journals and that such books are not typical of disciplinary practice. Interestingly, the books continued to be read long after most of the articles. Doubtless the books' greater convenience is in part responsible for this, but it may also have resulted from the wider scope of the books. The scholars seem more willing in these books to risk conjecture and speculation, and are therefore less bound by positivism than they are in their journal articles. In general, however, the books are consistent with the methods and concerns typical of *PMLA*.

What did *PMLA* publish? While it was the journal of an association devoted to the study of all modern languages, from its beginning in 1884 through its fiftieth year, 1933, 52.6 percent of the articles were on British language or literature. The figure increased from 36.4 percent during the first twenty-five years to 57.9 percent during the second quarter century. American literature accounted for another 2.4 percent, while comparative articles, which often include English authors and texts and were often written by scholars in English departments, add an additional 11 percent.[16] My own sample suggests that articles in English literature, excluding purely linguistic articles but including comparative and methodological ones, account for more than 50 percent of the essays between 1900 and 1930, and in some instances the rate of English literature articles is as high as 82 percent.[17] As such figures demonstrate, *PMLA* was overwhelmingly a journal of English studies. Among the English articles, medieval and Renaissance topics account for more than 70 percent of the articles between 1900 and 1920. During the 1920s, publications of articles in nineteenth-century literature begin to rival those of the other two periods, and by 1925, we recognize that the dominance of medieval scholarship has waned.

The early interest in medieval literature may not seem surprising given the origins of English literary research in philology, here defined as historical linguistics. Since the training of the first English scholars was heavily weighted in Anglo-Saxon and Middle English, it would make sense that such scholars would continue to work in that area. What is surprising is how little narrowly philological work turns up in *PMLA* in the period under discussion, especially in articles devoted to English. In the foreign languages, philological study accounts for a significantly higher percentage of articles, which include titles such as "Gender-Change from Middle High German to Luther, as Seen in the 1545 Edition of the Bible," but such narrow linguistic focus still accounts for a minority of articles on foreign languages. Of course, philologists such as Francis March understood philology to be the much wider project of a comprehensive science of language, including psychological, historical, and cultural contexts, and rhetorical, literary, and critical dimensions.[18] In this sense, virtually any article in English or American literature would be a contribution to philology. But the object of English scholarship was neither language nor culture, but literature. Language and culture were relevant tools for literary research, but they were most definitely tools and not the focus of research. And even at that, we do not find a great number of articles on literature that turn strictly on points of historical linguistics. The study of Anglo-Saxon and Middle English language was obviously necessary to treat texts in those languages as literature, but the evidence suggests that the study of the former soon came to be regarded as more of a test of a graduate student's seriousness than as something genuinely essential to work in the field. Even philological dissertations are comparatively rare, with only 10 percent of dissertations produced at Harvard and Chicago falling into that category.[19] As early as 1883, some scholars were questioning "the utility of Anglo-Saxon in a course of English literature."[20] After the turn of the century, we see a movement in discussion of method in English away from philology, which was typical of the 1880s, and toward literary history, which was increasingly the dominant practice during the period under discussion here. By the end of the period, it was well enough entrenched that it was widely under attack and defenses of it were published in books and articles.[21]

It is important to distinguish literary history from literary criticism. Because criticism became, after World War II, the dominant practice in English, we tend to assimilate literary history to criticism. The work of René Wellek provides an interesting case in point. Wellek's first book on the history of literary discourses (my term, not his) was *The Rise of English Literary History* (1941). In the preface to that book, he promises a more extensive sequel that would cover a wider cultural and historical range.[22] But Wellek never produced that work. Instead, as everyone knows, he went on to write *A History of Modern Criticism 1750–1950*, a work of six volumes with a seventh projected. As he said in a preface to a reissue of the earlier work, literary history is treated in the newer one as a branch of literary criticism.[23] But between 1900 and 1930 in English, academic criticism is a branch, and a fairly minor one, of literary history. My sample shows that articles in which critical evaluation or judgment represented any significant part of the author's argument amounted to a mere 7 percent. And none of these articles was purely critical. Even if one takes a wider definition of criticism that would include interpretation, the number of critical articles would still be only 16 percent between 1900 and 1920. After 1920, the number of explicitly interpretive articles increases significantly but the number of evaluative ones does not.

Wellek argues that the first works of English literary history, by the brothers Warton, emerged out of the project of textual annotation. According to Wellek, such history emerged in the context of an already established discourse of criticism, and it was offered as justification for critical argument. But as literary history developed in the nineteenth century, it came to be pursued for its own sake. Under the influence of philology, it seems to have returned to something like annotation. In the early part of the century, scholars did not conceive of literary works as something that needed to be interpreted in the special sense that we have since come to understand the term: "that a proper understanding of their meaning as works of art required also some understanding of the special ways in which language works when employed in literary or poetic discourse as distinct from scientific or historical discourse would never have occurred to" the literary historians we are concerned with here. These scholars "presented the texts, set them in their historical context, translated or explained difficult words, and in short made it possible for students to learn to read them accurately."[24] For the literary historian, the text is not a vessel of masked truth. Finding out what a text meant was a matter of discovering information, and thus not a matter that demanded elaborate argument. The literary historian's job was to make this information available to the reader, and not mainly to explain how the new information bears on the work's meaning.

Still less did the literary scholars of the period regard their objects of study as moral or aesthetic events in need of judgment or evaluation. That does not mean, however, that these scholars treated all English writing as equally interesting to literary history. Rather, they accepted the judgments of criticism, a longstanding practice outside of the academy. It is because the canon of English literature was so little in dispute that the domain of English as a discipline was very quickly established. Even in 1884, we find an outline of the field that, with minor changes and the addition of American and twentieth-century literature, could be accepted today: "The pupil would . . . make himself substantially conversant with First English Philology in Caedmon, Bêowulf and Alfred; to study its characteristics and structure; to mark its transition through middle English of Layamon and Langland to Chaucer and Spenser; to mark the great historical periods of Modern English from the Elizabethan to the Victorian."[25] If scholars rejected the evaluative "criticism of taste" that they found in journalism and the work of the men of letters, they did so because they wanted to establish their discipline on scientific grounds.[26] The history of criticism, with its repeated arguments over the merits of works and authors, led the researchers to believe that there was little chance knowledge could be advanced by that means. The new English professionals accepted the critical judgments of others, and thus focused their attention on an already constituted canon that was not an aspect of English literature, but was English literature itself. As constituted by the discipline, the domain of English literature is dominated by four figures: Chaucer, Spenser, Shakespeare, and Milton. In fact it would be more accurate to say of each of these what one scholar did say of Chaucer: "He *is* English poetry incarnate," while allowing that "only two, perhaps, of all his sons outshine his fame."[27] As work in *PMLA* becomes more literary and less philological, these figures attract more attention: in 1900, 22 percent articles in English concerned one of these figures, but by 1920, 37 percent did. During the 1920s, as nineteenth-century literature became a major topic of research, Chaucer, Spenser, Shakespeare, and Milton decline somewhat as subjects. In 1930, they represent 29 percent of articles in *PMLA*.

Earlier I insisted, following Williams, that the nineteenth-century concept of literature differs from the Renaissance concept of poetry in that the earlier concept meant something one made, while the later one meant something one read. But it is not an inconsistency to assert that for English in the early part of this century literature and poetry were nearly synonymous. Poetry was for these scholars something to be read, and it was almost the only form of literature that they studied. The four major figures were all called poets, even though Shakespeare's plays were far more frequently discussed than his other work. It is true that the Elizabethan stage was a major topic of research, but the drama of other periods was neglected. Fiction was discussed even less. My sample from *PMLA* shows no more than one article per volume on fiction through 1920, with the number increasing to four and three respectively for 1925 and 1930. The first *PMLA* bibliography of scholarship by Americans, published in 1922 for 1921, mentions only five articles and a handbook on fiction.

What did literary historians do with the literature they studied? A manual written by Harvard professor of French André Morize, but used in graduate courses in English as well, gives us a good outline of their tasks:

1. Questions of bibliography.
2. Questions of criticism of the text.
3. Questions of interpretation and of explication: "A text may be authentic and correct and yet be quite obscure, or decipherable only with difficulty. . . . Words may be obscure. . . . Perhaps grammar and syntax puzzle you. . . . Then there are many allusions. . . ."
4. Questions of versification.
5. Preparation of a critical edition.

6. Questions of date and of chronology.
7. Questions of authenticity and of attribution.
8. Questions of sources and of origins.
9. Questions of the formation and the transformation of a work.
10. Questions of biography.
11. Questions of success and of influence.
12. Relations of the history of literature with the history of ideas and of civilization.[28]

The training of graduate students is a strong indication of what a discipline considers most fundamental, and this list gives us a clear picture of the fundamentals of literary history. It is true the notion of mental discipline seems to have continued to have enough influence that some of what graduate students were asked to do was prescribed for purposes of "stiffening . . . mental processes" (Jones, 471). But consider for the moment the kind of mental habits students are being asked to acquire. All of the problems explained in the manual are in principle capable of objective resolution. Most involve mainly the accumulation of facts. Only in item 12 of the list is the student asked to perform synthesis, and none of the tasks call for theorizing or critique. One of the justifications for what critics charged was the pedantry of graduate school was that students lacked the factual knowledge and reading experience that would allow them to produce valuable independent essays in criticism or scholarship (Jones, 471). Given the pattern of graduate training, however, there is no reason to think that scholars would be capable of writing critical essays, and the record shows that they did not often do so.

While literature was held up by the culture and often by literary scholars themselves as an antidote to science and materialism, literary works are treated by scholars as material objects in need of explanation. "In the strict sense, literary history regards authors and masterpieces impersonally, either as incarnations in time of the human spirit which is eternal, or as phenomena, *materialien*, like the phenomena which political history uses as the basis of its interpretation" (Greenlaw, 87). In practice, few books or articles set out to demonstrate how an author or work manifests the human spirit; most do address works or authors as phenomena. Questions of textual criticism, descriptive bibliography, and the preparation of critical editions are obviously very much matters of texts as physical things. But questions of sources, authenticity, attribution, dates, formation and transformation, and interpretation in the narrow sense all also assume that the work is not mainly a medium, an expression, or a representation, but a discrete object. Literary historians believed that literary works were more than this, but insofar as such works were the objects of the discipline, that was how they were treated. The discipline's project was to add to the quantity of verifiable—if not entirely verified—knowledge about these objects. The project of literary history for which graduate students were trained and in which scholars were engaged emerges as thoroughly positivist.

Historical knowledge, far from being merely a parapedeutic to criticism, was highly valued for its own sake: "A sense of historicity, of the significance of time, is one of the rarest acquisitions of the human mind. . . . every sound scholar will distrust generalizations which do not proceed from a careful and candid study of the chronology of the period in which a work appears, of the life of the man who wrote it, and even of the composition of the work. . . . chronology . . . lies . . . at the very heart of literary study" (Jones, 475–76). Thus the graduate student is instructed that, despite the existence of useful reference works, "nothing . . . can take the place of chronological tables made by yourself" (Morize, 134). This suggests the rather impoverished sense of history that the discipline of English often manifests. The chronicle, originally a table of dates and events, is the most minimal representation of history. It is history without narrative. The history of English literature that the discipline took as its object was a chronicle rather than a narrative. Authors and works are historical events in need of insertion into the chronology. In the preoccupations with source and influence, we see that scholars recognized the interest of tying together the chronologically dispersed events. And yet these mini-narratives never add up to a general account of the development of the literature as a whole. English studies in America never produced a comprehensive history of English literature of the kind written by Taine. The importance of chronology seems also to have led scholars away from what we would now call synchronic studies of historical periods.

111

Such studies were performed, but they are far less common than ones that seek the past or future relations of a work.

All of the problems mentioned by Morize are represented in *PMLA* during the period under discussion, but they are not equally represented. Especially through 1920, research in English is preoccupied with issues of date, authenticity, source, and influence. Source and influence studies are the most common type of article found in *PMLA* at least through 1925, and it is clear that *PMLA* is not unusual in this. A study of Harvard dissertations, for example, showed that 63 percent of dissertations produced during the 1890s were source or influence studies.[29] Even one of the books most often described as breaking out of the usual limitations of literary history, Lowes's *The Road to Xanadu*, is a study of Coleridge's sources. It is not a coincidence that these tasks should be privileged. They are, for one thing, the most exact equivalents of philological questions transferred to literary objects. Literary scholars did not often use the history of the language to solve problems of literary history, but in their construction of their object of study they imitated the philologists' concern for genetic analysis, for questions of mutation and historical progression. In a word, the literary historians wanted *origins*. Articles sometimes traced works of English literature as far back as Sanskrit sources. More often, they settled for showing how a particular work had its source in an older work in English or another modern language. What I want to stress, however, is that we cannot attribute this practice merely to the influence of philology. Rather, philology and literary history were both products of the same set of assumptions about language, history, and knowledge, which we find expressed with different emphases in biology, economics, and other fields as well.

If a work is a historical event in a chronology treated "impersonally," one might expect authorship to be relatively insignificant. But among the elements or features of literature as the discipline of English constituted it, the author may be the most important. This may seem less surprising when we consider that authorship is one way to account for the text as a historical event. It is true that literary historians regard authors themselves as products of their times and therefore do not take biography to be the ultimate origin of a work. Nevertheless, Chaucer, Spenser,

Shakespeare, and Milton are regarded as geniuses, each unique in his greatness, and all authors are regarded as personalities. The importance of the author as a personality is suggested by the fact that three of the major books on Chaucer—those of Root, Kittredge, and Manly—begin with a chapter or chapters on the author's life, while the fourth, Lowes's *Geoffrey Chaucer and the Development of His Genius*, is biographical throughout. A theoretical article published in 1930 states a basic assumption of English: "A piece of writing that has nothing personal about it can be called literature only by courtesy. . . . The primary source of literary value being thus localized in the personality of the writer."[30] The personality of the author does not exist apart from his works, but rather in and through them, and cases of disputed authorship are held to be interesting because "the personality of an author might appear much modified if the disputed work were definitely assigned to him."[31] But the issue of authenticity works in the other direction as well. A work will become much more significant if it can be attributed to a major author. Literary historians seem to accept a version of the romantic conception of authorship, something they share with the men of letters of the period. The man of letters, however, took authorship to be sufficient to account for a work, while the literary historians did not.

We might describe these two potential origins of works—sources and influences on the one hand and authors on the other—as two forms of depth, two sources of authenticity. Yet it would be a mistake to regard either as the work of a hermeneutics of suspicion. It is precisely the surface of the text that the historian seeks to authenticate in the depths of personality or historical time. Plainly, however, these two origins are always potentially in conflict. In reviewing the conclusions at which literary historical articles arrive, we frequently find that it is this conflict they seek to resolve. But we will also find that it is both never and always already resolved. It can never be resolved because authorship implies originality, but history implies continuity; it is always already resolved because, in the discourse of English, authorship has priority. Since the major authors constitute the core of the object of study, they cannot be deprived of originality.

Consider, for example, this conclusion from a 1915 study, "Guillaume de Machaut and *The Book of the Duchess*":

> We have studied Chaucer's lovely and pathetic elegy, with some particularity, in comparison with its sources, not, one may trust, for the sake of accumulating parallel passages, but rather for the sake of getting a better insight into his methods as an artist. Whatever the result, one thing emerges triumphantly from our investigation—the essential originality of Chaucer's genius.[32]

The conclusion seems to betray some sensitivity to critics' charges that academic studies of literature were nothing more than the accumulation of useless facts, and perhaps not without reason. If the parallels do help us gain insight into Chaucer's methods, they do so only if we choose to make the connections. The article offers no explicit examples and makes no argument. Furthermore, no case is made for Chaucer's originality. Rather, the article's principal strategy is simply to present portions of the texts in parallel columns, adding in places some instructions about what we are to take from the comparison. The article's purpose is to document a source that someone else had previously identified "but with scanty quotations that by no means prove [the] case" (9).

Not all claims for originality are this flat. A discussion of Wordsworth's *Michael* as a member of the pastoral genre accounts for its originality in terms of specific changes in convention: "*Michael* was a novel pastoral partly because it dropped the convention of love and of amoebean contest, and because it dealt with a real English shepherd. These facts point to originality."[33] But unlike, say a Russian formalist analysis, this article is not mainly interested in demonstrating that a generic innovation came into being. Its purpose is to demonstrate Wordsworth's genius. The article begins with the assertion that "Wordsworth saw common things with 'unaccustomed eyes' " and proceeds to quote the poet on the proofs of genius (432).

Not all sources are earlier works or authors of literature. Sources could also be works in other genres whose ideas the author is alleged to have known and used: "From the material presented in this paper we may deduce the obvious conclusion,

I think, that in the drawing of the Reeve and Miller Chaucer makes ample use of the rules of physiognomy."[34] This article does use the rules of physiognomy to interpret the text it discusses, but it is clear from the sentence above that the scholar is more interested in demonstrating an origin than in showing its significance for reading the poem. Here originality need not be protested, since the source is not another author but an anonymous system of thought. Another example of such a system is the seven deadly sins whose role in *The Canterbury Tales* was debated. One scholar argued that in addition to many casual references to the sins "the poet finds these familiar conceptions of medieval theology so serviceable a framework that he recurs often to the well-known formula as a convenient and suggestive device of construction."[35] The other denied that the sins were defined precisely enough for them to have served such a function.[36]

Source studies, in the most narrow sense of the term, find the origin of a major work in the existence of one or more earlier minor ones from which the later author borrowed. By this definition, the article on physiognomy might not fit since it doesn't claim that Chaucer drew on particular physiognomies. The debate over the seven deadly sins would fit even less since the originating material can no longer be described as even a body of sources. Rather, it is the influence of widely known ideas and their role in the work that is at issue. Articles that identify a general body of texts or ideas might be called influence rather than source studies, although the terms were not used with great precision and are often synonyms for each other. Source studies rely on the similarity of textual and linguistic features of the works, together with supporting historical data showing that the source was or could have been available to the author, to make what were apparently taken to be convincing arguments. One rarely finds source studies being rebutted.

But influence was a much more slippery matter, in part because it is a much broader concept. The strongest sense of the term during the period attributes influence to the work of a major author on his contemporaries and those who come later.[37] Influence is also used in cases where the work of one author is believed to have an effect on another, but no particular sources can be established. If the two authors are contemporaries, relations of influence can be reciprocal, and the question of whether such relations existed between Spenser and Sidney was repeatedly addressed during the period. An article published in 1930 reviews the debate: "The present writer expects to do no more than to try to bring together the various opinions of Spenser's and Sidney's work and, by supplementing and modifying them, to clarify rather than to settle a problem which has suffered much from dogmatic assertion."[38] Here the problem is that two major authors are being considered as influences on each other. If either author is too much the influencer and the other the influencee, then the genius of one will suffer. Thus we have the scholarly equivalent of a tie game: "The extent to which one influenced the other is, at present, impossible of exact definition" (731).

This general conclusion is supplemented with a list of seven more particular ones that the scholar nevertheless describes as "tentative":

1. The remarkable parallel in the chronology and nature of the two men's writings seems to point to a genuine intimacy.
2. Although the "Areopagus" probably never existed as a club, the theories of poetry held by Spenser and Sidney coincide essentially, the former manifesting a seemly deference towards his patron's interest in classical metres.
3. The employment of the Italian *sestina* by both poets probably resulted from a *mutual* attempt to anglicize this exotic measure.
4. Spenser and Sidney agree upon the function of epic poetry, they employ many of the same devices, and they voice a similarly ethical ideal.
5. Sidney's cosmic views, expressed in a single chapter of the *Arcadia*, are not opposed to Spenser's, but distinctly harmonize with his both in their general character and in their sources.
6. The historical rather than the moral allegory of the Cecropia-Pamela in the *Arcadia* is paralleled by the Braggadocchio episode in *The Faerie Queene*. Except for this unique incident, the *Arcadia* betrays no evidence of historical allegory in the sense universally employed by Spenser.
7. Finally, political ideas found in *The Faerie Queene* and in the

Arcadia belong invariably to the traditional thought of the time. (712)

This list gives us, in a more-obvious-than-usual way, a good sense of the sort of statements that the discipline of English could produce ad infinitum. Each of the conclusions is historical, and none are evaluative. They are all, in principle, capable of objective resolution. Interpretation is implicit in most of them, but it is not the issue in any. In addition to authors and works, the list reveals the importance of genre and other formal classifications to the discipline. And yet such taxonomies are seldom the object of research, but are rather tools that permit the discussion of authors and works to proceed. Something similar may be said of politics and other extraliterary historical issues. In spite of the direct involvement of both poets in court politics, the interest of their political ideas lies in their similarity or difference from those of the other poet, rather than in their content. This is not to say that no article could take the politics of an author as its topic, but that this article indicates the typical distribution of interest in these matters. Larger history remains background for literature.

The article on Spenser and Sidney also gives us, in exaggerated form, the characteristic rhetorical structure of articles in English. The rhetoric is borrowed from the sciences and the articles follow the pattern of hypothesis, presentation of evidence, and formal conclusion. Most articles do not enumerate so many points, but virtually all assert some piece of knowledge that they have demonstrated. As this article attests, the pattern is followed whether or not anything definite may be concluded. The rhetoric allows the authors of scholarly articles to retreat behind the mask of disinterest and to appear to be conducting the sort of observation that could be performed by any properly trained individual. This rhetoric would make the articulation of dissenting positions on certain kinds of issues difficult. While matters that can in principle be resolved on the basis of historical evidence were open to considerable debate, issues of judgment were not. The rhetoric expected in scholarly articles would thus limit the ability to challenge the core assumptions of the discipline, those about the value of canonical texts and authors.

117

Reorganizing English

If "The Relations of Spenser and Sidney" exemplifies the rhetoric and discourse of English throughout the early part of its history, it also suggests a condition more typical of the end of the period than the beginning. After nearly fifty years as an organized discipline, English literary history was able to feed on itself. There was by 1930 a sufficient body of contributions discussing the issue that an article can be published that refers mainly to secondary sources rather than the works of the poets themselves. And, since the largest issue remains unsettled, there is no reason this article should be thought to obviate the production of further contributions on the same subject. The relative undecidability of influence, as opposed to "source" in the narrow sense, allowed for continuing controversies that gave scholars more occasions to intervene. Yet this state of affairs also contributed to some scholars' sense that, in spite of growing productivity, literary studies were not making progress.

This feeling was already expressed by MLA president John Manly in his address to the 1920 meeting in Poughkeepsie. He observed that, the many valuable contributions that had appeared in *PMLA* not withstanding, "no great outstanding accomplishments in the field of scholarship . . . can be placed to the credit of the Association. No one great author or period has been fully studied; no great text or body of related texts has been edited; no problem of literary history or criticism has been made the object of concentrated and consistent study. . . . the general impression produced by a survey of our work is that it has been individual, casual, scrappy, scattering."[39] Nine years later, a review of literary scholarship asserted that it was hard to answer the question "What has been the progress of literary scholarship during the past quarter of a century?" While admitting that "there have been no startling discoveries, no revolutions," the scholar describes the task as "an endless one. The study of letters is forever running a losing race." In this admission is perceptible the beginning of the end of the positivist dream in literary scholarship. The review finds hope for the future not in the achievement of truth, but rather in that progress "has been made through an enlarging view of literature itself. . . . it has been approached not by one method but by many."[40]

In retrospect, such diversity seems more a prediction than a description of the state of scholarship in 1929. Nevertheless, increasing diversity is perceptible between 1900 and 1930, but especially after 1920 when there is a general trend in published articles toward increased attention to more modern literature and less dependence upon source and influence studies. That trend seems to be a direct result of the "reorganization of the [MLA] meetings with a view to greater specialization and greater stimulation of research" that Manly called for in his address (lx). In the following year, the MLA initiated the inclusion on the program of annual meeting sessions of specialized research groups. Prior to this change, the program recognized only the divisions of English, Romance, and Germanic languages in addition to a general session. This effectively mirrored the discipline's conception of itself as a unified field of research. The changes Manly achieved were the de facto recognition that the field was too big to be unified in this way. Manly noted that the heterogeneity of sessions usually meant that every listener found one topic about which he knew something, but had to listen to three or four about which he did not. The result was that "discussion is rare, and usually brief and perfunctory—almost never vigorous and profitable" (lv). Real achievements could be made only by groups of specialists meeting together. The reorganization of the MLA meeting doubtless encouraged work in areas such as the nineteenth century that had received little previous attention, and we begin to see the results in *PMLA* shortly thereafter. In 1925, for example, there were fifteen articles on the nineteenth century, more than on any other period, and nearly as many as on medieval and Renaissance literature combined. The greater attention to such periods was also facilitated by the expansion of the journal around the same time, so that more than four times the number of articles were published in 1930 as in 1900. Manly's changes also allowed American literature to achieve its first formal recognition within the organization as one of the English research groups. Furthermore, the pattern of diversification was established that would allow the MLA to absorb even narrower specialities but also increasingly heterogeneous approaches.

In this section we have examined several different sets of practices that contributed to the construction of literature during the first third or so of this century. Outside the university, the power to produce, disseminate, and evaluate literature was at first concentrated in the hands of a few men of letters. While much of their power derived from their editorial positions and from their reputations as poets or novelists, their influence was also conveyed through criticism. Criticism was concerned not with aethestics only, but quite directly with social, moral, and political issues. The decline of the men of letters left this practice in the hands of the New Humanists and the literary radicals whose criticism, however, never carried the cultural clout of the men of letters. Nondisciplinary literary history was another discourse produced within the literary of this period. While some of this history was written for pedagogical purposes, much of it also served more broadly to preserve the cultural past and to encourage nationalism. In some sense, each of these histories worked at the same problem, the story of American literature as a whole. Finally, the discipline of English produced a very different kind of literary history. Instead of producing narratives or serial biographies that covered long stretches of time, scholarly historians most often sought to uncover the sources and influences of particular works or authors. This is typical of disciplines, which must produce an infinite number of problems for their practitioners to solve. In the next section we will see that the new subdiscipline of American literature imitates the literary historicism of the field of English.

Part II
Institutionalization

4
American Literature as
a Discipline:
Constituting the Object

The last section is properly understood as the prehistory of my subject, American literature as an academic field. In previous chapters I have described the place and function of the literary in American culture as it changes from a powerful, elite cultural sector to one at first divided against itself by the rise of mass media, and then increasingly marginalized as those media expand in number and influence. Literature, nevertheless, retains much of the value it had acquired—by serving particular ideological functions within bourgeois culture—even as it retreats from the market into the protection of the university. Beginning roughly in 1890, American literature becomes an increasingly important issue. A large number of histories and a much smaller number of critical studies are devoted to it, although they fall outside of the mainstream of English as a discipline. But it is from that discipline, the work of which consists almost entirely of narrowly positivist studies of a very small canon of English authors, that the academic field of American literature will emerge.

In this chapter, my focus will be the effects of that genealogy on American literature as an object of study. What I will show is how in becoming an academic discipline—in becoming disciplined by the academy—American literature was transformed into a new object, an American literature different from any previous one. That object was defined in large measure by the terms of English as a discipline, but the project of establishing the subfield was itself motivated by the ideological demands of the larger culture.

Those demands were transmitted to the subfield in many forms, but one of the most important and heretofore least recognized was the New Humanism. This form of conservatism was the foundation of Norman Foerster's reconceptualization of American literary history, and Foerster's version of the history remains with us today. The effect of the disciplinary model of knowledge was to prohibit or marginalize overt political discussion but at the same time to instantiate a particular politics in the very object the discipline studied.

Basic Assumptions and Conditions

There were, as we shall see, significant changes during the 1920s and 1930s in the object constituted by American literature scholars, but discussions of this period of professionalization have overrated some of them and neglected others entirely. Critics of the canon have tended to neglect what American literature inherited from its parents, the preprofessional study of American literature and the discipline of English. The claim that American literature became significantly more racist and sexist during this period, for example, does not bear up under scrutiny; the conception of American literature the discipline inherited, as we have seen, was already thoroughly classist, racist, and sexist. The dominant conception of American literature already included a list of standard authors, all of them white men, most of them from New England, and almost all of them of English ancestry. American literature had long been understood as the expression of a homogeneous American culture defined against the alien cultures of immigrants, blacks, and Native Americans. Even ideals such as democracy and egalitarianism were relatively insignificant. And if some representations of American literature did include some sense of cultural diversity, only a few radicals such as Randolph Bourne actually argued for the value of such diversity. In the end, even the work of the literary radicals, because of its cultural nationalism, would contribute to the new dominant conception of American literature.[1]

As we have seen, the American literature that the new subdiscipline inherited was not so well formed that it was predestined to be taken up by the new field. The *Cambridge History* reflected the possibilities for several radically different conceptions of the field. In that history, even the terms "American" and "literature" remain ambiguous. "American" could have included Native American and non-English writing. "Literature" includes a great variety of utilitarian writing, but in explicitly opposing a conception limited to "*belles-lettres* alone," the editors acknowledge that "literature" had already come to mean "imaginative works of great value" in English departments and in the culture at large. During the 1920s and 1930s, the restrictive definition will exclude the broad one from serious consideration within the discipline, but the broader definition will have its last hurrah.

The fact that American literature as an academic field emerged out of the MLA and English as a discipline accounts in part for the failure of the new subdiscipline to broaden the boundaries of its object. The Americanists were trained not only in a narrow definition of literature but also to accept a particular exemplar of it. A fundamental element of that exemplar uses a notion of authorship that came into being with "literature" in the nineteenth century. The author as a creative personality was in both the earlier histories of American literature and in the disciplinary study of English the fundamental unit of literary study. For historians of American literature in particular, the author was far more likely to be the focus than the text; historians of English literature were more able to make their arguments turn on philological points. "Authorism," as we might call it, undoubtedly helped to restrict American literature to texts that had authors. Authorless writings, such as Native American literature and folktales, were thus excluded or marginalized.

But an author was not any writer.[2] Authors in the English canon were original geniuses; they represented the mystery of creativity and art. Their works, or at least the ones that merited canonical status, were valued for their originality, rather than for conformity to some set of essential laws of art. In the absence of such laws, however, the most original of the geniuses serve to define what will count as originality, just as they define poetry itself. The English canon was not just a list of those authors and works commonly studied and taught. It was more even than a hierarchy. If English poetry was incarnate in Chaucer, Spenser, Shakespeare, and Milton, then they must define what English poetry was or could be. Other authors were judged by comparison to their work. The canon also had a temporal dimension, named "tradition," that such comparison helped to produce. Later authors built on the tradition represented by earlier ones. For American writers to count fully as authors, they had to be part of the tradition, that is, to fit the English model.

The dependence of the discipline of American literature on that model made it likely that a canon similar to that of English literature would be established. A recognized canon did not exist when the subdiscipline got its start, even though a list of standard authors was widely accepted. It would be one project of the new field to determine which authors would merit canonical status. Yet we will see that the field was ill-equipped to carry out this task, since very few of its members practiced literary criticism. Disciplinary work in English had very little to do with judging the originality or the value of authors. Since the canon was largely inherited from criticism produced outside of the university beginning in the eighteenth century, there was no reason for practitioners of English to address these questions. Criticism was not part of its task. Virtually all of the research was narrowly historical, with source and influence studies the dominant forms.

Given this background, it is not surprising that the American literature canon would emerge slowly, at the margins of the field, during the 1920s and 1930s, and that it would be sometime during the next decade before that process was ratified and recognized. The lack of critical training itself doubtless contributed to making the English canon both the model and the measure of American literature. That canon, dominated by poets, had long had the effect of focusing attention on American poets at the expense of prose writers, but the model also defined the essential author as being white and male. The proximate cause of the exclusion of African-American and women writers was the conception of literature implicit in the English canon, rather than an increase in racist or sexist discourse. Of course this conception of the author, of literary authority, was consonant with the ideology of American culture in general. Under these circumstances, the formation of the canon could not but be classist, racist, and sexist.

Predisciplinary treatments of American literature suffer from two weaknesses that members of the new subfield had to overcome in order to establish the interest and legitimacy of their endeavor: the lack of an aesthetic appropriate to American literature and the lack of a unifying conception or theory of that literature's meaning. The need for an aesthetic and a theory was both exacerbated and made more difficult to fulfill by the relationship of American literature to English literature. Both in and outside of English departments, certain British works and authors were taken to represent the pinnacle of literary achievement. American works either seemed to be pale imitations of the British or to violate the aesthetic standards by which British works were valued. Thus Emerson is often praised as the creator of beautiful sentences, but damned as one who could not put two of them together coherently. Emerson's essays did not fit the models provided by British essayists, from Addison and Steele to Carlyle and De Quincey. American poems and novels were often similarly deviant from British standards in form and subject. The assumption that American literature was a branch of English prevented a homegrown aesthetic from emerging.

On the other hand, American literature did not have to emerge in opposition to an explicit unifying conception of English literature. While such theories had been offered, most influentially by Taine, they were not fundamental to English literary scholarship in America. Indeed, in the first fifty years of the discipline of English in America, no general history of English literature was produced and histories even of single periods were rare. But there was, nevertheless, a theory of English literature against which Americanists were forced to struggle. That theory held simply that all literature written in the English language was part of a single body, a body that was the greatest of all national literatures. Americanists such as Fred Lewis Pattee could assert that English was the only language that had produced two national literatures, but it remained to be demonstrated that American literature was a national literature. Thus a theory that explained the unity and distinctiveness of American literature was needed even though no comparable theory of English literature existed or seemed necessary. Yet the production of this theory was inhibited by the fact that there were advantages to conceiving of American literature as part of British literature. These included not only association with this greatest of all literatures, but also, as Nina Baym has pointed out, the identification of "American" with the Anglo-Saxon race. Treating American literature as part of British literature allowed for the dominant American ethnic group to assert its superiority.

Criticism in the 1920s

Changes in the literary since its pre-World War I formation help explain the cultural necessity for America in the 1920s to understand itself to have a literature of its own. While the literary remained a powerful source of prestige and influence, it had suffered a real if perhaps unrecognized demotion. If we take Howells—who was feted by the nation's leaders, up to and including the president himself—to represent the cultural role of the literary in prewar America, we would have to take H. L. Mencken to represent the literary of the postwar period. He was recognized at the time as "the most powerful influence on this whole generation of educated people" and he has been understood since as "the leading champion of naturalism and the literature of the twenties."[3] But unlike Howells, Mencken was an outsider. Although Howells occasionally had left the mainstream by, for example, supporting the Haymarket anarchists, Mencken defined himself against that mainstream. Mencken's Germanophilia led him to support the Germans and oppose U.S. intervention against them in World War I. He favored aristocracy over democracy, immorality over morality; he was explicitly anti-Christian. Stuart Sherman captures the part Mencken played when he describes "Mr. Mencken's continuous tirade against everything respectable in American morals, against everything characteristic of American society, and against everything and everybody distinguished in American scholarship and letters."[4]

Rather than reflecting the unity of culture and society, Mencken both lamented and represented their divorce. Culture or civilization was what American society, in Mencken's view, lacked. But for Mencken the culture the old custodians had sought to preserve was not worthy of the name. The new culture that Mencken would help legitimate was critical and rebellious, though it lacked any consistent oppositional premise or program. How could so valuable a portion of cultural capital as the literary pass into the hands of opponents of the regime? Perhaps the most significant single factor was the decrease in the relative value of the literary. Thus while Mencken, literary radicals such as Brooks and Frank, and younger critics such as Malcolm Cowley and Edmund Wilson had taken over the critical function of the men of letters, the literary they now controlled was not as powerful as that of Howells. Furthermore, these intellectuals had a smaller role than their predecessors, the men of letters. Where Howells and his ilk had literary authority over the leading periodicals and direct connection with the major book publishers, the next generation were most significant as critics. While many of them served as editors, they worked for distinctly less powerful organs, at best journals such as the *Nation* or the *New Republic* read by the intelligentsia, but often little magazines with tiny circulations and even smaller incomes. Even the better journals lacked the cultural clout of the *Atlantic* or *Harper's* of 1900.

Stuart Sherman, one of the editors of the *Cambridge History*, professor of English at the University of Illinois, and later editor of the literary supplement of the New York *Herald Tribune*, was a rather different representative of the literary of the 1920s. We might think of him as a new sort of cultural custodian, a Howells for a new era. While Sherman had earned a Ph.D., he worked not as a literary historian but as a critic, contributing regularly to the *Nation* and publishing seven books of criticism between 1917 and 1927 (the last two posthumously). Sherman, a student of Babbitt's, in his earliest criticism took an orthodox New Humanist line highly critical of most contemporary literature and culture.[5] In that role, Sherman began an exchange with Mencken that Richard Ruland has analyzed at some length. During the course of this debate, Sherman changed from a New Humanist critic of American culture to what Ruland calls a "radical conservative" booster of it. Our interest in Sherman is not in his complex and changing political positions but in his defense of "the native tradition" in literature and in politics. Like his New Humanist teacher, Sherman was a moralist who came to identify Puritanism with everything that was positive in America. In the wake of the war, which seemed to have had a major emotional impact on Sherman, he came to find more and more positive elements in American culture. Throughout most of the debate, he attacked writers such as Theodore Dreiser and James Branch Cabell, whom Mencken supported. Sherman defended American writers of the past: Whitman, Emerson, Thoreau, Hawthorne, Franklin (whom he discussed in the *Cambridge History*), and James. Mencken liked some of these writers, but he regarded them as isolated from each other and the culture, rather than as representing a tradition. "Mencken looked to the major writers of America's past to demonstrate a conviction central to much of his work: the pursuit of an American tradition was self-defeating, for America had no tradition which was characteristically hers" (Ruland, 121).

Ruland argues that Mencken had won the debate with Sherman, and from a certain perspective this is indisputable. The naturalist and aestheticist positions that Mencken held certainly had more impact on contemporary literature than did Sherman's moralism and patriotism. Toward the end of his life, even Sherman began to find something of value in Dreiser and in Mencken himself. But in another sense, Sherman seems to have won, for, in the long run, American literature was conceived as a tradition. Where Mencken pictured his favorite American writers—Emerson, Hawthorne, Poe, Twain, Whitman—as antithetical to Americanism, Sherman regarded them as its chief representatives. Sherman's view would not prevail immediately nor exactly on his terms, but it would eventually become the dominant view of the literature. The specific writers Mencken championed—Sherwood Anderson, Sinclair Lewis, Joseph Hergesheimer, Dreiser, and Cabell—would be left out of the canon, or become increasingly marginal to it. The arguments advanced by Mencken and the literary radicals contributed to a growing gap between contemporary literature and American literature. American literature came to seem increasingly like a thing of the past, while contemporary literature was increasingly understood as international. The new subdiscipline would contribute to this distinction by discouraging work on contemporary writers, but the competition for the rights to the label "American literature" was won by the literary historians for their object.

The argument over an American tradition cannot be understood apart from the larger problem of an American civilization, a problem that preoccupied the literary culture of the 1920s. We recall that such civilization as was thought to exist in the United

States at the turn of century was identified with Anglo-Saxon or English characteristics and achievements, rather than with anything distinctly American. It was partly this sense of cultural humility or inferiority that provoked writers such as Brooks and Bourne to call for cultural nationalism. Their search for a usable past was meant to identify a tradition that could support the development of an American civilization. The radicals' position in this debate was articulated in Harold Stearns's collection, *Civilization in the United States*. Stearns's preface states that among the contentions of the volume was that "whatever else American civilization is, it is not Anglo-Saxon, and that we shall never achieve any genuine nationalistic self-consciousness as long as we allow certain financial and social minorities to persuade us that we are still an English Colony."[6] And yet, the literary radicals also participated in the denigration of American civilization. Thus Stearns also contends that "the most moving and pathetic fact in the social life of America today is emotional and aesthetic starvation. . . . We have no heritages or traditions to which to cling except those that have already withered in our hands and turned to dust" (vii). It was in large part this lack of a usable past that led Brooks in his essay "The Literary Life" to quote approvingly Samuel Butler's assertion that "America will have her geniuses . . . , but I do not think America is a good place to be a genius."[7] The radicals' attacks on the "professors" and the "genteel tradition" called into question those aspects of American culture that seemed the most redolent of civilization. There is, of course, a contradiction at the root of this position. If America had previously failed to produce a civilization, how could a usable past, a tradition, be discovered? In searching for a usable past they acknowledged an American tradition in spite of themselves. This contradiction explains, I believe, Brooks's strange career, which began by attacking the American tradition in *The Wine of the Puritans* and ended by embracing it in the *Makers and Finders* volumes. More important, it explains why the impact of the literary radicals' work was ultimately to shore up the tradition they originally hoped to tear down.

Not all of the contributors to the discussion of American civilization were so conflicted. Mencken's rejection of the American past allowed him to deny the existence of American civilization.

Thus he asserted that transcendentalism "produced no civilization, but only a tawdry pseudo-civilization—a codfish civilization."[8] Few contributors were willing to go this far. Yet even the conservative opponents of the literary radicals did not argue that American civilization had been successfully expressed in its literature. Some, like Babbitt and More, were as critical of American culture as were the radicals. More described America of the nineteenth century as a "half-civilization."[9] Even Sherman, who believed that he could identify America's "national genius" in Puritanism, felt that it was still not possible for the man of letters to "hold [America] first till her national genius expresses itself as adequately, as nobly, in . . . literature, as it has, on the whole, in the great political crises." Sherman was refreshingly honest about the political implications of literary nationalism: literary expression could stimulate national pride more effectively than Liberty bonds or universal military service: "Robert Burns and Sir Walter did the work more simply and cheaply for Scotland."[10]

Sherman here understands literature as an expression of the collective mind of a nation, and therefore as evidence of the nation's success or failure. A great literature—and in a very strong sense, that expression for him is redundant—meant a great nation. The literature of a nation gave it an identity; it was an expression of the nation's character. It could serve these functions particularly well because literature could exclude the divisive realities that could not be so easily purged from history. The aesthetic and nationalist functions of literature are in this conception combined. A civilization by definition produces literature of high aesthetic value. In light of this we can understand the cultural mandate to produce an American tradition. The principal cultural work of the new academic field of American literature would be to demonstrate the existence of an American civilization. That is, American literary studies were organized to show that America had achieved the highest level of development and was thus fit to join the exclusive club of ancient and modern societies that merit the name "civilization." Both an aesthetics and a theory of unity and distinctiveness were necessary if this mission were to be fulfilled. An aesthetics was necessary to demonstrate the quality of American literature; the theory was necessary to show what was American about American civilization.

The Outline of a Tradition

The rise of American literature studies in the 1920s cannot be understood apart from the debates over tradition and civilization, but there are, of course, a variety of more broadly cultural reasons for the debates themselves to have reached their height during the late 1910s and early 1920s. Doubtless the most important of these was the increased nationalism provoked by World War I. The rhetoric of the war meant "to make the world safe for democracy" must be reckoned as the source for the renewed strength of the identification between America and that ideal, which we find reflected in some of the propaganda supporting the study of American literature. The United States' decisive contribution to the victory over Germany contributed to the perception of America's increased importance on the world stage. The time was ripe for the dominance of the cultural nationalism that had been an emergent ideology prior to the war.

The development of an institutional base in 1921, the American Literature Group of the MLA, made possible an organized effort to invent an American tradition. If the new subdiscipline inherited much from its preprofessional predecessors, it did not inherit a coherent picture of American civilization. The newly organized Americanists did not share the literary radicals' view of their culture, but they just as strongly rejected the cultural humility of the prewar literary. The professional Americanists would have been less willing than Stearns to attribute Anglo-Saxonism to "financial and social minorities" but they were equally convinced that it prevented a needed "nationalistic self-consciousness" (vii). The academic Americanists did not identify the problem, as Brooks did, as a matter of finding "a usable past" since for them the past was a thing to be known rather than used. And given the positivist orientation that they learned in graduate study, most of them would not attack the problem directly. Nevertheless, the agenda is unmistakable as early as the ALG's third meeting, when Robert Spiller, serving as acting secretary, noted in his minutes that discussion following Fred Lewis Pattee's paper, "American Literature as a College Course," "favored presenting American literature as expression of national (historical) consciousness and not as aesthetic offshoot of English literature."[11] Jay Hubbell remembered the nationalist sentiments expressed at this meeting as a characteristic "emphasis" of American literature study at the time.[12]

But what was the national consciousness that the literature expressed? The beginnings of an answer were forthcoming two years later in Norman Foerster's paper "New Viewpoints in American Literature," presented at the 1925 ALG meeting. After it was read at the ALG session, it was published in substantially revised form in the *Saturday Review* and it would end up as the introductory essay in *The Reinterpretation of American Literature*. Foerster makes it clear that the debate over American tradition and civilization was a major stimulus to his call for the reinterpretation of American literature. Foerster acknowledged that such a project could derive "perhaps some light from . . . the critics who had been deploring the absence of 'Civilization in the United States.' "[13] He mentions Brooks, Bourne, Mencken, Sherman, and Henry Seidel Canby as critics who have dealt with "the absence of a national culture," but unlike most of them, he sees the problem as a historical one "that had its origin on the frontier" (31). As a New Humanist and student of Babbitt's, Foerster accepted a certain portion of that critique of American civilization: "Instead of seeking . . . growth of the spirit . . . , America gave herself up, with slight compunction, to materialism—a materialism colored with a conventional religiosity, which effected the ascendancy of middle-class philistinism" (30). But we also see in this treatment of the problem the beginnings of the end of the critique. In Foerster, the problem of a national culture is already on its way to becoming a theme in the American tradition, in other words, an aspect of national culture.

Nevertheless, the historical prominence of Foerster's essay demonstrates the importance of the issue of American civilization in the emergence of American literature as a discipline. Spiller explicitly traces the intellectual origins of the discipline to Foerster, attributing to his "philosophical perspective" half of major responsibility for the ALG's "sense of direction and purpose."[14] Spiller has correctly identified Foerster's significance where Ruland and so many other historians of criticism have missed it. It is not clear, however, that Spiller correctly interpreted Foerster's contribution. Spiller claimed that it was Foerster who introduced the perspective of the "New History" of Carl Becker, James Beard, and Frederick Jackson Turner, a history devoted to claims for America's uniqueness and rooted in the methods of the social sciences. It is true that Foerster mentions this history as having "given us a new vision of the forces dominant in our past" (25), but he takes up relatively little of that vision. The most important element of it for him is the replacement of the germ or Teutonic origins theory by the frontier origins theory. What the historians provide might be understood as a counterweight to the literary radicals: an account of an American culture. Thus Foerster's essay could demand that American literature would have to be studied in relationship to that culture. But Foerster's conception of the culture owed far more to the New Humanism than it did to contemporary historians. Vernon Parrington would give expression to their conception applied to literature.

Foerster's essay did not attempt to solve the problem of defining American civilization; on the contrary, its purpose was to make the problem the central task of the new academic field. He saw himself as offering a theory that would serve to direct future investigation. Unlike most literary historians of his day, Foerster recognized that "the secular progress of knowledge in the fields of science and history . . . indicates that important acquisitions of knowledge normally *follow* the formulation of a generalization or hypothesis."[15] He warned of the "aimless accumulation of small facts" as a danger to the new field of American literature, and noted that "additions to the sum of knowledge are rarely of value unless they are related with an important end in view." What was needed was "a number of fresh interpretations—the systematic exploitation of promising points of view. Each possible main factor should be extensively applied to see how much it really explains" ("Factors," 38). It should be made clear that what Foerster means by "interpretations" here is not readings of individual texts, but readings of American literature as a whole. As we will see, Foerster was much more the critic than most ALG members, but the program he proposed did not conflict with the assumptions of literary history. Foerster still understood literary history as a science—he just understood science differently. He acknowledged that "our literary historians are still seriously embarrassed by the paucity of known facts in which support may be found for generalizations. Our need of facts is quite as patent as our need for penetrating generalizations" (Introduction, xxi). This concession allowed that the project Foerster proposed could be understood in terms of the usual naive positivism of literary historical scholarship, even as he hoped to go beyond its limitations.

Foerster's paper originated, as a disciplinary project, the construction of a theory of American literature. Foerster made the agenda of that project explicit in his introduction to the *Reinterpretation of American Literature* when he named three broad problems "with which the student of American literary history is concerned. . . . 1) In what sense is our literature distinctively American? 2) In what ways does it resemble the literatures of Europe? and 3) What are the local conditions of life and thought in America that produced these results?" (xxiii-xxiv). It is astonishing to us now to think that Foerster's first question articulated a project that had not been pursued before. The "Americanness" of American literature was, as we have seen, valued in an Emerson or a Franklin, but it was not an organizing principle around which literary histories were constructed. Foerster complained that "there has been, since the war, an enthusiastic waving of the flag 'Americanism'; but obviously those who rally round this stirring symbol have commonly but the faintest idea of what it symbolizes" ("Factors," 24).

Foerster suggests that the answers to his three questions could be explained in terms of four "factors:" "1) the Puritan tradition, 2) the frontier spirit, 3) romanticism, 4) realism" ("Factors," 26–27). These categories have since become so familiar, that it is hard to imagine that we were ever without them. But the fact that Foerster offered an innovation here is demonstrated by the impact of his paper on the ALG membership. The group was so impressed that the next ALG program, titled "Factors in American Literary History," was devoted to papers on Foerster's categories. Out of plans for this session emerged the idea of the book project that would become the *Reinterpretation of American Literature*.[16] The heart of the book included essays by Hubbell on "The Frontier," Howard Mumford Jones on "The European Background," Kenneth Murdock on "The Puritan Tradition in American Literature," Paul Kaufman on "The Romantic Movement," and Parrington on "The Development of Realism." The first essay, however, was Pattee's "Call for a Literary Historian," reprinted from the *American Mercury*, which castigates the textbook timidity of earlier histories and holds up D. H. Lawrence's *Studies in Classic American Literature* as a model. *The Reinterpretation of American Literature* concludes with two essays, one by historian Arthur Schlesinger and the other by Harry Hayden Clark. Together these essays form something of a manifesto, an announcement of the program of the new discipline.

It is important to be specific about how Foerster's perspective reframed the study of American literature. As we have seen, most of the earlier treatments of the subject borrowed their periodization from political history, and their selection of authors was determined in part by the need to include representatives of different regions. Foerster specifically rejects both of these "political and geographic divisions" as the source of "our disordered interpretation of American literature" ("Factors," 26). In replacing these with the "factors" mentioned above, Foerster provided a periodization proper to literature itself and a conception of that literature as the reflection of the nation, rather than any of its regions.[17] The new periodization is important because it became the basis for a new narrative of American literary development. Literature no longer merely reflected other national events; it now could be seen to have its own events. On the other hand, Foerster's scheme could incorporate much of the received wisdom. Thus like Wendell, Foerster can claim that American romantic writers "virtually created American literature" ("Factors," 32). But if the same "events" continued to be recognized, there was a new conception of what sorts of things could count as explanations of literary events. Foerster's conception was novel enough that Hubbell could misunderstand it. He proposed that race, environment, and outside literary influences were the larger factors behind those Foerster named, thus going back to Taine and to most of the historians since, who had assumed such causes had to be physical.[18] Foerster's factors are, rather, mainly intellectual. He is, in a word, an idealist. Even where he invokes the American environment, the relevant factor is the frontier *spirit*. By shifting the ground of American literary historical explanation from the physical to the ideal, Foerster provides the opening for the new form of literary scholarship that will make itself felt around 1940.

Hubbell was apparently a quick study, for his essay on "The Frontier" is as pure an example of Foerster's program as could be imagined. The frontier, Hubbell argues, "should not be identified with the geographic environment."[19] Nor was the frontier mainly to be understood as something that was documented in American literature, since much of the writing that took the frontier as its subject was the highly conventionalized product of urban writers who had never left the city (46). The real question for Hubbell is the influence of the frontier on nonfrontier writers such as Emerson, Whitman, Mark Twain, and William James, but it is a question he cannot solve: "It is natural . . . to conclude that there is, in the writings of such men . . . something distinctively American which comes indirectly from the frontier; but it is no easy matter to put one's finger upon it" (49). The frontier becomes at most a distant and vague social reality, an influence on the national character—but we are well on our way here to treating the frontier merely as an idea.

Hubbell's essay demonstrates that even in the late 1920s, the issue of whether American literature was a national literature remained nominally open: "Our literature has always been less American than our history; possibly it is not even yet a national literature in the full sense of the word" (43). But Hubbell goes on to explain how a national literature did develop. Hubbell also traces it to the romantic movement, which he suggests may have felt the impact of the frontier through Jacksonian democracy. But it was the Civil War that finally brought about national literature: "In ante-bellum days American literature was little more than an aggregation of sectional literatures; after the War it became national in a sense of the word not applicable before that time" (53–54). The real question, then, is Foerster's—not whether American literature is distinctive, but what makes it so. The frontier is the most significant of the four factors, because it is the only non-European one. Thus the frontier gave "our writers . . . a new point of view, which we may call American" (44). Hubbell thus equates the development of American literature with the development of American nationalism. The frontier is one of three influences on such development, the other two being the mixed ethnicity of those who settled the country, which thwarted an English identity; and the standardization of culture created by the industrial revolution. Of these, only the frontier would become a significant category in American literary studies.

The other essays in the volume tell us less about where study of American literature will be going. Howard Mumford Jones, who was originally to be represented by an essay on another factor, "The Middle-Class Spirit," instead puts American literature in its place vis-à-vis its European background: "We have no American Shelly, no Godwin, no Gautier, no Heine and no Schopenhauer to deny conventional values, but in place of these, Emerson and Longfellow and Bryant and Lowell and Hawthorne, who have their merits doubtless, but who are not quite of the company of Nietzsche. . . . the American 'Romantic Movement' is a very correct romantic movement."[20] Jones's politics are clearly to the left of most of the contributors to the volume, but his position contributes to a rereading of the American romantics as conservative. Kenneth Murdock's essay is devoted mainly to attacking misconceptions of Puritanism rampant in contemporary literary criticism. While the British context is mentioned, it is not the focus of the essay. Neither is the influence of the Puritan tradition on later American literature, an influence Murdock seems to say can't be isolated.[21] Neither Paul Kaufman on romanticism nor Parrington on realism focus mainly on European sources. Both, in fact, provide surveys of the American literature of the respective types, but the surveys are strikingly different. Kaufman's is completely predictable, including some more obscure writers but focusing on the standard authors. Parrington, on the other hand, excludes Henry James and concentrates instead on Howells, Hamlin Garland, Stephen Crane, Frank Norris, and Theodore Dreiser, and numerous minor authors are also discussed. Unlike any of the other essays in the volume, Parrington provides a narrative of realism's development; he presents an interpretation, rather than calling for one. Henry Hayden Clark's essay, which was added at the last minute after Henry S. Canby had opted out, seems designed to refute those of Parrington and Schlesinger. For the new literary historian, Clark insists, "literature itself remains the true subject, and the proper focal center is finally the acknowledged masterpieces."[22] He complains of economic and other determinisms, and of misplaced emphasis on background rather than on the literature itself. Clark attempts to illustrate an alternative approach in which "one focuses his attention first squarely on the foreground—the specific book or poem under consideration; then let him view the background in this particular case through the 'windows' of the foreground" (197–98). While Clark's examples demonstrate that he has no notion about how to focus attention on a text and therefore simply repeats the pattern of literary history, his essay demands the reversal of the relations of text and history that New Criticism will bring about.

The importance of Clark's claims for the primacy of the masterpiece is revealed in Canby's review of *The Reinterpretation of American Literature,* which appeared both in the *Saturday Review* and then in the first number of *American Literature.* The opposition of history and aesthetics was one of the major theoretical problems to confront the new subdiscipline. With literary history the dominant research practice in English, scholars in American literature could be expected to have some allegiance to history. In fact, *The Reinterpretation of American Literature* is mainly a call for scholarship in the history of American literature. Similarly, the same issue of *American Literature* told prospective contributors that the most important articles are those that bring to light new materials or facts, and that articles that present new interpretations based on old information are less important.[23] While responding very favorably to the volume as a whole, Canby singles out Schlesinger's essay for disapproval and in so doing endorses Clark's argument. Schlesinger was the lone "outsider" to appear in the book, being a professor of history invited by the American Literature Group to discuss the relation of American history and literary history (Foerster, "Introduction," iii). Schlesinger argued for a "broadly social" understanding of literary history on the warrant that scholarship ought to serve democratic ends. He asserts that the literary historian has been "mainly interested in the picturesque, the unusual, and the superexcellent" and urges that he should rather be concerned with material he judges to have the widest influence on American culture.[24] Judged on these grounds, Schlesinger suggests, Emerson is perhaps less important than William H. McGuffey, creator of the

McGuffey school readers. Schlesinger wants to free the historian of letters from the domination of the aesthete: "It remains, however, that literary criticism and literary history are two distinct branches of scholarship, each with its own point of view and technique, and having no more in common than, say, history in general and the study of ethics" (163–64). This is a position that reflects accurately the work the literary historians did, but not their sense of the material they studied. Canby is horrified by the possibility that the McGuffeys of our history might displace the Emersons. He speaks for the disciplines that have been constituted around "literature" when he objects to Schlesinger's privileging of social over aesthetic significance. Such a criterion would render valueless the very project of literary study as it had developed in the university over the course of fifty years.[25]

Canby and Schlesinger represent more extreme positions than those of the other contributors to the collection. After all, Canby was the literary critic of the *Saturday Review*, and Schlesinger a professional historian. But Canby was also trained as a literary scholar and he was a member of the ALG. And Canby was not the only one to take this tack: F. O. Matthiessen, reviewing *The Reinterpretation of American Literature* in the *Yale Review*, warned that the historian of American literature "must not lose himself in his background, or forget that he is dealing primarily with literature. He must remember that his real quarry is aesthetic values. . . . Above all he must be aware that the imperative thing for American scholarship today is not so much the accumulation of small facts as a sensitive interpretation of them."[26] This endorsement of aestheticism over history clearly reflects the direction in which American literature studies were headed. If American writing were to be worthy of the name "literature," it must be shown to have characteristics such as the expression of original genius by which a literature is recognized. Schlesinger's plea was doomed to fall on deaf ears. It was only by demonstrating that there were "super-excellent" works produced by Americans that American literary historians could justify their own existence. Most ALG members would remain historical scholars in their practice, but like Clark they would regard their subject as the history of great works rather than of socially significant ones. Thus the publication and reception of *The Reinterpretation of American Litera-*

ture serve to define an important boundary for the new discipline, even though not all work on American literature in the 1930s will respect the boundary.

Foerster and his contributors established both the main boundaries of the field of American literature and the most significant subdivisions of that territory, its major periods and problems. But this did not result in an immediate solution to the question of American civilization. That project was severely limited by the assumptions and the practice of literary history itself, which would prevent the incipient demand for an academic criticism from quickly being answered. It is worth noting in this connection how radically the articles in *The Reinterpretation of American Literature* differed from those that would be published by *American Literature*, or for that matter were being published by other journals in English. Very rare indeed is the theoretical or critical article in American literature before the 1940s.

While Foerster, Clark, and others wanted more criticism and interpretation, they did not see any epistemological distinction between those activities and history. The word "factors" in Foerster's title tells us much about the kind of project the new subfield was conducting. In spite of his idealism, Foerster's model remained that of the sciences, and he continued to conceive of literary history in positivist terms. That Hubbell's version was even more reductive in naming race and geography, categories familiar from Richardson, suggests how little the conception of literary history had changed in the roughly fifty years that English had been a discipline. For most of the scholars who formed the ALG, a theory of American literature would have to fit the reigning positivist model for scholarship—yet such a demand ultimately stalled the development of such a theory. The kind of scholarship sanctioned by the positivist model could not produce the knowledge necessary to sustain a theory. The facts that literary scholars established could not by themselves add up to a picture of the whole.

There was another limitation in Foerster's conception of the problem that I would go so far as to say prevented its solution on his terms. Foerster's "factors" fell into two classes, "European culture" and the "American environment" ("Factors," 26). He contends that "American culture is derivative, and consequently the study of American literature is essentially a study of comparative literature, a study in the international history of ideas and their literary expression" (Introduction, xxiii). Foerster's insistence on an international perspective on a national literature is, if not inherently self-contradictory, at least not easily turned into a coherent practice. Foerster was aware, as were other ALG members, that the doctorate in English did not provide the kind of training that would support such study. The ALG discussed a plan for a separate Ph.D. in American literature that would have included modern European history and modern philosophy and religion.[27] Since the plan was not pursued, new specialists in American literature remained ill-prepared for comparative studies. More important, however, is the fact that the undertaking itself could not have produced the kind picture of American literature that nationalism demanded. It is precisely the conception of America as a derivative culture that the project of creating a civilization sought to refute. What American literature had to be was the expression of a distinctively American culture.

To be sure, some American literature scholars—Perry Miller and Jones come to mind—would study European sources of American movements, but this was not to become typical of research in the new field, and it was even less typical of teaching. Thus despite the importance that Foerster's four "factors" had in the constitution of American literature as an object of study, they did not function as he assumed they would. Consider the "Puritan tradition," for example. Murdock, Miller, and others would rescue it from the humanists and the literary radicals, but even in their work, the focus would be on New England as an isolated "experiment." Puritanism, though understood in increasing complexity, continued to be considered distinctly American. The other European factor, romanticism, was in the practice of research even less connected to Europe. American romantic writers were studied separately from European romantics, and romanticism as an intellectual movement was not a major topic of study. Rather than being understood in relation to their European influences, the writers of the romantic period in America were regarded as the most genuinely American authors.

Humanism and American Literature

As I have suggested in several instances above, I believe that the effect of Foerster's program for study of American literature was to render such study more conservative and to limit the possibilities for other interpretations. Here I think we have to recognize that Foerster's humanism influenced his conception of American literature, even though that conception was neither offered nor received as an expression of humanism. It was his humanism that led Foerster to emphasize European "factors" in American literature, since as a humanist Foerster believed that literature ultimately was the expression of humanity, not nationality.[28] This is not to say that the New Humanism ever became the official program of academic Americanists. Jay Hubbell reported that some ALG members disagreed strongly enough with Foerster to object to Hubbell's suggestion that he serve as coeditor of *American Literature*.[29] But the humanist agenda did point to a conception of American literature defined by ideas and values, rather than one defined by political and social conditions. Of Foerster's factors, only the frontier could be understood as a social condition, but it is not understood by Hubbell as such. Of the contributors to *The Reinterpretation of American Literature*, only Parrington sees his subject, realism, as the product of economic and social factors. In spite of Foerster's claims that humanism as a critical method seeks "historical understanding," it is in fact a program that renders historical differences uninteresting (*AC*, 252). What counts for the humanist are eternal ideas and the unchanging character of humanity expressed in the "*normally or typically human*" (*AC*, 241). American literature will increasingly come to be studied in these terms; the American tradition will be understood as a unique expression of these values or norms.

Most previous accounts suggest that the New Humanism was rejected both as a literary theory by the New Critics and as an educational theory by advocates of research. The New Humanism is treated as a force that was already spent by the time Foerster published his symposium, *Humanism and America*, in 1930 (Ruland, 184). Though some may admit that humanism's influence persists, it is treated as marginal. It is true that the New Humanism as a movement lost influence after 1930; but if it did not survive as a movement, its influence persisted in at least two different veins: through T. S. Eliot to the New Critics and through Sherman and Foerster to American literature studies. The reason that the New Humanism persists is that it codified much of the ideology of the literature that emerged in the nineteenth century. The important differences that separate the New Critics from the New Humanists are visible against a background of family resemblance. Similarly, humanism was the ground upon which the narrative of American literary history was written. That narrative includes not only the story of places and ideas, the movement from Puritan New England via the frontier to romantic New England and finally the realism of the machine, but also the story of authors as originators or bearers of the traditions.

Thus Foerster's humanist arguments and interpretations are integral to the project of securing the canon. This is not necessarily because his interpretations were widely accepted, but because they demonstrated how America's problematic standard authors could be understood and accepted from a conservative standpoint. Foerster was more influential than his theoretical masters, Babbitt and More, because Foerster read American literature more sympathetically than they did. While they regarded most American writers as pernicious—and when they found one such as Emerson redeemable, carefully distinguished the good from the bad—Foerster tended to find value even in the most antithetical authors, such as Poe and Whitman. The effect of this sympathy, however, is always to mitigate the offending elements in the author under discussion. Poe's criticism is praised for its rationality, its honesty, and its fidelity to principle. More important, Foerster reads Poe seriously; he works at elaborating Poe's arguments and revealing his assumptions. This treatment tends to render the author valuable even if, as is the case here, most of the arguments and assumptions are held to be in error. Thus Matthiessen can conclude from reading Foerster on Poe that "the reason for Poe's enormous influence on poets of the magnitude of Baudelaire and Verlaine and for his comparative neglect at home has never emerged so clearly as in this elaboration of his theory of art" ("New Standards," 182).

Foerster's interpretations are more significant when he is able to read the author as a humanist. In *Nature in American Litera-*

ture, Emerson is called a "true descendant of the Puritans" who was assured of " 'the eternal distinction between the soul and the world' and the ineluctable authority of moral sentiment."[30] Emerson here is made to bear the fundamental distinction of humanist doctrine, between the human and the natural. Of Thoreau, Foerster observes that "although the scientific temper of the age to a large extent directed his moods and activities, Thoreau was clearly enough not a skilled naturalist" (*Nature*, 88). One senses that this endears Thoreau to Foerster: "One must regret his indifference to Plato and Aristotle, who might have offset, if he had known them better, his tendency to absorption in nature" (*Nature*, 96n.1). Foerster's longest section on Thoreau is entitled "Humanist," and in it we find that Thoreau in the final analysis holds all of the right positions. Thoreau's discipline, for example, may be too extreme when it comes to meat or sex, but it distinguishes him from European romantics even when it comes to "obedience to his genius—not the 'genius' of the German romanticists but the Socratic inner witness, the 'heavenly monitor' of Milton" (*Nature*, 130). The romanticist conceives of man's genius or inner nature as single, but Thoreau, like all good humanists, understands it as a dualism of desire and spirit (*Nature*, 131). Foerster's final evaluation of Thoreau is that he "brought together much that is perennially vital in the leading traditions of the Western world—the classical and the Christian—at the very time when they were being assailed with all the weapons of modern science and of the natural man bent on utter emancipation" (*Nature*, 142).

The explicit humanist opposition to emancipation and social justice doubtless troubled some Americanists. But troubling perhaps to many more was the humanists' desire for an aristocracy and their explicitly antidemocratic views. For example, Thoreau, like Emerson, is valued because he exhibits none of the "extensive sympathy with all men that is typical of the modern democratic era"; both rejected charity or, as the New Humanists called it, "humanitarianism" (*Nature*, 137–38). Whitman, on the other hand, is seriously deluded about the masses: "We can discern few indications that democracy might show itself a substantial basis for any such grandiose structure as that which Whitman prophesied." On the contrary: "Everywhere reflective persons fear that the equalitarianism of democracy inevitably tends to depress the superior and raise the inferior'' (*AC*, 214–15). And yet Whitman is salvaged (though his theories are not) by the fact that he is exceptional. It is in this move that we see the connection between the New Humanist rejection of democracy and the ideology most Americanists shared. The Americanists wanted to establish the existence of an American literary aristocracy, and they could no more accept Whitman's appeal on behalf of the average than could Foerster. In the end, Whitman and his vision of democracy would be celebrated, but his theories would be more honored than they would be accepted.

Foerster, as a professor of literature who was more a critic than a historian, was an anomaly during the 1920s and 1930s. As such he is usefully revealing but not representative of American literature studies during the period. I am not claiming that Foerster or humanism is responsible for the disciplinary object, but rather that he made explicit assumptions that silently informed the constitution of that object. By focusing attention on the history of ideas by means of his factors, Foerster helped to define the kinds of questions that the discipline would ask, questions that were not directed to American social and political conditions. Yet these questions were motivated by nationalism, even if Foerster did not embrace it as his ultimate concern. What emerges then from the program announced in *The Reinterpretation of American Literature* is a covert political project. The task of "discovering" an American civilization as an expression of nationalism is inherently political, but it is presented as anything but political: as moral, aesthetic, philosophical, and above all objective. As literary historians, Americanists would not seek to express their mere opinions about the civilization, but to objectively explain it. Such an intention could not a priori exclude political explanations, but it could render them always already inadequate, politics being precisely the realm in which opposing interests or biases are openly expressed. In the next chapter, we will see how these considerations make Parrington's *Main Currents* and later left-oriented histories unacceptable, even while prohibiting their complete exclusion. We will also see how the practice of literary history prevents the new discipline from immediately developing a research program based on *The Reinterpretation of American Literature*.

5

Institutionalizing
American Literature

In chapter 3 we saw how English functioned as a research discipline and observed that both a learned society (MLA) and a central journal (*PMLA*) were necessary for it to do so. Without such disciplinary apparatus, English could not have held a significant place in the new university. It might have continued to be taught to undergraduates, as was composition within English departments, but it would have lacked the status of other subjects that claimed to produce, and not merely transmit, knowledge. For American literature to become a discipline, even a subdiscipline, it needed an apparatus paralleling that of English as a whole. The American Literature Group and its journal, *American Literature*, would allow practitioners of American literature to be judged by their fellow specialists. While scholars of American literature continued to be members of English departments, the subdisciplinary apparatus gave them a certain independence from the larger discipline. On the other hand, the ALG and *American Literature* held more power over Americanists than did other MLA divisions over their members. The ALG limited who could speak and with what authority about American literature. It also quickly established a standard research practice exemplified in *American Literature*, a practice that was consonant with the parent discipline but that involved some significant modifications.

This chapter examines the power of discipline to produce and to restrict. In the space of less than 20 years, academic Americanists produced an enormous body of scholarship, the very exis-

tence of which demonstrated that American literature was a fit
topic for research and teaching. But during these twenty years,
the form and content of contributions to the study of American
literature were restricted by the discipline. Nondisciplinary studies were stigmatized as such. Even studies produced by members
of the subdiscipline such as Lucy Lockwood Hazard and Vernon
Louis Parrington were marginalized because they did not reflect
the emerging disciplinary practice. Furthermore, the disciplinary
apparatus restricted access to power and influence within the
field, serving to formalize an "old boys network" that excluded
most women and others not properly connected.

Creating a Disciplinary Apparatus

American literature could not have become a successful subdiscipline of English on the strength of an intellectual program alone.
In fact, that program was only developed after an institutional
space had been created for it. Given the literary formation of the
period and the demands of ideology, it is likely that sooner or
later that space would have been created. It did not necessarily
have to be within English departments, however. It is true that
those departments had always regarded the literature in English
produced in America as part of their concern, and that there had
been a slow but steady increase in both research and instruction
devoted to such literature. Nevertheless, in 1921 English departments remained bastions of Anglophilia. In his brief memoir of
the period, Robert Spiller complained about the "predominantly
apologetic tone" of the *Cambridge History* that he finds typical
of preprofessional discussion of American literature.[1] Those in
English who were interested in American literature suffered
"from feelings of inferiority."[2] Before the formation of the ALG,
"an American specialization was hardly respectable; in fact, it was
close to professional suicide" (Spiller, 259). Formal recognition of
American literature occurred in 1921, when in the wake of the reforms of President John Manly, the MLA reorganized itself into divisions devoted to specialties. Even then, American literature was
included as the last of eleven English sections only after special
pleading by interested scholars. Prior to that time, American
works and authors were acceptable topics for literary-historical

research, but they were distinctly minor topics. Prior to 1922, there were only eleven articles published in *PMLA* on American literature and a total of fifty-one articles in all scholarly journals, excluding in both figures those on linguistics and folklore. There were a mere forty-four dissertations produced in English departments, and many of those were on figures or topics that would not fit into the new subfield.[3] Courses on American literature had come to be offered by many English departments, but they remained marginal to the curriculum. According to a 1928 account, "Only one out of eleven [literature] courses in the English departments is in American literature. In the graduate departments . . . the average is about one in thirteen."[4] While the relative absence of American literature from English studies had been lamented by a vocal minority both in and outside of the profession since the late nineteenth century, it was only after MLA's reorganization that significant changes occurred.

The reorganization provided several essential conditions for the creation of the subdiscipline. The fact that at least one convention session per year would be devoted to American literature guaranteed an outlet for scholarship on the subject and thus encouraged its production. Since *PMLA* typically published many papers read at the convention, an increased possibility of publication was also a likely outcome. Official professional recognition and an increased demand for scholarship both gave work in American literature a legitimacy it had heretofore lacked. Simple recognition by the MLA could provide respectability, forums for discussion, and opportunities for publication, but it was not a sufficient condition for the kind of success that American literature was to experience over the decades to come. The major impact of the ALG was to be organizational. The importance of having an organized body that promoted the interests of Americanists cannot be overestimated. Spiller argues that the ALG took advantage of the reorganization of the MLA in a way that few others could. The credit for the ALG's success at this, according to Spiller, should go to Jay B. Hubbell's organizational skills ("Early Days," 259). Hubbell not only proposed, organized, and edited *American Literature*, he was ubiquitous on ALG committees beginning in 1923. While most other groups simply elected a secretary and chair from the floor at each convention to serve for the following year, the ALG established committees and undertook numerous projects beyond organizing convention sessions. In 1926, a continuing leadership was established, including an Advisory Committee and Executive Committee, and provisions for a nominating committee. This organizational structure helped the ALG to establish what amounted to a second professional apparatus, which included most prominently a new journal, *American Literature*, "the only scholarly journal in the country devoted wholly to work in the national literature."[5] Even before the journal appeared in 1929 the group published in *Studies in Philology* (1926) the first cumulative bibliography of scholarship in American literature. In addition, the ALG made plans to compile lists of manuscript sources and, with less immediate success, to produce a comprehensive history of American literature to replace *The Cambridge History of American Literature*, which was perceived by many within the group to be inadequate.

The ALG may have been more prepared to take advantage of the changes in the MLA because Americanists perceived themselves as marginalized by the parent body. The ALG thus became something of an oppositional force, a counterorganization as much as a branch of an established one. By 1926 the ALG was discussing a plan for a Ph.D. in American literature that would have eliminated the Anglo-Saxon and Middle English requirements of the doctorate in English, and would have added substantial work in American, English, and European history, as well as in the history of modern philosophy and religion. This plan was never approved, at least in part because it would have met with resistance from others in English departments, and it was tabled at the 1928 meeting as "premature."[6] One can recognize in the plan, however, something quite similar to the American Studies or American civilization programs that began in the 1930s at Harvard, Yale, and George Washington universities. The ALG lobbied tirelessly within the MLA on behalf of American literature. One goal, first proposed in 1927, but not finally attained until 1966 when it didn't matter, was for American literature to have the same status as English, French, and German "sections" of MLA. Leaders of the ALG regularly discussed the possibility of forming a separate organization devoted solely to American literature. But Americanists finally did not want to leave the English fold; they elected to remain within the traditional Ph.D., as members of English departments, and as one of twelve divisions of the English section of MLA. A discipline is not only an object of study, the methods and procedures for studying it, and the body of statements that they have produced. Disciplines also discipline their practitioners, and the Americanists of the 1920s and 1930s proved to be well disciplined. Nevertheless, the ALG made American literature an indispensable element of English studies in America.

Who were the people responsible for this initiative? A group of established professors including Fred Pattee (Penn State), Killis Cambell (Texas), Arthur Quinn (Pennsylvania), and Foerster (North Carolina) served as leaders between 1921 and 1924. While these older men were called on again to serve on the Advisory Council when it was formed in 1929, only Foerster would have a major impact on the Group's activities. Beginning in 1925 the ALG was taken over by a group of young men whose primary devotion was to American, rather than English, literature. Most of the leading members of the ALG between 1925 and World War II finished American literature dissertations in the 1920s. It is not surprising that this generation of scholars should be well represented in the ALG. The increased interest in American literature after World War I resulted in thirty-five American dissertations being completed between 1922 and 1925, nearly as many as had been produced during the preceding forty years of graduate training in English. Among those finishing American dissertations during those years were Hubbell, Spiller, Sculley Bradley, Kenneth Murdock, T. O. Mabbott, Ralph Rusk, and Ernest Leisy, all of whom would play active roles in the ALG. Several others, including Howard Mumford Jones, Henry Pochmann, and Tremaine McDowell would finish American dissertations in the next few years.[7] What is surprising is the small number of individuals who held leadership positions. Between 1921 and 1940, a total of thirty people filled the positions of chairman, secretary treasurer, and bibliographer, the six seats on the Advisory Council, and four rotating seats on the Board of Editors of *American Literature*. Many of these same thirty also served on the advisory board of the journal. The rotation of the same few individuals into different ALG offices would seem to confirm the charge of "self-perpetuating elitism within the group" (Vanderbilt, 545–47). The restricted participation in the ALG leadership may have been responsible for the conservative character of the research that it sponsored and published.

Institutional hierarchies and networks were important in the formation of the ALG. Eastern private universities such as Harvard, Yale, Pennsylvania, Brown, and Columbia were regarded by many as representing the top of the pecking order. Geographical proximity to the Northeast seems to have conferred privilege on lesser-ranked institutions, a fact that makes more sense when we remember the difficulty of cross-country travel. Thus when plans for a journal were discussed, Nebraska was opposed in part out of desire for a "more central" location.[8] Hubbell was loath to include those located in the far West on the *American Literature* editorial board because they were "pretty far away to attend meetings or return manuscripts promptly," the latter remark suggesting that Hubbell imagined mail still being carried by the Pony Express.[9] On the other hand, Brown's journal proposal, though considerably less substantial than Duke's, received serious consideration because of its institutional affiliation. The Brown group proposed to have a board of editors, appointed by Brown, consisting of three from that institution and one each from Harvard, Yale, and Columbia. Not all of these institutions were leaders in American literature, however. Brown and Yale had produced few dissertations in the field. North Carolina, on the other hand, was by the mid-1920s already a major producer of American literature Ph.D.s. Vanderbilt, using Leisy's 1926 and 1929 reports, notes that Columbia (17), Chicago (14), Virginia (7), North Carolina (6), Pennsylvania (5), and Cornell (5) had produced the most American dissertations (260). If we look at the ALG leadership, however, we see a somewhat different picture. Columbia remains dominant, with Hubbell, Rusk, and Mabbott all being graduates, but Chicago produced only Jones. Pennsylvania, on the other hand, trained both Spiller and Bradley among its five. Finally, we can't ignore Harvard, recognized as the leading graduate program in English, even though in 1929, Murdock was the only ALG insider to have done a dissertation there in American literature. Foerster had trained there, but wrote a dissertation in English literature.

Interestingly, none of the faculty at Columbia who supervised those dissertations became active in the ALG, while Boynton at Chicago and Quinn at Pennsylvania were early leaders. Unlike the students of Kittredge, who dominated Chaucer studies for years, no senior Americanist produced a dominant line of academic descent in American literature during its first twenty years of institutional recognition. Perhaps the leading mentor of Americanists at Columbia, Carl Van Doren, was an adjunct faculty member who did not participate or publish in professional circles. This vacuum at the top was what doubtless permitted younger scholars to become so quickly established. Once in power, however, they saw older Americanists as allies who were useful in lending their reputations to a subject that was still suspect within English departments. The young Americanists saw their rebellion as embodied in their choice of subject matter, not in their methods, theories, or scholarly activities, all of which they seem to have modeled as closely as possible on the standard practice in the larger discipline.

American literature dissertations were perhaps less often influence or source studies than those in other fields of English, but such studies were nevertheless quite common. Henry Pochmann's study of the influence of German tales on the short stories of Irving, Hawthorne, and Poe is a representative application of standard literary-historical practice to an American subject. One account of a trend toward new types of dissertations seems only to confirm the limits of literary history: "Graduate schools are permitting prospective young doctors to concentrate on practical tasks—the writing of biographies of men of recent date, and even the editing of American classics like Poe's *Politian*."[10] Among American dissertations, the phrase "life and works" appears frequently in titles, suggesting that biography was becoming as important in graduate training as it was in published literary histories. Biographies and editions remain within the discipline that Morize had outlined, and critical or interpretive dissertations were very rare. This traditional training left its mark. As we will see, the standard research practices in American literature will follow the English model as nearly as they could. Of the leading members of the ALG, only Foerster and Jones seem to have contributed directly to the new conception of the field that would become dominant after 1945.

Between 1921 and 1940, two women served in the ALG leadership, Janette Harrington, a high school teacher from Little Rock who served on the Advisory Committee for one year, and Louise Pound, who although she proposed housing the planned ALG journal at her institution, Nebraska, was not elected to the ALG Advisory Committee until 1940. Obviously, the ALG had no formal policy that excluded women from the leadership, but just as clearly they were excluded. The problem was not a lack of trained women in the field. Of the dissertations listed by Leisy in 1926, fifteen were produced by women, and several of them, as we will see, became books. The ALG membership rolls, however, show that women made up a rather small minority (roughly 16 percent in 1927, for example). How do we account for the small role women played in the ALG in general—and in its leadership in particular? Two articles by Pound from the early 1920s give us a good idea of the situation that women faced in the academy. Pound notes that only a few decades before there had been a debate over whether women were capable of doing graduate work. That issue now settled, the questions were how to attract women to such work, the wisdom of doing so, and what to do with them when their studies were completed. These questions arose because women were having trouble finding jobs: "The National Bureau of Education reported . . . that the number of women holding positions in higher institutions of learning is actually decreasing."[11] Evidence of an exclusive "old boys network" is rife in the *American Literature* and ALG archives. Notes are frequently appended to letters asking if a "promising young *man*" is needed or available.

Other recent reports suggested that positions were "being quietly taken from the women of this generation in universities and larger colleges" (293). One explanation for this phenomenon was that as academic salaries began to rise in the 1920s, more men were willing to take those positions, and institutions preferred to hire them. The problem was not only with those doing the hiring; Pound quotes a graduate student who complains, "The interest of our professors wanes, we are recommended for no advanced positions" (294). When women did get hired, it was most often in positions that demanded much work for little pay—positions, in other words, that men would not take. The membership rolls of the ALG suggest the accuracy of this analysis. Most of the women members are located at small colleges or lesser public institutions where teaching loads were heavy. Under these conditions, they were able to find little time to do scholarly work. Pound notes that this limitation, together with the small prospect of advancement should successful research be completed, inhibited women from becoming "confident professional" researchers.[12] Pound concludes that women should be encouraged to become researchers only for the love of the work (313).

Three Books on the Frontier: A Case Study

In spite of these difficulties women produced substantial scholarship in American literature. Two of the three books on the frontier in American literature produced in the 1920s were by women. The careers of the three authors of those books are instructive about the possibilities for advancement available to men and women. The male student of the frontier was Ralph Rusk, whose book, *The Literature of the Middle Western Frontier*, was his dissertation at Columbia (1924).[13] He went on to become a leading member of the ALG, and to write what was for many years the definitive biography of Emerson. His first academic post was at Indiana University, but by 1925 he was back at Columbia, already an associate professor. Dorothy Dondore also finished a dissertation on the frontier at Columbia in 1924, and it appeared in book form in 1926.[14] She was hired by Elmira College, and never published another book. In 1925, Lucy Lockwood Hazard completed her Ph.D. at the University of California with a dissertation entitled "The Frontier in American Literature." Her book by that title appeared in 1927, by which time she was employed at Mills College.[15]

Though I do not have enough information to know for certain, it seems more than likely that gender bias kept Dondore and Hazard from having the kind of career that Rusk had. The books themselves lend credence to this hypothesis, although they also demonstrate that more than gender bias was at work. Rusk's book, issued in two volumes, is a very traditional literary history, with a decided emphasis on history. The book is even less devoted to literature in the dominant sense than was the *Cam-*

bridge History. It is perhaps not insignificant that both Van Doren and William Peterfield Trent are acknowledged as having "given invaluable advice regarding the conduct of this study from the time of its inception" (1:ix). The book's chapters give a strong sense of its content: "Cultural Beginnings," "Travel and Observation," "Newspapers and Magazines," "Controversial Writings," "Scholarly Writings and Schoolbooks," "Fiction," "Poetry," "Drama," and "The Vogue of British and Eastern Writers." Most of the second volume is given over to bibliography. The book has no unifying argument, and it offers only passing claims regarding aesthetic merit or historical significance. The body of the text is as much a catalogue as the bibliography. One can imagine that such a book helped establish Rusk's credentials as a researcher, but it otherwise had so little impact on literary scholarship that Hubbell could all but ignore it in his essay for *The Reinterpretation of American Literature*. To be fair, this was likely the result of Rusk's choice of subject: the literature of the middle western frontier through 1840. Since no standard authors and few recognizable minor ones were included within the scope of his study, Rusk's book could have had little but antiquarian interest. As one reviewer notes, "It goes, in a sense, to prove a negative . . . that the literary flights of the frontier were few, and rarely reached great heights."[16] Nevertheless, the book was published by Columbia University Press, and the institution thought enough of him to bring him back only one year after he finished his doctorate.

Dorothy Dondore's Columbia dissertation was finished the same year as Rusk's, but *The Prairie and the Making of Middle America: Four Centuries of Description* wasn't published until 1926 by the Torch Press of Cedar Rapids, Iowa. She also acknowledges the help and influence of Van Doren and Trent as the most important of her obligations, but she mentions historians Arthur Schlesinger and Frederick Jackson Turner as well. Their influence is apparent, for Dondore's book is closer to professional history than is Rusk's. Where his task was basically to chronicle the writing published and plays produced during the very late eighteenth and early nineteenth centuries in a sparsely populated region, Dondore is concerned with the history of descriptions of the prairie from the Spanish explorers through the writers of the twentieth century. Dondore's book is also a catalogue of sorts, but because it traces the history of literature about the prairie, it anticipates the kind of work that Henry Nash Smith would do in *Virgin Land*. There may not be an argument, but we get a strong sense of the conflict between romanticized or promotional perspectives on the one hand, and realistic or critical ones on the other. While the structure of both Rusk's and Dondore's studies means that very little can be said about any one author or work, Dondore is often able to give a better sense of why her subjects might continue to be of interest.

Both scholars, for example, praise Caroline Kirkland—a writer who would all but disappear from American literature until feminists rediscover her in the 1970s—as one who succeeded in offering realistic portrayals of frontier life in her fiction. Rusk says, "For realistic treatment of pioneer communities . . . perhaps the most notable work of fiction to appear before 1841 was Caroline M. Kirkland's account of society in the upstart villages of the Michigan wilderness" (284). Rusk notes that Kirkland was inspired by Mary Russell Mitford's sketches of English small-town life, that she had a bent for satire, and that unlike most other writers, she dispensed with adventure and the theatrical. Compare Dondore's treatment:

> Appropriately enough the first writer adequately to portray in fiction the discouraging aspects of the frontier was a woman— Mrs. Caroline Mathilda Kirkland. For it was the woman who suffered most profoundly in the great movement of peoples that populated the wilds. They dreaded most the breaking of old ties; they yearned in secret for the homes and friends behind them; they were compelled to labor beyond their strength in the weary days of "breaking" or "clearing"; they had the task of rearing a family far from civilization. (297)

Where Rusk is content to evaluate, classify, and historically connect Kirkland, Dondore explains her realism as a function of her gender, and then gives some account of the content of Kirkland's description.

> Everywhere around her the struggle for existence had overemphasized the physical. The spirit of intense practicality prominent throughout the country at large, she feels, is especially marked in the new regions. There she can find almost no

trace of idealism, almost no yearning for beauty. The mark of
progress to the settler is girdling every tree in
sight. . . . Nevertheless Mrs. Kirkland's heart goes out always
to the poor and oppressed. It is of the destitute families in the
little clearings that she thinks when the wildcat bank bubble
bursts and the hoarded notes prove useless. (298)

These remarks on Kirkland suggest a political or social perspective that Dondore did not allow free reign, but which nevertheless does enliven the volume. Whatever Rusk's attitudes, they are much more carefully buried beneath the veneer of scholarly objectivity. Furthermore, Dondore's interests are certainly a function of her own gender. Her concern with the hardships faced by women and children on the frontier is one that will not receive a serious hearing in the discipline until the rise of feminism and women's studies.

As befitting their common training under Van Doren and Trent at Columbia, Dondore and Rusk produced relatively similar books. The third study of the frontier, Hazard's *The Frontier in American Literature*, is striking in its differences from both the others. Hazard trained at California under B. H. Lehman, someone not known for scholarship in American literature. She also acknowledges Vernon Louis Parrington, her undergraduate teacher, "who first taught me the economic interpretation of American literature" (viii). Hazard's book appeared before Parrington's *Main Currents* (which we will consider in detail below), but her reading of American literature is considerably more modern than his. More than Dondore and Rusk, Hazard is a critic, both of American literature and American society, and she is fearless of tradition or reputation. Unlike them, she deals with most of the major figures; her focus is almost exactly what Hubbell would call for in his *Reinterpretation* essay, though Hubbell himself could not see it. He accuses Hazard of neglecting the interrelations of other influences.[17]

My guess is that while Hazard's overt politics and, even more important, her failure to treat the standard authors with the expected deference bothered Hubbell and other Americanists, it was the broad sweep of the volume and its more critical than historical approach that precluded her volume from serious influence. All these factors are illustrated in her treatment of Emerson: "It is time to decanonize Emerson; to recognize that however truly he may have been 'the friend and helper of those who would live in the spirit,' he was just as truly the friend and helper of those who want to annex a territory, or corner a market, or spread heretical propaganda" (152). Emerson at that time was, as we saw in Brownell and More, perhaps the single figure in American literature most likely to be regarded as canonical. Furthermore, he was perceived already as a personification of America. Thus Hazard risked taking the most heretical position possible. Her critique of Emerson, however, is not the work of a neophyte, as Parrington himself recognized.[18] In fact, in passages such as these she makes Parrington's treatment of Emerson seem like mere nationalist propaganda:

> Emerson and his circle were lending their moral support to the growing empire of the machine; their very scorn of government control, their admiration of individual enterprise, their assertion of absolute *laissez faire*, were destroying the safeguards that might have preserved a world in which the transcendental dream could become a reality. (165)

Not all of Hazard's remarks about the standard authors were damning, however. Hawthorne is treated in the chapter on "The Puritan Frontier," but he is depicted as one who, while transcribing "Puritan materials and Puritan attitudes . . . made the very transcription a commentary on the inadequacy of the Puritan world" (30). The Puritans were spiritual pioneers, "the radicals of their day," a radicalism lost when their "heroic adventure" became "an established church" (34). Hawthorne is also a spiritual pioneer, though a timid and ineffectual one. "The latent radicalism of Hawthorne may best be illustrated in one strain that runs throughout his fiction—his feminism. This differentiates him sharply from the Puritan who thought of 'good' women as childbearers and housewives, and of other women as snares of the devil" (36). Hawthorne's feminism is expressed not in a rejection of "feminine virtues" but in "recurrent wonder whether these virtues form an all-sufficient expression of woman's nature" (37). This is Hazard's reading of Hawthorne's oft-noticed doubling of female characters, both halves of which are present in Hester. If Hester is but a "faint precursor of the feminist type," she reflects exactly Hawthorne's role, pioneering timidly the remaking of human society (38, 39). Clearly Hazard's gender allows her to both see and value an aspect of Hawthorne not often discussed by male critics. Just as clearly, Hazard's progressive view of history and her radical politics are the basis of her evaluations. But it is perhaps less obvious that Hazard's whole discourse is outside of the project of academic literary history. Her tasks are interpretation and evaluation, while Rusk and Dondore were mainly concerned with cataloging and description. Hazard's doubly marginalized status as both a woman and a graduate of a marginal department perhaps allowed her to violate conventions that would otherwise have prevented a Ph.D. student from pursuing her project.

The frontier, of course, continued to be an important topic for Americanists, but it became curiously transmuted in the process. Instead of following Rusk's and Dondore's interest in literature produced on or descriptive of the geographic frontier, later works tend to follow Hazard's treatment of it as a broad cultural influence. Instead of reading that influence, however, as socially progressive or subversive of elite culture, later scholars treat it as foundational to such culture. As Hazard complains in her review of Percy Boynton's *The Rediscovery of the Frontier*, authors like Bryant, Brown, and Stowe are made to represent the frontier influence, while those such as Harte, Garland, and Cather are virtually ignored. "The frontier has been taken under the patronage of the elite and moves in the best circles of literary criticism."[19] Ernest Marchand's article on "Emerson and the Frontier" illustrates another way Hazard's argument gets transformed. Like Hazard, Marchand interprets Emerson's individualism as a regressive historical force, but his essay is concerned mainly to demonstrate that Emerson was influenced by the frontier. In place of Hazard's radical call for decanonization, we get Marchand's identification of Emerson and the frontier. Marchand does acknowledge Hazard as making the connection between Emerson and the frontier that others had missed, but he does not acknowledge her interpretation of that connection.[20]

None of the books by Rusk, Dondore, or Hazard had a major impact on the field, although all were well-received and widely noticed. All three have their strengths and weaknesses, but by the standards of the time, Rusk's may well have seemed to be the most valuable. Still there is nothing in the written record to indicate that it was perceived as so far superior as to warrant Rusk's so much greater reward. It is likely that the formidable barriers to women's success in the academy prevented these women from rising to the top of their profession in spite of their demonstrated abilities. Those barriers not only kept women on the margins of the field, they kept the kinds of issues women were better able or more prone to raise on the margins as well.

Parrington

The studies of the frontier produced during the 1920s reflect several possible patterns that research in the emerging subdiscipline might have followed. They are evidence that the field remained as yet undisciplined in that a standard practice was not yet established. In this still emerging disciplinary research environment, not all of the work produced conformed to narrow limits of the disciplinary discourse. The ALG program for the field had not borne significant achievements. Recall that Foerster's paper on "Factors in American Literature" was startling to the ALG. Less than two years later, in 1927, seemingly out of nowhere appeared the first two volumes of Vernon Louis Parrington's *Main Currents in American Thought*. Parrington had been at work on his history for nearly ten years, and he had been known well enough to have contributed a chapter on "Puritan Divines" to the *Cambridge History*. He had also been offering courses in American literature since 1909 at the University of Washington, making him a pioneer teacher of the subject. But Parrington was a figure marginal to the ALG. Although he was a member of the group and even served on the advisory board of *American Literature*, his geographically remote position at the University of Washington and his own work habits had made him relatively unknown. He did not take part in ALG meetings because he did not attend MLA conventions, suggesting marginality to the discipline of English as well. His attitude toward that field is revealed in his famous remark about Henry James: "Like modern scholarship, he came to deal more and more with less and less." Thus Parrington cannot be regarded as a figure typical of literature as a discipline even though he spent his whole life teaching in English departments.

Doubtless Parrington's geographical remoteness is partially responsible for his idiosyncrasies. He studied at Harvard, where he took a B.A., but graduated before coursework in American literature became available there. His lack of a Ph.D. meant that he would not be able to find a job at a leading research institution, and in fact his first position was at tiny Emporia College, where he had been an undergraduate. He went from there to the University of Oklahoma, where he was fired in a purge of "Eastern" faculty inspired by religious fundamentalists. He finally ended up at the University of Washington in 1908. He has been justly called "one of the most underprivileged of our famous academic men, a veritable waif of scholarship" (Hofstadter, 367). These circumstances suggest that we need to consider Parrington as an autodidact, and to realize that the method he developed in *Main Currents* he invented out of his own reading. While Parrington's bibliographies show that he kept up with current literary history, the more important influence on his approach came from history proper, especially in the person of his friend and colleague at Washington, J. Allen Smith. It was Smith who developed the dualistic interpretation of American history "as a long running quarrel between aristocracy and democracy" that progressive historians such as Beard and Parrington elaborated (Hofstadter, 192, 388). Parrington found the formula he had learned from Smith confirmed in Beard's *Economic Interpretation of the Constitution*, which he read early in his work on *Main Currents*.[21]

The influence of history on Parrington may seem surprising, but it should be remembered that the two fields were not so long separated as to be regarded as entirely distinct. William Trent, one of the editors of the *Cambridge History,* was trained as and always considered himself to be a historian despite teaching literature at Columbia for many years. The division of the two fields was an issue in *The Reinterpretation of American Literature,* where even Clark can admit that the field of American letters "is but part of a larger whole."[22] But whereas the study of American history became the principal concern of historians in America, the study of American literature was only beginning to become a serious subject for literary scholars. What Parrington borrowed from historians was a conception of American civilization far more coherent than any available to him from within the literary. As Gene

Wise has shown, Parrington applied the categories of progressive historians such as Turner, Beard, and others to materials they had largely neglected, and, in the process, "put together the broad sweep of the [Progressive] paradigm."[23] Parrington thus straddled the still lightly defended boundary between two increasingly distinct disciplines.

As a result both of his being embraced by the left in the 1930s and of his being the subject of red-baiting ever since Lionel Trilling's 1940 attack on him, Parrington's approach has often been misunderstood. Although he called himself "a good deal of a Marxian," he was not a Marxist in his politics or his theory of history, much less in his approach to literature. Parrington's well-known sloppiness with terminology is responsible for some misconceptions. Parrington called himself an economic determinist and everyone accepted this self-characterization. In one sense, Parrington described himself correctly. He believed that governments or politics were economically determined, but he believed that this view was held by many of the founding fathers. As he argued in *Main Currents*, "the current conception of the political state as determined in its form and activities by economic groups is no modern Marxian perversion of political theory; it goes back to Aristotle" (3: 408). His explanation of American historical development is based on a shift from economic dominance by an aristocracy at the time of the revolution to economic dominance by the middle class beginning in the mid-nineteenth century. But Parrington does not treat works of belles-lettres, or at least many of them, as if they were economically determined. Thus while he may dismiss Poe, Hawthorne, and James as being disconnected from social reality, he does not explain this failure in economic terms. Parrington lacked—or rejected—Marxist conceptions, such as "mode of production" and "ideology," that would have enabled him to extend his economic analysis. As it stands, "Parrington unwittingly behaves like a Platonist of sorts. Ideas beget ideas which go on to beget other ideas, without touching much of anything from the world outside" (Wise, 255).

While the negative comments by Americanists about *Main Currents* focused on economic determinism, the real objection was clearly to Parrington's conception of literature. Perhaps they saw Parrington's selection of texts as predicated on economic determinism. While this is undoubtedly true to some extent, E. H. Eby asserts that it was conceiving of "American literature as American thought" that allowed Parrington to escape belletrism.[24] What such a conception did was render formal issues insignificant. If, as Kermit Vanderbilt had demonstrated, Parrington did not refrain from aesthetic evaluation, it is clear that such evaluation was not his major principle of selection (325). That principle was political significance. Having constituted his object as thought, Parrington returned to a conception of literature closer to its pre-nineteenth-century meaning than to the then-dominant conception. Instead of being a repository of wisdom, however, literature became the record of political struggle. In this conception aesthetics had a role, but it was a minor one, especially when compared to its role in the dominant conception. Aesthetic success or failure could help or hinder the political effectiveness of a work. Thus Parrington's generally favorable treatment of Dreiser acknowledges the "failure . . . of art that does not merge" episodes concerned with business with others concerned with the erotic (3: 359). Dreiser's significance, on the other hand, "lies in the fact that he is an individual apart—one who has broken with the group and sits in judgment on the group sanctions. He is an anarchist who will be partisan to no taboos. This is a rare and perilous thing to do" (3: 356).

But it would be a mistake to see Parrington's selection process as a matter of choosing writers for their political value in spite of their aesthetic failure. In the majority of cases, aesthetics are not relevant. In the first volume, belles lettres are relegated to minor status, as in, "The revolutionary upheaval produced no polite literature in any respects comparable to its utilitarian prose" (1: 248). His discussion of the early years of independence focuses on the debate over the Constitution, with belles lettres being treated as an expression of that conflict. It is hard not to feel that Parrington's selection is eminently reasonable here. The writings of Hamilton, Adams, Madison, and the other founders are of more interest than the poetry of Freneau or Dwight, unless the standard of judgment assumes that poetry is always more important than political argument. But in other instances Parrington's focus seems strange. Consider his treatment of Emerson and Thoreau, two writers of whom he clearly approves. Emerson is represented by a strange mixture of *Journal* entries and passages from "Politics" and "The Present Age." Missing entirely are those most other literary historians typically cited: "The Poet," "Circles," "The Over-Soul," and, perhaps most significantly, "Self-Reliance"; *Nature*, "The American Scholar," and the "Divinity School Address" are merely mentioned. The Emerson who emerges from this treatment is "the man who was to become the most searching critic of contemporary America," that is, a political commentator (2: 386). Emerson the moralist and metaphysician who appealed to More and Foerster is nowhere to be seen. Thoreau is, if anything, treated even more narrowly. Parrington refers almost exclusively to the "Economy" chapter of *Walden* and to "Civil-Disobedience." "*Walden* is the handbook of an economy that endeavors to refute Adam Smith and transform the round of daily life into something nobler than a mean gospel of plus and minus" (2: 400). The book is understood to present a program, as if Thoreau were offering a plausible alternative to contemporary social arrangements. Thus, quite bizarrely, Hawthorne can be said to have "never grappled with economics as Thoreau did" (2: 449). "Civil-Disobedience" is, accurately though a bit dismissively, read as an expression of eighteenth-century liberalism, but here Parrington's history of ideas seems to get the better of him, since he misses entirely the possibility of a political strategy in that essay. But this omission is characteristic; Parrington, though so much preoccupied with political ends, is little concerned with political means.

Like most other historians of American literature before him, Parrington uses the biographies of the various writers as building blocks of *Main Currents*. The writers and not their texts are his fundamental objects. Parrington's treatment of individual biographies differs, however, in that it focused on intellectual rather than personal issues. Furthermore, Parrington's use of biography is unusual in its rhetorical effectiveness for two reasons. One is Parrington's gift for epitome: where other literary historians had merely recounted the lives of their subjects, Parrington made each of his stand for something. Each was given a name—"Herman Melville, Pessimist," "Brooks Adams, Rebel"—and a position to play on either the liberal or the conservative side of American thought. This gave literary biography a significance it had heretofore lacked, as the various figures came to be understood in relationship to the vast historical conflict that *Main Currents* describes. What allowed that conflict to be successfully presented were the inclusion of sections that explain and connect the biographies. Because these explanations and connections represent the main points that Parrington is trying to make, they do not come across as mere background. It is this combination that, in allowing Parrington to make sense of such an enormous quantity of material, accounts for the impact that *Main Currents* had on so many of its readers.

Perhaps the most significant characteristic of Parrington's treatment of the figures he discusses is that they are not constituted as authors in the sense common to both literary criticism and the discipline of English. None of Parrington's figures are geniuses and originality is never an issue. If Parrington seems at times to be pursuing in the history of ideas the literary historians' preoccupation with sources and influences, he never seems concerned to rescue his subjects from them. Of course, his stated commitment to environmental and economic determinism is incompatible with the romantic conception of original genius. It is well known that Parrington usually abandons such determinism in dealing with those he considers liberals, yet even in these cases influence is not denied. Thus Parrington's greatest praise for a figure is not given for innovation, but is reserved for those whom he can call children of Jean-Jacques. In Parrington's scheme, being on the right side is far more important than being inventive.

The reception of *Main Currents* in the realm of the literary was overwhelmingly positive. In addition to being favorably reviewed in most major organs, the first two volumes were awarded the Pulitzer Prize in history in 1928. Academic Americanists also gave the book generally positive notices, leading Bernard Smith to exclaim, "Rarely are works of literary history so widely praised as Parrington's. . . . the fact that the point of view was radical makes it astonishing."[25] Yet the academic reception of the book was more ambiguous than Smith's remarks would suggest. One problem was its violation of disciplinary boundaries. The book "was not at first taken by most historians to be a historical work, and (except for an obscure magazine in Parrington's own state) was not reviewed by the professional historical quarterlies" (Hof-

167

stadter, 376). Literary Americanists were clearly impressed by Parrington's effort, but they never regarded it as a satisfactory history of American literature. Spiller captures, I think, the general response when he depicts *Main Currents* "almost as a specific answer to [Foerster's] call for a new type of literary history."[26] The dominant, positive side of the Americanists' response to Parrington is explained by the degree to which *Main Currents* fit their own conception of a history of American letters and exceeded their expectations in having been written, rather than merely conceived. Perhaps most significantly, the Americanists recognized that Parrington had worked out in considerable detail the scheme that Foerster had only recently made available to them in his "Factors" paper. Foerster and Parrington seem to have arrived independently at the romantic/realist periodization of the nineteenth century that Foerster published first in his anthology *American Poetry and Prose*. Three of Foerster's four factors play leading roles in Parrington's history. Curiously, given Parrington's Progressive assumptions, the frontier plays only a minor role in his story. As Parrington explained it, "I gave, in reality, serious consideration to the whole question of frontier influences, but I could not forget that ostensibly I was writing a history of ideas expressed in literature, and so when I had followed the development of such things as frontier humor in David Crockett, I convinced myself that I had pushed my field to the limit."[27] Even more than Foerster, Parrington believed that the roots of American culture lay in Europe, and his book discussed specific European sources and influences for American thought, including its Puritan, romantic, and realist strains. But Parrington, like Foerster, also treated realism as a product of the mechanized condition of modern American life.

However radical its democratic perspective, *Main Currents* is very much a book of its own time. One sign of this is Parrington's sexism and the latent racism of his selection of subjects. This is not to say that Parrington would have thought himself sexist or racist. The one feminist he discusses, Margaret Fuller, is treated far more sympathetically than she is in earlier histories and she is praised as "the first since Mary Wollstonecraft . . . to undertake a reasoned defense of the claims of woman to emancipation from man-made customs" (2: 432). Still, Parrington's treatment of

Woman in the Nineteenth Century trivializes it by treating it mainly as shock to "Boston bluestockings." This single mention of nineteenth-century feminism and the absence of any mention of the successful suffrage movement is significant given Parrington's focus on politics. His sexism is perhaps more clearly revealed by his terms of evaluation. Like most other critics of the period, Parrington uses "masculine" as a term of approval. He praises the "intellectual honesty and masculine vigor" of colonial debate, and laments, "Our literary historians have labored under too heavy a handicap of the genteel tradition . . . to enter sympathetically into a world of masculine intellects and material struggles" (1: i, vi). It is hard not to associate the "genteel" here with the "feminine," and indeed we find Howells's failure as a novelist blamed on his living "in an atmosphere of complacent convention, a society dominated by women, culture, and conscience. . . . In such a world of refined manners and narrow outlook what should the realist do but report faithfully on what he saw and heard? And so Howells, perforce, became a specialist in women's nerves." (3: 250). It is not surprising that he is more forgiving but no less negative about the same kinds of prose written by women. So Sarah Orne Jewett practiced a "realism . . . as dainty and refined as her own manners—bleached out to a fine maidenly purity" (3: 65).

Parrington was perhaps more aware of racism as a social evil, and one finds no overt expression of it. Nevertheless, in a book that claims not to be bound by accumulated critical judgments, the absence of nonwhite writers is striking. Abolitionism is given prominent treatment, but Frederick Douglass is not mentioned. Neither are Booker T. Washington or W. E. B. Du Bois. Again, given Parrington's political criteria, it is hard to see how these figures ought to fall outside of the "main currents of American thought."

Neither race nor feminism were dominant topics in the postwar literary, and it is perhaps not surprising that Parrington should have responded to those that were. If the Progressive school of American history could be understood to have "inverted point by point" the views of the conservative nationalist historians "to yield a historical rationale for social reform," then Parrington can be read as inverting the history of the New Humanists and other literary conservatives (Hofstadter, 27). Thus just as Babbitt blames the influence of Jean-Jacques Rousseau for most of the ills of modern American culture, Parrington credits him with inspiring Jefferson and the democratic strain of American ideas.[28] While New Humanists such as Foerster and Progressives such as Parrington offered opposite solutions to America's problems, they agreed on the existence of many of the same problems and especially on the role of science and industrial culture in creating them. This, I think, explains the curious turn Gene Wise has observed in volume 3, where Parrington now finds his hope in the literary rather than in the properly political sphere: "It is the men of letters—poets and essayists and novelists and dramatists, the eager young intellectuals of a drab generation— who embody the mind of present-day America; not the professional custodians of official views. . . . Literature at last has become the authentic voice of this great shapeless America that means so much to western civilization" (3: xxvii). Parrington here reveals his own cultural affiliation, sharing with the literati, left and right, and with professors of English, a belief in the expressive and saving power of literature.

Since Trilling first raised the issue in 1940, a good deal has been made of Parrington's conception of reality.[29] When it was first published, however, *Main Currents* inspired no discussion whatsoever of its epistemology for the simple reason that Parrington held the same one as virtually every other literary scholar. Like other contemporary literary historians, Parrington understood his task as a matter of explaining literary events and giving interpretations of facts. He did not understand his job to be interpreting texts, the meanings of which he like other members of his field took to be largely self-evident. Wise says that Parrington and the other Progressive historians "were driven to unmask reality," a view that to some extent contradicts Trilling's assertion of Parrington's monodimensional conception of the real (271). But if it is true that Parrington looked for unarticulated political and economic motives for certain ideas, his can hardly be called a hermeneutics of suspicion. There is no sense in his work that a fundamental reality is systematically masked so that it is unavailable to the writer as well as his readers. Parrington doesn't claim, for example, that the Federalists failed to recognize their economic motives; on the contrary, he asserts that they held an economic interpretation of politics. Like other historians of his day, Parrington sees himself as correcting later misunderstandings of the past rather than, like a Marxist or Freudian, uncovering a reality unavailable at the time. If Parrington's sense of reality differed in any way from the norm in literary studies, the difference was ontological rather than epistemological or hermeneutical. Parrington holds economic and political life to be more real than such things as aesthetic experience or everyday life as rendered by Howells (see Hofstadter, 387). A Hawthorne, a Howells, or a James may perversely choose to ignore what is most real, rendering them trivial. Their work is not useful for getting at the most real, even though it may be entirely accurate in describing a lesser portion of reality.

Americanists could appreciate Parrington because, except for his overt political bias, they understood the task of literary history in much the same terms. They may have been most impressed by the fact that *Main Currents* addressed the question of American civilization head on. His stated goal was "to give some account of the genesis and development in American letters of certain germinal ideas that have come to be reckoned traditionally American" (1: iii). The Americanists may have disagreed with Parrington's characterization or complained about his limited conception, but they recognized in *Main Currents* a coherent and compelling version of an American tradition. For Parrington, American civilization is a product of the political conflict his book traces, but it is distinguished by its expression of liberal or democratic ideas. Parrington's book answered, perhaps in spite of itself, critics left and right who denied that there was an American civilization. Parrington himself can celebrate an "America that means so much to western civilization" even though he is not at all sanguine about the condition of contemporary America (3: xxvii).

Americanists were able to acknowledge *Main Currents* as a legitimate attempt. Parrington's book propounded a theory of the unity and distinctiveness of American literature, but it was one that the profession rejected. Despite the warm welcome for his book, Parrington lacked "influence within the institutional networks."[30] While his previously noted lack of contact with other Americanists doubtless contributed to this, *Main Currents* itself was the major problem. There are three features of Parrington's conception of American literature that prohibited his book from attaining definitive status. One was his very notion of literature. As we saw, Parrington's book entailed a residual conception of literature that literary historians were in the process of banishing. A history that regarded John Calhoun as more important than Poe was clearly not a *literary* history. The second follows from the first: *Main Currents* did not—it could not, given Parrington's assumptions—provide an aesthetic justification for the value of American literature. Finally, Parrington's picture of an American past in perpetual conflict did not suit the nationalist aims of the subdiscipline. While consensus history did not become dominant until the 1940s at the earliest, the different character of American literature studies made consensus its dominant conception as early as the 1920s. Parrington demonstrated that there was *an* American tradition, but Americanists saw it as partial. Parrington's book had included conservative figures, but it somehow rendered them less American than the liberals. The nationalist project demanded that *the* American tradition include all of the *major* figures, whatever their politics.

Establishing a Standard Research Practice

The past several sections have focused on several different kinds of research produced during the 1920s. The doctoral dissertations, the books by Rusk, Dondore, and Hazard, and the landmark study of Parrington together suggest a lack of an established research practice. It is not surprising that different practices should exist, given the small amount of work done in American literature before 1920. Those few, scattered academic studies had not established a set of problems, much less a method to solve them. Nevertheless, the different approaches remain distinctly literary-historical. Furthermore, if the larger problems that preoccupied the new field originated in the literary culture, the methods it first used came from the study of English literature. And those methods determined in practice the smaller problems to which individual scholars would devote their work. During the 1920s, American literature became a more frequent topic of academic articles. At the end of the decade, a standard practice emerged out of the application of the methods of English studies to American topics. Thus it would be method, rather than theory, that would define the typical article in the field's new journal, *American Literature.*

The founding of the journal *American Literature* marks the point at which the movement to establish American literature as a subdiscipline reached fruition. Many in English studies remained unconvinced that American literature deserved such recognition. Even in seeking support for the idea of a journal devoted to American literature, some of its supporters feared that the field "was still besieged by hostile critics who charged that it dealt in huge vaguenesses and lacked, as yet, sufficiently academic discipline" (Vanderbilt, 287). Even some Americanists felt that not enough scholarly work was being produced to fill the pages of a normal-sized quarterly. That must have been the belief of the Brown contingent, who proposed to publish four sixteen-page issues a year. To respond to such fears, Hubbell compiled a list of articles on American literature published during 1927. Although he was able to find "only about half of the 1927 numbers" of the magazines he consulted—the others were being bound—he counted 33 articles, or more than enough to fill four issues.[31] Hubbell's count is a bit disingenuous, since many of the articles could not have been published in *American Literature.* But his list presents another picture of scholarship in American literature prior to the creation of the journal. The nonprofessional quarterlies, such as the *South Atlantic Quarterly* or the *Sewanee Review,* published informal essays that expressed distinct authorial points of view. Such articles ranged from reminiscences such as "One Who Knew Poe" in *The Bookman* to discussions of contemporary subjects, such as "American Criticism To-day" in the *Sewanee Review.* Another distinct category was articles that promoted or attempted to define American literature as an object of study. One such article appeared in *English Journal,* a publication of the National Council of Teachers of English, and two others were published in the *Sewanee Review,* but none appeared in the strictly scholarly journals. Informal essays and field-building articles would not be published by *American Literature,* which modeled itself in most respects on journals such as *PMLA* or *Modern Philology.* On the other hand, seven of the articles on the list were by prominent ALG members—including two by Stanley Williams and three by Hubbell himself—and these articles typify the scholarship that will appear in *American Literature*: Williams, "Unpublished Letters of Emerson," *Journal of English and Germanic Philology*; Hubbell, "Cavalier and Indentured Servant in Virginia Fiction," *South Atlantic Quarterly*; Napier Wilt, "Poe's Attitude Toward his Tales: A New Document," *Modern Philology*. As these titles suggest, the emphasis is on the factual, to the point where the mere recovering of lost documents justifies a publication. The existence of such articles demonstrates that a distinct research practice had already been established in the 1920s by ALG members. *American Literature* would nurture and sustain this practice through the 1950s.

Hubbell was able to secure the acceptance of Duke's proposal to house the ALG's journal because the university was willing to provide far more financial support than was Brown. *American Literature* would be published by Duke University, which would appoint the editor from its faculty and provide the editorial offices, but it was the official organ of the ALG, with the editorial and advisory boards to be chosen by that organization. The financial commitment of a university (albeit a new one with little academic reputation) and the support of the MLA made the journal possible, while its very existence answered the critics. The threat of such criticism may have been partly responsible for the very conservative character of the journal, which eschewed articles on pedagogy and living authors and which demanded agreement of all five members of the editorial board for the acceptance of an article. Such a policy was designed to ensure that the journal represented the whole field and not just the perspective of an editor.

In practice, the policy served to exclude articles that did not follow widely shared methods. Although *American Literature* billed itself as "A Journal of Literary History, Criticism, and Bibliography," criticism was not a usual activity for most ALG members, and whatever critical articles they may have offered the journal had a gauntlet to run to get accepted. For example, on March 25, 1929, when the first number was still in press, Hubbell wrote to Ralph Rusk to ask him to reconsider his vote to reject an article by Frederick C. Prescott entitled "The Interpretation of American Literature." Rusk was the only member of the board who had voted "no," although another had recommended that the article not appear in the first issue. Hubbell admitted that he did not find the Prescott article up to his standards, but he wanted to publish it because "thus far we have got almost nothing in the way of criticism—and we need it. . . . we don't seem likely to get much —unless we ask the 'New Humanists' or the Menckenites to write it—and I am not enthusiastic about either of those camps."[32] It is telling that the article in question was never published in *American Literature.* Nor was Hubbell the only ALG member to worry about the absence of criticism. The next month, Stanley Williams wrote to Hubbell congratulating him on the first issue: "What impressed me most was its solidity. This was wise in the first issue, as in all others. Perhaps your next need will be some rather more critical articles to lift parts of the magazine into real constructive thinking. . . . I do hope you will include later one or two papers of pure criticism."[33] These sentiments were expressed by a scholar whom Hubbell had described in the letter to Rusk as one of those who "care nothing for criticism."

These discussions of the need for criticism are overdetermined. They suggest that criticism is generally accepted as a legitimate aspect of literary study, and they acknowledge the absence of criticism among the submissions to *American Literature* and in the first number. But they also suggest the difficulty of finding criticism that will be acceptable to literary historians. The Prescott article is recommended as an example rather than for its merit, while Williams seems to contrast the "solidity" of scholarship with the "constructive thinking" found in criticism. Hubbell disparages the major schools of criticism outside the university but acknowledges the lack of alternatives.

Given these attitudes, it is not surprising that so little criticism was published in *American Literature.* In the first six volumes, for example, there were perhaps a total of two or three articles in which evaluation was a major task. A few others were broadly interpretive, while perhaps one or two articles per volume were formalist descriptions of poetic rhyme, meter, or other techniques. By publishing mainly articles that could be justified in positivist terms and thus that resembled those published in *PMLA* and other scholarly journals of English, *American Literature* could demonstrate that the field it represented had sufficient academic discipline. But since the ALG was dominated by literary historians, there is little reason to think that they would have preferred to do things differently.

American Literature immediately became, as Hubbell had predicted, the leading journal in the new field, as the lists of articles on American literature it published clearly demonstrate. In fact, these lists suggest the journal was without rival and that its contents are typical in both method and content. A large proportion of articles on American literature in the early 1930s were published in historical journals, especially state or regional ones. The second-largest share appeared in literary quarterlies such as the *Sewanee Review* or the *South Atlantic Quarterly*, although these journals tended to include articles on contemporary literature that most scholarly journals, including *American Literature*, did not accept. Concern with the contemporary was much more common to general circulation periodicals, such as the *Bookman* or the *New Republic*, which, because of this, also account for a sizable share of articles on American literature. The traditional scholarly journals continued to publish relatively little in the field. The prominence of *American Literature* leads me to conclude that it is a reliable guide to the practice of Americanists during this period, and the following analysis is offered, as was the earlier one of *PMLA*, as representing the entire field.

Because it duplicated so closely the activity of the parent discipline, it is largely unnecessary to describe in detail the research practice of American literature. Influence and source studies were its bread and butter, even though the historical range of such studies tended to be considerably foreshortened. Where a typical article in English studies might have traced a source that antedated a work by a century or more, most sources of American works were discovered in the author's contemporary historical context. This rendered scholarship in American literature closer to the discipline of history than was scholarship in English generally. In fact, there is little to distinguish an article such as Hubbell's "Cavalier and Indentured Servant in Virginia Fiction" from history pure and simple, since the article treats fictional works as historical documents rather than as literary works.[34] The author continued to be the dominant element of the disciplinary object but, because the canon remained in question, the author may have tended to stand less distinctly in front of the historical background. A discussion of the sources of Emerson's "Divinity-School Address," for example, comments directly on the tension between the conflicting origins of author and source: "one of the most signal weaknesses of the historical method as applied to the study of American letters is the ever-present tendency to resolve the past into a series of personalities."[35] This article explicitly denies Emerson originality, concluding that the " 'Divinity School Address' had better be regarded as one of the concrete manifestations of a general attitude among Transcendentalists, and not as an extraordinary bit of spiritual pioneering" (31). While this treatment was permitted by the still questionable canonical status of American authors, such explicit privileging of source over author was rare. However, since many of the source studies dealt with distinctly nonliterary sources, the conflict itself was less prominent in scholarship on American literature.

If anything, the typical article on American literature seems even more positivist in its assumptions than the typical contribution on English literature. One reason for this is the lack of a long history of academic scholarship on the former. As we saw, by 1930 scholars of English literature could enter into longstanding discussions, such as the one about the mutual influence of Spenser and Sidney, and could write as much in response to the scholarship as to the primary texts. Such discussions conferred value on scholarly articles in that they became contributions to something more immediate than the general accumulation of knowledge about a subject. Without such continuing discussions, Americanists, editors and contributors, had little to guide their judgments of relevance or interest. The published record suggested that, in the absence of other criteria, the certainty of an article's information became the most important consideration. As the "Note to Contributors" in *American Literature* put it, "Articles of particular value, we think, are those that bring to light new materials or new facts," while those that presented new interpretations are regarded as "less important."[36] While such a policy may have fit the circumstances of the new field, the assumptions it reflects doubtless inhibited the emergence of scholarly debates. When scholarly controversy did enter the pages of *American Literature*, it was usually over a matter of factual inaccuracy. So, for example, a critique of Parrington on "The Sources of New England Democracy" demonstrates that in finding these sources in Luther Parrington got it wrong. The article shows not only that Calvin was more sympathetic than Luther to republican forms of government, but that Luther's teachings had little direct influence on the New England churches.[37] Parrington's treatment of the Puritans inspired others, such as Perry Miller, to construct rival interpretations of the Puritans' place in American cultural history, but this article was a dead end. Once its correction was accepted, nothing remained to be said.

As a result of the limitations of its epistemology, *American Literature* cannot be said to have explicitly endorsed the New Humanism or any other social or political position. But it is equally true that these limitations prohibited dominant positions from being effectively questioned or challenged in its pages. This is most obvious in the frequent articles that do no more than announce the existence of some new facts or materials. But even those few articles that proceed to some interpretation remain inhibited. Marchand's article on "Emerson and the Frontier" is unusual in the degree to which it offers interpretations of its subject. As we noted earlier, Marchand interprets Emerson's individualism as a historical force against social legislation, although he believes that as a "lover of justice" Emerson would disapprove of the use to which he has been put (161). Likewise, Emerson's attitude toward democracy is shown to be mixed at best. These readings, however, are only elements of an essay the form of which is determined by problems of historical causality. If the essay has an overall argument, it is merely that Emerson's thinking derives more from the frontier than from foreign sources: "The cardinal points of his teaching—optimism, melioration, democracy, individualism, self-reliance—derive chief sanction and meaning from the psychology bred by the American frontier" (174). Ultimately, then, whatever its criticisms of Emerson, the essay leaves the man all the more American, and therefore all the more important to American literature. The social impact of the doctrine of self-reliance becomes less important than the Americanness of the doctrine.

As a result of its positivist orientation, *American Literature* could offer little by way of a direct contribution to the two major tasks the subdiscipline faced: establishing an appropriate aesthetic and creating a theory that explained the unity and distinctiveness of American literature. If *American Literature* symbolized the achievement of disciplinary status, it did not contribute to solving the problems that *The Reinterpretation of American Literature* had established as central to that discipline. Instead, most articles in *American Literature* seem offered as contributions to a fact bank. It is impossible to discern in the journal any more pointed an intellectual project than this between its beginning in 1929 and its belated capitulation to criticism under Arlin Turner in the 1970s. While I suggested above that the precarious position of American literature as a discipline contributed to its editors' conservative editorial policy, there are several conditions that helped to determine what that policy would be. One of these was an epistemology that identified knowledge with verifiable facts; criticism had not yet reached the point where its judgments could be so verified. Interpretation beyond that derivable from historical research clearly violated this epistemology. Answers to questions such as those raised in *The Reinterpretation of American Literature* were always deferred. Someday, enough information would be gathered to answer such questions; in the meantime, all that scholars could do is gather. Second, the kind of training that literary scholars received gave them no tools with which to address the larger questions. They were not expected to be critics, and the special language of literary interpretation that would become the lingua franca of English departments later was now just being invented by T. S. Eliot, I. A. Richards, and a few others. The new field of American literature was bounded—disciplined, we might say—by the larger field of English in spite of the fact that American literature had already defined its mission as exceeding those boundaries.

Paradoxically, American literature was forced by the conception of literature that the discipline of English maintained to move beyond the kind of research practiced in English departments. Not only did American literature's status as a distinct national literature need continually to be reaffirmed, but the canonical status of American authors remained to be demonstrated. Yet even in this latter project, *American Literature* seems to have made little in the way of a direct contribution. Americanists recognized that the old list of standard authors no longer defined their field. As a review of "Trends in American Literary Scholarship" during the first decade of its disciplinary history put it: "Interest in Longfellow, Whittier, Lowell, and Holmes is apparently declining; Bryant, Irving, and Hawthorne seem to be holding their own; whereas Emerson, Thoreau, Cooper, Melville, Whitman, and Emily Dickinson are rising in the literary firmament."[38] Yet the discipline contributed little by way of direct intervention on these questions. The "Note to Contributors" in volume 1 of *American Literature* reveals the disciplinary prohibition against such behavior: contributors are warned against the use of superlatives. Elsewhere literary enthusiasm is rejected in favor of "unbiased critics to place the man and his ideas . . . in the main currents of American and world literature."[39] The positivism of literary history promised definitive knowledge and correct judgment, while in the present it permitted dealing only in the obvious and the transparent.

As a result, the American literary canon emerged out of judgments made outside of the academy, but more or less silently ratified by it. The two major elevations to canonical status of authors not previously regarded as standard, the cases of Melville and Dickinson, occurred without any support from the journal. Interest in Melville was raised first by biographers such as Raymond M. Weaver and Lewis Mumford, and the case for his importance was made most forcefully by the latter and his fellow literary radical Van Wyck Brooks.[40] By 1932, it could be asserted that "The vogue of Herman Melville is at its peak."[41] Yet during the first six years of *American Literature*, only three articles on Melville were published, all of them historical, although one did deal with Melville's historical reception, setting out to change "two erroneous conclusions: first, that Melville's contemporaries were blind to the significance of his work, and, second, that until the beginning of the revival of the last decade Melville was completely forgotten."[42] Another of the articles, on the sources of *The Encantadas* sketches, ends like many articles in *PMLA* with a defense of the author, who transformed his materials "with a magic wand."[43] There were also three articles on Dickinson during the period, one textual, one biographical, and one that uses contemporary reviews to demonstrate her *minor* status.[44] As a point of contrast,

Longfellow was the subject of four articles and considerably more mention than either Melville or Dickinson.

A few articles, while avoiding superlatives, do seem to bear directly on the canonical status of other writers. A discussion of "Lowell's Criticism of Milton" uses the former's lack of penetrative sympathy for the latter to question his critical rank. The article asserts that Lowell was, as he said of Milton, "far more rhetorician than thinker."[45] On the other hand, several articles on Whitman are among the few instances of interpretation published in *American Literature* during its first years. One works at establishing the pattern of Whitman's career, and in doing so seems to go out of its way to make the poet a safe cultural figure by claiming movement from the values of individualism, love of freedom, and materialistic pantheism to nationalism, love of law, and highly spiritualized idealism.[46] The second treatment of Whitman's development is more explicit in its critical endorsement of the poet: "Despite unevenness and audacities, [Whitman] was both a deliberate and a painstaking artist."[47]

Perhaps more important than their support for Whitman's canonization is the construction by these articles of a new concept of the authorial career. Where earlier careers were largely matters of simple biography, in each of these development or evolution occurs within the writing itself. This shift in the constitution of the author marks the increasing importance of the text as an object of study, and it helped pave the way for the New Criticism, the influence of which will make this textual conception of the author the standard one within English.

American Literature did contribute indirectly to canonization of the standard authors merely by printing articles about them. In the first 6 issues, Poe was the subject of 15 articles and Whitman 11, although Emerson rated a mere 5, and Hawthorne and Howells only 4 each. A few of these articles seem to argue against canonization, as does a formalist analysis of Poe that shows his narrow range of theme and technical inventiveness,[48] but in the face of such frequent serious and largely positive attention, the rare negative treatment of a Poe or Whitman could have little impact. The great disparity in the number of articles accorded Poe and Whitman compared to other standard authors reflects less the greater value accorded their individual achievement than the bias of English as a discipline in favor of poetry over prose. Obviously, such numbers can only be at best a rough guide to an author's standing. Clearly Americanists in general regarded Hawthorne as more important than Howells. But what such accounting does reveal is the absence of articles that attempt to recover authors who fell outside of earlier literary histories. Minor writers are regularly the subject of articles, but they are in general those who have been long recognized as meriting this status: Francis Hopkinson, Jeremy Belknap, James Kirk Paulding, George W. Cable, Richard Penn Smith, John Pendleton Kennedy, John Howard Payne.

One would have thought that recent work on the frontier by Rusk and Dondore would have prompted a spate of articles on minor frontier writers, but few of these were published. Furthermore, the minor writers are uniformly white and male. There were no articles on women writers other than Dickinson, although one does describe several series of nineteenth-century popular novels—many of which were written by women—that had been neglected by literary historians.[49] There is nothing on African-American, Native American, or non-English-speaking writers. Yet there are two books reviewed that suggest that the existence of African-American literature was well known and could have been researched without great difficulty. V. F. Calverton edited an anthology of African-American writers that was positively reviewed. The same reviewer, John Herbert Nelson, also reviewed Vernon Loggins's *The Negro Author in America*, which is described as a "successful pioneering journey into one of the fields which [according to Loggins] 'our literary historians almost without exception have neglected.' "[50] Nevertheless, Loggins is accused of being overly enthusiastic about his new discoveries, and the reviewer finds the volume more of interest to social, rather than literary, historians; even the author admits that he covers "little that is truly artistic."[51] The reception of Loggins's book can be usefully compared to that of Rusk's study of frontier literature. Both were Columbia dissertations that dealt with bodies of writing not regarded as having great literary merit. Rusk's book, nevertheless, was regarded as telling us something fundamental about American culture, and it was never dismissed as merely of social interest. In both cases, a narrow definition of literature excluded the authors each studied, but racism kept Loggins's authors even from attaining the status of minor writers. African Americans at least were organized enough to begin to demand cultural representation. After the success of the suffrage movement, women's political organization declined. While Amy Lowell and Mary Austin may have already begun to think literature in feminist terms, few recognized the initiative. If gay culture could be said to exist in the early 1930s, it was surely unrecognized by the dominant culture. The only references to homosexuality in the scholarship of Americanists are oblique and negative. One scholar found it necessary to defend Whitman from suggestions of being "sexual abnormal";[52] clearly an openly gay writer could not at this time be fit for the canon.

On the other hand, it should be remembered that artistic merit or pure literary significance were not the only criteria by which authors or works were deemed worthy of discussion. The academic canon was also formed by the demands that different historical periods and regions be represented there. Neither Edwards nor Franklin, for example, meet the generally accepted criteria that defined the literary, but they continued to be part of the literary canon so that pre-nineteenth-century literature might be included. The need to represent regions other than the Northeast—especially the South—continued to be grounds for the discipline's interest in materials it might otherwise have ignored. *American Literature* published articles such as "Sir Walter Scott and His Literary Rivals in the Old South" and "Notes on the Reading of the Old South," but also articles on William Gilmore Simms and Lanier, who might well not have merited attention were there not a need for Southern representation.[53] Thus the formation of the canon was a response to conflicting demands of aesthetics, nationalism, regionalism, and positivism, the latter manifesting itself in a demand for historical coverage.

Reading through the first volumes of *American Literature* is bound to disappoint one seeking out the promise of the essays in *The Reinterpretation of American Literature*. The articles demonstrate little more than competent literary-historical scholarship, and as a group they certainly do not contribute to any sort of reinterpretation. On the other hand, as Vanderbilt has noted, the reviews now seem to have been the more valuable feature (292). Certainly they are more interesting to readers looking back on the journal today; in the reviews there are clearly stated issues and controversies, while in the articles these are usually buried under the veneer of objectivity when they exist at all.[54] The very existence of these reviews is worthy of consideration. *PMLA* did not publish reviews, nor did most of the scholarly journals in literary studies. But Rusk, Leisy, and Spiller all urged Hubbell to include regular reviews of books in the field. It is not clear, however, that Hubbell needed any urging. The presence of the review section in *American Literature* may have resulted from his conception of the journal as something more than a professional organ. Although the ALG committee on publications insisted that "under no conditions should the journal be made 'popular' at a sacrifice of scholarly standards" (Hubbell, "American Literature," 34), from the beginning, *American Literature* has been conceived as a *magazine*, a conception that owes something to nineteenth-century periodicals such as the *Atlantic* or the *North American Review*, and to twentieth-century quarterlies such as the *Southwest Review*, which Hubbell had previously edited. Hubbell hoped that the journal would come to have a significant readership outside of the academy, and even arranged for Canby's review of *The Reinterpretation of American Literature* to appear in both the *Saturday Review* and the first issue of *American Literature*, in hopes of publicizing the journal (40). And, in spite of the fact that no significant audience outside of the academy ever materialized, Hubbell thought of *American Literature* as having a distinctive readership it served, a readership not identical to the membership of the ALG. Because the journal was devoted to "our national literature," its founders may have believed that it would attract readership where other journals of literary scholarship did not. Conversely, American literature did receive much more attention in nonprofessional periodicals and books than English literature. The large number of books was doubtless another reason for including book reviews in *American Literature.*

Reviews were an early source of controversy in the journal. Hubbell had asked his friend Foerster to suggest someone to review *American Criticism*, a favor Hubbell apparently extended to other insiders as well. Harry Haden Clark's review was perceived by William Cairns and Hubbell to conclude with excessive and unseemly praise for Foerster, and Clark was asked to change the review. Foerster found out about the request and complained to Hubbell that he was compromising Clark's independence as a reviewer.[55] In response to the flap over Clark's review, William Cairns suggested to Hubbell that reviewing not be done by board members. But if Cairns was aware of the problems that could be caused by incestuous editorial relationships, it did not seem to trouble many others. Insiders continued to be favored both in being reviewed and in being asked to review. The insiders rarely risked offending each other by contributing hostile reviews. Gregory Paine, for example, thought that ALG bibliographer Ernest Leisy's history *American Literature* was "very superficial," but he refrained from including this judgment in his polite review. When Pattee was attacked by Fred Millett, an assistant professor, Hubbell felt the need to write Pattee an apologetic note. There seems to have been little opposition within the ALG to these polices. In 1937 Oscar Cargill, a relative outsider, did complain about the journal's practices, telling Hubbell that senior scholars received more favorable treatment in the journal's reviews than did junior scholars without established reputations.[56] This critique, by its isolation, suggests the high degree to which the authority of the ALG leadership was accepted by the membership. It implies that the reviews themselves were understood as highly authoritative.

This is not to say that there was a coherent, conscious program that the reviewers worked to fulfill. In fact, the general policy of protecting and promoting insiders would have interfered with any attempt to advance an agenda not shared by most of them. The resolution of the Clark/Foerster problem—Clark's review was published virtually intact—suggests that the usual conventions governing reviews applied: the review was an expression of the reviewer's opinion, unlike a scholarly article which, as positivist epistemology mandated, must present only verified or verifiable statements. Nevertheless, the regular reviewers, with their common training and shared sense of the field, tended to agree with each other quite often and certain patterns clearly emerge. Perhaps the most important is the promotion of the positivist ideology of scholarship. This was a necessary mission of the *American Literature* Book Review section, not only to make sure the scholarship was "on par" with research done in other areas of English, but also to distinguish their scholarship from mere writing about American literature produced outside the academy. At every turn members of the ALG are giving advice and setting standards of style and historical accuracy that define what real scholarship is. The reviewers repeatedly assert their own agnosticism about theories applied to American literature, thus claiming the appropriate scholarly position of disinterest while at the same time accusing others of lacking it. For example, a review of Albert Mordell's *Quaker Militant: John Greenleaf Whittier* complains that "Mr. Mordell has allowed his personal bias and his anachronistic attempt to measure Whittier by Freudian and Socialist yardsticks to color if not distort the evidence. . . . It is unfortunate these views should confuse the issues in a biography, which, among other things, should be objective, non-partisan, historical, and genetic."[57] But in this case, the ideology of scholarship is also used to attack a book written from a political position of which the reviewer disapproves.

The *American Literature* book reviews were the major place where the discipline sought to assert its authority and control over its territory. This "boundary-work" was aimed not mainly at other disciplines but at nonacademic critics and literary journalists. Because so much nonacademic writing was devoted to American literature, journalists and intellectuals were regarded as significant rivals by the Americanists. In 1932, an article on "Trends in American Literary Scholarship" devotes more space to books by nonacademics than to those by members of the discipline. The explanation for such emphasis and the general line of attack are reflected in the following passage from the article's conclusion: "No field of literature is more open to the superficial appraisals by the uninformed than American literature. Almost anyone can, and many do, try a slapdash hand at it. Scholars are labeled as pedants, and the desire to attain originality, or ease in interpretation, as well as popularity with the general public, leads critics to attach tags, to pigeon-hole into neat compartments, both authors and books. . . . These are the tricks of the critics' trade." Earlier in the same piece, John Macy's collection *American Writers on American Literature* is described as "a strange melange of weighty judgments, impressionistic criticism, and shallow estimates" with "decidedly the best chapters . . . written by college professors."[58] We find a similar, if somewhat less explicit, stance in many *American Literature* reviews. A review of Canby's *Classic Americans* is used as an occasion to lament the proliferation of "experimentalist" (i.e., psychoanalytic, sociological, economic, etc.) literary histories and the resulting lack of a "good standard Literary history of the United States."[59] Such experimentalism is also attacked in reviews of Lewisohn's *Expression in America*, Brooks's *The Life of Emerson* and *Sketches in Criticism*, and Mumford's biography of Melville. Even Constance Rourke's *American Humour*, not identifiable with any damning bias or theory, comes in for a lambasting, its weaknesses finally being chalked up to the author's attempt to write for scholarly *and* general readers.

The ideology of the scholarship, however, also limited, even in reviews, the degree to which a "bias" or theoretical position could be expressed. The claim of disinterest sometimes allowed books presenting left-wing conceptions of American literary history to be received with interest and not rejected out of hand. The most important of these was, of course, Parrington's *Main Currents in American Thought*. The review of the third volume is critical of the "over-simplification" of the first two, but regards the last as "so much the superior" that it is "likely to prove an enduring monument to Professor Parrington's profound consideration and understanding of his country's intellectual and cultural development."[60] The review even defends Parrington against the charge that he "was blind to aesthetic appeal" (445). Perhaps this treatment of Parrington is less surprising when we remember that he had served on the journal's advisory board. But even complete outsiders, such as explicitly Marxist critics V. F. Calverton and Granville Hicks, are said to make valuable contributions. The interest of such critics was precisely the very strong sense of the unity and distinctiveness of American literature that their arguments asserted. For example, a review of Calverton's *The Liberation of American Literature* gives the book quite high ratings: "Far more significant than any technical perfection or imperfection is the thesis itself, a thesis so important that if it be correct, *The Liberation of American Literature* will hereafter be one of the landmarks in American literary criticism, worthy of a position above even the trilogy of Vernon L. Parrington."[61] The review of Hicks's *The Great Tradition* concludes that the "book is one to be referred to and reckoned with by any student who ventures into his field, but it has the virtues and the defects of an original piece of historical criticism rather than those which make for ultimate acceptance as authority."[62] These books may not be wrong, the reviews imply, but they are premature; their claims can only be adjudicated after the positivist promise of certainty has been fulfilled. Both of these reviews qualify their judgments by an appeal to the authority of scholarship over that of mere criticism. Thus, in spite of their relatively balanced tone, these reviews consign their subjects to marginal status.

The reviews also are more explicit than the articles about changes in the canon and the dominant aesthetics of the discipline. We might describe these changes as reflecting increasing elitism and exclusivity. Pattee serves as a kind of marker of this change, since he reflects an older, populist conception of the canon. A review of Pattee's *The New American Literature 1890–1930: A Survey* complains, "He is interested in such writing as reflects the tastes and ideals of the uncultivated reading public rather than those of a restricted and fastidious aristocracy of culture. It is undoubtedly a consequence of this social quantitative estimate of literature that he gives twenty-three pages to Jack London, nineteen pages to O. Henry, six pages to Edwin Arlington Robinson, dismisses T. S. Eliot as the 'leading eccentric of the period.' . . . On the whole, Professor Pattee's score on taste is not very high."[63] Two years later, we find Pattee fighting back. He condemns Carl Van Doren's *American Literature: An Introduction*: "Its title should be American Literary Rebels. It seems to be the fashion now to exclude from the roll of American authors of major importance all who were not condemners of the conventional, damners of Puritanism, shockers of *hoi polloi* readers who are old fashioned in taste and morals. Van Doren's little volume excludes Bryant, Longfellow, Whittier, Holmes, Lowell, Stowe, Harte, and the like, and fills one fourth of his space with Emily Dickinson, Henry Adams, Mencken, Dreiser, Lewis. Paine, Poe, Melville, Thoreau, Whitman, Mark Twain, and Emerson (who was feared by his own generation as a heretic)—these are the American writers worth a modern critic's ink."[64] Where Van Doren's position is elitist, Pattee's is populist: he calls for "a history of the American *people*" with due consideration of best-selling books such as *Little Women* and chapters on such topics as "The Gift-Book Era." Pattee's prophesy that "Melville will wane back to the fifth magnitude" and that the schoolroom poets will regain their honor reveals Pattee's commitment to pre-World War I aesthetics (380). On the other hand, Van Doren's book and the review of Pattee's reveal the aesthetic grounds upon which the new canon is being built.

The research practice we have just surveyed does entail some important changes in conception of American literature, even if these changes do not add up to a coherent, unified retelling of its history. In fact, the lack of a dominant narrative of American literary history implied the decline of older narratives and their explanations. Since researchers concentrated their efforts at microexplanations, broad, Tainean macroexplanations are rare, and occur mainly in books produced by nonacademics. Under the influence of Marx, Freud, and the Progressive historians, however, these studies introduced new forms of explanation that, as the reviews demonstrate, are regarded skeptically by the discipline. Meanwhile the old forms of explanation disappear. Race, which had already declined in importance by the time of the *Cambridge History*, is now virtually absent as an explicit "factor" in American literature. With the passing of racial explanations and with the developing sense of American literature as a distinct object, the English language and its literature also lose their explanatory appeal. The dominant social class is no longer, as in Wendell, conceived as producing the cultural aristocracy. Region, while remaining an important category, also loses explanatory power, except in the special case of the South. Microexplanation has little use for any of these macroforces, but it also is incapable of inventing new ones. The result is that the American literature that these older categories had already helped shape remains little changed, as most researchers ignore its overall character and become preoccupied with its parts. As race, language, class, and region—criteria in terms of which leading authors and texts were selected—are forgotten, such criteria remain embodied in those objects and the accepted wisdom about them. In other words, they now function almost exclusively as ideology.

Because the discipline contributed little in the way of new critical judgments, the older criteria continue to be the dominant influence on the canon. In spite of the addition of Melville and Dickinson, and of the demotion of the schoolroom poets, the canon the discipline is forming remains based on the standard authors. While outside the academy, social conditions during the 1930s helped produce an explicitly political criticism and attempts to found a canon on its terms, inside it the impact of these conditions was limited. But changes in aesthetics are noticeable within the academy. The canon produced there will reflect what both New Humanists and New Critics want to call "an aristocracy of culture" defined not, as it was in Richardson or Wendell, in terms of bourgeois proprieties and romantic clichés, but by originality and innovation. Where taste had previously been defined by the genteel tradition, it was now becoming the property of critics who shared the modernist assumption that great art alters, rather than merely reproduces, tradition. But these aesthetics also separate art from the social and political context in which it had long been understood to exist. The new canon might consist of rebels, but their rebellion was aesthetic and they regarded themselves not as the vanguard of a new social order but as the saving remnant of a decaying one. In the next section, we will look at the working out of the new aesthetics as the New Criticism makes criticism safe for the academy. Before that task had begun in earnest, however, anthologies and teaching practices already begin to reflect the emergence of a new object of study. The next chapter will focus on these pedagogical developments.

6

American Literature
in the Curriculum

The last two chapters have examined the way in which American literature became established as a research discipline. In that discussion, some consideration has been given to graduate training in American literature as a necessary element in creating a field of research. But undergraduate teaching is an important aspect of the institutionalization of American literature as well. It was by means of undergraduate teaching—and through it, high school teaching—that the research discipline's conception of American literature was most widely disseminated. Relatively few people outside of the profession read the academic articles and books it produced, but increasing numbers of college students were exposed to its American literature in surveys and more specialized courses. Such courses served a broadly ideological function, even if, on the whole, they were but a minor part of the ideological state apparatus. With regard to the literary, however, such courses were extremely important, for they defined literature for a large number of people, playing the same role as had magazines at the turn of the century. In this chapter, I will trace the development of the undergraduate curriculum in American literature from the 1920s through the 1960s, and the rise of American studies as a form of graduate training.

The Undergraduate Curriculum

As the discussion of the school histories in chapter 2 showed, when American literature was taught prior to World War I, it was

mainly as a series of biographies. While the school histories sometimes stated that they were meant to accompany the use of actual
works, little in any of these histories suggests what the point of
such assignments would be. While the school histories in general
seem intended for primary or secondary levels, they were used
in colleges as well. There is little evidence available about teaching methods, but there is no reason to believe that the teaching
of American literature before World War I would have often di-
verged from the two approaches then typical of English departments: lectures on historical backgrounds, and the reading aloud
of literary works, accompanied by brief celebratory interjections.
Courses in American literature had become standard at some colleges prior to World War I but were not offered at others; a third
of colleges responding to the ALG survey did not offer a course
in the subject until after the war. The scant information available
in course descriptions suggests that historical surveys were most
common, but the marginal status of the subject meant that it was
not governed by disciplinary rules. Thus American literature
courses were perhaps more likely to reflect the idiosyncrasies of
individual instructors than were courses in English literature.

It may seem strange that American literature did not more
quickly become a significant subject for college study. While English literature was thoroughly institutionalized by 1890, American literature did not become a regular part of the college curriculum until the 1920s, and it remained a distinctly minor part of the
curriculum until after World War II. Nor was the growth of American literature in the curriculum consistent, even though the number of institutions offering courses did increase consistently. Prior
to the turn of the century, American literature courses, though
sporadic, appear with some frequency, especially considering the
relatively small number of English courses. But between 1900 and
the end of World War I, the percentage of American literature
courses in the English curriculum declines. One explanation for
this is the consolidation of coursework under the rule of English
as a research discipline, from which, as we have seen, American
literature was largely excluded. Earlier, the ideology of nationalism together with greater freedom for personal preferences may
have combined to produce American courses. As Horace Scudder's arguments suggest, patriotism, civic duty, and public order

were explicit motives for teaching American literature in the schools since before the turn of the century; we know that patriotic works such as the "First Bunker Hill Oration" were among those most frequently taught in high school.[1] But before the war, the inculcation of patriotism or "good citizenship" was not regarded as central to college or university curricula.

Pattee suggests that this changed, however, as a result of World War I, which brought a "new insistence upon the teaching of Americanism in our American colleges, especially in the colleges which have been under government control" and "demands for patriotism-inciting subjects."[2] During and after the war, there is a notably increased identification between America and democracy in literary discourse. Baym notes that in nineteenth-century histories, "the word 'democracy' seldom appeared . . . given their Whig orientation,"[3] but the war rhetoric of "making the world safe for democracy" changed that. Pattee himself had proposed American literature as a means for teaching Americanism: "American literature must be taught henceforth not as a frill, not as a graceful accomplishment or a help toward English composition, but as an interpretation of American life. Every classic that has survived has survived because it emanated from a human soul during the national era. . . . My lecturer will say little about the beauties of style and the mechanics of art, but . . . he will tell of the romance of the Western march . . . he will say much of the true meaning of democracy and of the new vital individualism of the new world" ("Americanism," 276).[4]

The war doubtless did help provide the impetus for more courses in American literature, but the evidence suggests that there was no major increase in the late 1910s or early 1920s.[5] The greatest impact of war-inspired nationalism may have been the creation of the ALG itself, an event that would have enormous long-term effects on the curriculum. Pattee's narrowly political program could not have been sufficient to make American literature a standard college subject. The anti-belletrism of Pattee's position was unacceptable because claims for aesthetic value were integral to the nationalist project. The movement to include American literature in the college curriculum was not an explosion, but a slow building up over a period of thirty years. In 1928 the results of the first attempt to survey the teaching of American literature appear and they show that "only one out of eleven [literature] courses in the English departments is in American literature. In the graduate departments. . . . The average is about one in thirteen."[6] The ALG's own survey, conducted in 1946, reports success in adding American literature courses to the college curriculum during the years since 1919, but notes that such success did not come without a struggle.[7] While this struggle was repeated at each college or university, it was also conducted in the pages of the periodical literature of the period. The ferment of cultural nationalists outside the university was matched by persistent if less anguished demands from professors that the national literature receive its due. One argument called for American literature to have its own department: "It seems little enough to ask: that the national literature be granted a status equal to that now generally accorded such subjects as journalism, the Spanish language and literature" (Nuhn, 331). Some arguments for the study and teaching of American literature make explicit their nationalist motives: "The great throbbing civilization to which we belong is a thing apart from that of any other nation"; "It is only by using our native literature, by keeping it current, by making it saturate the national consciousness—it is only so that we can make history serve and enrich and inform us, and give to our culture the momentum of a vital tradition"; "We who have the responsibility of training the teachers of literature for the colleges and higher schools will fail in our duty, unless we impress upon them the importance of the study of our own literature."[8] Even a commentator who asserts that "our civilization has as yet produced relatively little fit to stand with the works of the world's greatest artists" argues that we should conceive of the subject as consisting mainly of historical and political material and therefore that we "shape our courses as to make them courses in American civilization, reflected in American literature"; the author announces that he plans "to give the young Americans who come into my lecture room a pretty stiff dose of Roosevelt and Woodrow Wilson."[9] What is significant about this position is that it helps us to realize that in spite of the repeated theme that American life is expressed in American literature, most commentators assume that the object of study is an aesthetic one. The arguments in favor of American literature met with little published opposition, although they surely were not greeted with open arms by English faculties. Nevertheless, the position these articles state was powerful enough that American literature would become a recognized component of the English curriculum.

There is also evidence of some changes after the war in the standard method of teaching American literature. Prior to the War, there were no textbook anthologies of American literature.[10] In 1919, Pattee's *Century Readings in American Literature* was published. It was an immediate success, and would appear in a total of three editions before 1930. A second college anthology, Foerster's *American Poetry and Prose* appeared for the first time in 1925. During the 1920s, these anthologies seem to have been assigned in conjunction with handbook histories. Pattee's "Introductory Note" suggests the novelty of his collection; he refers to it as a "handbook"—the same term that was used for the old histories. "For courses in literature, as literature is now taught, handbooks are necessary. The insistence now is not upon facts *about* authors and masterpieces, but upon the masterpieces themselves."[11] Pattee's claim here is more a seller's puff than an accurate account of contemporary teaching practices. But over the course of the next two decades, it would become increasingly true. During the 1930s and 1940s, many new anthologies were published, and they replaced the handbook histories, which largely disappeared from the textbook market. This pattern parallels the slow shift in research from biography and background to oeuvre and text. Still, the use of an anthology did not guarantee that the presentation of facts and background would not dominate the course. As late as the 1940s, the complaint was still made that survey courses presented students with "biographical data about authors whose works they . . . had not learned to understand."[12]

The anthologies reveal changes in the canon and in dominant critical positions. Before 1930, the anthologists were, in general, hospitable to the established critics (Poe, Lowell, and Whitman); to the genteel critics (Stedman, Howells, and Brownell); and to the traditionalists (More and Sherman). Viewpoints of critics such as Macy, Mencken, Lawrence, Brooks, or Eliot "would not come through to the student using any of these textbook anthologies."[13] Yet these earlier anthologies do offer a broad conception of American literature, though it is broader in Pattee than Foerster. Pattee's "Introductory Note" sounds many of the themes of his nationalist articles of the period: "More and more clearly it is seen now that the American soul, the American conception of democracy,—Americanism, should be made prominent in our school curriculums, as a guard against the rising spirit of experimental lawlessness which has followed the great war." This orientation is reflected in Pattee's stated principles of selection:

> first, literary excellence and originality; second, style and individuality of the author; and, third, light thrown upon the period of the author and upon the growth of the American spirit. The last of these has been kept constantly in mind. . . . The book . . . is, if the compiler has done what he considers his duty, a handbook in Americanism, an interpretation of the American spirit by those who have been our spiritual leaders and our Voices. (*Readings*, v)

Pattee's claims here far exceed the critical and historical discussion of the period, and they predict a conception of American literature that won't find articulation until Matthiessen's *American Renaissance*. Pattee himself offers nothing in his standard biographical headnotes to direct the reader toward an understanding of the American spirit.

In terms of its selection of authors, Pattee's anthology has much in common with its contemporary, *The Cambridge History of American Literature*. Like that work, *Century Readings* reflects an emerging rather than an established canon. The large number of pages given to Longfellow, Whittier, Holmes, and Lowell is more typical of prewar than postwar tastes. Although he had complained about Wendell's New England bias, the era Pattee labels "The New England Period, 1830–1860" takes up 287 pages and includes the works of 25 authors. The years 1787–1830 get a mere 161 pages for 28 authors, while 1870–1914 is accorded 294 pages to cover 46 authors. It is in this last section that Pattee's selection differs most strikingly from the representations of the period that will follow his. Pattee includes women such as Sarah Orne Jewett, Emma Lazarus, Constance Fenimore Woolson, Mary Noailles Murfree, and Edith Matilda Thomas, who will disappear quickly from textbooks. His poets of the period—Hovey, Mitchell,

Gilder, Tabb, Wilson, Sherman, Cawein—will all soon be forgotten. No major figures—not even Mark Twain, James, or Howells—stand out from the background. In other words, beyond the New England group, Poe and Whitman are the only writers *Century Readings* accords major status. The selections that represent authors currently canonized differ from the works now typically anthologized. Hawthorne, for example, is represented by "The Birthmark" but also by "David Swan," several sketches, and the Preface to *The House of the Seven Gables*. From Melville we have only three chapters from *Moby-Dick*, while the selections from Henry James are "Alphonse Daudet" and "Greville Fane." In spite of Pattee's heavily nationalist rhetoric, there is relatively little space accorded to statesmen and other political authors, who total a mere five: Washington, Webster, Lincoln, Grant, and Roosevelt. Perhaps the most significant inclusion compared to later anthologies is the large number of songs. These include a few folk songs, but more typical are "The Star-Spangled Banner," "America," and "My Old Kentucky Home." Not only do such texts reflect Pattee's nationalist mission, but they also suggest that the boundary between lyrics and poetry was less rigid than it would soon become.

Foerster's anthology, published a mere six years after Pattee's, suggests a rapid shift in judgment. Where Pattee addressed the still scattered and unorganized teachers of American literature, the core of Foerster's audience was the new ALG. His goals reflect the prevailing view of literature within the new subdiscipline: "My object has been to provide materials for a study of 1) the literary achievement of our writers, especially the major writers of all periods, and 2) the historical development of our literature."[14] Where Pattee had been explicitly nationalist, Foerster's focus is on literary achievement and development. And although they both claim allegiance to literary excellence, their judgments of this derive not only from differing tastes but also from differing politics. As we have seen, Pattee was a populist, while Foerster a New Humanist. Thus Foerster's first principle of selection, "literary value," is for him a justification for the greater attention given to major writers such as Poe, Emerson, and Whitman. Minor writers, on the other hand, are represented only to fill gaps where history has provided no major figure. Foerster is explicit about the narrower definition of literature that he invokes: "Seeking to do full justice to all writing that is part of *literature* in the usual rather than in the virtually unlimited sense of the word, I have made bold to exclude work of statesman, orators, journalists, authors of popular or patriotic songs, unless their work really possesses literary distinction" (iii). Under the heading of his second principle of selection, "historical importance," Foerster offers his ground-breaking reconceptualization of the periods of American literary history. Pattee had relied on a mixture of the old regional divisions—for example, "The New England Period"—together with such nondescriptive names as "The Period of Beginnings" and "The Period of Transition." We have already discussed the influence of Foerster's periodization (Puritan, revolutionary, romantic, and realist) and the resulting shift in the conception of literary history from the material to the ideal. The effect of the criterion of historical importance, however, is to introduce some material, especially in the Puritanism section, that would have been regarded as lacking in literary value by most previous authors of textbooks. John Smith, William Bradford, Anne Bradstreet, Nathaniel Ward, Michael Wigglesworth, Samuel Sewall, and William Byrd are added to Cotton Mather and Jonathan Edwards. Pattee had excluded colonial literature entirely from his anthology, which begins at 1787. Foerster's representation of this period is dominated by Franklin and Freneau, who account for 38 of the 68 pages, and his selection of authors from these early periods will become standard in later anthologies. Yet, like Pattee, Foerster includes far more minor writers from the nineteenth century than later anthologists, and this seems surprising after Foerster's claims about his principles. There are fewer orators and statesmen in Foerster, but Webster and Lincoln are represented, as are historians Prescott, Parkman, and Motley. There are also songs from the Revolutionary and Civil wars. Foerster gives us the organization that American literary history retains to this day, but his canon remains transitional. One major difference between Pattee and Foerster is the much greater space given to the major writers. Emerson gets 28 pages in Pattee, but 92 in Foerster, while for Poe it's 28 versus 71, and Whitman, 26 versus 78. This reflects Foerster's "sympathy with the present tendency in 'survey' courses to prescribe intensive study of greater authors," a tendency that will grow continuously into the 1960s. Another difference is the more recognizable selection of authors from the early twentieth century. Foerster's poets include Amy Lowell, Carl Sandburg, Robert Frost, Vachel Lindsey, Edgar Lee Masters, and Edwin Arlington Robinson. On the whole, Foerster's anthology is more restrictive: it includes only 96 authors to Pattee's 117, and there are fewer women represented. The differences in the selections, however, reflect the editors' differing principles rather less than their claims would suggest. Anthologies and other textbooks need to reach a wide audience of teachers, and that restricts the degree to which they may differ from each other.

During the 1930s, we find that the anthologies begin to separate into two general types: those that seek to represent through literature, including documents of social or political importance, American cultural history; and those that seek to represent only America's aesthetic achievement. Three that fall into the former category are Oscar Cargill's *American Literature: A Period Anthology* (1933), Warfel, Gabriel, and Williams's *The American Mind* (1937), and Thorp, Curti, and Baker's *American Issues* (1941). The Warfel anthology has sections under each of its major period divisions with titles such as "Economic Thought," "Frontier Thought," and "Nationalism and Sectionalism." All of these more historically oriented anthologies contain writers not normally included in the literary canon, although nonwhite and female writers are not much more in evidence in them than in the more aesthetically oriented collections. These historically oriented anthologies might be regarded as "Parringtonian," until one looks at a genuinely Parringtonian collection, Bernard Smith's *The Democratic Spirit*, which represents only the Jeffersonian current of American thought.[15] The other historical anthologies strive for balance, and none of them follows Parrington's rigorous exclusion of aesthetes who fall outside of the main currents. Thus economic thought of the early national era is represented in Warfel mainly by a few pages of Alexander Hamilton, while Poe gets more than 30 pages in the same anthology. The second volume includes presidents Theodore Roosevelt, Taft, and Wilson and radicals Emma Goldman, Eugene Debs, and Daniel De Leon. The Cargill anthology, five volumes with five different editors, includes some political writing, but it is distinguished by its representation of minor poets, dramatists, and fiction writers.

The existence of these anthologies demonstrates that the object of American literature remained contested, but it is misleading about the outcome of that contest, which by the late 1930s was no longer in doubt. The historical anthologies were successful enough to appear in revised editions after the war, but the form represents a distinct minority of the total number of anthologies and an even smaller proportion of adoptions. The most popular anthologies have from the beginning been those that were based mainly on aesthetic criteria. Pattee's *Century Readings* was the most popular during the 1920s, while Foerster's *American Poetry and Prose* was perhaps the dominant text in the 1930s and remained a popular text well into the 1950s, with adoption by more than 1,000 colleges and universities over its life of five full-length and several "shorter" editions. The 1930s also saw the creation of anthologies that are not only narrowly literary but which mark a distinct shrinking of the canon. The first of these may have been Jones's and Leisy's *Major Writers of America* (1935), but it was soon followed by *The Oxford Anthology of American Literature* (1938) edited by Benét and Pearson, who assert that "there has been no effort to be all-inclusive, and no timidity in adjusting selections to valuations now generally accepted."[16] These two collections represent distinctly different versions of the American tradition, however. Jones and Leisy still includes Bryant, Lincoln, Longfellow, Whittier, and Lowell among the major figures. In the *Oxford*, the schoolroom poets have clearly receded to second rank, and Lincoln merits only the inclusion of "The Gettysburg Address." On the other hand, the canon of American modernism emerges in this anthology in roughly the form it has today, with poets Ezra Pound, H. D., T. S. Eliot, W. C. Williams, e. e. cummings, Hart Crane, and Wallace Stevens; and fiction writers Gertrude Stein, William Faulkner, John Dos Passos, and Ernest Hemingway.

The selection of minor writers in the *Oxford* remains large compared to postwar standards, but these writers are largely white male poets and fiction writers. It is worth remarking on the role minor writers play in the pre-World War II anthologies. In general, the same names and works appear in each collection.

Thus John Hay's "Jim Bludso" appears in each of the anthologies I've discussed so far. Joseph Rodman Drake and Fitz-Greene Halleck are nearly always represented by "The Culprit Fay" and "On the Death of Joseph Rodman Drake," respectively. It is clear that anthologists routinely rely on each other as guides in the selection of authors and works. It costs little in time or resources to continue to reprint a few poems or a story by a minor writer, and there is always the fear that omitting the writer teachers have come to expect will cost the publisher adoptions. This sort of inclusion seems better described as habit than tradition. Though there is little hard evidence from before the war, the odds are that these minor writers were seldom assigned by teachers who used the anthologies. Unlike the handbook history, the anthology's format encourages the teacher to use its contents selectively. The presence of the minor writers is thus much less significant as a marker of diversity or even historical difference in taste than it might at first seem.

The proliferation of anthologies reflects the role of American literature within the English curriculum. While the number and assortment of American literature courses varied widely among different institutions, the American literature survey was far and away the single most frequently offered course. The survey was already familiar enough in 1925 for Foerster to mention it in his Preface, albeit in quotation marks. The American survey had become a fixture in English departments by 1940. According to a small poll appearing in *College English*, "there is hardly a college or university today that does not present at least one survey course in this field."[17] The usual survey described here is still with us, save for the cut-off date. It "begins with Captain John Smith and continues down toward 1900. The end of the Civil War, 1870, 1880, 1890, and the death of Whitman in 1892 are conventional termini. When the earlier dates denote the end of the survey, a continuation course is usually offered to bring the work down to present writers" (Flanagan, 515–16). The survey is the perfect curricular reflection of the positivism of literary historical scholarship. It assumes that literary knowledge can be surveyed as if from an external vantage point, and it implicitly denies that there are significant problems of interpretation or judgment.[18] If the anthology by its very existence reflects the increasing importance of texts in literary instruction, prior to World War II the survey course continued to constitute texts as objects of objective historical knowledge.

The ubiquity of the American survey did not convince most Americanists that their subject had finally achieved its rightful place in the curriculum. Prior to the war, departments typically offered an English survey during the sophomore year and an American survey during the junior year.[19] The English survey was foundational to the curriculum as a whole, including the American survey, and it was a prerequisite for more advanced courses in historical periods or major authors. The American survey was typically followed by few if any advanced courses. This pattern clearly suggests the subordinate place of American literature, since the survey of it was merely a more or less important addition to the English edifice. In 1935, Howard Mumford Jones addressed the English section of the MLA on "American Scholarship and American Literature," and he accused the discipline of continuing to ignore the national literature in both research and teaching:

> in twenty-five leading colleges and universities, I find that in most of these there has been only the most elementary treatment of the subject, and I know of only two or three in which the distribution of emphasis is something like what it should be. The national literature not only receives much less proportionate attention than British literature—a fact that is perhaps justified by its relative youth—but it actually receives less attention than any of the periods of British literature, a fact for which there is no justification whatsoever. In this country education in English literature is education in British literature.[20]

Jones supported this contention by describing the typical distribution of faculty by specialty within an English department. In a department of 15 or 16, only one "man" is typically assigned to American literature, while the Renaissance might typically have three, including specialists in Shakespeare and Milton ("Scholarship," 117). His arguments in favor of increased attention to American literature are both aesthetic and nationalist. Jones is willing to mention American writers in the same breath with the greatest Englishmen: "If the United States has not developed a Shakespeare or a Milton, Great Britain has not developed a Whitman or a Mark Twain. . . . The constant tendency among specialists in British literature to deprecate the Americans is a mark of ignorance" ("Scholarship," 120). Jones also warns that preoccupation with British literature had fostered imperialist visions in American leaders and made some of them less willing to defend American interests against the British. He then returns to themes first articulated by Horace Scudder:

> In a period of intense social strain the country needs the steadying effect of a vital cultural tradition; it needs, in Van Wyck Brooks' phrase, a "usable past." . . . I firmly believe that unless this organization sees the need of associating itself with the cultural history of our common country, it will come in time to count for less and less in the intellectual life of the United States. Shall we leave the field to the social scientists, or shall we accept the challenge which the situation gives us? ("Scholarship," 123–24)

I have quoted Jones at some length here because his arguments give us a clear sense of how the teaching of American literature was promoted and how it was positioned vis-à-vis other disciplines competing for academic and cultural influence. Like Pattee, Jones is willing to assert that political benefits will accrue from teaching American literature, but he is unwilling to concede anything on the aesthetic front. It is a failure to recognize the aesthetic merit of American literature of which he is accusing English professors and politicians alike. In taking up Brooks's call for a usable past, Jones demonstrates how the literary radicals' demand for the transformation of tradition was now used in the service of that tradition, and to provide a "steadying effect" no less. Brooks himself was by this time leading the way in this regard. The clear conservatism of Jones's argument is especially noteworthy when we consider that Jones was by no means one of the more conservative ALG members and that his class-based analysis of American literary history was rejected by Foerster for inclusion in *The Reinterpretation of American Literature*. But besides Anglophilia and anarchy, Jones mentions a third enemy: the social sciences. As Elizabeth Wilson has argued, English and the modern languages had recently begun a "border war" with the social sciences.[21] Jones raises the threat of losing that war if American culture is ignored by the MLA. Jones's arguments produced no change in the organization, but the war with the social sciences did eventually lead the MLA to accept pedagogy as part of its concern, something it had rejected in 1903.

In the meantime, the American literature curriculum continued to grow. If the survey was the only American literature course that every English department offered, a more extensive American curriculum was taking shape at many institutions, including genre and period courses. Such courses are another indication that the curriculum in American literature was developing around aesthetic concerns. The courses that English departments offered in American literature rarely were organized around thematic concerns, and seldom did they betray a Parringtonian perspective on literary history. Only after the war did single-author courses in American literature become commonplace, although they were traditional in English literature. At institutions that offered survey, genre and period, and single-author courses in American literature, it became a curriculum parallel to the one in English literature, which shared the same architecture.

By 1940, the American survey had become standard enough for it to be already under attack from several different directions. One complaint is that the usual survey is not historical enough: "Usually the survey is a thinly disguised pretext for an examination of the 'golden period' of the nineteenth century. The rest goes by the board. The course is initiated with a formality and concluded with a weak flourish. The conscience of the teacher is appeased, but the historical perspective of the student has hardly been established."[22] According to this commentator, in order to establish historical perspective, more attention to both colonial and modern periods is necessary, including authors such as Eliot, Pound, and Stein whom we would now call modernists. This complaint suggests that a canon exists and argues that it should be expanded in a particular way. Historical coverage, rather than historical depth, is the motive behind this critique. Still, this position holds that American literature can only be understood from the perspective of its historical development, and it assumes that many teachers will "use American writing as a partial guide toward a definition of the American mind" (Pearson, 585).

Both of these assumptions would be rejected by those who sought New-Critic-inspired reforms in the teaching of American literature. They believed that the survey was too broad to allow for close reading of major authors and thus sought to replace it with a different kind of course. An account of the American literature curriculum at the University of Oklahoma reports that the

> survey has been converted into a course dealing with the writings of seven or eight major authors a semester, arranged logically rather than chronologically. The first semester begins with eight weeks on Franklin, Paine, Freneau, Irving, and Bryant, followed by three weeks each on Longfellow, Hawthorne (including *The Scarlet Letter*), and Poe. Additional figures may be assigned for supplementary reading, but the course pretends to deal with writers through their writings, and the staff has concluded that the material must be rigorously limited if it is to be studied intensively. The second semester gives three weeks each to Emerson, Thoreau, Melville (including *Moby Dick*), and Whitman, two to Mark Twain, one to Howells, and one to Lanier. (Shockley and Walcutt, 682–83)

This course simply advertises its coverage as that which, according to the historical critique, the usual survey presented anyway. But the justification for the limited number of authors is a goal that that critique does not recognize: teaching students to read. "The poem is not regarded as a historical fact in the development of English literature but as a work of art which presents a problem in intelligent understanding and appropriate response. Some progress has been made toward displacing the Amusing Anecdote and Significant Fact. We are trying to teach literature; not facts about literature" (Shockley and Walcutt, 681).

What made this kind of course possible were the reading strategies and techniques presented first in Cleanth Brooks's and Robert Penn Warren's *Understanding Poetry* (1938). This book showed how the poem might become the center of systematic, precise inquiry. Its impact is recorded in numerous testimonials suggesting that many more converts to the New Criticism were won by its success as a classroom strategy than by its theoretical pronouncements. By treating the poem as an organism rather than an artifact or representation, New Critical reading strategies made it possible to implement the goal Pattee had articulated in 1919: to focus "not upon facts *about* authors and masterpieces, but upon the masterpieces themselves." This resulted in a change not only in course content from historical background to textual interpretation but in pedagogical method as well. A class organized around discussion was a good way to teach reading strategies; while it never entirely displaced the lecture, the discussion format attained widespread popularity. Provision was made for it even where large lecture classes remained by assigning graduate assistants to lead discussion sections.

The success of New Critical teaching strategies did not lead to the general adoption of courses such as the one implemented at Oklahoma. The year-long survey continues even today to be the most important way in which American literature is represented to undergraduates. Immediately after World War II, the NCTE conducted a study of American literature in the college curriculum. It found that "the two-semester survey, meeting three times a week (6 credits), is offered by slightly more than half of our colleges and universities."[23] Including other variations, the most common being the one-semester survey, a total of 94 to 97 percent of colleges and universities offered an American survey. Statistics about the authors included on the 90 syllabi that the committee examined reveal that the canon was narrowing faster —or perhaps had always been narrower—than evidence from anthologies shows. Only seven authors (listed in order of frequency of appearance: Emerson, Hawthorne, Whitman, Poe, Twain, Thoreau, and Melville) were included in a majority of courses. That Longfellow and Irving were included more often than Henry James suggests that the influence of the New Critics and the New York Intellectuals—who were James's strongest champions—was not yet very strong among academic Americanists. Of the 37 authors mentioned on at least 4 syllabi, it would be hard to classify any of the authors as certifiably minor, though William Bird, mentioned seven times, comes the closest. The realists, whom Lionel Trilling and other critics claimed that Parrington had elevated to dominance in American literature, are quite marginal. Howells was included on only 15 syllabi, Crane on 11, Dreiser and Garland on 6, and Norris on 5. Of women writers, Dickinson is predictably the most often taught, appearing on 24 lists, the equal of J. F. Cooper and Oliver Wendell Holmes. The only others are Edith Wharton and Willa Cather, at the bottom of the heap with 5 and 4 mentions respectively. It is worth noting, however, that F. Scott Fitzgerald, William Faulkner, and Hemingway did not appear at all, though they will soon come to replace Wharton and Cather as the chief representatives of twentieth-century American fiction. Jefferson and Lincoln were included in 11 and 8 courses, but no other statesmen or explicitly political writers make the list. It is possible that minor writers included in anthologies were assigned but not listed by name, but no mention of this is made.

Lecture and discussion were combined in 80 percent of the survey courses, though the NCTE report tells us nothing about the proportions in such combinations. Another 10 percent of the surveys were taught by lecture alone. The dominant approach to the material was literary-historical, though only 14 percent of the surveys are said to have used this perspective alone. Literary history was included by 44 percent, with combinations of aesthetic appreciation, social history, philosophical implications, or economic forces, while another 39 percent combined only aesthetic appreciation with literary history. Another blow to the myth of Parrington's dominance is that social history was included in just 20 percent of those courses combining several points of view, and economic forces in a mere 5 percent of such combinations. A solely aesthetic approach was taken by 5 percent of the courses, and none of them are described as having taken a specifically critical or interpretive approach. Not surprisingly, the American literature survey course in the immediate postwar years appears firmly in the grip of the literary historians that the profession had been turning out since the 1920s.

The NCTE report suggests that a standard curriculum in American literature beyond the survey had not yet emerged. After the survey, students were most likely to receive instruction in American literature in courses in contemporary drama, poetry, literature, or fiction. The very existence of these courses is a marked change in the English curriculum, as is the increased importance of American literature. At the turn of the century, William Lyon Phelps's course on the contemporary novel was regarded as so unusual as to merit attention in the newspaper. *PMLA* only started publishing significant numbers of articles on nineteenth-century literature in the 1920s. The university in the 1940s was already beginning to regard even contemporary writing as part of its domain, and to think of reading contemporary literature as something that might demand formal training. American literature usually took up about one-half of the time in contemporary literature courses. The most common course other than the survey offered in American literature alone was the American novel, but only 19 of 100 institutions offered such a course. Single-author courses, theme courses, period courses, and courses on American humor, folklore, and language are offered at a mere 1 to 2 percent of institutions.

These statistics suggest a mixed picture of the role of American literature in the college curriculum in the 1940s. While virtually all colleges and universities now offered courses in American literature, less than 5 percent of them required it for the bachelor's degree, and few of these were research universities or elite liberal arts colleges. Only 24 percent made American literature a requirement for English majors (*ALCC*, 23–25). In spite of the nationalist content of American literature scholarship and anthologies, and the nationalist rhetoric used to promote the teaching of such literature, these statistics suggest that American literature did not play a very important role in the general maintenance of Americanism. But this may say less about the significance of American literature to American culture than it does about the importance of any literature to that culture. While an English course was almost universally required of first-year students, that course was intended to teach students to write, and therefore cannot be considered a course in English literature. In other words, seldom were literature courses of any kind required for graduation. Since those attending college at this time still represented a very small minority of their age group, very few Americans could have experienced literary study at the college level. Though English may be said in one sense to have replaced classics in the college curriculum, it never dominated the curriculum in the same way. All of which suggests that the state could have gotten on quite well without the literary as an ideological apparatus; it does not suggest, however, that the literary was constituted any less ideologically as a result.

The inherently nationalist character of American literature as a discipline becomes apparent in the context of World War II and the Cold War. If it is unclear whether World War I produced a significant increase in the teaching of American literature, there is no doubt that World War II and its aftermath did so. During the war, interdisciplinary programs in American civilization sprang up at many universities and colleges. Some programs of this kind had begun earlier at institutions such as Yale, Harvard, and George Washington, but the war inspired an explosion of interest. As we will see in a moment, the primary impact of what would soon be known as the American Studies movement was on graduate training, but during the war such programs or courses were understood as part of the war effort. They were among the responses to President Roosevelt's challenge that our colleges should help "preserve the culture that our soldiers were fighting for."[24] The popularity of American civilization programs grew as the war continued, feeding and feeding on the nationalism of the era. The military itself ordered Jay B. Hubbell's anthology, *American Life in Literature*, for the U.S. Armed Forces Institute home study program. The American victory raised the nation to the role of world leader, and the ensuing Cold War presented a new enemy against which it would be judged. The government, through both overt and covert means, began to promote American literature at home and abroad as an expression of the success of American civilization. The vast increase in courses in American literature during the 1950s cannot be divorced from this political climate, though it must also be tied to the growth of the universities themselves in the wake of returning servicemen seeking education on the GI Bill.

Conditions in the fifties were thus ripe for the expansion of American literature in the curriculum. Nationalism provided an ideological motive, government money provided more students and faculty, and the New Criticism provided an approach that proved congenial to both the students and the literature. The argument that New Critical methods were especially suited to the large number of relatively uneducated students who entered college after the war has often been made. In Jane Tompkins's version of it,

> the emphasis on formal properties accommodated another feature of the academic scene in the 1950s, namely, the tripling of the college population, brought about by the GI Bill, postwar affluence, and an increasing demand for people with advanced degrees. The theory of literature that posited a unique interrelation of form and content justified close reading as an analytic technique that lent itself successfully to teaching literature on a mass scale.[25]

Students did not need deep historical background or wide reading in order to master New Critical methods. The New Criticism also may have made advanced courses in American literature easier to imagine and to carry out. While single-author courses in English literature go back to the nineteenth century, the authors —usually Chaucer, Spenser, Shakespeare, and Milton—were historically distant enough from the students to require, or seem to require, philological elaboration. No major American author needed the kind of glossing that English teachers borrowed from classicists until the New Criticism showed how all texts consisted of layers of meaning existing in the formal properties of the works. As we will see in the next chapters, however, it was not just the New Criticism that conceived of the text in this way. The entire project of criticism now sought meaning buried under the text's surface. Suddenly, it was easy to find enough to say about Hawthorne, Melville, or even Hemingway.

The survey remained the usual prerequisite for these new advanced courses, though given the New Criticism it may seem an anachronism. The survey doubtless did change during the 1950s from an emphasis on background and history to one on the text and its meaning, but literary history did not disappear entirely. Moreover, the character of the survey meant that no matter how little historical knowledge was presented, more than isolated readings of individual texts were being taught. The continuity that the survey willy-nilly imposes on its sequence could of course be explained in an infinite number of ways, but it is likely that most teachers would have relied on the conceptions of continuity proposed by prominent Americanists. Such continuity remained understood in terms of a succession of the periods Foerster had articulated (supplemented with a fifth period, the modern) but larger principles of connection were by the 1950s a major topic of scholarly discourse. Books such as Richard Chase's *The American Novel and its Tradition*, Roy Harvey Pearce's *The Continuity of American Poetry*, and R. W. B. Lewis's *The American Adam* doubtless bear a circular relation to the survey course. These scholars were young enough to have experienced the American survey as undergraduates and to have taught it as young professionals; their books appeared at a time when they would have immediately fed other instructors' hunger for themes that tie

American works together. It would be a mistake, then, to assume that the prevalence of New Critical reading strategies deprived American literature courses of the 1950s and 1960s of their nationalist content and mission. Rather, such content simply shifted to a new locus: the myths, symbols, and other structures of meaning that works shared. History didn't so much disappear as recede into the text as literary material, while continuing to remain outside it as chronology.

The anthology remained the basic tool of the survey course, and in its conception the anthology changed remarkably little between the 1920s and the 1960s, when anthologies continue to be based on the same patterns we saw in Foerster (Bibb, 433). While a few of the more historically oriented anthologies remained, they represented a tiny fraction of the nearly 50 in print in 1964 (Bibb, 14). These anthologies in the main differ little from each other, presenting pretty much the same works by the same major and minor writers. In general, however, most anthologies contained fewer authors from the nineteenth and early twentieth centuries than did their predecessors of the 1920s and 1930s. Jane Tompkins has described these changes in considerable detail, though her choice of Perry Miller's *Major Writers of America* (1962) to demonstrate the narrowing of the American canon is somewhat misleading (*Sensational Designs*, 186–201). As Tompkins acknowledges, Miller's text is typical of one of three types of anthology, but she does not indicate that this type, which excluded all minor writers, was not the most popular. More typical of the majority of anthologies was the leading text from the late 1950s through the 1970s, Bradley, Beatty, and Long's *The American Tradition in Literature* (*ATL*, first edition, 1957). In its first two editions this text does include "Negro Songs" and "Cowboy Ballads" along with Mary Wilkins Freeman, O. Henry, and William James, all of which will disappear in later editions, though Freeman will come back. However, the picture of American literature is radically different in this book than it was in anthologies of the 1920s. In 1957, there were 89 authors included in *ATL*, but 28 of these are writers of more recent birth than any included in the first editions of Pattee or Foerster, leaving 61 authors to represent a period the earlier anthologists had taken 117 and 96 to cover. By the third edition of *ATL* (1967), this number had been reduced to 47, a mere 10 more than the authors the NCTE had found most frequently taught just after the war. One conclusion that could be drawn from these numbers is that anthologies became increasingly reflective of what actually went on in the classroom. Nevertheless, insofar as the contents of anthologies are some kind of recommendation about what should be taught, Tompkins's point that considerable diversity of race, gender, and class was lost in 1950s and 1960s anthologies remains persuasive.[26]

We should wonder that as American literature became the subject of more courses, fewer authors were taught. But if one considers the ideology of nationalism that demanded that America understand itself as a unified people, rather than a society of different classes, races, and genders, then such narrowing makes perfect sense. It also makes sense if we understand English literature as the model for the American canon. The more American literature came to resemble English literature, the more it could be taught as having its own masters and masterpieces, the larger the role it could have in English departments. During the 1950s and 1960s, American literature came to make up more of the English curriculum than at any previous time. This is especially true if we consider not just the number of courses but their popularity. During this period courses in American literature attracted students in much larger numbers than previously, such that enrollments in American literature came to rival those in English despite the relatively smaller number of American offerings. This is a strong indication of the success of Americanists in creating American civilization.

Graduate Education and American Studies

If the American literature survey had become an established course in the undergraduate English curriculum by the late 1930s, there is no such obvious change in the graduate curriculum that might mark American literature's recognition. To be sure, there were increasing numbers of Ph.D.s on American topics. In 1946, there were 88 students pursuing the Ph.D. in American literature compared to 146 seeking the degree in English literature (*ALCC*, 31). That nearly 38 percent of doctoral students in English were writing dissertations in American literature, an area often remote from most coursework, bears strong witness to the cultural and disciplinary prestige of the subject. In the 1940s, there were also more American courses offered at the graduate level. But college catalogues suggest that such courses were still understood as marginal to the doctoral degree, which remained patterned on the model that emerged from the philologically based discipline of the turn of the century. Anglo-Saxon and a course in the history of the language were still required. Standard courses continued to reflect the periods of English literature, with an American course or two added to these. In other words, in English department graduate training, American literature had yet to attain even full subdisciplinary status.

As we noted earlier, the ALG had discussed in the late 1920s the idea of a separate doctorate in American literature but had decided against promoting the idea. There would never be a separate doctorate in American literature, though by the 1960s some institutions permitted "concentrations" in this field that allowed students to avoid most British literature and to omit Anglo-Saxon and Middle English entirely. The reason for the glacial pace at which this change occurred was the commitment of most English department faculty to a disciplinary object of which American literature could only be a minor element. While the proportion of Americanists in English departments slowly increased, the organization of the discipline's specialties meant that there would be more British specialists needed for coverage. In the 1930s, however, a solution to the disciplinary limitations of English departments was invented: the interdepartmental and interdisciplinary program in American civilization. There is some argument about where the first of these programs began. While Yale is known to have awarded the first Ph.D. in 1933, for a dissertation on the American cult of success, Harvard claims to have established "the first formal degree-granting program in 1937."[27] George Washington University, the University of Chicago, and several other institutions also offered graduate work in American civilization prior to 1940. Some undergraduate programs began in the 1930s as well, but, as noted earlier, the war produced enormous growth in their numbers, and it had the same effect on graduate programs. As of the academic year 1946–47, there were at least

15 institutions offering graduate work in American civilization, 13 of which had Ph.D. programs. Over the next twenty years the growth would continue, so that by 1968 there would be more than 100 institutions offering graduate and/or undergraduate programs in American Studies, as it would by then be known.

My focus here will be on the early programs. I will reserve comment on the scholarship produced by students in these programs until chapter 9, when we will see how important they were in the process of creating American civilization out of American literature. Here our concern is with creating American civilization in the more prosaic sense of program building. Nevertheless, the choice of "American civilization" as the most common early name for such programs is significant. As I have suggested, "civilization" is an honorific term, the applicability of which to American life had been debated since the turn of the century. In choosing this name, scholars were identifying America both with enlightened and progressive development and with an achieved state that might be defined as having produced "culture" in the Arnoldian sense. Both identifications might be conceived as tendentious responses to those who doubted the existence of civilization in the United States. To study American civilization was thus to study "culture" in the Arnoldian sense, but also to study the progressive development of the society that produced that culture. The name thus entails the two often conflicting impulses that characterized the movement throughout much of its life: to take the whole of American life as the object of study, but to privilege the products of that experience that are most distinctive. The latter quality might be found in economic conditions (e.g., affluence), a political system (i.e., democracy), or the national character (e.g., individualism), but it could just as easily—perhaps more easily—be discovered in aesthetic achievements, the most impressive of which were literary.

It is perhaps not surprising, then, that literary Americanists dominate the early graduate programs in American civilization. It is true that these programs were mainly interdepartmental, and that the most active departments included history as well as English. But perhaps because historians and social scientists were less in need of an extradepartmental affiliation—since their disciplines did not, like English, define themselves in terms of another national culture—American civilization programs tended to be more often staffed by literature professors and to produce dissertations on literary topics.[28] Many of the leading programs were started by ALG stalwarts, including Stanley Williams (Yale), Robert Spiller (Pennsylvania), Willard Thorp (Princeton, undergraduate only), Kenneth Murdoch, Howard Jones, and Perry Miller (Harvard), Randall Stewart (Brown), William Charvat (Ohio State), and Tremaine McDowell (Minnesota). Since all of these scholars were trained as literary *historians*, one can understand why they would have been interested in pursuing American civilization beyond its purely literary manifestations. Yet it is a bit unusual that individuals so recently involved in the creation of one new field should seek to found yet another. Clearly many Americanists, even some of those most traditional in their scholarship, remained dissatisfied with the position of American literature within English departments.

Most American civilization programs built their curricula as a variation on the "synthetic approach," in which a student majored in a traditional department and took minors in two or more others, emphasizing American aspects in each field.[29] Administratively, the programs were "under the jurisdiction of committees, deans, and special advisers," though in a few institutions a single department had control; some programs offered courses representing the cooperative efforts of two or more departments (*ALCC*, 33). Many of the programs specified requirements in representing a wide range of disciplines. Brown, for example, listed "History of American Economic Life," "American History to 1789," "American Political Theory," "Studies in American Literature," and a cooperatively conducted seminar in American civilization (*ALCC*, 35). Most Ph.D. programs were less specific in their requirements, allowing individual students more freedom to develop their own combinations of disciplines and courses.

The Harvard program, the History of American Civilization, is widely regarded as having set the direction for the American studies movement, its faculty, and the doctoral students producing the work that came to define the new field.[30] In addition to Jones, Miller, and Murdoch, Harvard's program included F. O. Matthiessen and Bernard DeVoto, as well as philosopher Ralph Barton Perry. Of the major contributing faculty then, there were four literary scholars, one novelist and literary critic turned social historian (DeVoto), and one philosopher. During the first years of the program, Miller's *The New England Mind: The Seventeenth Century* and Matthiessen's *American Renaissance* were published. Though these books were conceived well before the program began and thus cannot be considered results of its formation, they were to become the "exemplars" of American Studies, and indispensable works in American literary studies generally. Harvard's American Civilization students during its first decade included Henry Nash Smith, Daniel Aaron, Edmund S. Morgan, and Richard Dorson, while Leo Marx arrived somewhat later, finishing his degree in 1950. Smith and Marx both went to the University of Minnesota, which became the next major center of American Studies scholarship. Harvard thus not only founded the scholarship of American Studies, but was the spring of an academic genealogy that would dominate the field until the early 1970s.

It is important to try to assess the impact of graduate programs in American Studies on American literature in the academy. Such programs produced some of the most important studies of American literature to appear between 1950 and 1965. Furthermore, through the founding of the American Studies Association and its journal, *American Quarterly*, they encouraged the production of similar kinds of scholarship by those who trained in, and taught in, traditional departments. Wise has described this scholarship as being produced under a paradigm he calls the "intellectual history synthesis," but that designation is misleading, as it assumes that the scholars are historians rather than critics. Wise, mistakenly in my view, regards Miller as the most important founder of American Studies; it is Miller who used the phrase "the New England mind" in the titles of his two most important books. Miller was an intellectual historian, and he was concerned to portray the content of the explicitly intellectual labor of Puritan theologians, divines, and statesmen. Few other leading figures in American Studies adopted this strategy.

The typical American Studies project, rather, is a hermeneutics of suspicion that seeks to get beneath the surface of the text to its symbolic or mythic pattern of significance. As we will see, this makes American Studies scholarship of a piece with the literary criticism produced in English departments at the same time. What distinguished work in American Studies was not its method or theory but the texts on which it worked. What students in American Studies did that their counterparts in traditional English departments generally did not do was read subliterary or nonliterary texts, not as historical evidence or artifacts, but as if they were in need of the special interpretive strategies normally reserved for literature. Thus Henry Nash Smith studied dime novels, Richard Dorson, popular tales and legends, and Alan Trachtenberg, the Brooklyn Bridge. Furthermore, at a time when the dominant theory of literature, New Criticism, insisted on isolating the literary text as criticism's only proper concern, American Studies took as its object American culture. It thus continued to assume the general historical relationships that had always been assumed by literary historians. Nevertheless, history played a subsidiary role to interpretation of individual texts in the most familiar works of American Studies.

But American civilization programs and the American Studies movement that they spawned did not radically transform the academic field of American literature. Rather, they contributed to the course of development that the field was already bound to take. How could it be otherwise when American civilization emerged mainly from literary studies with a subject matter but no research program? If American Studies scholars sometimes studied things English departments rejected, they much more often studied the same texts that preoccupied those departments. When in the late 1960s and 1970s social scientists began to assert their opposition to the dominant scholarship in American Studies, they could justly point to the assumption of literary scholars in the field of the "privileged position" of "great" literature in understanding the culture as a whole.[31] American Studies scholars and teachers placed this literature in a larger context than their New Critical counterparts, but their focus remained largely on the literature.

Moreover, insofar as American Studies scholarship did differ from typical work in English, such innovations had relatively little effect on American literature as a field. Why was the impact of these innovations so muted? For one thing, although the discipline of English and the university structure as a whole have welcomed innovations, they have tended to so isolate them that their effects on disciplinary knowledge have largely been nullified. Gerald Graff has argued that this "patterned isolation" of new approaches and objects of study has allowed English departments to incorporate heterodox materials and methods without reconceiving or even reexamining the whole.[32] Even when American literature was studied apart from English in programs of American Studies, the structure of the university helped established disciplines prevent the reorganization of knowledge. Second, most American Studies scholars remained in English departments and shared the professional and disciplinary biases, especially the aestheticism, of other members. Finally, as we will see later, American Studies shared the cultural commitments and function that American literary scholars had held since the beginning of the field. They would contribute to the same conception of American civilization during the 1950s and 1960s. We will come back to American Studies in the last chapter, but we must first consider two other forces that shaped the way American civilization would be imagined both in and out of American Studies: the New Critics and the New York Intellectuals.

Part III
Creating American Civilization

7

The Triumph of the Aesthetic

The development of the American literature curriculum demonstrates a historical predilection toward an aesthetic conception of literature. Such a conception was already the dominant understanding of literature at the turn of the century, but the residual identification of literature with learning or knowledge remained influential. That broader conception of literature helped define the object of the *Cambridge History of American Literature*, Parrington's *Main Currents*, and many anthologies of American literature from Pattee's through Warfel, Gabriel, and Williams's *The American Mind* (1937). As we have seen, in the 1930s this broader conception continued to decline, and the object of study was increasingly defined aesthetically. Yet the practice of such study remained literary-historical. The final triumph of the aesthetic would be the transformation of that practice into criticism. But it would not be the same sort of criticism that had been practiced by the men of letters, the literary radicals, or the literary journalists. Instead of being explicitly political or at least didactic, criticism would now be disciplined and would appear to be disinterested. In fact, however, criticism in the academy would be covertly conservative, its conservatism being located in the very terms and themes by which texts were read.

New Criticism and the Revolution in Academic Practice

In the last chapter we noted the powerful impact of Brooks and Warren's *Understanding Poetry*, which provided a system by which close reading could be taught. But William Cain points to a paradox in the history of the New Criticism. While the New Critics are correctly understood to have developed and disseminated the "close reading" of literary texts, the leading New Critics, including T. S. Eliot, Allen Tate, and John Crowe Ranson, did relatively little close reading. Cain asserts, "the New Critics are significant less for the critical practice they sometimes did . . . than for the assumptions about criticism and literary study that they propagated and popularized."[1] In other words, Cain is arguing that the New Critics are most significant as theorists. In terms of the history of criticism, Cain is certainly right, especially in the long run. But the impact of New Critical theory was not felt most significantly as a contribution to a theoretical conversation. Such a conversation did exist, and the New Critics certainly gave it new life. But although the practice of theory became more important, it did not become a major element of the discipline of English during the 1940s or 1950s when the New Critics' influence was at its peak. The major impact of that influence was establishing the practice of literary criticism in English departments. Prior to World War I, English departments practiced literary history; by the middle 1950s, the dominant practice had become close reading.

This book is not a history of criticism or literary theory, and thus my treatment of the New Criticism will not be focused on its major theoretical statements. That the practice of close reading follows from that theory cannot be denied. And, as I will argue in the next chapter, the New Criticism reflects a fundamental theoretical shift from positivism to hermeneutics. But the New Critics did not argue for this epistemological transformation, which occurred more as the result of the invention of the techniques of close reading than of specific theoretical arguments. Such techniques were what triumphed within English departments, as criticism came to displace historical scholarship as the dominant academic practice. In the context of the English department, the value of New Critical theory was not that it taught critics how to read but that it could be used to defend the practice of close reading against competing theories and practices. Perhaps more to the point, New Critical theory was a defense of *criticism*, just as close reading was the practice of criticism. What the history of criticism misses by treating literary history as one among many critical schools is precisely the radical shift in practice that occurred in English departments. As we have seen, few scholars within the discipline of English practiced criticism. It was only after World War II that what is often described as the critical revolution of the 1930s had a major impact in the academy.

The shift in English from literary history to criticism deserves to be considered as a revolution, a paradigm shift in which one form of "normal science" or puzzle solving replaces another.[2] Yet Kuhn's account of scientific revolutions does not fit in all its details. For one thing, literary history was never banished from English. That is an important exception, because it indicates that the earlier practice was not discredited. The New Criticism did not win by demonstrating the shortcomings of the dominant practice; it did not need to offer such a critique because such shortcomings were widely perceived. As we have noted, already in the early 1930s literary historians were complaining that their fifty-year-old project had not achieved its goals. This dissatisfaction, however, cannot by itself explain why twenty years later English was willing to give up not only the old methods but the old goals as well. So great is the change that I am not sure it is entirely explicable; in fact, it may represent a fundamental epistemic rupture such as those Foucault describes in *The Order of Things*. To note that the shift from positivism to hermeneutics in literary studies could be seen as part of a larger epistemic change in which various representational media—language, symbols, signs, myths—replace simple reference in the constitution of knowledge and experience is not to explain an event in literary studies, but merely to note that it may be part of a larger, still unexplained event. Nevertheless, we can at least attempt to describe the conditions under which the changes in literary studies occurred.

Perhaps the most important of these conditions is that English had never disowned criticism. As we noted earlier, English departments even in major research universities continued to include a few liberal culturists who wrote criticism rather than scholarly articles. Moreover, we saw that the entire edifice of literary research assumed a set of critical judgments that scholarship continued to ritually reaffirm. English studies didn't deny the importance of criticism, and its habitual dependence on received critical judgment is reflected in the negative reaction to Parrington's lack of appreciation for Poe or James. As we have seen, aesthetically oriented anthologies dominated the textbook market. But English regarded criticism as preliminary to scholarship and outside of its own scientific activity. Hubbell might have been speaking for the unconscious of the discipline when he urged a "remarriage of scholarship and criticism" and asserted, "It would be better, however, to make every course we offer to a large degree a course in criticism. We can encourage our students to form their own estimates and form them intelligently, and we can cease handing out to them ready-made critical opinions." But if research and criticism should always go together, criticism is also the "most complicated of intellectual operations."[3] It was this difficulty that kept research and criticism divorced, since positivism demanded a degree of certainty critics could not supply. Finally, there were, even prior to the rise of the New Criticism, a few genuine "scholar-critics." Among Americanists the most important of these was none other than Norman Foerster. As we have seen, Foerster's critical work did not always endear him to his colleagues, but neither did it disqualify him from a leadership role in the subdiscipline. In retrospect, we can see that it was Foerster's willingness to be a critic that enabled him to redefine the field of American literature. Thus even while the discipline of English did not practice criticism, criticism remained a very present absence and, among some members of the field, a repressed desire.

How did that repression come to be lifted? Two simultaneous developments are at work here. One is a change in the social situation of the literary that allowed—or forced—criticism to become increasingly academic. The other consists in the specific intellectual innovations that the New Criticism entailed, including the paradoxical combination of a criticism that claimed to be scientific together with the rejection of science as the model for all knowledge.

What enabled the academicization of criticism was the fragmentation of the literary. If in the 1920s the literary came to be represented by the literally eccentric figure of Mencken, during the 1930s it lacked any single representative figure. To understand this change we need to look at the explosion of mass media during the two decades. During the 1920s, the circulations of major daily newspapers grew exponentially. The development of wire services helped create the first consistent national news culture. Perhaps more important, radio and newsreels provided alternative sources of news and information. In a certain sense, the popular conception of news or current events did not exist much earlier than this period. Previously, only war or the threat of it was important enough to push local matters into the background. But with the content of "news" being increasingly determined by national organizations, all kinds of "events" could become news everywhere. The books that Frederick Lewis Allen wrote about the 1920s, 1930s, and 1940s could not have been written about the 1910s because the majority of readers would not have recognized the events out of which Allen manufactures nostalgia.

The literary was not much directly affected by these changes, although one effect they did have was the invention of the literary star. During the late nineteenth century, Howells had enormous cultural influence, but he had reached this status as a result of a long career of literary activity. Mark Twain, on the other hand, is a precursor of the literary stars; he attained great celebrity largely as a result of tireless self-promotion. But the stars of the 1920s and 1930s, preeminently F. Scott Fitzgerald and Ernest Hemingway, were creatures of the media. In fact, authors such as these came to completely displace the older conception of the author as a man of learning. Having extraordinary experiences was now understood to be the most important training for authorship. The status of these new literary stars was not unrelated to the judgments of critics, but it was far less dependent upon such judgments than earlier authorial status had been. Hemingway is the more important figure here, since he combined critical approval with popular adulation—but the latter came to overwhelm the former. Hemingway's personality guaranteed interest in his books no matter what the critics said about them, and that personality was made available in media other than books to vast numbers who never read them. At the same time as celebrity writers like Hemingway came to define the popular image of the literary, the literary marketplace came to be increasingly dominated by what were thought to be subliterary forms. If *Gone With the Wind* was in most respects a typical historical romance of the sort that had been leading best-seller lists off and on since the

1880s, the power of the mass media turned it into a cultural event of major proportions. Even before the movie appeared, the book was the largest-selling novel in American history.

But we cannot forget the indirect influence of nonliterary media—including newspapers, the new photo magazines such as *Life*, sound films, and radio—on the literary. Prior to the rise of these media, the literary was the dominant form of cultural communication. Even after the rise of the mass market magazine, serious discussion of cultural and political issues continued to be conducted in literary magazines. Fiction and the theater were the major forms of representational entertainment; working-class diversions, such as vaudeville or the nickelodeons, whatever their social significance, did not compete with the literary for cultural influence. The new media did not challenge the cultural status of the literary, but they did mitigate its influence. For one thing, the creation of new personalities by these media diluted the celebrity of literary figures. Besides writers there were now movie stars, filmmakers, newspaper columnists, radio announcers, and magazine photographers. The movies, radio, and the picture magazines also came to take over some of the functions of the literary. All of them represent new means of telling fictional and nonfictional stories. They made these stories available to audiences far larger than the largest-selling author had ever reached. Each of these factors reduced the economic significance of the literary. As a sort of compensation, however, the value of the literary as cultural capital may have actually increased as it came to be identified as the property of an elite. Paradoxically, the literary grew in status as it declined in economic value and political clout. This paradoxical condition made the university the most viable of the institutional formations competing to control the literary.

Criticism may have been the biggest loser in the decline of the literary as a cultural force. Where criticism had been perhaps the most important discourse of the leading magazines, it was increasingly relegated to book reviews in newspapers and to periodicals on the margins of the mainstream print media. It is the marginal condition of criticism in the 1930s that allowed it to be dominated by groups to the right and left of mainstream American politics.[4] Politically marginal groups and individuals had relatively little influence in other media. The mainstream press and the film industry were closed to them, while the sectarian press provided only limited public access. Literary criticism was a discourse that was available to be captured by those on the margins, and it was worth capturing because of the cultural capital it continued to carry.

As a result, criticism during the 1930s became much more divided than it had been in the 1920s. During the earlier decade, critics seemed to fall into more or less conservative or liberal camps, with the New Humanists, Sherman, and surviving men of letters representing the former, while Mencken, the literary radicals, and newcomers such as Edmund Wilson constituted the latter. There were two new forces that would emerge in the criticism of the 1930s to join a variety of others left over from the 1920s. The most successful of these during the 1930s was Marxist criticism, the success of which is explained by the social and political conditions of the Great Depression. We will look at that criticism more carefully in the next chapter. At the same time as the rise of a newly influential left criticism, there also emerged a new critical force on the right. The New Humanists had represented the right wing of literary culture since before World War I, and we have seen that they remained influential enough in 1930 to produce a collection, *Humanism and America*, that yielded a volume in response, *The Critique of Humanism*. The more important 1930 volume for the future of criticism was *I'll Take My Stand*, a manifesto of twelve Southern Agrarians, four of whom were formerly associated with *The Fugitive*, the literary magazine that has been called the "embryo" of the New Critical movement.[5]

The formation of *The Fugitive* has much in common with the creation of little magazines that sprang up everywhere in the 1910s and 1920s. Whatever their very real differences in style and intent, these little magazines reflect the cultural marginalization of literature, especially poetry. *The Fugitive* was neither avant-gardist, nor politically engaged, nor even alienated as were the magazines of Greenwich Village intellectuals. Although it was supported by and centered at Vanderbilt University, the magazine was clearly the work of individuals who styled themselves not as professional academics but as "amateurs writing for the fun of it and addressing their poems to some ideal citizen of Nashville like themselves (Vanderbilt graduate, classicist, gentleman, admirer of nineteenth-century English verse)."[6] Of course, *The Fugitive* was in fact almost as marginal to the culture of Nashville as it was to the culture of America. Its chief literary success may safely be said to be the nurturing of writers who would publish their most important work later. Among their writings would be not only the poetry and fiction of Allen Tate, John Crowe Ransom, and Robert Penn Warren, but also Agrarian essays, and some of the most influential literary criticism and theory of the twentieth century.

The Agrarianism represented by *I'll Take My Stand* marked the metamorphosis of the Fugitives from literary amateurs into full-fledged intellectuals. Ransom actually stopped writing poetry about this time and would not return to it until his retirement from Kenyon College in the 1960s. Tate, Warren, and Donald Davidson continued to write imaginative works, but in their contributions to Agrarianism they participated in a right-wing version of the same kind of general criticism of society that Northern intellectuals typically produced from the left. While the Agrarians in the main continued to be associated with Vanderbilt, their work was no more the product of academic culture than was *The Fugitive*. Their Agrarianism garnered the Fugitives their first significant attention in national literary culture, even though such attention was largely negative. It was their playing the role of general intellectuals that gave these men the position from which their call for a new literary criticism could be heard. When it came, that call would reflect another metamorphosis, from intellectual to professor, but the former stage was necessary to the mission that would be undertaken in the latter.

Thus in spite of the fact that by the time New Criticism got its name in the early 1940s, the New Critics had left Agrarianism behind, the two movements are theoretically linked. The underlying assumptions of Agrarianism, best articulated in Ransom's *God Without Thunder*, are consistent with the assumptions of the New Criticism.[7] Like many right-wing ideologies, including the New Humanism, Agrarianism idealized the past, inventing a highly romanticized image of the South destroyed by the Civil War.[8] Like the New Humanism, Agrarianism was a politics of culture, but the Twelve Southerners offered a much more far-reaching political and economic alternative in Agrarianism. Their goal was to reinforce the "ancient integrity" of agriculturally based communities of the South, "the chief instance of the stationary European principle of culture in America, . . . as centers of resistence to an all-but-devouring industrialism."[9] The political force of Agrarianism, however, was nil even in the South, and its impact was therefore ironically more restricted to literature than was New Humanism's. That impact occurred mainly later in the form of the New Criticism. Because of this, the specific economic solutions proposed by the Agrarian group are its least significant feature. Much more important are the general right-wing assumptions that the Agrarians shared with New Humanists and other cultural conservatives —the two positions have much in common. Both movements regarded science as the enemy, and its unchecked expansion in industry as the chief bane of modern life. Both movements were aristocratic or royalist, rather than democratic; they took for granted the natural inequality of different races, cultures, and classes. But while the New Humanists understood themselves to represent the best of American culture, the Agrarians were willing to think of themselves as outside of it. They spoke from the economic and cultural periphery, identifying themselves with an internal colony, the South. Where the New Humanists saw their chief enemy in Rousseauian liberalism, the Agrarians identified their primary opponent as Marxism. Several of the contributors wanted to title *I'll Take My Stand* "A Tract Against Communism." Just as the New Humanists saw liberalism as a pervasive force in American civilization, communism to the Agrarians was not an oppositional political movement but the telos of industrial civilization itself. Neither movement was anticapitalist, but opposed only what they regarded as its contemporary excesses. Both were ultimately individualists, even though each regarded order as the central problem of modern culture.

These connections between Agrarianism and the New Humanism are frequently overlooked because the New Critics and the New Humanists differed radically in their literary criticism and theory, and the two movements are therefore usually regarded as antithetical to one another. The standard explanation is that "the New Critics did not lose interest in politics and theology, but rather, following the early Eliot, tried to compartmentalize their concerns and separate their literary criticism from their analysis of American life."[10] This is an accurate reflection of New Critical theory, but such a separation is impossible to maintain in practice.

So even in criticism there are some important continuities between the New Humanists and New Critics. Both movements were fundamentally moralistic in their criticism, though the application of their moralism differed. The New Humanists were puritanical in their objection to literature that did not represent the correct influence on society. Almost all modern literature fell under this condemnation. The New Critics, on the other hand, saw morality as a drama played out in literature, and thus did not treat literature as an instrument of moral intervention. But both groups accepted the traditional Christian view of human evil and thus rejected the assumption common to both liberals and Marxists that human nature could be improved given the right social conditions. The assumption of human depravity is as important a distinguishing feature of New Critical practice as the assumption of textual autonomy that it to some extent mitigates. New Critical articles don't just identify formal features; they interpret texts in terms of the moral categories that the critic assumes to be the ultimate sources of meaning. As Ransom acknowledges in his insistence on mimesis, the New Criticism never treated the text as a purely formal system.[11] The poem represented the world, but not a particular historical or social world, since the truth of literature transcended those conditions. Rather literature represented precisely the conservative picture of a world torn between good and evil, a condition beyond social remedy. The organically related components of literary works—theme, plot, character—became in New Critical analysis the means by which this drama was played out.

The New Critics thus picked up the banner of the intellectual right, carried it into the universities, and raised it over their English departments. How did the New Critics succeed where the New Humanists had failed? In the first place, they conducted an organized campaign to make criticism an academic enterprise. Ransom's essay, "Criticism, Inc.," proposed an explicit strategy for professionalizing criticism:

> It is from the professors . . . of English . . . that I should hope eventually for the erection of intelligent standards of criticism. It is their business. Criticism must become more scientific, or precise and systematic, and this means that it must be developed by the collective and sustained effort of learned

persons—which means that its proper seat is in the university.[12]

But Ransom and the New Critics did more than merely argue this course of action. They pursued it vigorously using a variety of means. Ransom himself made Kenyon College, where he was appointed professor of English in 1939, a center from which the movement could be directed and built. In addition to *The Kenyon Review*, which Ransom founded and which was the movement's most important theoretical organ, there were also "The Kenyon Review Fellowships" and "The Kenyon School of English," which trained current and future professors for work as critics (Fekete, 87).

The *Kenyon Review* was only the most prominent of the journals that were instrumental in furthering the New Critical agenda. Others included *Hound and Horn*, the *Southern Review*, the *Sewanee Review*, and the *Hudson Review*. These journals constituted an alternative medium for professional publication. As we have seen, scholars had contributed to literary quarterlies all along, but by the late 1940s, the New Critics had made the journals they controlled a rival market to *PMLA*, *ELH*, and *Modern Philology*. The New Critical journals were organs of professional academic criticism. Even more important, as I have already argued, was the appearance in 1938 of *Understanding Poetry*, and the subsequent anthologies by Brooks with Warren and other collaborators that revolutionized the teaching of literature.

The New Critics' campaign could not have succeeded, however, had the practice they advocated not been well suited to the demands of the academy. Victory in the English departments came at the price of the specific content of the Agrarian agenda. Ransom's and Tate's plan to "found criticism" in the university marked an explicit abandonment of the role of the humanist intellectual, and adoption of the more limited one of the literary specialist.[13] By the time it came to be called "the New Criticism," the movement had lost its overt political character. If it had retained an overt politics, its chances of succeeding in English departments would have been slight. The New Criticism transformed the practice of English from historical scholarship to criticism because it made criticism seem to be empirical and disinterested. New Critical theory claimed that "the formal qualities of a poem are the focus of the specifically critical judgment because they partake of an objectivity that the subject matter, abstracted from the form, wholly lacks."[14] This claim for the objectivity of form allowed for the possibility of an empiricist criticism: "The object is separated from the categorical modes of its appropriation, and this independence of the object serves as the basis for a thoroughgoing empiricism that becomes most explicit in New Critical practice" (Fekete, 77). Criticism had heretofore been marginalized in the university because its claims could not be distinguished from the interests of the critic. The theory of the poem as an autonomous object and the practice of showing how the object worked as an organic whole made criticism look like a kind of science. That is, it became a form of knowledge production that could fit the disciplinary model of the university.

We might say that earlier critical practices, both left and right, could not be disciplined—could not become a discipline—because they could yield but a finite set of statements. A critic's job boiled down to judging whether the work served the interests that literature ought to serve. Once the work became not a medium of communication but a system of meanings and formal structures, then it became capable of sustaining an infinite number of statements. Knowledge could be compiled about the form of a work just as it had been compiled about its history. To a limited extent, of course, such a possibility had long been recognized within English departments. Articles describing rhyme and meter were a consistent if minor element of literary scholarship. By treating literary works as systems or structures of meaning, the New Criticism was able to make the whole work seem amenable to formal study. It became an object because it was no longer itself interested. Great literature was ironic, ambivalent, dualistic, ambiguous, multidimensional, and so on. It no longer did anything in the world except to be literature in this sense, and yet, because literary works were systems of meaning, the critic's politics or theology could not be excluded. This is true not merely because the exclusion of politics is a politics, but because the structure of a work still had to be construed, and the New Criticism tended to construe it in terms of the oppositions that defined the conservative point of view. But because the structure was understood to be intrinsic, the critic's reading nevertheless appeared disinterested.

Having insisted upon a specific political valence in the New Criticism, I do not want to leave the impression that every professor who came to use New Critical methods did so in awareness of—let alone in sympathy with—the political tendencies they embodied. While genuine left criticism is very rare in the 1950s, some left-leaning critics such as Maxwell Geismar did adopt New Critical reading strategies.[15] More important, the pedagogical program of *Understanding Poetry* was seen by many as a liberation from the oppressive teaching practices typical of literary history. New Critical methods allowed students to quickly develop the competence to have something to say about literary works, and thereby made the discussion class a real alternative to the lecture. Since those methods were perceived to be disinterested and formalist, they doubtless were adopted by many teachers who did not understand their political implications. Moreover, some teachers may well have substituted left-wing categories of experience for those that the New Criticism assumed. Yet we must regard such modifications as a subversion of the New Critical project, a subversion that, even if it may have succeeded in the long run, failed to produce a significant impact during the 1950s.

Since the New Criticism had disguised its politics, most teachers and students probably perceived it as treating literature apolitically. The usual reading of the New Critical transformation is that it made criticism a purely aesthetic enterprise. That is, after all, what New Critical theory often asserted. As Ransom put it, "the business of the literary critic is exclusively with an esthetic criticism."[16] Such a theory doubtless did have a significant impact on criticism, since it had never been purely aesthetic in its concerns. Criticism, however, was practiced outside of the university. Inside the university aesthetic considerations had long governed the character of the literary object, even if such considerations were not the concern of most literary scholarship. As we saw in our discussion of teaching American literature, aesthetically oriented anthologies prevailed over socially oriented ones even before the New Critical program was announced. The New Critical conception of literature did not so much change the academic conception of that object as it insisted on its essential character. Furthermore, the New Critics claimed for the aesthetic a far greater importance than earlier theories had granted it. Thus they felt free to grant literature virtually scriptural status. Tate's claim that "literature is the complete knowledge of man's experience" is more extreme than most New Critical statements on this point, but it reflects the spirit of the movement.[17] Such sentiments were doubtless heartening to English professors who found the boundaries of their field increasingly besieged by the social sciences. And, since the aesthetic conception of literature was the most widely shared, reducing literature to the aesthetic meant giving up only what properly belonged elsewhere anyway. The New Criticism marked the triumph of the aesthetic, but the victory was the culmination of forces long at work in literary study.

But if the New Criticism only reinforced an older notion of literature as an aesthetic object, it introduced the notion of literature as an object of interpretation. Criticism may have entered the university under the sign of objectivity and empiricism, but the theoretical problems that were raised in the process remain with us today. The uncontested positivism of the previous half-century came to be undermined from within. Although the New Critics would not have admitted it, their theories were as much contributions to hermeneutics as to aesthetics, and New Critical practice came to have interpretation rather than judgment as its chief goal. The effect of the paradigm shift in English departments was not only a radical change in practice but perhaps an even more radical break in epistemology.

That break, even though it was largely misrecognized, produced a need for literary theory. As we have seen, there had been some work on questions of theory almost from the start of English as a discipline in the 1880s, but theory was until the middle part of this century a very minor discourse. Theory was unnecessary because literary study shared assumptions about knowledge and language with the rest of the university. Literary historical scholarship had neither to evaluate nor to interpret literary texts, but merely to establish facts about them. Literary theory became important when this conception of literary study came under attack. Thus it was the New Critics who introduced literary theory into the American academy. They did so in order to justify criticism as a distinct method of study that did not need to be governed by positivism. Since they could not invent a discourse out of whole cloth, they borrowed from the primary discourse opposed to positivism in the Western university, philosophical idealism, a borrowing most clearly reflected in John Crowe Ransom's call for an ontological criticism.[18] The impact of the writings of Ransom and his fellow Agrarians inspired a lively discussion of literary theoretical issues in journals such as the *Kenyon Review* and the *Partisan Review*.[19] The New Critical theory was codified in Wellek and Warren's *Theory of Literature*, a book that could not have been written without Wellek's background in phenomenology and linguistics. English departments began to offer graduate courses in literary theory.

Literary theory came to prominence in the 1940s because literary studies came to regard literature as a special form of language. To be understood, literary language had to be not merely read but interpreted. Hermeneutics, the theory of interpretation, arose out of philology in the eighteenth century to cope with those special instances where ordinary reading did not yield a clear meaning. In the New Critics' conception, all literature presented special problems of interpretation. Literary study under their influence became a hermeneutic enterprise, and it remains such today. Once the practice of interpretation, or close reading, became the standard one in English departments, the practice of literary theory lost its urgency, and it retreated to the marginal status it had previously held; English departments stopped offering courses in it. But the character of literary study had been permanently altered, and the issues that theorists had raised remained potentially relevant. The more recent turn to European theory was to be expected, not only because theory had continued to be discussed but also because American literary practice derived quite recently from European theory. We live today in a theoretical world that we have inherited from New Critics such as Ransom, Eliot, and Tate, and, as we will see, their contemporaries such as Philip Rahv, Trilling, Richard Chase, and William Barrett.

The success of New Criticism definitively marks the capture of the literary by the university. Criticism became an academic specialty because the literary institutions that once supported it could do so no longer. The 1930s represent the last decade of a vital criticism outside the university. After World War II, virtually all of the older critics who remained influential took academic positions, while younger critics now began their careers in academia. As we will see in the next chapter, the New York Intellectuals resisted complete identification with the university longer than the rest, but they too would succumb before the 1950s were out.

F. O. Matthiessen and a New Criticism of American Literature

The New Criticism, it has been alleged, exhibited an "almost total disregard of American literature" (Ruland, 281). While this assertion may seem overstated, it would be hard to contradict if we restricted it to American literature prior to Henry James and Emily Dickinson. The New Critics' antipathy to romanticism meant that they were unlikely to find much of interest in most nineteenth-century American writers. No earlier writers met their aesthetic standards, and neither did the realists and naturalists of the turn of the century. More important, perhaps, the New Critics were not much interested in national traditions. Only Tate, in *American Harvest*, seems to have offered a version of an American tradition. Strictly speaking, then, the New Critics had rather little impact on the premodern American canon. Their support for James and Dickinson was influential, but their disapproval of Emerson, for example, had no effect on his status within the subdiscipline. As I have just shown, the New Critics did much to change the study of literature in the academy from literary historical scholarship to criticism. Even here, however, it is important to recognize that the techniques of close reading that the New Critics helped to institutionalize were developed during the 1930s by critics other than the Agrarians. Of course, these critics owed much to T. S. Eliot and I. A. Richards, whose theory and criticism are usually regarded as foundational to the New Criticism. "What resulted from the joint influence of Eliot and Richards was a criticism that aimed to give the closest possible attention to the text at hand, to both the structure and texture of the language."[20] Among those influenced were Richards's student William Empson, left-leaning critics such as Edmund Wilson and Kenneth Burke, non-Agrarian conservatives R. P. Blackmur and Yvor

Winters, and a few literary historians, such as Austin Warren and Matthiessen himself. In Matthiessen's case, it can safely be asserted that Eliot's direct influence was more important than that of the Agrarians, since Matthiessen's criticism develops simultaneously with their own. Still, by the time Matthiessen came to write *American Renaissance*, he was practicing a style of criticism that had much in common with that of Ransom, Brooks, and Tate.

F. O. Matthiessen may have been the first person to apply a New Critical approach to the problem of an American literary tradition. Whether he was indeed the first, however, is less important than the fact that his attempt was the one that successfully recast that tradition. Matthiessen's importance in the history of the field is second to none, yet his real significance has often tended to get lost. Matthiessen is easily the single figure in the history of American literary scholarship who has been the subject of the most discussion. Much of this discussion concerns Matthiessen the man, his politics, his sexual orientation, his tragic suicide. An enormously influential teacher as well as critic, Matthiessen seems to have produced an unusual loyalty in students and readers alike. Such a powerful personality is likely to inspire strong opponents as well, and Matthiessen became first the butt of New York Intellectual attacks for being soft on Stalin and then, more recently, the symbol of the failure of American literary scholarship to reflect social struggle. Such treatment has provoked staunch defenses by his proponents, who call attention to the complexity of his conception of the human condition and to his credentials as a Christian socialist. It has been hard for many critics to separate Matthiessen the man from his work. Ruland, for example, claims that *American Renaissance* is "an articulation of the total man; it *is* F. O. Matthiessen, with all his compassion and all his commitment to the wide world around him" (231).

Regardless of whether Ruland's reading can be sustained, our interest in Matthiessen here does not concern the total man, or even the flesh-and-blood individual, part or whole. Like the other figures treated in this book, Matthiessen is for our purposes best considered a historical necessity, the sort of person whom the discipline would have to have invented had he not existed. In removing Matthiessen's personal life from consideration, however, his contribution to the discipline of American literature seems all the greater. I am not arguing that Matthiessen succeeded in keeping his politics and his criticism separate, but that the connections that are present are hidden, albeit, like the purloined letter, in plain sight. In order to accomplish this, the political had to become naturalized, to take on the coloring of the dominant. Cain makes Matthiessen a tragic lesson for those who would try to keep politics and criticism separate.[21] But however much we might agree with that lesson, it must be understood that if Matthiessen had not by and large kept overt politics out of his criticism, he could not have played the role he did in creating American civilization. On the other hand, I will argue that a covert conservatism exists in *American Renaissance*, a legacy of both the New Humanism and the New Criticism. Furthermore, *American Renaissance* is the place where a convincing theory of the unity and distinctiveness of American literature is first articulated, a significant political enunciation.

What is worth noting of Matthiessen the man is how slight his connection was to the organized activities of the discipline. His contributions to *American Literature* consisted of three book reviews. He was for most of his career not a member of the MLA and therefore did not participate in the ALG. Matthiessen complained that the MLA convention had too many papers, most of which were presented merely "to gain jobs or show off," and this sense of the profession led him frequently to use "academic" in a pejorative manner.[22] Though in many respects *American Renaissance* is a quintessentially academic work, its lack of citations may represent an explicit rejection of academic conventions. More important, Matthiessen's distance from the discipline certainly must have helped him to resist its demands and to write a book that would be the principal exemplar of a new disciplinary practice.

There is little dispute about Matthiessen's importance. The definitive statement of it was made in 1963 by Roy Harvey Pearce when he described the criticism of American literature after the appearance of *American Renaissance* as "post-Matthiessenian."[23] Matthiessen is the central figure in Ruland's narrative of rediscovery and he has been the subject of three book-length studies. No other academic Americanist, including Parrington, has received anywhere near this much attention. But if Matthiessen's importance is universally proclaimed, it has not been satisfactorily explained. Generally Matthiessen is credited with two achievements in *American Renaissance*: to have produced "the first study of American literature to apply New Critical analytic tools to American writing as a whole";[24] and to have established the canon of major American authors (Cain, 69). Both of these claims are partially true, but even that truth is not self-evident.

There has been considerable discussion of Matthiessen's relationship to the New Criticism, which is complicated by his stated political position, Christian socialism, and his explicit critique of the New Criticism in "The Responsibilities of the Critic" (1949), where he accuses the movement of having produced a "new scholasticism" (5). This has led various historians to assert Matthiessen's successful separation of New Critical method from any of the restrictions it may have imposed on other critics. Ruland claims that Matthiessen mastered New Critical techniques but was not limited by New Critical theory, so that he became a "cultural historian" rather than a mere literary critic (230). Similarly Gunn asserts that the "new formal orientation that Eliot helped to introduce into modern American criticism . . . was intended primarily to correct certain abuses, and that its most able representatives used it primarily not to further theoretical speculation but rather to develop stricter methodological discipline and greater critical refinement. Such, at least, was its influence on F. O. Matthiessen."[25] Cain, on the other hand, clearly believes that the New Criticism had deleterious effects on Matthiessen, leading him to keep his politics and his criticism separated: "He is not a socialist cultural historian, but a socialist *and* a historian *and* a New Critic" (28). Unlike Ruland and Gunn, Cain admits that Matthiessen made "the formalist approach and method his central focus" and that "he persistently invoked and remained obeisant to New Critical, formalist principles" (41). Cain, I believe, is right as far as he goes, but in emphasizing formalism it is easy to overlook the covert political biases of the New Critical approach.

Cain agrees that Matthiessen was adept at close reading, but argues that he did not very often practice it. Yet, as we have seen, Cain also claims that the leading New Critics themselves did not often practice close reading. The explanation for this phenomenon is that none of these critics is adequately described as a pure formalist. All knew, even if they sometimes argued otherwise, that compelling criticism always moves beyond the particular text. For many of the New Critics, that "beyond" was the theory of criticism. Thus close readings by Ransom and Brooks usually turn out to be lessons about how to read or what good poetry is. The latter is, of course, a formalist question, but in answering it the New Critics had to make value judgments, and thus abandon in practice if not in theory the objectivity close reading claimed. If we compare Matthiessen's approach to earlier treatments of American literature, we do find far greater attention to texts. But it is less the quantity of close readings than the particular aesthetic on which those readings are based that sets *American Renaissance* apart. What Matthiessen took from the New Criticism was more than bare technique; just as important were modernist aesthetics, which enabled him to make a new case for the aesthetic achievement of his five authors, and an idealist theory of tradition, which allowed him to conceive of American literature as having a radically different kind of history than had Tyler, Wendell, or Parrington.

American Renaissance is not a discussion of American literature "as a whole" that these men would have recognized. Although there is an enormous range of reference to literature of other periods and detailed treatment of works by its five major subjects written at other times, the book explicitly focuses on only five years, 1850 to 1855. Not even the whole of the nineteenth-century romantic canon is treated, since Poe is absent. And yet *American Renaissance* does present itself as representing American literature as a whole, in the sense that it treats individual works and authors as organically related to each other and to a broader American culture. The point is that the character of the whole has changed. The "whole" is now the organically related elements of the tradition, rather than the positivist "whole" of all the facts about all the authors.

Matthiessen was most directly influenced, not by Tate, Ransom, or the other Agrarians, but by Richards and, especially, T. S. Eliot. Not only did Matthiessen learn how to read by studying these critics, he also learned many of his theoretical assumptions from them. Eliot's theory of tradition is an important component of Matthiessen's approach. The importance of "Tradition and the

Individual Talent" to Matthiessen is suggested by the fact that he begins *The Achievement of T. S. Eliot* by discussing it, even though the book is not directly about Eliot's criticism. He asserts that the essay has become as much a classic as Arnold's "The Study of Poetry," and that "Eliot's criticism has quietly accomplished a revolution" in the evaluation of English poetry.[26] In "Tradition and the Individual Talent," Eliot depicts the literary tradition as an ideal order of eternal objects. Floating above more mundane history, the tradition is nevertheless itself historical. New works alter the tradition as they become part of it.[27] This defined for Matthiessen the relations of the literary past and present:

> The first awareness for the critic should be the works of art of our own time. This applies even if he is not primarily a critic of modern literature. One of Eliot's observations which has proved most salutary is that of the inescapable interplay of past and present: that the past is not what is dead, but what is already living; and that the present is continually modifying the past, as the past conditions the present. ("Responsibilities," 6)

There may be no book more faithful to this principle than *American Renaissance*. Unlike most academic literary historians, Matthiessen moves effortlessly among great writers of all ages, from Dante, Spenser, Shakespeare, and Milton to Henry James, Thomas Mann, Eliot, James Joyce, D. H. Lawrence, and other moderns. It is a perfect representation of Eliot's notion of the contemporaneity of great literature. One significant effect of this is to canonize Emerson, Thoreau, Melville, Hawthorne, and Whitman by association. Another is to make a potentially synchronic study of five years of literary history into a description of an event in a vast narrative that is not told but simply assumed. That is not to say that Matthiessen neglects the actual context of his renaissance, but that context is largely represented by figures who are themselves not connected to any social, political, or economic system—or indeed, even to particular institutions or communities. The discussion of Horatio Greenough, for example, does not depend on his historical connection to Emerson or Thoreau (although such a connection may license the reference—Emerson mentions Greenough in *Nature* and recorded some passages of his in the journals). Rather, Greenough represents the democratic ideals that Matthiessen believes define American culture, and he articulated an aesthetic of "organic growth" that Matthiessen himself shares. Greenough is a minor but representative American who shares distinguishing traits with Emerson and other major figures. The illustrations are even less historically relevant. From the daguerreotype of shipbuilder Donald McKay that serves as the frontispiece to paintings by W. S. Mount and Thomas Eakins, the illustrations give the impression of a unified American aesthetic tradition floating like Eliot's literary one, above history.

Whatever his failure to realize a cultural whole, it is important to recognize that Matthiessen, like Eliot, was attempting such a realization. Although one can find statements in Eliot that imply as rigorous an isolation of the poem as any proposed by Tate or Brooks, Matthiessen believed that Eliot's early work established the proper scope for the critical enterprise ("Responsibilities," 6). In fact, Eliot's statements on this issue remained contradictory throughout his life. Eliot did not want literature to be forced to do society's bidding, whether that be moral, political, philosophical, or any other. But like Tate when he asserted that "literature is the complete knowledge of man's experience," Eliot wanted to insist on literature's relevance. In Eliot's view, literature remains a key to the cultural and social whole even if it is not in any way bound by that whole. Literature seems to function on the model of Plato's ideal realm. The literature of a single nation and literature in general are "organic wholes."[28] Thus Eliot assumes a nationalist foundation for literature. He argues that the important moment for criticism is "when poetry ceases to be the expression of the mind of a whole people."[29] Thus he does not deny a connection between literature and culture, but argues that literature contains or represents what is most important in culture or in human experience. The result of such a theory could only be an extreme form of idealist intellectual history. The mind of a people for Eliot has nothing to do with the material conditions of a particular era, but exists above these as an essence. The mind in question is not a construct of what the people think at a given historical moment, but is an Idea that gives the nation its telos.

American Renaissance is Matthiessen's attempt to work out a conception of American literature in terms of this theory. We need to take Matthiessen at his word when he describes his project as "cultural history" (*Critic*, 242). Cain's formulation is misleading because it suggests that Matthiessen engaged in two different kinds of writing, cultural history and literary criticism. But in fact, in *American Renaissance* the two are one and the same. "The history of an art," says Matthiessen quoting Ezra Pound, "is the history of masterwork, not of failures or mediocrity."[30] But he also claimed,

> An artist's use of language is the most sensitive index to cultural history. . . . Emerson, Hawthorne, Thoreau, Whitman, and Melville all wrote literature for democracy in a double sense. They felt that it was incumbent upon their generation to give fulfillment to the potentialities freed by the Revolution, to provide a culture commensurate with America's political opportunity. (*AR*, xv)

The "culture" of which Matthiessen is a historian is Arnold's "culture": not a whole way of life, but the best that was thought and said. The success of "our democracy" is measured by the achievement of our writers.

In writing *American Renaissance*, Matthiessen understood himself to be attempting to "repossess" that achievement. When he asserted that "you cannot 'use' a work of art unless you have comprehended its meaning," he made plain what such repossession entailed (x). *American Renaissance* is then explicitly a work of interpretation. Unlike earlier literary histories, it regards literary texts as requiring special acts of understanding. Whatever the proportion of "close analysis, and . . . instances from the works themselves," *American Renaissance* is always and everywhere concerned to tell us what works mean (*AR*, xi). "Attention to the writers' use of their own tools" is an approach to their themes and is not undertaken as pure formal analysis (*AR*, xv). The achievement of American writers will be demonstrated by interpreting their work far more often than it will be by explicit evaluation of it.

In some sense, Matthiessen believed that the judgment has already been made: "the successive generations of common readers who make the decisions, would seem finally to have agreed that the authors of the pre-Civil War era who bulk largest in stature are the five who are my subject" (*AR*, xi). As the earlier chapters of this book have shown, Matthiessen misrecognizes the process of canonization, but he correctly perceives its results. By the time Matthiessen came to write *American Renaissance*, the canon was already very close to being established. All of Matthiessen's five writers were recognized as major figures, and only Melville's recognition was recently granted. Matthiessen did not significantly alter the standard evaluation of the importance of any of these writers. Yet, as we have seen in our discussion of the English canon, a canon is more than a list of authors. What *American Renaissance* did for the American canon was to give it a definite shape by naming the American Chaucer, Spenser, Shakespeare, and Milton. It is not a coincidence that three of those four writers are associated with the Renaissance proper. In borrowing his title from Wendell, Matthiessen was claiming an analogous status of the authors and the period he covers. In successfully inventing an American renaissance, Matthiessen brought the long project of legitimating American literature to a close. *American Renaissance* represents the culmination of a process of creating an American canon.

Matthiessen's use of Emerson is fundamental to the shape *American Renaissance* gives to the canon. It is important to insist on the centrality of Emerson in *American Renaissance* since Matthiessen's treatment of Emerson there has attracted more criticism than any other aspect of the book. The general verdict is pronounced in *Eight American Authors*, where Matthiessen's judgment that Emerson is limited by his virtues of optimism and cheerfulness is cited as having "seminal influence on many younger scholars."[31] Ruland calls Matthiessen's portrait of Emerson "clearly the least successful portion" of the book, but he also notes that

> Matthiessen realized its centrality. He applied to Emerson the figure Emerson had chosen for Goethe: he was the cow from which the rest drew their milk. Emerson's theories of expression were basic principles for Thoreau and Whitman, while Hawthorne and Melville developed strength by pushing against his philosophical assumptions. But Matthiessen admits that the lack of a masterpiece on which to focus has forced him to range more widely in his Emerson essay than in any other section of his book. A more basic difficulty is acknowledged in

[Matthiessen's] opening sentence: it is perhaps impossible to
present a unified picture of a consciousness which was itself seldom whole. (Ruland, 232)

Ruland is acute in his diagnosis of Matthiessen's problem with
Emerson, whose avoidance of "foolish consistency" was no less
troubling to the New Critical sensibility than it was to the genteel.
Furthermore, Matthiessen is explicit in his condemnation of
Emerson's political naiveté in his failure to recognize the realities
of capitalism. When we add to this Matthiessen's complaints
about Emerson's lack of a tragic sense, it would seem that Matthiessen's treatment of Emerson, whatever his influence on the
other figures, is very close to a condemnation. Clearly some
readers have read Matthiessen in this way, but it is just as clearly
a misreading, not just of Matthiessen, but of the impact of *American Renaissance*. It is precisely because Emerson is not easily
pinned down that Matthiessen can both criticize his political innocence and still regard him as a genuine "philosopher of democracy." But here Matthiessen is merely in agreement with the critical tradition. What Matthiessen adds, despite the lack of an
Emersonian masterpiece, is the beginnings of an aesthetic justification of him.

Like most critics before him, Matthiessen complains of Emerson's "want of continuity," but instead of attributing it to a defect
in Emerson's craft or character, Matthiessen chalks it up to the
special conditions of American culture: "He was a symptom of his
age's expansiveness . . . the increasingly violent divergence between the world of transcendentalism and that of the industrial
revolution" (*AR*, 56). Emerson's preference for the symbolic over
other forms of expression is attributed to his need to "bring the
two separated halves of his consciousness into unity" (58). Notice
how in his very lack of organic wholeness, Emerson becomes an
organic element of his culture, the divided fruit of a divided plant.
Furthermore, this divided consciousness defines Emerson as a
modern. If he had been an undivided Platonist, he could not have
commanded anything of us save an antiquarian interest. As it is,
Emerson's dividedness makes him one of us, says Matthiessen,
and it is the source of (or perhaps merely the name for) the ambiguities by which the New Critical mind defines literary expres-

sion. Thus Emerson, though he remains a failed poet, becomes something far more significant: the very representation of the dilemma of the artist in the modern world.

But if Matthiessen agrees with the history of judgment about Emerson's poetry, he offers some of the first successful aesthetic justification for Emerson's prose. In 1941, despite the literary-historical attention that Emerson had received, there had been few critical studies of his work. The generally negative assessment of Emerson by Eliot and the leading New Critics meant that he was not among the first to be read closely. The lack of a master-piece meant that Matthiessen would not offer an extended reading of any of Emerson's works, but he does offer readings of individual passages that point the way to the more general aesthetic approval that would be granted during the 1950s. As he does with the poetry, Matthiessen finds Emerson's prose to lack continuity: "All of Emerson's books can be reduced to the same underlying pattern. They are hardly constructed as wholes. . . . The problem of Emerson's prose was the same as that of his philosophy, how to reconcile the individual with society, how to join his sentences into a paragraph. Since his chief preoccupation was to demonstrate identity beneath all manner of variety, his formula for an essay was an abstraction instanced by an indefinite number of embodiments" (64–66). Matthiessen may cite in agreement Woodberry's remarks on the limitations of Emerson's prose constructions, but Matthiessen's focus is on the pattern, which the earlier critics had not seen. Furthermore, some of Emerson's works turn out to have a compelling "unity of tone": in *Nature*, for example, he is said to "succeed . . . in clothing his abstractions in the colors of the visible world" and "to sustain . . . the art of the rhapsode. No one could demand a composition more satisfactory for its purpose than that of *The American Scholar*" (68).

At his best, Emerson turns out to exhibit one of the leading qualities of modernist aesthetics, condensation. There are paragraphs "that assume wholeness in the reader's mind" (68). One from "Illusions" uses Plotinus's image of the soul alone "to provide a frame for [Emerson's] Neo-Platonic thought and to condense it . . . into an effective parable" (68). If the passage does not quite put Emerson in Hemingway's league, it is for Matthiessen an undeniable example of a well-crafted paragraph. But condensation is only one principle of Emerson's technique; its inevitable opposite is to be found in "the Heraclitean doctrine of the Flowing. [Emerson] saw himself, in a recurrent image, standing on the bank of a river watching the endless current upon which floated past him objects of all shapes and colors. . . . Similar images were the special signatures of nineteenth-century poets" (69). Matthiessen mentions Wordsworth, Arnold, Whitman, Baudelaire, and Rimbaud, putting Emerson in the best of company. Finally, the heterogeneous Flowing also helps make Emerson whole: "Emerson's work is as permeated with images of flowing as you would expect from his declaration that 'the philosophy we want is one of fluxions and mobility.' In *Nature* the earth becomes 'this green ball which floats him through the heavens.' Nothing solid is left secure, since all matter has been infiltrated and dissolved by thought" (69–70). The paradox of Emerson's writing is the same one he sought to solve in his metaphysics, the unity which emerges out of difference: Emerson's "strongest writing emerged from his recurrent themes" (70).

Emerson thus emerges not as America's greatest artist, but as one who most embodied the peculiar national genius. Given this role, Emerson need not be treated uncritically in order to be accepted wholeheartedly. Emerson is all the more important because he embodies the national faults as well as the national virtues. Whatever Matthiessen's particular reservations about Emerson's craft or thought, they are overwhelmed by the place Emerson is given in American literature and culture. To regard Matthiessen's treatment of him as having "influenced young people against Emerson" is a view that can only be taken from within the priesthood (Stovall, 62). It ignores entirely the meaning of Emerson's centrality, but it does so precisely because by 1956 that centrality was so completely accepted that Matthiessen's demonstration of it carried no weight.

Henry David Thoreau is the most important exhibit in that demonstration, and, in *American Renaissance*, Thoreau comes off as Emerson's greatest creation. Emerson and Thoreau are treated in the same section, while Hawthorne, Melville, and Whitman are each treated separately. Thoreau rose to major status later than Emerson or Hawthorne, and it was for the content of his writings that he was valued. Matthiessen begins his discussion by asserting that "Thoreau has not ordinarily been approached primarily as an artist," and then proceeds to reject the other ways Thoreau has been approached, as a naturalist and as a reformer (*AR*, 76). Instead of "appraising the vigorous paradoxes of his social thought," Matthiessen asserts that "we can judge his contribution most adequately if we heed his single remark, 'My work is writing,' and come to *what* he created through examining his own *process of creation*" (79–80, italics in original). Perhaps the greatest change in reputation produced by *American Renaissance* was the new perception of Thoreau as consummate artist.[32]

One reason that Matthiessen was better able to appreciate Thoreau was the modernist conception of the artist as craftsman. Where romantic aesthetics had depicted the artist as a genius, one endowed with a special sensitivity to beauty or emotion, modernist poets like Pound and Eliot regarded great artists as having superior craft. Modernism did not dispense with the cult of the artist in this move—on the contrary, the cult was never more fervent than among the modernists—but it did shift the burden of greatness from substance to form. Thoreau's insights appeared to earlier generations of critics to be derivative of Emerson, and this fact alone consigned him to secondary status. Furthermore, both the genres and the subjects that Thoreau chose seem to make him too mundane and practical—too much the economist or natural historian—to be a great artist. But these very qualities make him all the more the craftsman, an identity that matches in many respects the persona Thoreau created for himself in *Walden*. Matthiessen demonstrates, for the first time, that *Walden* is not a simple record of Thoreau's experience but an elaborately crafted work of art, its structure all the more artistic for seeming natural. Organic form, Matthiessen makes clear, does not come naturally; it comes only to those, like Thoreau, who are devoted to the work of writing.

Another quality valued by modernist aesthetics was important to Matthiessen's reevaluation of Thoreau as artist. Modernist writers had in a variety of ways regarded the primitive as the indispensable ground of their own work. Eliot borrowed heavily from *The Golden Bough* in conceiving *The Waste Land*. Conrad located the dark heart of human experience in the African jungle. Lawrence extolled the need for the vestigial animal in modern man to burst the barriers of repression. If this veneration of the primitive is largely borrowed from the romantics, it was nevertheless an aspect of romantic aesthetics that did not become dominant in the United States. In the nineteenth century, Thoreau's primitivism put him on the border of respectability. In the twentieth, it had prevented critics from perceiving Thoreau's artistry. But for Matthiessen, recognition of the primitive is the condition for Thoreau's artistic success: "It was Thoreau's conviction that by reducing life to primitive conditions, he had come to the roots from which healthy art must flower" (*AR*, 171).

Unlike Thoreau, both Hawthorne and Melville were understood as artists prior to Matthiessen's discussion of them. Hawthorne, as we recall, was often cited as the one true artist of the nineteenth century. Matthiessen's treatment of these two figures would result in a shift in ranking, so that Melville for the first time comes to seem the more accomplished writer. Yet Matthiessen's treatment of Hawthorne hardly constitutes a demotion. Both are regarded as bringing to American culture a tragic sense that it otherwise largely seemed to have lacked. This judgment grants Hawthorne and Melville a cultural significance that had heretofore eluded them. Matthiessen is able to demonstrate this significance by creating a binary opposition between Emersonian innocence and the novelists' recognition of evil. Earlier conceptions of American literary history had tended either to see particular periods as unified rather than divided (Foerster) or to identify the tradition with one side of an opposition (Parrington). Matthiessen's strategy, which strongly reflects New Critical and modernist appreciation for ambiguity, is to argue that the tradition is defined by the tension between the poles of the opposition.

Though R. W. B. Lewis is guilty of hyperbole in claiming that Matthiessen "invented the romantic movement"—as we have seen, if anyone invented it, it was Foerster—there is a strong sense in which Lewis is right (quoted in Ruland, 204). Early conceptions of the romantic movement considered it more or less unified. It was defined by characteristics, qualities, and to a lesser extent beliefs that most of the writers shared. Matthiessen begins with this premise, asserting that "the impulse from Emerson was the most pervasive and far reaching, and that Whitman's extension of many of Emerson's values carried far down into the period after the Civil War" (*AR*, 179). But then Matthiessen goes on to show that the literature he is discussing was produced out of a conflict between the dominant Emersonian optimism and the tragic sense of Hawthorne and Melville. As he makes clear in explaining the organization of his book, Matthiessen defines the American romantic era dialectically: "We may stay closest to the pressures of the age, as its creative imaginations responded to them, by going from transcendental affirmation to its counterstatement by the tragic writers, and by then perceiving how Whitman rode through the years undisturbed by such deep and bitter truths as Melville had found. It would be neater to say that we have in Emerson and Thoreau a thesis, in Hawthorne and Melville its antithesis, and in Whitman a synthesis. But that description would distort especially the breadth and complexity of Melville" (*AR*, 179). It would also distort Whitman, who Matthiessen has just described as extending Emerson's values. More to the point, perhaps, this Hegelian version of the dialectic would be out of keeping with Matthiessen's own conception of life. His dialectic is, like Kierkegaard's or Karl Barth's, one that cannot be resolved in human history. Human life is defined by the perpetual opposition of good and evil, not by "the everlasting Yea," but by an "oscillating Yes and No."[33] This conception of human experience unites Matthiessen with the New Critics and, as we will see, the New York Intellectuals at a more fundamental level than either critical practice or political position.

In treating his period dialectically, Matthiessen succeeded in unifying American literature as no critic had done before. Emerson's milk may have nurtured Thoreau and Whitman while it gave Hawthorne and Melville colic, but it originated both. Matthiessen's conception of the period is illustrated by the way he poses and solves its chief problem: "How an age in which Emerson was the most articulate voice could also have given birth to *Moby-Dick* can be accounted for only through reaction" (*AR*, 184). Earlier treatments had taken Hawthorne's personal isolation as a sign of his lack of connection to Emerson and the rest of the Concord group. While Parrington and the left-wing critics simply found Hawthorne's work out of touch with a reality that did not include tragedy, other critics complained that he failed to achieve a genuinely tragic vision.[34] Mumford recognized that "Melville's work, taken as a whole, expresses that tragic sense of life which has always attended the highest triumphs of the race."[35] He was also aware of Melville's disapproval of Emerson, but he does not treat that fact as the point of departure of Melville's work. It is Matthiessen who established the now-dominant view that (as Irving Howe recently stated it) "flaws in [Emerson's] vision . . . become the themes of Hawthorne and Melville."[36] In spite of the critique of Emerson that this conception entails, it made him all the more central to American literature.

Matthiessen's image of Emerson as the "cow" of his renaissance suggests that he has not given up the literary-historical concern with influences and sources. Wellek's designation of Matthiessen as a "scholar-critic" is thus more accurate than one that would consider him a critic pure and simple.[37] Matthiessen was, of course, trained as a literary historian. His dissertation, a study of Elizabethan translation, was produced under the supervision of John Livingston Lowes, and Matthiessen received considerable advice from Kittredge (Gunn, 32). Lowe's *Road to Xanadu*, perhaps the most revered single work of source study produced by the discipline of English, took the method to a higher level than it typically attained. The complexity of Lowe's analysis of Coleridge's sources and the poet's use of them meant that the book could not avoid the sort of interpretation most source studies ignored or sought to preempt. Matthiessen may have learned as much from Lowes as from Eliot and the New Critics, as Coleridge's prominence in *American Renaissance* may suggest. Although Matthiessen makes frequent reference to his author's sources, his work is not itself a source study. In fact, Matthiessen usually relies on other literary historians for this information. It is, like almost any work about a literary tradition, however, inextricably bound up with problems of influence. Emerson is the presiding influence over the renaissance, but Hawthorne is almost as important as the presiding influence in American fiction. After noting Hawthorne's own predecessors and potential influences among American fiction writers, Matthiessen goes on to place Hawthorne at the beginning of a tradition that would produce not only the mature Melville, but Henry James, T. S. Eliot, and (through Melville) James Joyce and Thomas Mann. But in these conceptions of influence we see mingled the academic notion of historically documented influence and Eliot's idealist conception of tradition. Thus Matthiessen could assert "we are no longer dealing with an ordinary 'influence,' but with a rare case, in which Shakespeare's conception of tragedy had so grown into the fiber of Melville's thought that much of his mature work became a re-creation of its themes in modern terms" (*AR*, 435). Hawthorne's influence on Melville and James is historically documented by evidence of these authors' own statements, but his relations to the modernists involve an undocumentable argument about the development of symbolism as a literary technique. Furthermore, Matthiessen's use of influence runs counter to the way it typically worked in academic literary histories: "The connections between [Hawthorne] and James . . . are so fundamental for throwing Hawthorne's contribution into its proper light that they demand explicit statement. . . . the value of an author cannot be wholly separated from the tradition to which he has given rise, especially when the presence or absence of an American example to build on was precisely the factor that differentiated the early developments of these two" (*AR*, 292). Rather than belittling Hawthorne, this view of his role as an influence on several greater artists actually increases his value.[38]

Matthiessen's treatment of Melville was of considerably greater significance than his discussion of Hawthorne. While canonicity was not an issue in either case, Hawthorne's artistry had been a staple conception of American literary histories since the turn of the century even if some more recent critics had demurred. Matthiessen falls somewhere between these two positions in his judgment of Hawthorne. While he finds a genuinely profound sense of tragedy in Hawthorne, he does not regard him as having entirely succeeded in finding expression for that sense. Melville, on the other hand, is the hero of *American Renaissance*. He is for Matthiessen, quite literally, the Shakespeare of our renaissance. Matthiessen's reading of *Moby-Dick* and *Pierre* both proceed by comparison with Shakespearean tragedies—*King Lear* and *Hamlet*, respectively. Such comparisons obviously serve to elevate Melville's status, and elevate in the process all of American literature to allow it to stand shoulder to shoulder with British literature. The comparison between Shakespeare and Melville is not entirely ungrounded. *American Renaissance* makes extensive use of Melville's library and the marginalia he left in those volumes. This is the major scholarly discovery the book exploits, and Matthiessen's treatment of Melville is as much a reading of Melville's reading as it is of his works themselves. In addition to meeting Hawthorne, "Melville started to go through the whole of Shakespeare in the winter of 1849," not long before he began work on *Moby-Dick* (*AR*, 412). Yet Matthiessen's historical argument is relatively trivial, if largely convincing. It matters much less that Melville's work was affected by his reading of Shakespeare than that he became the virtual reincarnation of the Bard's tragic sense.

Matthiessen's readings may also be the first to argue that these works are unified wholes. Although his reading of *Pierre* seems to have been largely unpersuasive in this regard, we tend to forget that *Moby-Dick* was also perceived to be a formal disaster, whatever its thematic power. The wholeness of *Moby-Dick* could only be perceived in the light of modernist works and the criticism that interpreted them. Thus *The Waste Land*, with its "fragments I have shored up against my ruins," and *Ulysses*, especially as read through Eliot's "Ulysses, Order, and Myth," allowed Matthiessen and other twentieth-century readers to find a unity in *Moby-Dick* that earlier critics had missed. The idea of myth, which Matthiessen seems to borrow as much from the Ransom of *God Without Thunder* as from Eliot, will be the place where *American Renaissance* ends and the creation of American civilization finds its vehicle.

Interestingly, however, even myth and other modernist strategies for lending order to chaos could not give Matthiessen a way to find organic unity in most of Whitman's major works, "When Lilacs Last in the Dooryard Bloom'd" being the major exception. Nowhere in *American Renaissance*, for example, is there a reading of "Song of Myself" parallel to those offered of *Walden* or *Moby-Dick*. Rather than attempting that kind of reading, Matthiessen chooses to argue for a kind of unity of oeuvre. Whitman lends himself to such a reading, of course, since the poetic oeuvre was continually republished as *Leaves of Grass*; Matthiessen claims, "he came to think . . . of his whole book as an organism" (*AR*,

594). Yet it is not the unity of that book that Matthiessen explores, but rather the language that constitutes the poems and the themes that characterize both poems and prose. The importance of such a reading should not be minimized. While some work had been done on Whitman's rhythm, very little close reading of any kind had been applied to his work. Matthiessen's treatment was impressive enough that in 1956 *Eight American Authors* could proclaim that "The best critical study of Whitman in English is the long fourth book of F. O. Matthiessen's *American Renaissance*" for having in the section "Only a Language Experiment" gotten at "the secret of Whitman's penetration and force as a poet."[39] Given the aesthetics of the New Criticism, it was essential for Matthiessen to make this case. The New Critics themselves, including Eliot and even Pound (whose own line, Yvor Winters noted, "is in part a refinement of Whitman's line") could find nothing of aesthetic value in Whitman's poetry. By focusing his discussion on Whitman's diction, Matthiessen becomes perhaps the first critic to provide a coherent argument for Whitman's aesthetic success.

But this is not to deny that Matthiessen finds a unity of form and theme in Whitman. In fact, the heart of Matthiessen's discussion of Whitman's diction is the belief that it is the proper embodiment for the poet's democratic vision. Whitman's words reflected his belief that "living speech could come to a man only through his absorption in the life surrounding him. He must learn that the final decisions of language are not made by dictionary makers but 'by the masses, people nearest the concrete, having most to do with actual land and sea' " (*AR*, 520, quoting Whitman). Thus Whitman's use of what he understood as the language of the masses is organically related to his acceptance of "the ideals of democracy" (*AR*, 537). Whitman's work goes beyond a particular politics, however, to achieve a transcendent humanism: "Whitman's ability to make a synthesis in his poems of the contrasting elements that he calls body and soul may serve as a measure of his stature as a poet. When his words adhere to concrete experience and yet are bathed in imagination, his statements become broadly representative of humanity" (*AR*, 526).

This last point leads us to the question of the politics of *American Renaissance* itself. There are two distinct views of this. We have seen that Cain's major criticism of Matthiessen is the separation of his politics and his criticism. Wellek, on the other hand, complains that Matthiessen's identification of his renaissance writers by " 'their devotion to the possibilities of democracy' [*AR*] (xi), [is] a trivial conclusion obsessively repeated" (74) and he speaks of *American Renaissance*'s "overriding political theme" (79). My view is that Matthiessen's political conception is so thoroughly humanist that democracy tends to become a name for that way of thinking, rather than a particular political system or program. Cain shows that Matthiessen took particular political stands that do not show up in his literary criticism. But he does describe a politics expressed in *American Renaissance*:

> Matthiessen sought in his own way to assemble a secular scripture that would, first, compensate for the deprivations and cruelties of the Depression in America, and, second, shore up men and women where, as was becoming increasingly clear by the late 1930s, doctrinaire communism, if not socialism, had failed them. . . . From this point of view, "democracy" has for Matthiessen, a concretely "American" political resonance, but it also transcends politics. . . . It signals resistance to the cult of ideology. . . . Democracy is organic, leading to an art that expresses . . . the aspirations of the common man, whereas ideology is alien and artificial, mechanically imposed from the outside." (150)

As Cain notes, the meaning of "Democracy" in *American Renaissance* is "oddly unparticularized" (151), and he illustrates the political consequences of this problem when he observes that "In *American Renaissance*, Matthiessen sought to stand with 'all the people'—which is different from standing with 'the workers' in their class struggle" (155). It is a mistake typical of the New Historicism's method of microhistory to make this position a product of the politics of the Popular Front.[40] It may be that Matthiessen was influenced by the rhetoric of that episode in American communism, but to make the Popular Front the origin of Matthiessen's discussion of American democracy is to ignore the fact that his rhetoric fits perfectly with the rhetoric of American nationalism as it had been articulated since Wilson's "war to make the world safe for democracy."[41] The Popular Front adopted its conception of American democracy ready-made. The more important issue here is not origin but application. Matthiessen's identification of America with democracy allowed him to name the distinction that defined the American literary tradition. But it also made democracy something that always already exists in America and thus need not inspire struggle or political action. Democracy becomes in *American Renaissance* the essence of American civilization.

This is why *American Renaissance* concludes with Whitman. In him, Matthiessen finds an author who explicitly identifies himself with America and America with democracy. This is the synthesis that Whitman represents. Whitman himself, like the words he carefully chose for his poems, was common: "Whitman did not 'espouse' the cause of the masses through any self-conscious gesture of identification. The relation was simpler and more natural, for he was quite literally one of them himself. As the son of a common man, as a casual worker in his own turn, he knew how the poor really lived" (*AR*, 542). Matthiessen contends that Whitman "veered inevitably" from individualism to socialism, but he provides no evidence of this movement, and as the following description suggests, such socialism could only be the natural outgrowth of America:

> Whitman's confident vision led him to fulfill the most naive and therefore most natural kind of romanticism for America, the romanticism of the future. He formulated directly what was often implicit in Emerson: "The Poetry of other lands lies in the past—what they have been. The Poetry of America lies in the future—what These States and their coming men and women are certainly to be." (*AR*, 543)

The Whitman Matthiessen describes is incapable of opposition even if his own position—as defined by his class, his sexuality, and even his poetic style—is in various ways marginal. He is rather a singer of nationalist celebration with a "prodigious faculty 'in making America as it was . . . into something grand and significant' " (*AR*, 519, quoting T. S. Eliot).

All of the writers Matthiessen discusses are in his view democrats; Whitman is only the most thoroughly self-identified as such. But ultimately their politics is less important than their Americanness, democracy being merely the most important aspect of that quality. Matthiessen never tires of pointing out how the distinctive conditions of the United States contributed to the writing of each of his subjects. As we saw in our discussion of Wendell, many of these conditions had been observed long before. One of them, the paucity of materials, was already an old saw when Henry James applied it to Hawthorne in 1879. But in Matthiessen, the exceptional conditions of American life are no longer presented either as excuses or explanations, but as *distinctions*: traits that are not only unique to America but also produce the value of its cultural productions. Thus "Whitman reveals the peculiarly American combination of a childish freshness with a mechanical and desiccated repetition of book terms that had had significance for the more complex civilization in which they had had their roots and growth" (*AR*, 531). "The passion that drove [Melville] into the discovery of his ambiguities was peculiarly American" (*AR*, 474). "No art that sprang from American roots in this period could fail to show the marks of abstraction. . . . The tendency of American idealism to see a spiritual significance in every natural fact was far more broadly diffused than transcendentalism" (*AR*, 243). "The heart of Thoreau's revolt was his continual assertion that the only true America is that country where you are able to pursue life without encumbrances" (*AR*, 79). "Emerson's growth was fostered not merely by the renascence of idealistic philosophy, but likewise by his eager apprehension of the possibilities of American democracy" (*AR*, 13).

And yet, this outpouring, this expression of America, was not enough. There remained "The Need for Mythology," as Matthiessen titled one of the sections of his final chapter, itself seemingly named for an American myth, "Man in the Open Air." Here the fundamentally ahistorical character of Matthiessen's work becomes clear.

> Where the age of Emerson may be most like our own is in its discovery of the value of myth. The starting point is in Emerson's "History," the opening essay of his first collection. He believed that history can be re-created only by a man for whom the present is alive. He had reached his initial premise of "the identity of human character in all ages" as a schoolmaster of nineteen. . . . his chief desire was to translate the Then into the Now. In the academic sense, his interest was unhistorical. (*AR*, 626)

Like Emerson, Matthiessen's interest in history is a rejection of the academic. He approves of Lawrence's account of the burden of the historical method: "The merely critical mind had become so desiccating that he could find his renewal only in the realms of the unconscious, and declared that the great myths 'now begin to hypnotize us again, our own impulse towards our own scientific way of understanding being almost spent' " (*AR*, 630). *American Renaissance* displays everywhere Matthiessen's mastery of literary-historical scholarship, but the book as a whole represents the abandonment of that practice. It is not in history but in myth that truth is to be discovered. Thus Emerson's belief that "we need a theory of interpretation or Mythology" is Matthiessen's as well (*AR*, 626). It might stand as the motto of literary study ever since.

"The Need for Mythology" stands as the conclusion of *American Renaissance* because Matthiessen does not persuade us that he had found the mythology he was seeking. Matthiessen is explicit about myth entailing a theory of history. It is telling, I think, that he finds the theory through which the "age of Emerson found its myth" best articulated not by any of his five authors but by Theodore Parker, a writer far more interested in social change than any of the makers of the renaissance:

> Parker believed that an American historian must write in the interest of mankind, in the spirit of nineteenth century. He must be occupied with the growth of institutions, not with glamorous spectacles. "He must tell us of the social state of the people, the relation of the cultivator to the soil, the relation of class to class. It is well to know what songs the peasant sung; what prayers he prayed; what food he ate; what tools he wrought with." (*AR*, 633)

According to Matthiessen, the American myth that this view of history produced is the myth of the common man; *he* is the American hero according to Emerson, Thoreau, Whitman, Hawthorne, and Melville. But Matthiessen is nowhere so feeble in his argument and interpretation as here. In spite of the repeated reference to democracy in the previous 600 pages, Matthiessen did not in his readings of any but Whitman prepare us for this claim. In fact, the heroes of *Representative Men*, *Walden*, *Moby-Dick*, *The*

Scarlet Letter, "When Lilacs Last in the Dooryard Bloom'd," and even "Song of Myself," are not common but extraordinary.

To show that American writers found value in the common life, or even that they sometimes expressed solidarity with workers, is not to demonstrate that the stories they told coalesce around such figures. The weakness of Matthiessen's case is exposed by his rapid turn to American folklore of the nineteenth century. Davy Crockett, Mike Fink, Sut Lovingood, and Johnny Appleseed are mentioned as embodiments of the myth. Not only are these figures absent from the renaissance Matthiessen has described, but their essentially humorous character makes them distinctly unsuitable to bear, as myth must, the burden of "elemental human patterns" (*AR*, 631). Nor does Matthiessen persuade us that the writers of his renaissance used Eliot's "mythic method." He comes the closest when he points out the explicit parallels Thoreau drew between himself at Walden and the heroes of Greek and Roman antiquity. But even here, Thoreau's references are to a large number of different narratives. There is no single mythic narrative, no story of Ulysses or a Fisher King, that orders Thoreau's work.

In announcing the quest for an American myth, Matthiessen set the agenda for much of the study of American literature in the next three decades. The American Studies myth-symbol school—many of whom were Matthiessen's students—pursued this agenda most directly. But even critics such as Richard Chase and Roy Harvey Pearce, who were not identified with American Studies, take myth as a major problematic. The agenda Matthiessen left his heirs is less the explicit focus on myth, however, than on the problem that that focus was designed to solve: " 'How to coordinate whatever is peculiarly American with the tradition of the ages' " (*AR*, 647; quoting Odell Shepard). The project that Matthiessen and his critical/scholarly progeny attempted is rooted in assumptions articulated by Thoreau:

> Thoreau learned that "the perennial mind" did not die with Cato, "and will not die with Hosmer." This mind was nothing rarefied; it was an integral part of the functioning of the human organism. What interested Thoreau most in literature was the expression of this mind, the insight it gave collective existence: "it is the spirit of humanity, that which animates both so-called

259

savages and civilized nations, working through a man, and not the man expressing himself." Thoreau had come to that fundamental understanding while studying the Indians, just as Mann came to it at the close of his essay on Dürer, in whose deep humanity he had found "history as myth, history that is ever fresh and ever present. For we are much less individuals than we either hope or fear to be." (*AR*, 648)

Assumptions like Thoreau's might have produced, as they did in France with Lévi-Strauss, the attempt to excavate the savage mind. In America, however, the perennial mind was understood via Arnold rather than the Thoreau of this passage. And, in spite of his numerous appeals to the organic and the common, Matthiessen's treatment of it is usually quite rarefied. America's peculiarity is for him a matter of ideas. The history Parker called for is utterly absent from Matthiessen or the discipline of American literature his book redefined. That practice was humanist in the sense that it assumed an essential standard for culture. Great works differed only in the positions they took toward perennial human(ist) concerns: innocence and experience, hope and tragedy, good and evil. Differences of region, class, race, or ethnicity could not be comprehended by this practice. "Democracy" and "humanity" stand for the irrelevance of these differences in American culture.

Where Barrett Wendell had failed, Matthiessen succeeded in making the literature of mid-nineteenth-century New England not only the literature of America but a distinct national literature fit to stand with those of England, France, and Germany. But this success was achieved at a price. The peculiarities of American literature Wendell identified were explained in terms of social and political conditions. However insufficient Wendell's treatment, it was genuinely historical. *American Renaissance* represents not merely the death knell for historical scholarship in American literature, but for history itself. For many years to come, Americanists would conceive of their object as a part of that contemporeneity that for Eliot distinguishes literature. History becomes merely the background and chronology of an essentially timeless canon.

8

Left Criticism and the New York Intellectuals

If the right-wing criticism of the 1930s was eventually to radically alter academic practice, the left-wing criticism of the same period would not in itself have much impact on American literature as an academic field. But one branch of the literary left of the 1930s would come to have a significant influence on literature in the academy, and on the study of American literature in particular. The New York Intellectuals are a group that has come to have almost mythic significance in American cultural history. Like the New Critics, the New York Intellectuals formed outside of the academy, but though they also moved into it later have continued to be identified as independent intellectuals. In the largest conception of the group, it is defined as emerging out of the anti-Stalinist left of the 1930s and to have moved to the political center by the 1950s. The larger group included such influential figures as Sidney Hook, Dwight Macdonald, and William Barrett, but my concern is focused on those New York Intellectuals who wrote mainly about literature, especially William Phillips, Philip Rahv, and Lionel Trilling, a circle best defined by involvement with *Partisan Review*. Trilling, Phillips, and Rahv all contributed to the new conception of American literature that emerged during the 1940s and 1950s, including the transformation in disciplinary practice from history to criticism. Their intellectual progeny, Richard Chase and Leslie Fiedler, produced two of the most significant versions of the tradition of the American novel. On the other hand, the New York Intellectuals also played a leading role in establishing the canon of modernism, which they proposed as a countertradition to American literature.

The New York Intellectuals cannot be understood except in the context of their emergence from the left criticism of the 1930s, even though some of them tried in their memoirs to bury the Marxism of their youth.[1] On the other hand, the fact of their thirties radicalism has tended to lead many commentators to the conclusion that the group remained a critical or oppositional force long after most of its members had become apologists for America. Thus left-leaning critics such as Vincent Leitch or Mark Krupnick continue to insist that the New Yorkers produced a genuine cultural criticism. Even more insistent is Russell Jacoby, who describes the New Yorkers as "the last intellectuals," an interesting claim, since they saw themselves as the first American intellectuals. To Jacoby and those who share his view, the New York Intellectuals embody the ideal of an independent intelligentsia.[2] I will argue that this view represents the simple acceptance of the New Yorkers' own self-serving misconception of their role. While the New Yorkers did insist on links between culture and society, literature and politics, even during the 1930s they were unable to move beyond criticism of vulgar Marxism to a sophisticated theory of these relations. After abandoning their 1930s Marxism, they failed to develop another position from which to critique American culture. While the New York Intellectuals' rejection of pure aestheticism is usually used to depict them in stark opposition to the New Critics, the two critical camps should properly be understood as two sides of the same coin. Both groups, unlike their critical and scholarly predecessors, were hermeneuts; they understood themselves as interpreters rather than as enforcers of aesthetic rules or compilers of facts. Thus the New York Intellectuals will also help transform the academic study of American literature from history to criticism. By the late 1940s, their politics had become so radically changed that they found themselves defenders of American civilization, and thus they would also contribute to the covert conservatism of the subdiscipline of American literature.

Marxist Criticism of the 1930s

The left-wing criticism of the 1930s did not arise spontaneously in response to the Depression; it was preceded by an earlier left criticism beginning with the literary radicals of the 1910s. They had identified themselves as socialists, but, as we have seen, their literary criticism was motivated more by nationalism than by class identification—or indeed by any explicit political program. In the wake of the Bolshevik revolution, the Communist Party broke off from the Socialists during the early 1920s. In the early 1930s, the Depression gave the Party's message a much greater appeal and its call for revolution much greater plausibility. But increased support for the Party does not tell the whole story of the rise of Marxist criticism. Socialist parties in the United States had lacked explicit cultural politics. Socialist writers, such as Jack London, used their work to communicate political messages, and avant-garde magazines often endorsed socialist positions. Neither the writers nor the magazines, however, developed anything like a socialist literary criticism. Nevertheless, there did develop an indigenous left criticism in the form of literary radicalism. By the 1920s some of the radicals had begun to adopt Marxist principles and to join the Communist Party. But neither of these influences would displace the nationalism that the radicals had long held.

The history of American left criticism has been distorted by the New York Intellectuals' retelling of it. Lionel Trilling begins the most important of these narratives, his essay "Reality in America," in this way: "It is possible to say of V. L. Parrington that with his *Main Currents in American Thought* he has had an influence on our conception of American culture which is not equaled by that of any other writer of the last two decades."[3] Of course, it is possible to say many things; the question is: Why would Trilling want to say this when, as other contemporary observers had recognized, Parrington's influence had waned?[4] In 1950, when *The Liberal Imagination* appeared, it certainly was inaccurate to describe Parrington as the most significant influence on America's conception of its own culture. Richard Ruland was far more accurate when he asserted that "the most influential reordering of America's literary tradition before Matthiessen's *American Renaissance* (1941) was Vernon L. Parrington's three-volume *Main Currents in American Thought* (1927–1930)."[5] And yet, even this assertion is somewhat misleading. Ruland himself describes *Main Currents* as "a capstone to one whole movement of literary criticism" (186) that began with Van Wyck Brooks and John Macy in the early 1910s. Parrington was only the most prominent of pre-Depression critics on the left, who included Max Eastman, Floyd Dell, Michael Gold, and Joseph Freeman.[6] Parrington is thus more correctly conceived as both being part of a movement and coming at the end of it.

Parrington thus should not be understood as typical of the left criticism of the 1930s, which is distinguished by its explicitly Marxist character. Socialism was a name for a variety of political programs, including Marxism. Marxism, on the other hand, is a philosophical discourse that not only supported a political program but claimed to ground scientifically knowledge in general. Those claims resulted in the production of several different Marxist aesthetic theories, and in different literary criticisms based upon them. The Communist Party's line on literature held that it was economically and socially determined by class interests and, more important, that it was an instrument of political action. The Party regarded literature as important enough to sponsor literary magazines and to feature literary criticism in its other periodicals. The Party probably did not have much direct influence over the rise of Marxist criticism in the 1930s, but it did indirectly support such criticism by providing a political program with which left-wing intellectuals could identify. I have already mentioned the two major Marxist treatments of American literature, Calverton's *The Liberation of American Literature* (1932) and Hicks's *The Great Tradition* (1933).[7] Neither writer was a Communist Party member when these books were produced, and Calverton was already an anti-Stalinist.

The 1930s certainly represented the high-water mark of the influence of Marxist criticism in America, but it ought to be remembered that Marxist criticism was never dominant. We have already seen that the impact of such criticism was successfully marginalized by the academy on what we might call quasi-epistemological grounds: it failed to meet the literary historian's requirements for certainty. Given the faulty cultural memory of the 1930s, it is worth stating what is perhaps obvious given my previous chapters: there was almost no Marxist literary scholarship or criticism produced within the academy.[8] Outside the academy, Marxist and other left critics wrote reviews and essays for mainstream organs such as the *New York Times*, but they represented only one element of the spectrum of opinion such periodicals featured. And much left criticism was restricted to little magazines or party organs that did not reach much beyond the intellectual and political culture of the left. It may have been the hothouse atmosphere of this culture that caused the New York Intellectuals to overrate the influence of Stalinism in American literary culture. Still, the overall marginalization of literary criticism allowed left criticism to represent a far larger fraction of the now smaller pie.

What is most striking about the two major 1930s Marxist treatments of the American tradition is their consistency with the nationalist project that we have encountered in both the criticism of literary radicals and in the ambitions of the academic Americanists. Calverton's narrative of "the liberation of American literature" tells the story of the development of a "native tradition" and a "national literature." Calverton differs significantly from Parrington in his account of this development. Where Parrington had discovered Americanness as early as Roger Williams, Calverton finds it to be no more recent than the later nineteenth century. His diagnosis of the problems of American culture resonates with those of Brooks and Bourne, Spiller and Pattee. In Calverton's view, America has long suffered from feelings of cultural inferiority, which he names "the colonial complex." The development of a national literature out of a colonial one follows, according to Calverton, four stages: adaptation, modification, struggle, and independence. In words that echo Pattee's of thirty years earlier, Calverton asserts that "American literature . . . is the only colonial literature ever to reach the fourth stage in the colonial process," that is, "to create a national literature." And yet "no colonial literature ever succeeds in completely separating itself from its maternal origins" and American literature is "in certain respects still a colonial literature" (Calverton, 2–3). Curiously, Calverton's Marxist conception of the liberation of American literature coincides precisely with the ALG's project of building an American literary tradition.

But Calverton's own account of the development of such a tradition could not have been acceptable to the new subdiscipline. Since Calverton writes off all literature prior to Walt Whitman and Mark Twain as merely derivative of England, his tradition could not justify any of the standard authors from which a canon would be formed. Like other literary radicals, Calverton persists in regarding Puritanism as the historical root of American philistinism. He gives this a Marxist twist by insisting that the American Puritans were of lower-middle-class origins, and thus petty-bourgeois in their ideology. But this class analysis renders no change in the standard liberal conception of Puritan influence on American culture. The "self-denying, pleasure-hating ideology of the petty-bourgeoisie" continues to be dominant even in the 1930s: "The importance of petty bourgeois origins of American psychology, insofar as our art and literature are concerned, can hardly be overestimated. . . . On the whole, we continue to be a nation of petty bourgeoisie in our attitudes and convictions. While the opposition to all art which did not serve a religious end has disappeared . . . the American public as a whole . . . has not escaped the aesthetic—or unaesthetic—philosophy of that class" (49–50). It is worth pointing out in this connection that Calverton also produced vulgar Freudian critiques of American marriage and sexual attitudes.[9]

Petty-bourgeois ideology is not merely expressed in Puritan writing, however. For Calverton, it turns out to be the ideology of the age of Emerson as well. Not being able to accuse Emerson of being entirely "unaesthetic," Calverton now makes radical individualism the hallmark of petty-bourgeois ideology. Given Calverton's Marxism, it is strange that what is missing from his critique is the material. Even more than Parrington's *Main Currents*, *The Liberation of American Literature* is fundamentally a history of ideas. It fails to discern any fundamental historical events or developments, save the emergence of America as a world power, to account for changes in American writing. Insofar as the nineteenth century does produce native characteristics, it does so on the frontier:

> The frontier began the revolt in favor of Americanness, but it did not crystallize that revolt into a tradition. . . . While the frontier provided the first source of real Americanness in our literature, it was the accumulative growth of power of the nation as a whole which made it possible for these American-nesses to be capitalized into a nationalistic tradition. It was only when America arose to the position of a world power among nations of our time, a rival in rank with its mother country, that it was able to release itself from the colonial complex and actually begin the development of a native literature of its own. (31)

One can discern a vaguely Marxist/Hegelian notion of historical progress behind Calverton's narrative of American literary development. The connection is vague because there is little sense of dialectic in Calverton's story, but there is a strong sense of telos. Nationhood appears to be a necessary step on the way to an international brotherhood of the proletariat. But the effect of this conception of history on Calverton's book is to endlessly defer that goal: "Radical literatures the same as bourgeois literatures will take on their caste from the national environment for some time to come" (36n.57). Such a position makes the development of "Americannesses" and of a "nationalistic tradition" unambiguously positive events.

Granville Hicks's nationalism is assumed rather than advanced. Rather than telling a story of a literature's liberation, he describes a tradition that may lead to the proletariat's liberation. It would perhaps give an undeserved impression of complexity to their perspectives to describe Hicks and Calverton as having differing theories, but they do at least emphasize two different theoretical orientations in Marxist criticism. While Calverton is mainly interested in classifying literature by the class interests it expresses, Hicks is interested in identifying literature that contributes to the project of a proletarian revolution. While Calverton tends to treat literature as a reflection of social conditions, Hicks judges it by the degree to which it approximates reality as Marxism understands it. Hicks can find a place for Emerson in the great tradition by virtue of his "confidence in the common man" (328), because that tradition leads to proletarian literature. That literature will obviously be international, but Hicks nevertheless celebrates a specifically American literature: "Revolutionary literature marks a new beginning. It is, in part and however imperfectly, something unprecedented in human culture. . . . But it is also the only possible fulfillment of the spirit that moves in the noblest creations of all American writers" (328). Hicks lists—in addition to Emerson —Thoreau, Whitman, Howells, Henry James, Mark Twain, Hamlin Garland, William Norris, Robert Herrick, David Graham Phillips, Upton Sinclair, and Jack London: "This is the great tradition of American literature. Ours has been a critical literature, critical of greed, cowardice, and meanness. It has been a hopeful literature, touched again and again with a passion for brotherhood, justice, and intellectual honesty" (329). Hicks thus claims American literature for the revolutionary cause. Yet if one attends at all carefully to what Hicks says about each of these writers earlier in the book, one might suspect that Hicks's title is meant ironically. None of the writers on this list are described predominantly in positive terms. All are failures because they turn away from economic and social reality. One committed to revolutionary literature would have a hard time finding reasons in Hicks to read this great tradition.

Both Calverton and Hicks find proletarian literature to be the most important contemporary form, but this literature was quite literally an afterthought in Hicks. He added a chapter discussing it in the second edition of *The Great Tradition*. Both books regard the more or less realist writing of the late nineteenth and early twentieth centuries as the most important aspect of American literature. In many respects this is consonant with the perspective that emerges from Parrington's final and unfinished volume. Of the three, only Calverton recognizes the diversity of literature during this period. He notes "a dynamic interest in the literary possibilities of indigenous materials provided by the Indian, the cowboy, and the Negro" (433). He has rather little to say about the former two, but his discussion of black writing shows familiarity with a large number of authors. (Calverton had edited one of the first anthologies of African-American writing, published in 1929.) Still, it is white, working-class writers whom Calverton regards as most important.

In considering the significance of Calverton's and Hicks's studies of the American literary tradition, it is important to keep in mind the underdeveloped character of contemporary studies of this kind. As Matthiessen pointed out, except for Parrington, there had been "only the usual handbook method of . . . listing the names and achievements of every possible author." While he disagreed a good deal with Hicks, Matthiessen called *The Great Tradition* "the first comprehensive analysis of our literature since the Civil War which throws all its various tendencies into a logical pattern."[10] Matthiessen thought Calverton's work a failure, but *Liberation* too is not a handbook history. Even more than Parrington, both of these critics move literary history away from the pattern of serial biography. Marxism provides these critics with an alternative conception of history and thus gives their work a coherence their competitors lacked. Biography becomes less important because class, society, and ideology now account for differences among authors and works. If the two critics' use of these concepts is not sophisticated by standards of later Marxist theory, it is considerably more subtle than Parrington's notion of the economic or his simple opposition of liberal and conservative.

Given these virtues, we might expect that the Marxist histories would have a significant impact. The books were widely known and read, but there is little evidence that the views of the American literary tradition they propound were ever widely accepted beyond Marxist circles. Certainly the books had no appreciable impact on the subdiscipline. While Hicks taught at Rensselaer Polytechnic Institute from 1929 to 1935 (when he was dismissed for political reasons), his writing had been addressed to literary rather than professional audiences. Calverton had no university affiliation. As we have seen, this did not prevent academic Americanists from reviewing the Marxist histories with some sympathy. But it does indicate that Calverton and Hicks were personally marginal to the subdiscipline, just as their books were marginalized by it. This is not to deny the importance of Marxism in the literary world of the 1930s. Numerous influential critics announced themselves as Marxist and many of these joined the Communist Party. But these critics remained largely outside of the university. When one looks at the anthologies, dissertations, and articles in *American Literature* and other scholarly journals, the Marxist point of view and the Marxist version of the American tradition are not to be found.

The New York Intellectuals

In the long run, perhaps the most important impact of these early Marxist critics was on those other leftists who would become known as the New York Intellectuals.[11] Hicks became an editor of the Party's main intellectual organ, *New Masses*, in 1934, a position that brought him into conflict a few years later with the *Partisan Review*, which by 1937 was in open opposition to the Party. The *Partisan Review* began in 1934 as the organ of the Communist Party's John Reed Clubs, which were started "to encourage both the creation of proletarian literature and the training of radical writers" (Bloom, 59). The original *Partisan Review* promoted this agenda, which was shared by its editors, Philip Rahv and William Phillips. However, from the beginning the editor's articles distinguished themselves from contemporary Communist writing:

> They generally pursued three objectives: a desire that proletarian fiction and criticism should incorporate certain aspects of the literary achievements of the 1920s; an opposition to schematic, sectarian, and reductive applications of Marxism; and a concern with developing a full Marxist aesthetic that acknowledged the special needs of radical intellectuals. . . . Of course, both [editors] gave allegiance to the Communist International's call for a consciously proletarian literature and art. They also believed in building an organized movement of anti-capitalist and pro-Soviet intellectuals. (Wald, 78)

In fact, Phillips and Rahv seem to have taken a position more explicitly Leninist than Hicks's or Calverton's on the role of critics, regarding them as a vanguard charged with directing the course of the spontaneous proletarian literary movement.[12]

The next year, however, the Communist Party's official endorsement of proletarian literature came to an end. In the same year that the revised edition of *The Great Tradition* appeared, Hicks found himself compelled, as editor of *New Masses*, to implement the Party's new Popular Front strategy. Politically, the "People's Front" was announced in Moscow on August 2, 1935, but the new literary policy was already anticipated by the American Writer's Congress held earlier in the year. The John Reed Clubs were disbanded in favor of the League of American Writers.

After the latter organization failed to make the *Partisan Review* its official organ, the journal was left without financial support and was forced to suspend publication in 1936. By the time of its emergence as an independent journal in 1937, Rahv and Phillips had rejected the Party's new line on both political and literary grounds. The Popular Front strategy called for alliances not only with other left parties but with progressive capitalism. In literary terms, this translated into an endorsement of a simple literary nationalism stripped even of the proletarian slant we found in Calverton. Newton Arvin argued for this new version of the American literary tradition at the Second Writer's Congress in 1937, where he urged attention to "The Democratic Tradition in American Letters" as represented by Thomas Hooker, John Woolman, Theodore Parker, Hamlin Garland, Howells, and Whitman. When this conception of "progressive literature" was adopted then almost anyone speaking positively of American literature could fit. Van Wyck Brooks and Archibald McLeish could be understood as expressing the Popular Front line, and so later could F. O. Matthiessen, even though he was an early contributor to the new *Partisan Review*. But of course all of these critics had developed their literary nationalism long before the Popular Front.

Phillips and Rahv had previously regarded themselves as serving the goals of a revolutionary movement, and their criticism of Party direction of writers and intellectuals was a matter of content, not policy. After 1936, however,

> Phillips and Rahv arrived at a new assessment of the relationship between revolutionary politics and radical literature. Above all, they concluded that writers and critics must be free from all partisan political and organizational pressure. Yet they also felt that they had been duped by the appealing simplicity of the notion that writers must ally themselves with the revolutionary working class. (Wald, 81–82)

Phillips and Rahv began to treat the literary avant-garde as a cultural and political vanguard. Their breaking with the Party and the proletarian literary program allowed their incipient elitism to flower. Always cosmopolitan and internationalist in their literary tastes, they were unlikely to find literary nationalism attractive under any circumstances. The effect of the Popular Front strategy was to allow the *Partisan Review* to attack both its Stalinist and its bourgeois opponents in the same breath. Later the two would often be conflated.

The New York Intellectuals were created by the split in the American left. They identified themselves from then on as anti-Stalinists, a position that would for most become simple anticommunism after the war. Without denying the importance of their anti-Stalinism, however, it can be argued that both the aesthetics and the politics of the New York Intellectuals shared an even more fundamental antipopulism. The American left since the nineteenth century had long had strong populist leanings. While the Leninism of the Communist Party represented a repudiation of populism as a political strategy, the Communists retained a populist conception of culture. The advocacy of proletarian literature derived from the view that culture should be the voice of the masses. Phillips accused the Party of "mouthing many of the populist platitudes of Upton Sinclair" even before the advent of the Popular Front.[13]

The New York Intellectuals, on the other hand, wanted a cultural vanguard, and they came to see themselves as being that vanguard. But by the late 1930s, they gave up even this hope and began to advocate "intellectual retrenchment," an embrace of the role of an alienated minority (Bloom, 94). They came to conceive of themselves as writing for a coterie. Such a position was justified by the need for an independent intelligentsia. The New York Intellectuals developed a theory of the intellectual based on this premise. It was the first such theory to be articulated in America, and it remains the dominant conception of the intellectual today. It runs directly counter to Gramsci's conception of the intellectual as inevitably serving the interests of one class or another. It is no coincidence that the New York Intellectuals eventually began to speak of themselves, that is, intellectuals, as a *class*.[14]

The New York Intellectuals' conception of themselves and the theory that justified it need to be understood as a product of the cultural position that this group occupied. As we have seen, the literary of the 1930s was no longer the dominant bourgeois cultural institution it had once been. Having lost popular influence to magazines, newspapers, radio, and film, the literary remained important mainly as a form of cultural (rather than economic or political) capital. The group of men—in the 1930s they were almost exclusively men—who came to be known as the New York Intellectuals began at the margins of this increasingly marginal sector of society. The *Partisan Review* was one of many little magazines started with little money and mostly donated labor. As an organ of the Communist Party, the journal at least had an affiliation with an important political force. Once it became independent, however, the *Partisan Review* now found itself on the margins even of the political and cultural left, the margins of the margins. Given this lack of political and cultural influence, it was perhaps necessary for the group to invent a theory that would explain their importance in the face of their seeming irrelevance. Thus they came to see an independent intelligentsia as the sine qua non of cultural achievement. In a view articulated by Phillips in 1941, American literature becomes "a kind of negative illustration of the relation of the intelligentsia to art. For the outstanding features—not to speak of failures—of our national culture can be largely explained by the inability of our native intelligentsia to achieve a detached and self-sufficient group existence."[15] The New York Intellectuals saw themselves as rectifying this situation.

It would be a mistake to think that this self-conception emerged purely from the Intellectuals' own imaginations. It was no doubt greatly abetted by the Communists' attacks on them. The Stalinist tactics of the Party led it to treat its left-wing opponents more harshly than its right-wing ones, or to simply collapse the distinction and call all of its opponents "fascists." The editorial that opens the first independent issue of the *Partisan Review* complained, "Already, before it has appeared, *Partisan Review* has been subjected to a series of attacks in the Communist Party press; already, with no regard for fact—without, indeed, any relevant facts to go by—they have attributed gratuitous political designs to *Partisan Review* in an effort to confuse the primarily literary issue between us." Yet this editorial also greatly exaggerates the Party's cultural influence in claiming the existence of "an authentic cultural bureaucracy," dominated by the Communists, which will try to "*excommunicate* the new generation" that the *Review* represents. *Partisan Review* is to its editors the organ of the genuine opposition, not merely to the Communists but to a conspiracy of "academicians from the universities," "yesterday's celebrities, and today's philistines . . . official critics [who] will revive the petty bourgeois tradition of gentility." By contrast, the *Review* "aspires to represent a new and dissident generation in American letters"; it stands for true art, for independence, for artistic innovation and experimentation, and for the future.[16]

The intellectual warfare with the Communists gave the *Partisan* group a clear sense of mission and purpose. Since the Communists were not understood as merely the dominant left group but as controlling a "cultural bureaucracy," opposition to them was opposition to the status quo. It made the aesthetic and theoretical issues that preoccupied the New York Intellectuals seem important in ways that in other contexts they would not be. It became a political act to assert their importance in the face of the Communists' dismissal of them. This may have helped make it possible for the New York Intellectuals to withdraw further into purely literary concerns while at the same time claiming political significance. Thus the editorial is curiously divided between claiming, on the one hand, "responsibility to the revolutionary movement in general" (3), and asserting the relative independence of literature and politics on the other. Furthermore, the formative experience of opposition to the Stalinism of the Party provided the model for the postwar conception of a Manichaean world consisting only of Stalinists and their opponents. The Intellectuals' position of the late 1930s that the Communists controlled American literature is a direct ancestor of the culturally dominant conception after the war that Communists secretly controlled everything from the State Department to the public schools.

It is worth noting that the Intellectuals' conception of the cultural bureaucracy included "academicians from the universities." Unlike their Nashville contemporaries who consciously planned to transform the teaching and study of literature in the academy—to form "Criticism, Inc."—the New York Intellectuals always claimed independence from academia. Like the literary radicals of the 1910s, the New Yorkers understood the professoriate as competing for control of the literary. Just as Brooks had depicted an alliance between the genteel men of letters and literary scholars, so Phillips and Rahv conceived of a hegemony of academicians, bourgeois critics (who ironically include Brooks), and Communists, whom they continued to associate with the "petty-bourgeois tradition of gentility." While the intellectuals' opposition to the academy was, in my view, structural—that is, a function of their relations in the struggle for control of cultural capital—this opposition was articulated along three lines of cleavage. First, where academics regarded themselves as preserving a tradition—whether classical, English, or American—the Intellectuals saw themselves as remaking literature. Their project thus involved a remaking of the canon, one that was potentially far more drastic than the similar project of the New Critics. The writers we now call modernists—Mann, Lawrence, Eliot, and so on—and their few historical predecessors made up the Intellectuals' canon. Second, where academics sought knowledge about literature of the past, the Intellectuals wanted to bring into being the literature of the future. The function of criticism is to make a "revolutionary literature," which is not literature that leads to political revolution, but literature that is "the product of an emerging civilization."[17] Finally, and most important, academic scholars claimed for themselves the mantle of science, while the Intellectuals understood themselves as dealing in values and interpretations. The Intellectuals could never accept the academics' claims for or even the ambition to create "modern fool-proof historical inquiry and explanation."[18] While the Intellectuals saw themselves as contributing to the collective project of building a new literature, they understood those contributions to represent their individual perspectives; they believed that much of the value of a critic's or of a writer's work derived from his or her individuality.

The New York Intellectuals' modernist conception of the artist and critic as outsiders was incompatible with the social perspective of Marxist theory, and the New Yorkers rapidly abandoned Marxism at least as a literary theory. Starting in the late 1930s, the oppositional stance they claimed for themselves grew increasingly isolated from any social movement. As an oppositional intelligentsia, the New York Intellectuals came to stand for art, for intellect, and for independence from politics, while they opposed the popular, the middle-brow, and all positions that they could term provincial or parochial. Their very isolation may have contributed to their sense of themselves as serving timeless and spaceless Literature. Their cosmopolitanism—unlike, for example, Bourne's transnationalism—did not value the separate contributions of different cultures, but imagined one "world" culture, consisting mainly of contributions by European males. The New Yorkers defined themselves as universal intellectuals. As is well known, Trilling declared his Jewish background irrelevant to his work, and only Kazin—a peripheral member of the group—seems to have frequently thematized his ethnic identity. National, racial, and finally class positions are obstacles to criticism; the intellectual claims to speak from a disinterested space that transcends these mere historical conditions. In their practice, this meant not only claims to universality but a lack of interest in history itself. What has been said of Trilling could be said of most of the New York Intellectuals: "The political history to which he was responsive was one that had become abstract, coagulated, and general. . . . In the decades after the 1930s . . . historical and political detail constantly lost weight in his evaluations."[19]

This diminished historical sense fit perfectly with their new cultural position after the war. By the 1950s, the Intellectuals themselves had become spokesmen for the culture they had as little as ten years earlier been relentlessly excoriating. The *Partisan Review* symposium "Our Country, Our Culture" (1952) demonstrated how affirmative the New York Intellectuals had become.[20] It was in this symposium that Trilling embraced the notion of the intellectual in power. Noting that intellectuals were then "better off" than ever before, Trilling claimed that the intellectual realm "associated itself with power as perhaps never before in history."[21] No longer content with their roles as mere interpreters, the New York Intellectuals increasingly sought and found roles as legislators, to put the matter in Baumann's terms. While not in the main taking up official government positions, the Intellectuals collaborated in the government's efforts to "legitimize its political power by demonstrating a corresponding greatness in culture."[22] They contributed to CIA-financed journals such as *Encounter*, and during the 1950s participated in CIA-funded organizations such as the American Committee for Cultural Freedom, of which the New York Intellectuals became leading members. Where they had once regarded everything American as suspect, they now regarded any criticism of America as a virtual form of treason, that is, giving aid and comfort to the Stalinist enemy. For example, a majority of the New York Intellectuals associated with the American Committee for Cultural Freedom refused to take a strong stand against McCarthyism until it became popular to do so. Communism was the only threat to cultural freedom most of the New York Intellectuals were able to recognize. For their service in opposition to communism at home and abroad, they earned greater access to teaching and publishing possibilities (Wald, 218). By the end of the decade, all of the major literary critics of the New York group held teaching positions.

During the 1950s, Lionel Trilling emerged as the leading literary critic among the New York Intellectuals, and it has often been claimed that he was then the most influential literary critic in America.[23] If we take Trilling to be the leading critic of the 1950s, how does he compare in that role to predecessors such as Howells and Mencken? One comparison that seems relevant is the media by which these critics reached the public. Howells published his criticism in the most influential medium of his time, the elite magazines. Mencken reached the public through newspapers and magazines of all sorts, including *Smart Set*, a specialized magazine that he edited. By the 1950s, Trilling, on the other hand, seldom published the sort of literary journalism typical of the earlier critics. His essays usually appeared first in little magazines such as *Partisan Review*, but reached a much wider audience when republished in book form. *The Liberal Imagination*, for example, sold more than one hundred thousand copies in its paperback edition. Trilling also reached the public through a relatively new medium, the book club. He wrote reviews and selected books for the Reader's Subscription and the Mid-Century Book Society. Thus Trilling was not merely an academic critic, but his role as a literary critic was less important in the American culture of the 1950s than that role was when it was filled by Howells or Mencken. Furthermore, whatever Trilling's access to the public at large, he remained a professor. He represents not the last "independent critic," but the first—and perhaps still the only—American academic literary critic to achieve broad cultural influence. Indeed, his variety of affiliations—with journals, book clubs, and especially Columbia University—belie any claim to independence.

If Trilling was the leading literary critic of the 1950s, then *Partisan Review* was the most important literary magazine of the time. If we compare *Partisan Review* to the *Atlantic* of the nineteenth century, or even to *Smart Set* or *The Nation* during the 1920s, we chart another way in which the cultural reach of the literary had diminished. No "little magazine" had ever before been accorded so much importance, but *Partisan Review* remained small in circulation and advertising. Its influence stemmed from its readership of other intellectuals, including professors, literary journalists, editors, and the like. As a literary magazine, *Partisan Review* differed from academic quarterlies in that it published a mixture of literary works and criticism. From its position outside of the academy, *Partisan Review* became one of the dominant organs in literature inside as well. Its original position on the outside enabled the journal to develop as it did, but during the 1950s the fact of the journal's independence was increasingly made irrelevant by the academic associations of its contributors. Even today the journal continues to give the impression of independence from the academy, but it has been university-sponsored since the late 1950s. Beginning even before that, most of the criticism published in *Partisan Review* was by professors. This is not to say that *Partisan Review* became just another *PMLA* because of its academic associations. On the contrary, like the *Kenyon Review* and other journals of criticism and letters, *Partisan Review* helped to bring these activities into academic acceptability. As Leslie Fiedler observed of himself and Richard Chase, "the rise of such critics is one symptom of the academization of formerly nonacademic journals, and of the complementary acceptance of articles written in them as academic credentials."[24] Criticism became in the 1950s a practice dominated by the university, and the writing of fiction and poetry increasingly took place there. Ironically, then, we see the antiacademic New York Intellectuals bringing more of the literary under academic control.

The New York Intellectuals moved in the course of about twenty years from the margins of an already marginal radical movement to the center of American literary life. What allowed them to make this journey was their willingness to become apologists for America, and the declining economic and political importance of the literary during the period in question. Nevertheless, the literary continued to represent valuable cultural capital, and the New York Intellectuals came to control a significant portion of it. But if they continued to imagine themselves in competition with the university, in fact their cultural influence derived from alliances with it.

The Other New Critics

The New York Intellectuals are sometimes understood as staunch opponents of the Nashville intellectuals and the New Criticism they introduced into the university.[25] During the 1930s, the Nashville critics did regard the literary left as their principal opposition, but their major arguments seemed to be with Hicks, Smith, and others more devoted to proletarian literature. When *Partisan Review* became independent, an exchange between the two camps began that continued well into the 1950s, after which it continued by virtue of their common association with English departments. During the 1930s, the New York Intellectuals, like other Marxists, clearly regarded Allen Tate and the other Agrarians as political and aesthetic opponents. But Rahv asked Tate for a contribution to *Partisan Review* in 1938, and as early as 1939, the New Critics and the New York Intellectuals began to show up in each other's journals. Lionel Trilling was an original member of the editorial board of the *Kenyon Review*, and Rahv, William Barrett, and Richard Chase published there. R. P. Blackmur, Cleanth Brooks, Robert Penn Warren, and Tate appeared in *Partisan Review*. Trilling, Chase, Rahv, and Alfred Kazin were fellows of the Kenyon School of English in the late 1940s. In Cooney's analysis, "the 'Agrarians' helped provide the *Partisan* critics with a sustaining network of intellectual and social ties as their bonds to the left unraveled" (209).

To note this connection is not to minimize the differences that remained between the two groups. It does demonstrate, however, that both groups contributed to the same discursive formation. The differences of theory and practice between the New Critics and the New York Intellectuals represent two positions defined by a shared set of assumptions, those of hermeneutics rather than positivism. The similarities between the two groups are thus far more significant than the differences, especially when contrasted with standard academic practice of the 1930s.

The New York Intellectuals, partly as a result of their own protests, are often thought to be historically and socially oriented critics. It would be a mistake, however, to think that the literary critics among the New York Intellectuals were ever much interested in history, and especially historical detail. Despite their claims to historical materialism during the 1930s, there is precious little historical analysis in the pages of *Partisan Review* or in other of their published work. "History" is most often used to invoke the Marxist metanarrative of modes of production and class struggle rather than to point to particular events.

Phillips, Rahv, and Trilling were not historians, or even mainly evaluative critics, but theorists. As early as 1935, Phillips and Rahv were arguing explicitly for theory. The development of a Marxist aesthetic is in their view "being seriously hampered by the prevalent vociferous aversion to theoretical analysis. Usually such analysis is dismissed as 'bourgeois estheticism,' 'academicism,' and what not. This distaste for theory reveals a misconception of the role and nature of criticism" ("Criticism," 17). What we find in *Partisan Review* during the 1930s and 1940s is a developing body of theory that, although never worked out with equal rigor or consistency, nevertheless paralleled the simultaneous development of the New Criticism. Like the New Critics, the New York Intellectuals were hermeneuts who saw literature as a special problem for interpretation and evaluation. Phillips and Rahv portrayed their leftist opponents as treating literature as simply another form of politics, and themselves as regarding literature as "a social instrument," but not one that worked in the same way as political and economic writing. Criticism should properly be concerned with "creating a new aesthetic" and "revaluating literary history" rather than with promoting new proletarian novels or plays ("Criticism," 18).

If the New Yorkers complained about the overemphasis on form and technique in the New Critics, they also complained about the neglect of these matters by most Marxist critics. The *Partisan Review* may have been the place where the problem of "vulgar Marxism" was first noticed and addressed in America. Like the New Critics, the New York Intellectuals valued complexity. Vulgar Marxist criticism failed because it was given over to "empirical observations," and "obvious truths"; it insisted "on elementary political lessons" rather than advancing our understanding ("Criticism," 16). Both literature and the world were too complex to be comprehended by simple formulas, and Stalinism comes to operate as a name for that mistake. It is perhaps only in this way that we can understand how it can still be asserted in 1948 that "Stalinism becomes endemic in the American middle class as soon as that class begins to think."[26] The New Yorkers believed that the world was fundamentally ambiguous, and the authors whom they championed were understood to share this view.

None of the New York Intellectuals was so devoted to complexity as Lionel Trilling. "Moral realism," the value Trilling most sought in fiction, is the antithesis of Stalinism, and it has been defined as "the imagination of complication" (Krupnick, 64). It might be argued that Trilling's most typical rhetorical move is to assert that "it's more complicated than that."[27] Trilling's famous attack on Parrington—titled, in *The Liberal Imagination*, "Reality in America"—boils down to little more than the assertion that the world is more complex than Parrington can comprehend. In making this attack, Trilling invents something that could be called "Parringtonism," although he does not use the name. It might seem at first that Parringtonism would be some kind of explicit political interpretation of American culture. Trilling says that "Parrington formulated in a classic way the suppositions about our culture which are held by the American middle class" (Trilling, *Liberal*, 3). Yet Trilling tells us little about what those suppositions are. He characterizes Parrington's interpretive strategy as a simplistic economic and social determinism, yet that is not the focus of Trilling's attack. Rather, Parringtonism consists in this doctrine:

> There exists . . . a thing called *reality*; it is one and immutable, it is wholly external, it is irreducible. Men's minds may waver, but reality is always reliable, always the same, always easily to be known. And the artist's relation to reality [Parrington] conceives as a simple one. Reality being fixed and given, the artist has but to let it pass through him, he is the lens in the first diagram of an elementary book on optics: Fig. 1, Reality; Fig. 2,

Artist; Fig. 1', Work of Art. Figs. 1 and 1' are normally in virtual correspondence with each other. (4–5)

It is interesting that Parrington's failure turns out to be epistemological and that faulty epistemology, a cultural condition: "the chronic American belief that there exists an opposition between reality and mind and that one must enlist oneself in the party of reality" (10). But Parringtonism is also given a particular social location. Parrington's "coadjutors and disciples" are said to "make up what might be called the literary academicism of liberalism" (10).

Trilling inflated Parrington's importance because it served Trilling's political agenda to do so. Parrington is used by Trilling as a stand-in for the leftist criticism of the 1930s, aka Stalinism. In the original article, published in *Partisan Review* in 1940, Communist critic Bernard Smith is depicted as a second instance of Parringtonism. In the later version Granville Hicks replaces Smith, and Hicks is actually quoted more often than Parrington. Even Matthiessen—probably because he was a Popular Front supporter—is depicted as expressing Parringtonism in defending Dreiser, even though Matthiessen's epistemology has much more in common with Trilling's. Rather than seeing Parrington as the end of something, Trilling treats him as the initiator of a movement.

If one accepts Trilling's claim that Parringtonism dominates Americans' understanding of their own culture, then one is likely to regard Trilling's attack on Parrington as having the effect of overthrowing Parringtonism. Thus Reising describes "Reality in America" as "dealing a death blow to the Parrington school of social criticism" and Gene Wise calls *The Liberal Imagination* a "threshold moment" of a paradigm shift.[28] But by 1950, "the Parrington school," if such a thing had ever existed, was long since in decline. The progressive paradigm that Wise believes governs Parrington's work (along with that of Charles Beard and Carl Becker) was by this time no longer dominant in the field of American history, and this paradigm had never been dominant within the field of American literature in the first place.[29] As we have seen, the majority of textbook anthologies, including the best-sellers, produced by Americanists and used in American literature courses based their selection on aesthetic considerations. By 1941, Matthiessen had already provided the exemplar for a new conception of American literature.

Though it did not overthrow its predecessor, Trilling's *The Liberal Imagination* is an expression of a new paradigm. But what is that paradigm? Wise calls it counterprogressive, which leads him to define it quite literally as the opposite of the progressive paradigm. This tactic allows Wise to make some interesting generalizations about studies of American history and literature produced in the 1950s, but it ultimately explains the rise of the counterprogressive as a reversal of and reaction to the progressive. There *is* a paradigm shift reflected in *The Liberal Imagination*, but that shift is epistemological at root and it is as much reflected in the New Criticism as it is in the work of the New York Intellectuals.[30] In fact, I would argue that literary studies are still working under that same paradigm. The most fundamental difference between Parrington and Trilling is that Parrington is a positivist, while Trilling is a hermeneut. Wise comes closest to understanding this point when he quotes Matthiessen's dictum that "you cannot 'use' a work unless you have comprehended its meaning. It is well to remember that although literature reflects an age, it also illuminates it" (quoted in Wise, 239). Parrington's conception of the relation of literature to society can be described as "billiard-ball causality." But it is important to insist that in this Parrington was typical of the literary scholarship of his era. It is true that most of his fellow Americanists were uncomfortable with Parrington's theory, but like him they assumed that the literary historian's job was to find the causes that were responsible for literary works. Thus Foerster's four "factors"—the frontier spirit, the Puritan mind, romanticism, and realism—are causes of the particular character of American literary works. Only later, after the paradigm shift, will they become what the literature expresses. There is, of course, an important difference between Foerster and Parrington: the former is an idealist and the latter a materialist. But neither regards the meaning of a literary work as his central problematic. Foerster and Parrington share some of the epistemological assumptions of earlier historians who followed Taine in believing that physical causes such as geography and race determined literature. We saw how Wendell gave this theory a new basis in society and language, but he retained region and race as secondary categories. Race and region both drop out for Foerster and Parrington, but the intellectual problem remains the same: to explain the existence of the literature.

In this light, I think it can be argued that we put too fine a point on Trilling's objections to Parrington if we understand them, as Reising does, as a response to "the errors of a crude base/superstructure model" (100). As we have seen, the New York Intellectuals had rejected such a conception all along. Trilling, himself a Marxist only for a brief moment, cannot be understood in 1950 to be concerned with revising the Marxist model. Rather, base/superstructure is for Trilling just one instance of an epistemological position that he finds characteristic of American culture and of American literature studies. Trilling complains that "American literature as an academic subject is not so much a *subject* as an *object* of study: it does not, as literature should, put the scrutinizer of it under scrutiny but, instead, leaves its students with a too comfortable sense of complete comprehension."[31] Literature, for Trilling, does not fit under the scientific conception of an object to be known. The proper experience of literature would seem to entail the experience of ambiguity, and the necessity of interpretation is the result.

Trilling had been explicitly endorsing interpretation for some time. In the first version of the essay on Parrington, where Trilling seems at some pains to be evenhanded, he asserts that "Parrington's conception of economic determinism was a useful one," because "it could really interpret."[32] Several times in the essay this interpretive conception of literary study is contrasted with one that would claim to apply the methods of science to literature. This is the same kind of error as assuming a "solid and irrefutable" reality (34). Though Parrington is judged guilty of the latter misconception, he is granted the recognition that his own work is not science. The other target of this essay, Bernard Smith, is guilty of claiming science, however. Trilling is willing to grant "a kind of science" to the "classifications" and "definite connections" of German philology, but in

> literary history, even though the ideal of checked data as complete as possible is the essential equipment of the literary

scholar, the 'science' has already a certain metaphorical flavor. After all, there are only certain things in literature that are indisputable and very few things indeed that are measurable. A spelling, an edition, a date, a form, the length of a line—we can be definite about these, even when incorrect. *But a meaning is not indisputable*, nor a quality either, and we find ourselves in a realm in which science cannot apply. (35, italics added)

Trilling here presents a statement more explicit than any of those of the Agrarians concerning the assumptions that will come to govern the practice of literary study in the university. Both the New Critics and the New York Intellectuals helped to establish a new practice of criticism based on the premise that literature requires special means of interpretation. This criticism explicitly or implicitly assumes that differences of interpretation and evaluation will be the rule rather than the exception. That is why both groups can regularly appear in each other's journals, become part of the same social networks, and teach in the same summer institutes. The two groups agree about the work's epistemological and ontological status.

One marker of that changed status is the new concern with "myths" and "symbols" in literary works. "Myth" had been a preoccupation of the *Partisan Review* starting in the late 1930s. The term came to criticism via the work of modernist writers such as Eliot and Lawrence, who influenced not just the New York Intellectuals but the Nashville intellectuals and university critics such as Matthiessen as well. The concern with myth was also related to the more general conception of mind as the realm of symbols. Though "myth" was not a term for which Phillips or Rahv had any use during the 1930s, their journal published numerous essays that discovered myths in modern literature. William Troy, for example, contributed articles on myth in the works of Lawrence and Mann.[33] At that time, Troy's invocation of myth was attacked by several members of the journal's inner circle, including Phillips, who insisted on science as a necessary ground for both criticism and literature.[34]

As it moved away from Marxism, however, *Partisan Review* also moved away from its defense of science and rationalism, and increasingly embraced a conception of culture and literature in which nonrational experience—myth, emotion, personality, the unconscious, and so on—became central. This is in part because the journal and the New York Intellectuals came to be represented by Trilling more than Phillips or Rahv. "Myth" was not a key term for Trilling himself, and he in fact remained wary of myth criticism. Myths were for him not real enough; he attacked Wellek's and Warren's claim that ideas become effective in literature only as symbols or myths ("Meaning," 283). However, when "myth" did become a key term in the discussion of American civilization during the 1950s and 1960s, Trilling was not overly dismayed. His own criticism of the 1950s "makes major concessions to the tendency represented by myth criticism even in opposing it, and his opposition is of the mildest kind" (Krupnick, 115). One of those myth critics was Richard Chase, whose *The American Novel and Its Tradition* defines American literature as tending toward the mythic and symbolic as opposed to the real. Earlier he had published *Quest for Myth*, his Columbia doctoral dissertation, for which Trilling served as one of the readers. The book is organized as a historical study of various modern conceptions of myth, from the Enlightenment to psychoanalysis. Chase's point, however, is to insist that myth is literature and art, and cannot be properly understood in mere functional terms. His references to anthropologists such as Franz Boas and Bronislaw Malinowski, to neo-Kantian philosophers such as Ernst Cassirer and Susanne Langer, and to Freud indicate the broader intellectual movement in which myth criticism has its roots. Chase quotes from Trilling a statement about psychoanalysis that also explains the more general interest in myths and symbols: "It was left for Freud to discover how, in a scientific age, the life of the emotions is lived by figurative formations, and to create, what psychoanalysis is, a science of tropes, of metaphor."[35] In other words, psychoanalysis, like literary criticism, is the interpretation of a special "language" normally impervious to understanding.

Chase, Trilling, and other New York Intellectuals share with the New Critics the project of interpretation. Their methods of reading literary works were often quite similar: "Trilling's dialectical method is like the 'tension' and 'irony' by which, in the New Critical theory, the contraries of a poem are bound together in an organic unity" (Krupnick, 54–55). Furthermore, by the late 1940s, the New York Intellectuals were increasingly interested in the same sorts of moral drama that the New Critics found in literary works. Trilling, for example, was concerned with obstacles to the intellect and imagination that he "typically located . . . within man himself, in some fissure that divided man from his very essence."[36] Both groups thus tended to read literature ahistorically and without regard to specific social contexts. The two groups differed significantly, however, in their conception of literature.[37] While the New Critics often expand the importance of literature—as Tate does when he says that "literature is the complete knowledge of man's experience"—they always insist on literature's specificity. But "literature" for Trilling and the other New Yorkers seems to incorporate some of the earlier broader meaning of the term. While "literature" most emphatically excluded "low culture" or mass culture, it included criticism and other forms of discursive prose. The generic specifications here are less important, however, than the frequent use of the term to stand for culture or for important beliefs or ideas. In other words, literature ideally should continue to function as knowledge or learning: "The literature of contemporary Europe is in competition with philosophy, theology, and science . . . it seeks to match them in comprehensiveness and power and seriousness" (Trilling, "Meaning," 293). Often, the "literary" is used as a synonym for "intellectual" or "cultural," so that reading many of the contributions to the *Partisan Review* symposium "Our Country, Our Culture" one is hard put to find any acknowledgment of intellectuals who are not literary critics. This easy slippage, if not simple identification, between literature and culture will be taken up in the 1950s and 1960s by many others who were creating American civilization. Here we will find that American culture comes to be conceived as figurative forms in need of interpretation.

The Invention of Modernism

As we will see in a moment, Rahv, Phillips, and Trilling did contribute directly to the project of inventing an American literary tradition, but they did not do so intentionally. Rather than make an effort to find a usable past, the New Yorkers sought an alternative tradition, modern European literature, which they initially hoped would transform future American literature. American literature is depicted as suffering from the same liabilities as the scholars who study it. American literature is "essentially passive," while modern European literature is "active" and puts "the scrutinizer under scrutiny" (Trilling, "Meaning," 292). It was this literature to which the New York Intellectuals devoted the greatest part of their attention. The result was the creation of an alternative canon that eventually received official recognition in the university.

Perhaps the most important literary role of the New York Intellectuals was as American inventors of what has come to be called "modernism." It is important to stipulate that in the mid-1930s, the New York Intellectuals had only the most inchoate conception of modern literature. Consider Phillips's account of what we now call the moderns as the second of "three generations." He recognizes a connection between, on the one hand, European avant-garde movements such as the symbolists and surrealists and, on the other, the lost generation, especially Eliot and Stein. However, he asserts that already "the lost generation has slipped into literary history."[38] The connection had been asserted several years earlier by Edmund Wilson in *Axel's Castle* (1931), widely recognized as the first book to provide an argument for what distinguished "modernist" literature (though Wilson called it "symbolist"). Wilson, for reasons of his very different background and development as a critic, should not be considered one of the New York Intellectuals, but this book and his critical work in general were major influences on them. If Wilson's book was the first survey of the terrain of modernism, however, the New York Intellectuals, in essays published from the late 1930s until the early 1960s, provided the definitive map of the field. Modernist literature came to be promoted by the New York Intellectuals as an alternative literary tradition to the one that academic Americanists and Popular-Front critics more or less shared.

At first, however, Phillips and Rahv imagined something beyond the literature we call modernist, a third generation. Most studies of the Intellectuals suggest that their first literary love was the experimental or avant-garde writing of the 1920s. During their first period of political radicalism in the 1930s, however, they espoused the cause of proletarian literature without abandoning their interest in the avant-garde. The first of the three generations consisted of the prewar group of writers, such as Dreiser, Lewis, Edwin Arlington Robinson, and Carl Sandburg, defined by their social interests. The third, the "proletarian," generation, the current group of writers associated with the radical movement, would combine the social awareness of the first generation with the artistic sophistication of the second, that is, the lost generation, to produce a revolutionary literature (Phillips, "Generations," 49–55). After the split with the Communist Party, *Partisan Review* dropped its endorsement of proletarian literature entirely. The new line identified radical politics with avant-garde writing. Marx himself comes to be represented, against "dogmatic Marxists," as an intellectual and a cosmopolitan. Articulating their opposition to literary nationalism in terms familiar from debates within Marxist politics, Phillips and Rahv opposed "the futile attempt to create a literature in one country—futile because inevitably a contradiction arises between the international consciousness of intellectual life and the provincial smugness of literature itself."[39] Phillips's and Rahv's alternative to American literary nationalism was their call for the "Europeanization of American literature."

It was essentially this project that *Partisan Review* and the New York Intellectuals would work at well into the 1950s, but the project evolved into something that its founders could not have foreseen. The desires to create a revolutionary literature or to Europeanize American literature were aimed at transforming what was written more than what was being read. The literature of the "emerging civilization" would be new kinds of fiction and poetry. Criticism was intended not merely to evaluate and interpret existing literature, but to guide and instruct new writers. In this project of building a new literature, the New York Intellectuals had much in common with the men of letters of the turn of the century who sought to build an American literature. The New Critics also wanted a new literature—and, indeed, helped create an entire generation of American poets—but the majority of literature professors continued to ignore contemporary literature entirely. The New York Intellectuals' championing of modernist fiction writers may have had as much influence on postwar fiction writing in America as it had on the study and criticism of modern literature. Still, as the New York Intellectuals themselves saw it, such influence did not produce the new literature they sought. In the absence of a recognizable contemporary American renaissance, the New Yorkers focused their attention on the second generation, who became the most important concern of *Partisan Review* after the break with the Communist Party. Not all of this commentary was celebratory, but all of it was respectful. By making the modernists the center of their attention, the New York Intellectuals canonized them.

As they moved into the academy in the 1950s, the New Yorkers brought their canon with them. The irony of this was not lost on members of the circle. One of the reasons this literature had appealed to the young Intellectuals was precisely its difference from the literature then typical of university literature classes. This literature was to the New York Intellectuals the antithesis of the academic, even though some of it—the poems of Eliot and Pound, the fiction of Joyce—was itself dependent on knowledge produced by the modern humanities. It has been argued that such literature was the perfect material to be grist for the New Critical interpretive mill. The New Yorkers' antiacademicism made them ambivalent about finding modernism becoming a university subject. On the one hand, they see modern literature as resisting the practices of academics because it does not "consent to be merely comprehended. . . . We as scholars and critics try to discover the source of its effective energy. . . . But inevitably we become aware that it happily exists beyond our powers of explanation, although not, certainly, beyond our powers of response" (Trilling, "Meaning," 292). Here modernist literature is still presented as an alternative to the official literature of the bureaucracy, but by 1961, Trilling was worried that the acceptance of modern literature by the academy could easily deprive the literature of its distinctive character. That character Trilling names as the goal of "freedom from society itself. . . . the idea of losing oneself up to the point of self-destruction, of surrendering oneself to experience without regard to self-interest or conventional morality."[40] Trilling's advice to the teacher of modern literature is that this element must not be left out, even if its inclusion seems paradoxical given the mission of the university. This latter concern points up Trilling's Arnoldian side. Krupnick argues that "Trilling took seriously the notion that he was educating young men—he was never much concerned with the education of young women—who would, as he put it, be 'responsible for the welfare of the polity' " and concludes that Trilling did not want to turn his Columbia undergraduates into *"Partisan Review* intellectuals."[41] Thus Trilling the humanist and cultural conservator conflicted with Trilling the modernist and cultural critic—or at least Trilling experienced such a conflict. But once modernist literature became canonized, it too became something to conserve, as New York Intellectual descendants such as Hilton Kramer illustrate. Furthermore, the radical claims made on behalf of the literature obscured its own historical connections to Arnoldian humanism.

But the New York Intellectuals nevertheless treated modernism in Arnoldian terms as a transhistorical condition of literature. Even Irving Howe, generally more historical in his approach, uses Catullus as an example of a modern poet. The New York Intellectuals did believe that the last 100 years had imposed special difficulties on man, but this did not necessarily make them especially historical critics. As we have seen, the New Critics too found special difficulties in the modern world, even if they disagreed about how those conditions might be relieved. The creation of "modernist literature" occurs in terms of the problematic of universal human nature facing unnatural conditions. If those conditions were sometimes in the 1950s still named by the New York Intellectuals in Marxist terms, this was a mere holdover from the rhetoric of the 1930s. Modernity was not a mode of production but a state of spiritual degeneration. Books were pretexts, not for discussion of politics, history, or society, but for discussions of abstractions such as "the spiritual circumstances of the modern world."

Like the New Critics, the New York Intellectuals came to the position that the ultimate reality of literature transcended history and society. In 1961, Trilling still sees modernism as dangerous, but the danger is now understood to be personal, where it had been understood in the 1930s by Phillips and Rahv to be social. This new interpretation fits perfectly with the increasing conservatism of the New Yorkers after the war, and with the newly acquired cultural capital that modernism had come to represent. Whatever radical significance modernist literature had in the 1920s and 1930s, little remained. The 1950s saw "the emergence of academic modernism at the center of an elite culture of the intellectual establishment, in the universities and in publishing circles" (Wald, 226). By the late fifties, at least one of the New York circle recognized that modernist literature was now "in power" (Wald, 221; quoting Delmore Schwartz).

Whatever their misgivings, the New York Intellectuals played a major role in "institutionalizing modernism."[42] By the early 1960s, the members of the group were writing not merely criticism but literary histories of modernism. Irving Howe, who lamented "the decline of the new," nevertheless contributed an important work in this genre, "The Idea of the Modern."[43] Trilling accomplished one of the most significant acts of any literary institutionalization, the creation of a textbook anthology, *The Experience of Literature* (1967), about 50 percent of which is made up of modernist literature.[44] The textbook was hailed (in the New York Intellectuals' own *Commentary*) as "a significant document in contemporary American culture" and more recently Krupnick called it "a massive summation of the literary taste of an entire generation."[45] This text made modernist works available for ready use in beginning literature classes. By 1970, modernism would have its own specialized academic journals, and courses devoted to it as a specific literary period would become commonplace.

But if the New York Intellectuals' favorite books became, not only the taste of an entire generation, but firmly implanted in the groves of academe, these books did not displace other canons in the latter. If modernist literature came to be widely taught, it did so within the already existing structure of the literary curriculum. Thus American modernist works were most likely to be taught in American literature courses, British modernist works in British literature courses, and so on. The alternative canon was not merely institutionalized, but intellectually absorbed by the university. Furthermore, British and American literature surveys remained the most widely taught courses within the curriculum of English departments. At the high school and junior high levels, these were often the only historical frames literary works were given. Thus, in spite of the influence of the New York Intellectuals, modernism never displaced the nationalist organization of literary study, nor did it endanger the canon that academic Americanists had created.

Defending American Civilization

In spite of themselves, the New York Intellectuals did contribute to that canon. Perhaps the major contribution of the New York Intellectuals to American literature as an object of study was the selection of Fitzgerald, Hemingway, and Faulkner to represent American fiction of the twentieth century. Trilling wrote one of the essays most influential in reviving Fitzgerald's reputation, and Howe's *William Faulkner* was one of the first book-length studies of that author.[46] Trilling refers to Hemingway and Faulkner as exceptions to the general "passivity" of American literature ("Meaning," 296). Yet even these writers never quite found their place in the New Yorkers' canon. They were exceptions to the general condition of American literature, but for one reason or another, neither did they seem central to modernism. Among American-born writers, only T. S. Eliot and Henry James were central.[47]

It is not surprising, given both their background and their beliefs, that most of the New York Intellectuals would fail to embrace American literature. Most of the group were first- or second-generation immigrants who grew up in urban Jewish neighborhoods, often speaking Yiddish as a first language. They experienced themselves as alienated, not only economically or spiritually as other literary radicals had, but culturally as well. Their conception of literature was international, and they valued the cosmopolitan over the local or provincial. As a result, in Howe's judgment, "not many *Partisan* critics were sufficiently grounded in the native cultural tradition" (*Margin*, 142). This is not to say that the New York Intellectuals ignored American literature entirely, but that they conceived of it in a distinctly different way. For one thing, American literature began for them around the turn of the century. The literature of most of the nineteenth century and earlier was either anathema or irrelevant to them. Instead of dealing with recent American literature as part of a national tradition, they approached it from the perspective of modern European literature.

Yet in order to become cultural legislators, they had to first become defenders of American culture, a transformation that required them to abandon their Marxist critical position and most of their earlier interpretations as well. They began to modify their antipathy to most things American. The transformation seems to have occurred during the war, although we begin to see signs of such a change even in the late 1930s, with Rahv's essays on American culture. But prior to the war, the *Partisan* group continued to associate Stalinists with the American bourgeoisie and the literary establishment. In 1939, Rahv could still charge that "supporting our decrepit social system, including the wars it gives rise to, cannot but lead in practice to the same consequences as fascism itself."[48] After the war, as they became the literary establishment, these critics now saw Stalinism as the leading threat to the American culture they had previously rejected. It is not surprising, then, that their literary criticism should become increasingly celebratory of American writing. Nevertheless, the New York Intellectuals did not become literary nationalists, even if some of them did become political nationalists.

In spite of their opposition to literary nationalism, the New York Intellectuals are often credited with offering some of the most important "theories of American literature," theories that do encompass the nineteenth century. This claim is made in part on the strength of contributions by more peripheral members of the group, including Alfred Kazin, Richard Chase, and Leslie Fiedler, but Rahv and especially Trilling are also cited. The latter offered ideas about American literature that were intended to explain its shortcomings, and they entailed conceptions of American culture as a whole. We have already noted how, like other radicals of the 1930s, the New York Intellectuals regarded the United States both as a failed civilization and as a dying social system. It was the association of capitalism with American cultural production that served as the ideational basis for the rejection of the Popular Front project of reclaiming progressive elements in an American tradition. In 1939, Rahv could still complain of a "new gentility" among American writers, a gentility "not based on a growing economy and a rising civilization; it is based on a downward-curving economy and an exhausted civilization" ("Twilight," 10).

But the problem of American civilization was a starting point for the New Yorkers' treatment of American literature. As we saw even in Foerster, the problem of national culture became a theme in the American tradition, in other words, an aspect of national culture. Thus Rahv begins to make American civilization an object of study. In "Redskin and Paleface," Rahv proposed a theory of the failure of American literature, the notion that "the national literature suffers from the ills of a split personality."[49] Henry James and Walt Whitman represent the purest instances of the two halves of this split between the highbrow, patrician paleface and the lowbrow, plebeian redskin. While Rahv clearly shows more affinity for the paleface than the redskin, the essay's major point is that American literature is defined by the radical division between the two kinds of writers. In spite of himself, then, Rahv is helping to construct a national literature.

A year later in "The Cult of Experience in American Writing," without using the terms "paleface" and "redskin," Rahv further develops the theory proposed in the earlier article. "The disunity of American literature, its polar division into above and below or highbrow and lowbrow writing" continues to be asserted, but now this condition is no longer treated as fundamental:

> There is . . . a common ground . . . an essential American-
> ism subsuming them both that is best defined by their mutual
> affirmation of experience. . . . plebeian and patrician are
> historically associated in the radical enterprise of subverting,
> each from his own end, the puritan code of stark utility in the
> conduct of life and in releasing the long compressed springs of
> experience in the national letters. In this sense, Whitman and
> James are the true initiators of the American line of modernity.[50]

Experience thus distinguishes modern American literature from its failed ancestors. Rahv finds himself agreeing with "genteel literary historian Barrett Wendell" that early American literature is a " 'record of the national inexperience' marked by 'an instinctive disregard of actual fact' " (415). Rahv invokes the romance/novel distinction to illustrate this disregard, asserting:

> Brown, Cooper, Hawthorne, and Melville were "romancers"
> rather than novelists. They were incapable of apprehending the
> vitally new principle of realism by virtue of which the art of fic-

tion in Europe was in their time rapidly evolving toward an hitherto inconceivable condition of objectivity and familiarity with existence. (415)

By invoking this distinction, Rahv can claim a radical break in American literary history; in the twentieth century, "the urge to experience at last overwhelmed and decisively transformed literary art" (418). In this sense, "The Cult of Experience in American Writing" may be seen as another version of the narrative Phillips told in "Three Generations." But instead of asserting development toward a revolutionary amalgam of realist and modernist literature, the narrative now ends with American literature's failure to reach the level of achievement of European modernists.

"The Cult of Experience in American Writing" seems to have initiated discussion of the theme of American inexperience and of the romance/novel distinction among the New York Intellectuals. One is led to wonder why Barrett Wendell's old chestnuts were revived in 1940 and took on a life of their own in the 1950s. Geraldine Murphy argues that they served Cold War politics well, with "romance" standing for freedom, "the novel" for social restrictions.[51] The importance of the romance/novel distinction in later discussions of American literature is usually credited to Trilling, who first mentions it in "Manners, Morals, and the Novel," a lecture delivered at Kenyon College in 1947 and first published in 1950 in *The Liberal Imagination*. Trilling's book doubtless reached a much larger audience than Rahv's essay, but Rahv's precedence in this matter should be acknowledged. Richard Chase, of course, made the romance/novel distinction the basis of *The American Novel and Its Tradition*, and, as a result, the distinction became a standard element of American literature as an object of study. In defining the romance as the American form of the novel, Chase opposes reality to the "mythic, allegorical, and symbolistic."[52] The meaning of "reality" in this opposition is problematic, as it already was in both Rahv and Trilling. Rahv's distinction, upheld by Chase, seems to locate reality in social and historical fact, a position that seems very close to the one for which Trilling condemns Parrington.

But Trilling's own use of the term "reality" in "Manners, Morals, and the Novel," is also inconsistent with his use of it in

"Reality in America."[53] The novel, Trilling claims in the former essay, "is a perpetual quest for reality, the field of its research being always the social world" (212). Nineteenth-century American romances ignored this quest because nineteenth-century America offered "no opportunity for the novelist to do his job of searching out reality, not enough complication of appearance to make the job interesting" (213). It is as if nineteenth-century America were adequately described in terms of Parringtonism. Reality in America was then so obvious that novelists had to ignore it in order to have something interesting to write about. But twentieth-century American writers do not have the same excuse: "Life in America has increasingly thickened. . . . become more complex and more pressing" ("Manners," 213). Still, novelists such as Dreiser and Lewis are inadequate to the task of recording social fact, and thus Trilling can claim that "Americans have a kind of resistance to looking closely at society" ("Manners," 213). Trilling fails to explain the unreality of the realists; he simply assumes his audience will agree with his dismissal of them. What we can infer, however, is that the realists are interested in the wrong sorts of social facts. While they acknowledge the existence of classes, they don't focus on how that reality is expressed in manners.

Reality, it would seem, is manners, except that, of course, "it's more complicated than that." Manners provide the field against which moral realism, that is, the imagination of complexity, may be displayed. "We have no books that raise questions in our minds not only about conditions but about ourselves, that lead us to refine our motives and ask what might lie behind our good impulses" ("Manners," 219–20). Here Trilling calls for a hermeneutics of suspicion, and he even invokes Freud as an example in the next paragraph. But he might just as well have invoked Matthiessen, who treats Hawthorne and Melville precisely as authors who lead us to "ask what might lie behind our good impulses." He could also have invoked Marx, who asks us to see what lies behind the "good" impulses of the ruling class. But the "good impulses" of which Trilling is suspicious are democracy and egalitarianism. Many of Trilling's favorite authors—James, Austen, Forster, Fitzgerald—fuel this suspicion by depicting the ruling class sympathetically. One is led to the conclusion that Trilling's hermeneutics is meant to affirm the moral value of class divisions, rather than to question them. The nineteenth-century romancers won't do because they ignore class; Marx and the American realists fail because for them class is the reality behind appearances. Thus, Fitzgerald's notion that the rich are different passes in Trilling for shrewd social observation, while Dreiser in depicting class oppression is merely stating the obvious.

Rahv and Trilling made the oppositions of innocence/experience, romance/novel, and unreality/reality structural to the discussion of American literature and culture during the 1950s. They continued to valorize the second term even if they recognized that it contained some elements of the first. The work of other critics, however, such as Richard Chase and R. W. B. Lewis, would question such privileging without quite managing to reverse it. Chase's *The American Novel and Its Tradition* is the most important book on American literature to have emerged mainly from this discussion.[54] According to Reising, Chase transformed "Trilling's insights into a new definition of American fiction which elevates its supposed radical alienation from society into a generic norm" (124). In Reising's view, Chase uses Trilling's aesthetic of complexity to affirm the value of American romance, which "pictures human life in the context of unresolved contradictions" (Reising, 129, quoting Chase, 224). But Reising neglects to mention that Chase uses Trilling against his own judgments, Trilling having not found the requisite complexity in the nineteenth-century romancers. In arguing for a national tradition, Chase explicitly rejects the New York Intellectuals' internationalism. Furthermore, his valuing of complexity puts him in agreement with the dominant critical paradigm of the period, and not merely with Trilling. Chase's project, like Fiedler's in *Love and Death in the American Novel*, represents a direction of study that the older members of the New York circle refused to follow very far. The first generation of New York Intellectuals, we might say, backed into inventing an American tradition. It was younger members of the circle who developed systematic versions of the American tradition. As we will see in the next chapter, the themes that the New York Intellectuals found in American literature become central to its reconceptualization in a new disciplinary object.

9

Civilization "Discovered"

One goal of the organized study of American literature almost from the founding of the ALG had been to discover what it was that made American literature a single entity, and what it was that distinguished this entity from other national literatures. We have seen that the Americanists' scholarly practice and the assumptions on which it rested prohibited them from attaining these goals. The new hermeneutics that characterize the work of the New Critics, of academic critics such as Matthiessen, and of the New York Intellectuals made it theoretically possible for these questions to be addressed successfully. This explains much, but not everything, about why it was only after World War II that a sense of the unity and distinctiveness of American civilization came to be embodied in American literature as a disciplinary object. To changes in theory and scholarly practice must be added the new political climate of the postwar world, and the response of a variety of American institutions to that situation. Calverton had argued that "it was only when America arose to the position of a world power among nations of our time, a rival in rank with its mother country, that it was able to release itself from the colonial complex and actually begin the development of a native literature of its own."[1] As it turned out, when America attained world power, it was finally able to "discover" that a native literature already existed.

While victory in the war doubtless produced its own surge of nationalism, cultural nationalism became an official policy of the

United States government during the Cold War. Foundations sought to aid in the fight against communism by supporting the study and dissemination of American culture. The Cold War rhetoric of politicians and journalists tended to identify everything American with the forces of good, and everything un-American with evil. Given these conditions, it is not surprising that American civilization could now be created. These conditions doubtless also contributed to the character that would be assigned to that civilization. However, in my view the Cold War has been a bit overrated in its impact on studies of American literature during the 1950s. The Cold War virtually eliminated the left criticism outside the university, but it had barely existed inside the university before the war. The ideology of American literature in the 1950s is consistent in many respects with that which had dominated the subdiscipline since its emergence in the 1920s. What did differ in the 1950s were the means by which this ideology could be embodied in academic discourse.

Previous treatments have recognized the late 1940s as a transitional moment in the history of the American literature subdiscipline. Ruland concludes *The Rediscovery of American Literature* with a short, epilogic chapter entitled "The Rediscovery of American Literature: From AL to AQ." *American Quarterly* was the journal of the American studies movement, which got its first extended treatment in Tremaine McDowell's *American Studies*, published in 1948. Kermit Vanderbilt's *American Literature in the Academy* is framed by two cooperative histories of American literature, the *Cambridge History of American Literature* and the *Literary History of the United States* (*LHUS*), the latter project published in 1948. Writing in 1966, Ruland could wonder whether *American Quarterly* might represent the beginning of what would become a new institutionalization of American literature in departments separate from English literature. Ruland, however, seems generally bemused by American Studies and its journal; he is unable to assess, or uninterested in assessing, the turn in American literature studies it represents, except to assert that it begins with Matthiessen. Vanderbilt, on the other hand, uses the *Literary History of the United States* to bring closure to his narrative. He notes that the ALG had long sought an adequate history to replace what they regarded as the deeply flawed *Cam-*

bridge History. While the *LHUS* was not finally a formal project of the ALG, the idea for it did emerge out of that group. For Vanderbilt, the *LHUS* represents the maturity of the profession of American literature. I will argue that it might best be regarded as a monument to the passing dominance of literary-historical scholarship. After World War II, American literature definitively "ceased to be a history and became a tradition," even if literary-historical scholarship did not cease.[2]

The usual story about the history of literary studies in the United States is that the New Criticism replaced literary history during the 1940s and early 1950s. If the story is told from the point of view of theory, it can be claimed that the New Criticism was already in decline by 1957.[3] But if we tell it as the history of practice, we find that in 1957, the New Criticism—or indeed criticism of any kind—was not yet firmly in control of the profession's major journals. It was only in 1957 that Charles Fiedleson replaced Stanley Williams as lecturer in Yale's introduction to American literature and the course shifted focus from literary history to interpretation.[4] But the standard history also tends to see the New Criticism as one among many competing critical schools, thereby missing the more important point that criticism in general was replacing literary history as the dominant practice in English. Critics shared a common set of assumptions and goals that historical scholars did not. However great the epistemological change it represents, criticism did not come to power in a "revolution" wherein the centers of intellectual authority within English capitulated or were seized. As we have seen, the New Critics, the New York Intellectuals, and other practitioners of criticism developed an alternative set of institutions, including journals, institutes and schools of criticism, and a few sympathetic English departments. A few such institutions were independent of the academy, but all relied on its members more than that fast-disappearing breed, the serious literary journalist. Only after these alternative institutions had become well established and a new generation of scholars came to power in the profession did the traditional bastions of authority fall. Even after they did, literary history remained an acceptable, if unfashionable, scholarly practice.

To these general conditions, one must add another in order to understand the specific development of the criticism of American literature: the American Studies movement. This movement is often understood as antithetical to the New Criticism, but it in fact cannot be understood except as an offshoot of New Critical theory and practice. As we will see, *American Quarterly* was during the early 1950s far more hospitable to criticism than *American Literature*. In American literature during the 1950s and 1960s, however, the most important contributions did not appear in journals, but as books. This in itself would represent a significant shift in scholarly practice, but the contents of the books also differed radically from the scholarship that most ALG members had been producing. Although not all—perhaps not even most—of these books were produced by scholars identified with American Studies, that enterprise is representative of the constellation of forces that brought about the long-awaited "discovery" of American civilization.

The Waning of Literary History

The ALG began at its 1938 annual meeting to plan formally for a new cooperative history of American literature. At the suggestion of Henry Canby, it formed a committee chaired by Robert Spiller and including Scully Bradley, Ralph Rusk, Stanley Williams, T. K. Whipple, and Canby. After polling selected ALG members about how the project should be administered and organized, there was little consensus on these issues, but only a few of those responding opposed the idea of a cooperative history entirely. At the 1939 meeting, the committee presented its report, which called for a strong editor supported by a small editorial board who would shape material provided by expert contributors into a coherent whole. The appeal of this plan was that it was thought likely to prevent the history from becoming a shapeless mass like the *Cambridge History*. The proposed history would run to a maximum of twelve volumes and was to be published by an established house. The report was accepted, and the original committee, minus Whipple, who had died in 1939, and with the addition of Howard Mumford Jones, Jay Hubbell, Percy Boynton, and Louis B. Wright, were empowered to sign a contract and establish a procedure for selecting the editorial board.[5]

The committee prepared a report for the 1940 meeting, but it was never delivered. The ALG had devoted one of its convention sessions that year to "Problems and Aims in American Literary History." In an unusual move, the papers for the session were published prior to it in the November issue of *American Literature*. According to Spiller, the three essays led the committee to withdraw its report and to propose instead a Committee on the Materials of American Literary History.[6] But these essays were not the only evidence of widespread objections to the project among ALG members. Perhaps most important, three of the new members of the committee—Jones, Hubbell, and Wright—wrote to Spiller to caution that the scholarship in American literature had not progressed sufficiently to allow a definitive history to be produced. Jones and Hubbell also objected to the proposed plan of organization for the project, claiming that it would give the editor-in-chief too much power and the ALG itself too little control.[7] The idea to publish the papers in advance of the sessions seems to have been Napier Wilt's, who was to be ALG chair in 1940. In a letter sent to Spiller during the fall of 1939, Wilt warned, "I rather expect the plan, whatever it is, will come in for quite a bit of criticism, and I suggest that one member of your committee be formally appointed to defend the plan" (quoted in Spiller, "History," 606–8). Though Spiller believed his support helped to get the committee's report accepted in 1939, Hubbell had to approve of the advance publication of the papers for the 1940 meeting, and one is led to wonder whether he had decided much earlier than the fall of 1940 to try to derail the cooperative history.

While the contents of the three papers themselves do not suggest a coherent position in opposition to the proposed cooperative history, they do reveal the range of opposition that the project did or might engender. Harry Hayden Clark's essay supports a cooperative history, but argues that such a project can only succeed if it accommodates both social and aesthetic orientations within the field. He proposes a plan and a theory that will solve this problem, but these differ considerably from the plan and theory that Spiller's committee was putting forward.[8] Yvor Winter's essay reflected—albeit in extreme form—the perspective of the literary critic, a disapproval of any literary history not based on sound critical judgment. Winters believed such judgment to be lacking in academic Americanists.[9] Wright's essay is by far the most important of the three and not only because he was a member of the committee. The major objection among the ALG inner circle to a cooperative history had long been their belief that such a project was "premature." Spiller himself in 1935 had presented a paper at an ALG session that argued this very point.[10] Wright's "Toward a New History of American Literature" also argues that the discipline was not ready to produce a definitive history, but he does so on quite different, more widely shared grounds. Spiller had argued that the main problems that needed to be solved were large ones that have to do with relating literature to society and culture. Wright, on the other hand, asserted that not enough information had been discovered yet. Thus he proposed, "An inventory of what is known about American literature should be the first task of a committee of editors of the proposed history. Then a plan could be made for filling in gaps in our knowledge before actual composition of the history is undertaken."[11] One strong bit of evidence that Wright's view was the dominant one is that it is the inventory project that the Committee on Materials was charged to carry out.

Wright's argument represents the assumptions of literary historical positivism in their purest form. In this way of thinking, a literary history will be possible when enough information is accumulated. Spiller shared many of Wright's assumptions, but he also seemed to see that the mere accumulation of information would not be enough, and that attention therefore must be paid to generalizations—theories—that might frame a history and allow its facts to become meaningful. Most literary historians seemed to regard such theories as properly the products of historical investigation. They remained empiricists in the sense that they did not believe that they needed to bring theories to their material. A cooperative history of American literature would have represented the culmination of the work most academic Americanists had been *contributing* to *American Literature* and other journals since the ALG began. It would have been the embodiment of their own conception of their scholarly mission of adding to the edifice of knowledge, for it would be that edifice. But the argument of Wright's essay and the support for it among other leading ALG members suggests that the group would never have been ready to undertake a definitive history; there are an infinite number of possible facts that may be collected about any historical subject. The literary historians may also have resisted an "official" and definitive cooperative history because successful completion of such an enterprise could have been understood to suggest that their own work was largely complete, thus making them obsolete.

The *LHUS* that Spiller, Thorp, Johnson, and Canby did produce was not official but independent, and it was not intended to serve as the definitive scholarly history of American literature. The history was planned for "neither a professional nor a popular audience. The readership [the editors] visualized was 'a *National* public of intelligent lawyers, scientists, journalists, etc., as well as specialists in the literary field.' "[12] This intended audience accounts for the attempt to give the volume elements of narrative continuity and to make its style fluid and readable. The imagining of this audience is significant, and it puts the *LHUS* editors on a common wavelength with both the New Critics and the New York Intellectuals. Nevertheless, my guess is that the *LHUS* reached few in that broader audience. On the other hand, it became in spite of itself the definitive history of American literature for at least the next 40 years.[13] Spiller describes well the function the work served when he comments humorously on his identification with it: "Now, when I meet new people—often those who owe their Ph.D.'s to good cramming sessions with this book— their faces momentarily expose their surprise that I am a real human being and not merely a name on the library shelf" ("History," 602). The work came to embody the literary history that Americanists needed to learn in order to be credentialed, but which they no longer were likely to perform as a scholarly practice. It became, in other words, a reference book.

This status meant that the *LHUS* would not have a major impact on conceptions of the unity and distinctiveness of American literature, though it does have such a conception, Spiller's theory of the two "cycles" of American literary history.[14] But as Spiller himself admitted, "Much of this rationale is buried in the vast mass of data subsumed by the final work" ("History," 606). More important than its explicit and relatively peculiar theory, however, was what the *LHUS* shared with the field of American literature in general. Spiller cites its debts to Parrington, but asserts that Foerster's "four factors" were even more important in the conception of the history. In so doing, Spiller acknowledges that the cooperative history is very much the product of the theory and practice of academic Americanists. But the *LHUS* was produced by more than just academic discourse. In one of the most genuinely self-reflective assessments by anyone in the field, Spiller notes the cultural motivation for the history:

> *LHUS* shared, of course, in the impulse of radical nationalism, social ferment, and reassessment of the native tradition that has followed every successful American war—the Revolution, the Civil War, and the two World Wars—and in the argument that political independence and world power should be followed by cultural independence and a position as one of the world's literatures. However fallacious, this argument provides an impelling incentive to self-respect and self-evaluation. The movement toward cultural nationalism that began in the twenties of this century had achieved worldwide acknowledgment by the forties and undeniably influenced the *LHUS* editors to answer an insistent call for a new literary history at that time. ("History," 604)

Spiller's assertion of the influence of a long-standing cultural nationalism is a precise reading of the motives for the academic field of American literature, but it does not give enough emphasis to the particular conditions that resulted from World War II and the ensuing Cold War with the Soviet Union. Having been conceived prior to World War II, the *LHUS* was doubtless not entirely the product of those conditions, but benefited from them nonetheless. As we will see, the postwar surge of cultural nationalism would produce not only the capstone of more than a quarter-century of literary history, but also new scholarly practice that would yield numerous books claiming to define American literature and culture. Taken together, these books would create the first widely accepted conception of a unique American civilization.

If in retrospect we can see that the *LHUS* marks the culmination of the literary-historical era of the field of American literature, one could not have guessed this from reading *American Literature*. In 1948, the journal was in its twentieth year, all under the editorship of Hubbell, who would remain in that post until 1954. Its editorial policies, stated or unstated, changed little during Hubbell's tenure. The prohibition against articles on living authors was removed only after it had already made the journal very late in taking up modern literature. Bibliographical essays were still welcome, and in practice this continued to mean the publishing of newly discovered materials with little or no comment. Between 1948 and 1952, bibliographic recoveries accounted for 15 of the 98 articles published in the journal. Of those 98 articles, only 18 were predominantly critical, while 4 additional articles combined both historical and critical purposes. The remaining 76 (including the bibliographical) were literary-historical, most often source and influence studies little different from those that typified the discipline of English during its first 50 years. A typical influence study is Vivian Hopkins's argument that "Ralph Cudworth's *The True Intellectual System of the Universe* (1678) deserves to be re-examined as a shaping influence upon Emerson's concepts of nature and art."[15] Sidney Lind's source study, "James's 'The Private Life' and Browning," uses James's own comments on Robert Browning to show how he was the model for Clare Vawdrey, a character in James's story. Here Lind is not even revealing a source, since James had acknowledged Browning as the model for Vawdrey in one of his prefaces.[16] Many articles simply describe a historical event or state of affairs that relates to a major literary figure or work. Thus, for example, Marie P. Harris's "Henry James, Lecturer," makes no claims for the artistic significance of James's lectures, either in themselves or in connection with fiction. Rather, the article simply describes James's lectures during his stay in America during 1904–5 and notes reactions to them.[17] Clearly articles "that bring to light new materials or new facts" remained of the highest value, and literary-historical positivism went unquestioned.[18]

The relative absence of criticism from *American Literature* should not be taken as a measure of that practice among academic Americanists after the war. As we have seen, ALG members had been commenting on the absence of criticism in the journal beginning before the first issue appeared. While the absence of criticism continued to be noticed every so often in the meantime, it became a major issue in the early 1950s. In 1951, Howard Jones wrote to managing editor Clarence Gohdes, reporting:

I do not find that younger men 'in the field are altogether happy about *American Literature*. I do not quite understand the gravamen of their complaints—largely, I think because I have never taken the trouble to find out. . . . Nevertheless . . . there does seem to be abroad a vague impression that *American Literature* has innocently fallen into a rut. Certainly the articles in the current *American Quarterly*, or at least some of them, might just as well have appeared in *AL*. Possibly they were not offered because of the superior attractiveness of novelty in a new periodical. Possibly they were offered and turned down. Possibly they were not offered because the legend arises that *AL* is interested only in one sort of material. . . . I think that *AL*, though theoretically a journal of critical expression and not of scholarship only, has on the whole not done very much on the critical side. Of course, *nobody knows what criticism is*.[19]

Jones called for the opinions and suggestions of the advisory board to be solicited on this matter. In response, Hubbell wrote to the editorial and advisory boards asking for members to write to him regarding the question of the journal's policies and their feelings about critical articles. Hubbell told the boards that he believed *American Literature* was unlikely to get many more acceptable critical articles. His reasoning implies what was most likely a valid critique of the state of graduate education in the early 1950s:

Most of what we publish in *AL* comes from young instructors and graduate students, and much of it comes out of doctor's dissertations directly or indirectly. Am I right in thinking that when the younger men and women write critical articles, they abandon the topics on which they have done real research and try their hands at interpreting Eliot or Faulkner or James, using one of the popular modern approaches—psychoanalysis, the "new criticism," symbolism, semantics, nature myths, etc.?

Most graduate training remained limited to the old historical scholarship; students had to learn to read and write criticism on their own. Hubbell acknowledges that there was "the danger" that the editors, all members of the older generation, were "unduly unsympathetic" to the interests of younger scholars. Yet the lack of sympathy is apparent in Hubbell's own opposition of "real research" and "popular modern approaches."[20]

Several months later, Hubbell again wrote to the editorial and advisory boards, exerpting the letters he received in response to his previous memo. The responses ranged from suggestions that critical articles be solicited in various ways, to assertions that the dissatisfaction that Jones reported was unreal or unfounded. Only Charles Anderson is reported to have favored the meeting of the boards that Jones had suggested, and James D. Hart is the only one who mentions good critical articles published elsewhere. Opposition to criticism was expressed by Theodore Hornberger, who does not want "to make *AL* another *Kenyon* or *Partisan*." Rusk, who in the journal's first year had vetoed the Prescott article, now complains that "we cannot afford to print papers whose chief recommendation is that they are sprinkled with such stuffed-shirt diction as 'myth,' 'psychosomatic,' 'dichotomy,' and 'ambivalent.' " If the dominant tone is unsympathetic to the new hermeneutical practices, however, a majority of respondents still indicate their support for more critical articles. Nevertheless, Hubbell summarizes the responses as being "pretty well agreed that 1) whatever some of the younger men may think, *AL* has not been inhospitable to critical articles and has rejected few if any good specimens of the New Criticism and 2) a good many of the newer sort of critical articles published in other magazines are of dubious value." He added an offer to publish a notice soliciting critical articles, but questioned its necessity by pointing out that "Professor Gohdes and some of you feel no new announcement of our policy is needed."[21]

Perhaps the most telling piece of news in Hubbell's memo, however, is Spiller's report that as an American literature reader for *PMLA*, about half of the submissions he received were critical articles. While *PMLA* at this time published more criticism than did *American Literature*, more than one member of that journal's boards reported that the criticisms made of *American Literature* were also made of *PMLA*. Spiller's remark, and *PMLA*'s record, give credence to the complaints that were dismissed by Hubbell, his editors, and advisers. While we do not know how many critical articles were submitted to *American Literature*, the comments of those who controlled the journal strongly suggest that the younger scholars' perceptions of a bias against criticism were accurate. The same complaint was raised again to Gohdes, now editor-in-chief, in December of 1954 by William Charvat, who asked for the representation of "a wider range of scholarship and criticism" on the Board of Editors.[22] This suggestion seems to have met with success, since Charles Feidelson soon became a member of the board. However, the board remained dominated by literary historians, and, while *American Literature* published more criticism during Gohdes's tenure (1954–69), the journal remained committed to literary history. Only under the journal's third editor, Arlin Turner, did criticism become the predominant discourse.[23]

The prolonged resistance to criticism by *American Literature*, especially the interpretive variety discussed in the last two chapters, is evidence of the radical disjunction between the old and new scholarly practices. The majority of scholars trained in literary history were prevented by their epistemological assumptions from recognizing either the purpose or the value of the new hermeneutics. They were not opposed to criticism in principle, but in practice they seldom found criticism of which they could approve. It always lacked "solidity" because it could not be grounded in unambiguous facts. Even the criticism *American Literature* did publish bears this out. The most unambiguously New Critical article published in *American Literature* before 1953 is Mary E. Dichmann's "Hawthorne's 'Prophetic Pictures.'" Like the other critical articles in *American Literature*, Dichmann's justifies itself as a reevaluation of a hitherto neglected work. In this case the neglect is relative to the critical attention paid to other works by the author: "Although Hawthorne scholars usually mention "The Prophetic Pictures" in their discussions of the writer's art, they have always, I believe, given it too summary a treatment to provide an adequate exploration of its theme and central problem." The problem is "the problem of the artist . . . the dichotomy of the act of artistic creation, which Hawthorne seems to have felt is man's most spiritual achievement, and of that 'dark necessity,' which, he feared, impels the artist by virtue of his very artistry towards the unpardonable sin, the violation of the human heart. The essential paradox of this position cannot be resolved."[24] The article thus exhibits characteristic interest in paradox and ambiguity, as well as the New Critical assumption that moral questions are subjects of great literature. Furthermore, the argument is advanced not by reference to external evidence, but by close reading of the story itself. What is significant about this essay is that it resembles the typical contribution to *American Literature* in several key points. Like most such contributors, Dichmann keeps her claims modest, her main point being that the story tells us more than other critics have noticed. Moreover, her object of analysis is limited to fit with the positivist temper of *American Literature* even if the method of her argument does not. She is concerned only with a single story, and makes no speculative leaps from it to larger theoretical or historical assertions. As a result, Dichmann's claims do not challenge historical analysis, but simply ignore it.

American Literature's failure to keep pace with the times meant that its significance in the discipline would decline. But this was not entirely the fault of the journal's commitment to literary history and its epistemology. The scholarly journal, which during the first fifty years of literary study had been the most important medium for professional publication in the humanities, began to lose ground to book publication during the 1930s and 1940s. By the 1950s, book publication had displaced the scholarly journal, and even *PMLA* no longer had the importance it once did. This occurred in part because scholars like Lowes and Matthiessen produced books that exhibited the detailed scholarship typical of an article together with the sweep of argument only an extended treatment can provide. Younger scholars planned their careers using these books as exemplars. But another factor in the decline of older scholarly journals was the enormous increase in the number of periodicals publishing academic literary studies. I've mentioned in previous chapters the New Critics' and New York Intellectuals' journals, but there were also new academic organs devoted to periods, subperiods, genres, regions, and even individual authors. As a result, publishing an article even in the most highly authorized organs such as *PMLA* or *American Literature* no longer carried as much professional weight. Moreover, some of the new journals claimed a new kind of authority, a readership beyond the confines of a single discipline and even the academy itself. As we will see, *American Quarterly* was conceived in this latter mode.

American Studies and *American Quarterly*

In chapter 6 we saw the emergence of the American Studies movement in the form of graduate programs in American civilization. In 1951, slightly more than ten years after the first of these programs was started, the movement was strong enough to form a national organization, the American Studies Association. Unlike most learned societies, the American Studies Association was first organized as a confederation of regional chapters, which quickly became 18 in number with a total membership of 2,000. The war effort caused major growth in American civilization programs in the early and middle 1940s. Similarly, the growth of the American Studies movement in the late forties and early fifties was spurred by the Cold War. Having just completed work on the *LHUS* and now serving as Chair of the American Civilization Department at Pennsylvania, Robert Spiller was in a strong position to capitalize on the cultural nationalism he would later so accurately identify. John Gardner, president of the Carnegie Corporation, approached Spiller in 1953 when he had become president of the ASA "to discuss what his foundation might do for 'American Studies.' "[25] The result was a grant to the organization that allowed for the hiring of an executive secretary and for a series of small, regional conferences. But it was not only the ASA that benefited from the foundation's newly discovered interest in promoting the study of American culture. The Carnegie Corporation made substantial grants to Brown University, Amherst College, the University of Minnesota, and the University of Pennsylvania in 1949, and Spiller managed to win a second grant to Pennsylvania from Carnegie, as well as one from Rockefeller. Yale was willing to say of its American Studies program that it was "designed as a positive and affirmative method of meeting the threat of Communism." This statement enabled Yale in 1950 to win from the Coe Foundation $500,000 for American Studies, "as a safeguard against Communism, Socialism, Totalitarianism, and for the preservation of our System of Free Enterprise." William R. Coe later requested that the professor who held the chair he endowed believe in free enterprise and oppose Socialism and Communism.[26] The newly organized Fulbright program also looked with special favor on scholars identified with American Studies, perhaps again because of Spiller's influence in governmental circles, though also doubtless because American Studies was what the government most wanted to encourage abroad.[27] When we add these grants and programs to the more direct but often covert government support for the spread of American culture we noted in the last chapter, it becomes clear that the cultural nationalism of this era was more than an outpouring of postwar euphoria. It must be seen as a concerted effort to secure American hegemony by increasing the symbolic capital of its culture. The Cold War environment made the claims of American literature scholars suddenly much more interesting and valuable.

The impact of the Cold War registered even in the pages of *American Literature*, though only in the book reviews was it explicit. When Ralph Gabriel asserts in a review of a book on one of the central themes of American Studies, *Characteristically American* by Ralph Barton Perry, that "today, when America has become a giant, a giant enemy has launched a world-wide campaign to disparage American civilization," he articulates the political rationale for promoting American culture.[28] But given *American Literature*'s editorial predilections, it could do little directly to serve that end. *American Quarterly*, on the other hand, was tailor-made for the job. Founded in 1949 at the University of Minnesota under the editorship of Tremaine McDowell, the journal moved to the University of Pennsylvania in 1951 and became the official organ of the ASA under Spiller's editorship. From the beginning, *American Quarterly* sought to distinguish itself from older scholarly journals. It was able to do this more readily because its position outside the disciplines helped to free it from disciplinary expectations. Furthermore, *American Quarterly* positioned itself not merely outside of established disciplines, but also explicitly astride the boundary that distinguishes disciplinary from nondisciplinary discourse: "Contributors, academic and nonacademic, will write for the lay reader who wishes to avoid the thinness of much popularization and the excesses of ingrown specialization."[29] This sense of an intelligent, nonacademic community of readers is much reminiscent of the *LHUS* editors' intended audience. By the third issue, the opposition to specialization was strengthened in the following addition, which urged contributors to write about "not only the areas of American life

313

which they know best but the relation of each of these areas to the entire American scene and world society."[30]

Antispecialization, one of the senses that the term "interdisciplinary" carried during these early days, was a major force within American intellectual life during this period. We have seen that the New Critics and the New York Intellectuals offered critiques of the overspecialization of academic literary study. There were two versions or tendencies of the attack on specialization, which might be labeled elitist and populist. The elitist tendency, the one shared by the New Critics and the New York Intellectuals, opposed the narrowness of academic work. This position urged the role of cultural leadership upon intellectuals, who were to make appropriate value judgments for the population. Academics had failed to play this role because they wrote only for each other, and because they tended to abdicate the throne of judgment. The populist position, in the early days of ASA associated most strongly with Carl Bode, also regarded academic work as overly narrow, but it held that scholars had also imposed a too-narrow range of judgments on culture. The populist position wanted to do away with cultural distinctions and academic ones as well.[31] The elitist view always seems to have held sway in *American Quarterly*, which despite its proclamations remained a medium for professors by professors at elite institutions. Within ASA, the populists held more influence, but their defeat was signaled by the convening of national conventions beginning in 1967. Henceforth, power was increasingly centralized and the regional chapters became much less important. The populists' response to their defeat in ASA was the founding of the Popular Culture Association in 1969. The populism of that organization was a matter of more than its choice of nonelite objects of study, as the title of Ray Browne's history of the organization, *Against Academia*, suggests.[32] But however much the Popular Culturists may have been against academia, they did not succeed any better than ASA in reaching beyond an academic audience. The intelligent general reader imagined by the editors of *American Quarterly* and *LHUS* may have existed, but he or she was unlikely to be reading quarterlies, however unspecialized, and was perhaps even less likely to want to read serious discussions of mass culture.

Thus, whatever its ambitions, *American Quarterly* remained

an academic journal. But the direction in which *American Quarterly* would develop was determined in part by the meshing of these ambitions with the greater cultural importance of the figure of the intellectual. We have seen how the New York Intellectuals had become important cultural spokesmen precisely as self-identified intellectuals while at the same time they became increasingly members of university faculties. *American Quarterly*'s instructions to contributors strongly suggests that its contributors should position themselves as intellectuals, a role that entails the right to speak authoritatively on all subjects. Criticism is a characteristic discourse of intellectuals, and I have already noted the Nashville and New York groups' affinities with each other. The intellectual, unlike the academician, has a self-imposed mission to address society at large, criticize its shortcomings, and prescribe alternatives. The literary historian, working under positivist assumptions, operates under no such burden. His task is merely to add to the total of human knowledge.

One way to gauge the difference between the academic and intellectual models is to look at the authors who appeared in *American Literature* and *American Quarterly*. *American Literature* published few articles by scholars with established reputations, and it did not repeatedly publish the same scholars. Between 1948 and 1952, only 4 out of a total of 94 contributors were represented by more than one article, and in each case only 2 essays were published. One reason for the lack of established scholars may have been the journal's policy of not publishing material that would appear elsewhere. Hubbell complained about the difficulty of getting established critics to contribute to *American Literature*, asserting that they could get paid for their work elsewhere, or were putting their time into books.[33] It was probably the combination of these forces together with the fact that literary historicism would soon become a residual mode that accounts for the relative insignificance of scholars published in *American Literature* during this period. On the other hand, *American Quarterly* published many leading scholars and many others who would become leaders: in addition to Trilling, these include Henry Nash Smith, Daniel Aaron, Frederick Hoffman, Richard Hofstader, David Reisman, Susanne Langer, and Norman Holmes Pearson. Many articles in *American Quarterly* are portions of books, some of which were already in print when the article appeared. This suggests that the journal was not primarily intended to be a repository of knowledge. Under an intellectual—rather than an academic—model, the author of an article is far more important, since it is his or her particular viewpoint and not the mere accretion of knowledge that is valued. This results in relatively frequent publication of second or even third articles by a single contributor. Of the 34 contributors representing literature in *American Quarterly*, volumes 1–4 (1949–52), 4 had 2 articles published, and this does not include multiple articles by contributors outside of literature. The ideal *American Quarterly* contributor seems to be the "leading or representative intellectual" while the ideal contributor to *American Literature* is a mere researcher adding to the store of knowledge.[34]

As their different missions would require, *American Quarterly* was to be radically different from *American Literature*. In *American Quarterly* we find very little of the kind of historical scholarship that was typical of the older journal: influence and source studies, bibliographies or recovered documents. On the other hand, there are articles by professional historians such as Richard Hofstader, and there are articles that combine elements of the disciplines of history and literature, as does Henry Nash Smith's article, an excerpt from *Virgin Land*. This is not to say that literary scholarship is lacking, however. Indeed, based on departmental affiliation, English has the largest representation of scholars, and, while some members of English departments published articles on subjects other than literature, there are more essays in literature than in any other discipline. In addition, there are articles by sociologists, philosophers, musicologists, art historians, and so on. Given the disciplinary diversity, it is difficult to discern very much common ground among the articles, but what many of them share is speculation. Where articles in *American Literature* seem to be chosen for the facts they establish, the typical article in *American Quarterly* advances a polemical claim that may be about something as narrow as the meaning of a single work or as broad as America as a whole, although, as we will see, even ostensibly narrow claims tend to expand.

New Criticism is not the dominant form of literary study in *American Quarterly*, but it is represented more often there than in *American Literature*. Donald Weeks's "Two Uses of *Moby Dick*" makes a useful comparison with Dichmann's article, because, while both are clearly New Critical, they reflect the differing agendas of the journals in which they appeared. The similarity in the two articles is reflected in their interest in formal and moral questions. Thus Weeks begins, "The paradox in the fame of *Moby Dick* is this: At a time when criticism is esthetic, our deepest interest in *Moby Dick* is moral."[35] But Weeks is just as concerned with the novel as an example of formal innovation as he is in its representation of good and evil. Where Dichmann's claims were modest, Weeks makes large claims that threaten historical scholarship by answering what are essentially historical questions ahistorically. Weeks's claims for *Moby-Dick* as an innovation in prose fiction could in principle be adjudicated in historical terms—as the Russian formalists have shown—but Weeks makes no attempt to do so. Rather, he simply asserts that the novel has been consistently misunderstood, even though he cites a contemporary source that seems to recognize its genre violations. Finally, Weeks's article represents a return to overtly nationalist rhetoric that most of the founders of *American Literature* would have labeled chauvinist. Weeks is explicit about claiming the highest status for American works in the canon of Western literature. Thus his article ends by asserting that "Melville indeed served as a kind of American Shakespeare. In many ways *King Lear* and *Moby Dick* are comparable" (164).[36] The argument for the greatness of American civilization was a project that *American Quarterly* could carry on in a more overt way than *American Literature* because it was not subject to the disciplinary authority of literary historians.

My focus on *American Quarterly* here is not meant to give the impression that it assumed the place *American Literature* had held in the 1930s as the dominant journal in American literature. After the proliferation of journals in the 1940s and 1950s, no single organ would ever dominate in the way the ALG's journal did when it was virtually the only game in town. In spite of its literary-historical orientation, *American Literature* itself published some significant articles during the fifties and sixties, including one of the first precursors by Leo Marx of his *Machine in the Garden*.[37] Nor do I wish to give the impression that American Studies replaced the American literature subdiscipline as the dominant institutional setting for the study of American literature. On the contrary, while American Studies gave strong impetus to the work of creating American civilization by making that its central problematic, it never gained enough institutional power to take over the study of American literature or history or any other field. The work done by literary scholars affiliated with American Studies by training or employment had its greatest impact on the study of American literature in English departments. That impact was significant and distinctive, but the work itself was not radically different from that produced by Americanists who were not affiliated with American Studies.

Yes, Virginia, There Is an American Civilization

The question of the status of American civilization had been on the floor more or less continuously since the late nineteenth century, even if it was not often directly addressed in scholarly articles before World War II. The dominant position at the turn of the century held that American civilization, insofar as there was such a thing, was English or Anglo-Saxon civilization. The literary radicals rejected that analysis, but complained of a general lack of civilization. America needed a tradition of its own, a usable past. Academic Americanists began in the 1920s to invent such a tradition, but their disciplinary commitments to English and to positivism made it impossible for them to complete the work. They continued to think of the question of American civilization as one that would be solved by the accumulation of facts. Outside the academy, vulgar Marxists, New Critics, and the young New York Intellectuals agreed on little else but the general absence of civilization in the United States. On the other hand, by the late 1930s, Van Wyck Brooks had discovered the civilization he earlier could not find, but those inside took little notice. Finally, Matthiessen in 1941 published *American Renaissance*, the study that established a conception of the unity and distinction of American tradition that would become widely accepted and built upon.

Given this history, those scholars who after the war came to address questions of an American literary and cultural tradition were not in a position to start from scratch. For example, these writers by and large contributed little to discussions about which writers belonged in the canon. Rather, their job was to explain how the canonized writers fit together into a literary tradition or cultural pattern, and sometimes to find connections between these writers' work and other forms of cultural expression. This was less likely to be what the subdiscipline had called minor literature than material that had not been regarded as literary at all: dime novels, political tracts, transcendentalist theology and philosophy, and so on. The critics of the fifties and sixties embraced the object of American literature that the subdiscipline gave them not only passively, as a result of their graduate training, but actively: it suited their goal of discovering a unified American civilization. The cultural diversity that was first actively suppressed and then, in the *Cambridge History of American Literature*, included on the margins, and finally simply ignored as American literature became more clearly identified with the work of a few white and mainly Northeastern writers, was simply not one of the things that American literature represented when the war ended. Nothing in the dominant culture of the era would have led the postwar generation to seek such diversity, and they did not. Thus the American tradition that they invented had little to say about the multiplicity of American racial and ethnic groups, about the reality of class divisions in American history, or the differences that had been defined by gender. Like their counterparts who were inventing modernism, these new Americanists were concerned with that metaphysical creature "man" and his "experience" in the New World. By posing their questions in these terms they prohibited themselves from attending to the differences among the experiences of men and women.

The books that established the "nature" of American civilization are often understood as offering theories of American literature or culture. In this conception, most successfully worked out by Russell Reising, each critic is seen as presenting a competing theory.[38] It is by no means illegitimate for a Reising to treat these books as theories that he may "review and revise," for such treatment is necessary if the case for a new understanding of American literature is to be made (6). But his treatment does mislead us if we imagine that Reising's concerns were typical of the contemporary audience for these texts. Those who discuss competing

319

theories may group them into schools or discern some shared goals or characteristics, but they do not treat them as constituting a single practice. Yet that is, in my view, how they are best understood. Contemporary readers clearly recognized this, as the perception of a "myth and symbol" method attests. I think that the books I will discuss in this section were also more often read as vague contributions to a single conception than they were read as competing theories. Nevertheless, they were not understood as adding up to anything so coherent as a "national narrative," even if this conception gets us closer to the way these texts were read. According to Donald Pease, the books' "images interconnect an exceptional national subject (American Adam) with a representative national scene (Virgin Land) and an exemplary national motive (errand into the wilderness)."[39] Such a narrative may well have existed in the political unconscious of American literature professors, their students, and perhaps other citizens, but it would have seemed sophomoric to the professors to hear it stated so baldly. Pease is able to put together this narrative now because he sees the critical studies out of which it emerges as cultural artifacts, rather than as authoritative interpretations.[40]

Pease's version is perhaps the most extreme conception of what many have understood as consensus history.[41] On this reading, what distinguishes the American studies of the 1950s is a particular conception of culture in which conflicts are understood as integral to the whole. Such a vision of culture is nearly always contrasted with the conception of American history held by the progressive historians, in which conflicts are depicted as opposing "currents" or intellectual forces rather than as tensions. In practice this meant that the progressives tended, like Parrington, to divide history into opposing camps, while the consensus builders saw tensions within works, movements, or individuals. The former view is seen to value those figures or works that fall into the correct camp, while the latter values those that express the cultural tensions in the greatest complexity.

There are several problems with this as a history of American literature as a discipline. For one, as I have already argued, progressivism was never dominant in that field. What little argument there was over cultural politics was relegated to the review section of *American Literature*. The dominant model was Foerster's, and it presented American literary history as a series of periods of consensus. Perhaps more important, however, is an erroneous explanation of what came to be dominant during the Cold War. The politically significant change between pre- and postwar criticism is not a new conception of culture as consensus but the extreme dominance of a conservative politics, often called "liberal." Thus, as we have seen in the example of Trilling, critics of the period showed a preference for works that expressed conservative or right-wing positions, for instance, the intractability of human nature, the desirability of class divisions. We have previously seen the various ingredients that determined this new conservative hegemony: the New Humanism, the New Criticism, the New York Intellectuals' anticommunism and "liberalism," McCarthyism, and direct financial support by government and foundations of anticommunist and pro-free-enterprise scholars and programs. To be sure, such influences wiped out much scholarly dissent, producing what might be called a consensus. What it did not produce in the academy was a conception of American literary history that was radically more monolithic than the prewar conception.[42] As we will see, though Americanists now could proclaim the unifying characteristics of their tradition, this led not to unified scholarship but to disciplinary dispersion.

In order to understand the specific character of the tradition-building of the fifties and sixties, we must return to two earlier contributions that have been neglected so far. The first of these has already been mentioned as an influence on the contributors to *The Reinterpretation of American Literature*, D. H. Lawrence's *Studies in Classic American Literature*. It is ironic but perhaps understandable that an Englishman should contribute so much to the invention of the American literary tradition. Unlike most of the critics of his day—the era of Mencken and Sherman—Lawrence was able to discuss America as if it did not signify either absolute good or evil. Lawrence was ambivalent about America, a state that lent itself to a dialectical understanding of American culture. While many critics at that time talked about America in terms of two opposing intellectual or social forces, they tended to identify the real America with one of them. Lawrence understood American culture as the dialectical interaction of pairs of elements, none of which may in itself be taken to represent

Americanness. We have already noted similar reading strategies in Matthiessen and Trilling, but they would become all the more prominent in later studies.

Lawrence was also a self-conscious practitioner of the hermeneutics of suspicion. Though Lawrence like other modernists saw art as a source of truth, he explicitly located that truth below the surface: "Art-speech is the only truth. An artist is usually a damned liar, but his art, if it be art, will tell you the truth of his day. . . . Away with eternal truth. Truth lives from day to day."[43] Lawrence regards "art-speech" as truth because it reveals the hidden meanings that are for him more significant than those that are consciously announced. This hermeneutic Lawrence thinks is especially appropriate for understanding Americans, who, he argues, "refuse everything explicit and always put up a sort of double meaning" (viii). Such an assumption would characterize the postwar interpretations of the American tradition.

Lawrence was also more self-aware than his contemporaries about his own activity in constructing a tradition where none existed before. The new man whom later critics seem to seek in history, Lawrence admits to helping to be born, calling himself a "midwife to an unborn homunculus" (viii). Lawrence forges a tradition by demonstrating that the Americanness of the literature is more than a matter of setting or subject matter. He defines patterns of continuity among the writers he discusses and takes them to stand for the culture. America promises genuinely new experience—a new voice that is present in the old American classics (1), but that new experience is not present on the surface because America, to begin with, was the oldest nation on earth (53–54). Cooper's Leatherstocking novels embody the paradox:

> They go backwards, from old age to golden youth. That is the true myth of America. She starts old, old, wrinkled and writhing in an old skin. And there is a gradual sloughing of the old skin, toward a new youth. It is the myth of America. (54)

The phrase "myth of America" has a double force. On one level it refers to a narrative pattern that sprang up from native materials: the frontier with its promise of rebirth, the doctrine of progress, the experience of European people in an authentically new world. Myth, here, does not mean a literary structure or genre: the narrative pattern that Lawrence finds is not present in any one of the Leatherstocking novels; it may be seen only by taking these novels in order of composition. Leatherstocking's life seen from this perspective is emblematic of America herself. Thus, on another level, the myth of America refers to the meaning of America in the course of Western civilization; that is, America for the European world is as a nation the source of regeneration. What Lawrence is talking about is not a literal description of American culture or experience as a whole, but the symbolic significance of America.

Lawrence's book had been widely recognized as important and influential, but the degree of his influence on the individual critics has not generally been recognized. At least two major books of the postwar period expand on ideas found in Lawrence's own little, slim volume. R. W. B. Lewis's *The American Adam* takes as one of its three epigraphs the lines about "the myth of America" quoted above. The following passage about *The Deerslayer* makes it clear that Lewis owes his description of the Adamic hero to Lawrence:

> The action of the story as distinct from plot—what is really going on in the novel—is something far more significant: it is the birth of an archetypal, still finely individualized character, which Lawrence identifies as "*the* essential American soul . . . an isolate, almost selfless, stoic, enduring man. Natty Bumppo is the full-fledged fictional Adam."[44]

Leo Marx's *The Machine in the Garden* may be seen as enlarging on the following passage from Lawrence, which he uses as an epigraph to his chapter entitled "The Machine": "The most idealist nations invent the most machines. America simply teems with mechanical inventions, because nobody wants to *do* anything. They are idealists. Let the machine do the thing."[45] Lawrence did not write in approved academic style, and he might be the antithesis of an academic literary historian. It is not surprising, then, that the academic Americanists would praise Lawrence's originality, but keep him at arm's length. Lawrence would not have a major impact on American literature in the academy until criticism became widely practiced there.

If Lawrence's importance in the development of American

literature as the object of interpretation has been somewhat underrated, Perry Miller's importance to that same project is often overrated. By this I do not mean to comment on the value of Miller's work or to deny its importance in establishing a commonly accepted narrative of American literary history. In fact, on this latter point, I want to insist on Miller's foundational role. His *The New England Mind: The Seventeenth Century* (1939) put forever to rest—at least within the academy—the simplistic conception of Puritanism that his first book, *Orthodoxy in Massachusetts 1630–1650* (1933) had explicitly attacked: "My contemporaries and I came of age in a time when the word 'Puritan' served as a comprehensive sneer against every tendency in American civilization which we held reprehensible."[46] The later volume made the case much more persuasively without polemics by demonstrating the intellectual richness of Puritan writing. This work together with the second volume, *The New England Mind: From Colony to Province* (1953), established the Puritans as having made a substantial contribution to American thought and letters. The chronology of American literature now had an intellectual starting place, rather than the mere date that John Smith provided.

Miller's work made it possible for others to discuss the Puritan origins of American literature, but, with the important exception of "From Edwards to Emerson," he mostly avoided such speculation. Reising provides a good overview of the most important discussions of Puritan origins in Yvor Winters, Richard Chase, Leslie Fiedler, and Sacvan Bercovitch, showing that Puritan origins play a role in the work of each of these critics. It is important to keep in mind, however, that neither *The American Novel and its Tradition* nor *Love and Death in the American Novel* is about the Puritans. Rather, Puritanism remains merely an origin, a way to explain the distinctive characteristics of American fiction that are the real subject of each text, and which have themselves little to do with Puritanism. Since Bercovitch's studies were produced after the period I am dealing with, that leaves Winters's book as the only major argument for Puritanism's definitive role in American literature. But since Winters was writing against the aesthetic and moral value of American literature, his argument was unlikely to be adopted by those seeking to demonstrate those values in American literature.

What Miller's work did not do, at least among literary critics, was to make Puritan writing a frequent object of interpretation or analysis. It is telling that Miller's most successful doctoral students were historians, that Miller's own work has been the subject of significant discussion, pro and con, by historians, and that Puritanism continues to be a subject to which historians still devote a good deal of ink.[47] Miller has not been treated with anything like the same seriousness by literary scholars, but, more important, they have also not been very interested in the Puritans. Miller is accepted by historians as one of their own because he shares with them the assumption that Puritan writing will tell us about Puritan reality. Historians thus may argue about whether Miller in his focus on mind neglected material conditions, but they do not doubt that he sought to understand events outside of texts. Thus, in spite of Miller's "close reading," he has much more in common with historians than with literary critics and scholars, whose goals are much more likely to be explaining the works themselves.[48] Puritan writing, while eminently in need of interpretation, did not seem worthy of it to most literary scholars because it was not seen as aesthetic. The importance of Edward Taylor, the Puritan poet whose poems were published for the first time in the 1930s, was that he represented for the first time a genuine aesthetic figure among the Puritans. But even Taylor was much more likely to be read in the context of Emerson than in his actual historical context. Matthiessen was much more important than Miller to the development of the postwar field of American literature because he showed how to read the writers most critics wanted to read. American civilization needed an origin, and Miller provided one; but it needed even more a body of writing that seemed to be of lasting value. Despite his own artistry as a writer, Miller could not make Puritan writings of interest to other literary critics.[49]

If Miller's work for all intents and purposes came to represent the first period of American literary history and the first of Foerster's "four factors," no single individual would come to dominate the discussion of the other periods and factors. Matthiessen would continue to be foundational to discussion of the romantic period, but his work did inspire other critics to tackle the same material. As I argued in chapter 5, the second of Foerster's factors, the frontier, was from the beginning more spirit than place. As the studies of frontier literature by Rusk and Dondore suggested, the frontier could not be "done" in the same way as Miller did Puritanism. If both continued to seem subliterary, at least Puritan writings were intellectually complex. Yet Matthiessen dealt with the frontier as a subject and inspiration for his five major figures. Perhaps as a result, the frontier becomes a more central theme than Puritanism in the American literature that postwar scholars invented. Consider R. W. B. Lewis, who claims that American culture is defined by a dialogue among three intellectual parties that he names memory, hope, and irony. The party of memory includes the intellectual descendants of the Puritans, but Lewis says almost nothing about it. On the other hand, the frontier is the space where the Adamic hero of the party of hope is portrayed in the novels of Charles Brockden Brown, Cooper, and Robert Montgomery Bird, and it is more abstractly the condition of the possibility of radical innocence in general.

One of the most important books of the 1950s, Henry Nash Smith's *Virgin Land*, takes the frontier as its focus. Smith treats the frontier as symbol and myth propagated in the writings of politicians, explorers, land developers, dime novelists, and such literary figures as Whitman and Cooper. This represents a major epistemological shift. If Americanists of the 1920s and 1930s did not regard the frontier as a direct environmental influence on major American writers, they did regard it as such an influence on American history. The frontier spirit in, say, Emerson was thus an indirect manifestation of the real historical process that Turner had described. Smith, on the other hand, treats Turner's thesis as itself an outgrowth of "the myth of the garden," a narrative projection that envisioned a "vast and growing agricultural society in the interior of the continent . . . centering about the heroic figure of the idealized frontier farmer."[50] Turner's argument is here treated as part of an "intellectual tradition" that expressed the "beliefs and aspirations" of Americans, and it thus becomes another version of the myth. According to Smith,

> Turner's most important debt to his intellectual tradition is the ideas of savagery and civilization that he uses to define his central factor, the frontier. His frontier is explicitly "the meeting

point between savagery and civilization." For him as for his predecessors, the outer limit of agricultural settlement is the boundary of civilization.[51]

This suggests that the frontier represents an alternative origin of American civilization. For Turner this meant democracy born of free land, that is, land occupied only by savages. Yet in American literature, this meeting of civilization and savagery just as often produces images of a civilization born of savagery. Either way, the special character of American civilization is explained. Furthermore, as Smith as since acknowledged, he continued to assume Turner's notion of civilization with its "doctrine of inevitable progress so deeply buried it was almost inaccessible to critical examination." As a result, he was unable to acknowledge "the tragic dimensions of the Westward Movement."[52]

Smith's book is just as important for its methodological innovations as it is for its reinterpretation of the frontier. The book was a revision of the dissertation he produced at Harvard's American Civilization Program. Its extensive use of nonliterary writing makes it unusual among the books I am discussing here, and it makes *Virgin Land* something closer to history than most of them. But unlike Miller's intellectual history, concerned as it was with explicitly developed systems of thought, Smith introduces the terms "myth" and "symbol" as means to talk about "collective representations" that exist not as well-articulated systems, but as a part of "the consciousness of Americans" (*Virgin Land*, xi, 4). "Myth" and "symbol" are "larger and smaller units of the same kind of thing, namely an intellectual construction that fuses concept and emotion into an image" (xi). While those critics who follow Smith will not keep strictly to his definition, the terms "myth" and "symbol" will become central to their project. There are two reasons for their centrality. One has to do with finding the historical significance of imaginative writing. As science, especially social science, increasingly defined knowledge on its terms, literature seemed increasingly irrelevant to history. Science also seemed to be defining nonrational experience out of existence. Talking about myths and symbols in literature was a way to get at irrational and often disguised meanings that were what people really felt about things. Literature no longer gave us truth, but it did give us access to feelings and beliefs that were not expressed in rational arguments.

The second reason for the importance of "myth" and "symbol" plays a lesser role in *Virgin Land* than it will in later works such as *The American Adam* and *The Machine in the Garden*. In Lewis's work, the dominant sense of the term "myth" is something like "the definitive artistic work of a culture or civilization." Lewis compares the Adamic myth, the outlines of which he has discovered in American intellectual history, to the *Aeneid*, a myth consciously created by Virgil. "The Roman myth received its final magnificent and persuasive form" in that work, but it was a dramatization of ideas that Romans had been discussing for centuries (4). Though America lacks a Virgil (unless Lewis is applying for the job), Lewis contends that we do have a dialogue or cultural conversation regarding "the matter of Adam." The major nineteenth-century writers turn out to contribute to this dialogue along with historians, theologians, and other "articulate thinkers." The definitive work of a culture need not be a work, but the collective intellectual labor of those whose concerns are central to the culture. When used in this way, the existence of a "myth" becomes one of the markers of cultural success. To have a myth is to be a civilization such as Rome.

The important point is that the senses of "myth" as collective representation and as cultural achievement tend to become conflated, so that the myth of the garden becomes, at least in the professional and cultural appropriation of *Virgin Land*, another work of American civilization. While *Virgin Land* is on the whole a *critical* study of American culture, its critical position pretty much was lost on its contemporary audience.[53] Doubtless that was partly because Smith announced no position from which his criticism issued, and little in the way of consequences that might derive from it. No New York Intellectual ever produced an extended work of cultural criticism to rival the detailed analysis of Smith's book, but the New Yorkers' widely known political stands, be they the Marxism of the 1930s or the conservative "liberalism" of the 1950s, meant that even their increasingly apolitical writing still seemed critical. Unlike Smith, Lewis did not discuss the epistemological status of myth, but he did not need to because he makes no explicit claims for the wide influence of the

Adamic myth and thus says nothing directly about larger history.[54] Yet *The American Adam* is not merely a testimony to American intellectual achievement; as Lewis's own words allow, it tells us about "experience in America," a formulation that takes Lewis's argument beyond the narrow definition of culture as a dialogue among articulate thinkers and artists (8).

Lewis might be seen as the representative figure for postwar studies of American literature. In him come together the three historical strands out of which the new disciplinary formation emerged. His graduate training at Chicago was both critical and historical. Lewis published essays in the *Kenyon Review* and the *Hudson Review*, one the chief organ of the New Critics, the other a kind of combination of New Critical and New York Intellectual sensibilities. *The American Adam* acknowledges the influence of both Matthiessen and Trilling. The book itself relies on New Critical reading strategies. While it perhaps entailed but a minimum of literary historical research, it is a work of intellectual history in the manner of Miller that develops a much more elaborate context and historical frame than did Matthiessen, Chase, or most other critics. The book's concern with the innocence/experience opposition reflects a New York Intellectual preoccupation, but Lewis's focus on irony and tragedy in Hawthorne and Melville is clearly Matthiessenian New Criticism. Of course, in combining all of these elements, Lewis is also unusual; most Americanists leaned more in one direction or another, and the practice of American literary study could not be said to be so unified a combination as Lewis embodies.

The themes and oppositions that structure the criticism of the postwar era were mixed and matched in the work of the different critics. Noting the "library" of books by Smith, Matthiessen, Trilling, Wilson, Pearce, Lewis, and Chase "in the movement toward a modern view of American literary history," Robert Spiller made a useful distinction between the two patterns that such critics had discovered in American fiction, a "Manichean dualism of good and evil" and "pastoral nostalgia," the former typically found in Melville, Hawthorne, and James, the latter in Cooper, Mark Twain, and Faulkner.[55] Spiller's distinction is an economical classification of different conceptions of American literature that at first might seem widely disparate "theories." His point is that no critic prior to Chase, not even Lewis, whose *American Adam* was based on the first pattern, nor Smith, whose *Virgin Land* relies on the second, "developed a cultural pattern common to the thinking of all of these writers" (83). According to Spiller, the advantage of Chase's notion of romance as the tradition of the American novel is that it does provide a conception that can accommodate all of these novelists.

A few years later, Leo Marx would make it clear that there are other ways to combine the two patterns. *The Machine in the Garden* deals with works that might be said to put the dualism of good and evil in a pastoral setting. In Marx, however, the pastoral is not merely an image or a longing but a genre. By placing American works in the context of a tradition that goes back to classical antiquity and includes a great many British poets, Marx elevates the status of American literature. By arguing that the impingement of industrialization becomes the particular problem of the American pastoral, Marx demonstrates the distinctiveness of American literature. He also reveals how seemingly antagonistic theses about American literature fit together better than first appeared.

The Machine in the Garden, more directly than either *Virgin Land* or *The American Adam*, comments on the problem of civilization itself. Pastoralism, as Marx himself has recently observed, is a longstanding attempt to mediate between civilization and nature.[56] As we have seen, since the nineteenth century, civilization has carried the contradictory meanings of enlightened and progressive development on the one hand and, on the other, the threatening results of such development, which conflict with the spiritual development signified by "culture," or, later, in Freud's formulation, with nature as manifested in human instincts.[57] *The Machine in the Garden* associates civilization with industrialization and the machine, and opposes it to nature as represented by the preindustrial landscape. Marx reads the pastoralism of American literature as a response to "the unbelievably rapid industrialization of an 'underdeveloped' society. Within a lifetime of a single generation, a rustic and in large part wild landscape was transformed into the site of the world's most productive industrial machine" (*Machine*, 343). The pastoral seeks to resolve in literature the contradiction between the waning preindustrial order and the newly dominant technological one. Yet the effect of

Marx's argument is to relocate American civilization from its embodiment in industry to the pastoral literature itself. American writers fail as they must to mediate the real conflict that motivates their work, but they succeed in producing "Americanness" and hence great literature.

Smith, Lewis, and Marx all extend their arguments in various ways into the twentieth century. Smith does this by commenting on the continuing effects of the myth of the garden on agricultural policy. Marx and Lewis both append epilogues dealing with the existence of the nineteenth-century patterns they discovered in twentieth-century fiction. In general, however, 1950s and 1960s critics tended to locate American civilization in the nineteenth century, and especially in the romantic writers. In this they seem to repeat Foerster's claim that the romantics invented American literature. After Matthiessen, who influenced all three of these critics, it was no longer necessary to make the case for the preeminence of the romantics, although Spiller's *Cycle of American Literature* (1955) did so. Rather, critics such as Lewis and Marx simply took for granted that the writers of Matthiessen's renaissance were the major American authors. The mid-nineteenth century thus became the temporal center of American literary history. If one stretches that center far enough, it can include in its orbit Brown, Washington Irving, and Cooper on the one side, and Twain and James on the other. While the New Critics and New York Intellectuals read James in the context of international modernism and as a forerunner of twentieth-century American fiction, Americanists were more likely to read James as a descendent of Hawthorne. Marx reads *The Adventures of Huckleberry Finn* as an instance of the pastoral design. What disappears almost entirely from these discussions of the Americanness of American literature is Foerster's fourth factor, realism, and the period with which it is identified. Dreiser, Crane, Norris, and Howells are not even afterthoughts, and thus apparently are not really American.

Discussions of myths and symbols that are typical of "the consciousness of Americans" (Smith) or American "culture" (Lewis) were two ways that the unity, distinctiveness, and (it must be added) importance of American literature were asserted. To those terms we must add one that encompasses them but that may be used without them as well: tradition. All of the myth-oriented criticism of American literature was explicitly concerned with traditions, but other studies take a particular genre and place it in a tradition of its own. The most influential of these studies is Chase's *American Novel and Its Tradition*, but others include Fiedler's *Love and Death in the American Novel*, Roy Harvey Pearce's *Continuity of American Poetry*, and Hyatt Waggoner's *American Poets: From the Puritans to the Present*. These sorts of studies take a longer view than do the myth-symbol books. Although they continue to make the nineteenth-century romantics central to American literature, they also typically take their stories up through the modern period, and begin them with the Puritans. This sort of tradition-building seems eminently historical, but it is an odd sort of history. Both Chase and Fiedler claim that Puritan origins permanently mark the character of the American novel. Since there are no Puritan novels, however, they must operate at some remove from the source. Of course, the old literary historians could make chains of influence covering equal or greater stretches of time, but they demanded documentary evidence. Chase treats Puritanism as simply there in "the American imagination" or "the national consciousness."[58] Puritanism here is in fact closer to the ahistorical meaning the term had in popular usage than it is to anything produced by Perry Miller. As Chase describes it, his work is "an essay in definition and appreciation, and although it often takes an historical view, it is not a detailed literary history" (vii). The "historical view" is mainly that of long-term historical continuities, rather than historical contextualization of individual works. Those Chase selected because they fit his requirements of "originality" and "Americanness," the latter apparently meaning that they were romances and therefore supported his argument.

Chase's use of history is a perfect example of the way history will increasingly figure in the study of American literature. As criticism becomes more dominant, history doesn't disappear in the way that some misreadings of the New Critics suggest it would; rather, history becomes a sequence of texts that are themselves events that beget future texts. Tradition and continuity, discovered intrinsically, replace influence and source, which are by definition extrinsic. And since tradition is the source, the tension between influence and originality that troubled the old literary history is avoided. To be original is now understood as adding to the tradition.

The Continuity of American Poetry is more deeply historical than most other treatments of American literary traditions, but its conception of continuity is finally little different from Chase's tradition. Pearce discusses Puritanism in enough detail to actually isolate a real intellectual issue of that era, antinomianism, but it quickly becomes transcendental: "The history of American poetry is the history of an impulse toward antinomianism."[59] The only real poet Pearce finds among the Puritans is Edward Taylor, in whose work antinomianism turns out to exist not as an issue but as an unrecognized force:

> Antinomianism will out, if only because the making of poems demands that the poet, in spite of all his beliefs to the contrary, be a maker. Saying this we surely gainsay Taylor and the others. But then, it is really not we who gainsay them; history, a history which they helped make, gainsays them—as it will be the burden of this book to demonstrate. (54)

In other words, the meaning of Taylor's poems is their place in the continuity of American poetry.

If Puritanism is "the continuing nature" of American poetry, that nature finds its definitive expression in the mid-nineteenth century: "The continuity of American poetry moves . . . from Taylor and his kind to Emerson and thence to Whitman. All American poetry since is, in essence if not in substance, a series of arguments with Whitman" (Pearce, 57). Pearce's claims for Whitman's central role in our poetic tradition is paralleled by Hawthorne's in many studies of the novel. While Chase does not give us a central man in his tradition, "Hawthorne figures not just as an author in a tradition but as the agent of its constitution: Chase establishes American fiction's difference around the antithesis of novel and romance, a distinction taken directly from Hawthorne's prefaces."[60]

Neither of these figures, however, has been as important in the overall conception of American literature as Emerson. We saw that even in the late teens and twenties, Emerson was emerging as the representative figure of American literature. We still find him playing that role in the *Literary History of the United States*, where, in a chapter Spiller himself wrote, it is asserted that "Emerson emerged as the delegated intellect" of his era and was "spokesman for his time and country."[61] In *The Cycle of American Literature*, Spiller calls Emerson the "recorder of the American mind" and "its poet and its prophet" (53). The traditionally historical Spiller treats Emerson as central to his own era, but there were much stronger claims made on Emerson's behalf. Hyatt Waggoner argued that "Emerson is the central figure in American poetry."[62] Waggoner traces everything of importance back to Emerson, and, following the odd logic of literary tradition-making, he even traces the poetry of Edward Taylor forward to Emerson (16–24). This move is explicitly borrowed from Leslie Fiedler, who argued that "without understanding Emerson" one cannot "appreciate the true meaning of Edward Taylor."[63]

Perry Miller's essay "From Edwards to Emerson" might have been the point of emergence of this sort of thinking. First published in 1940, the essay doubtless reached a wider audience when it appeared in *Errand into the Wilderness*. Miller, unlike Waggoner, is attempting a kind of influence study within a loosely knit but clearly identifiable institution, the New England church in which Emerson trained and briefly served as a minister. But a misreading that Miller reports in his headnote to the essay in *Errand* suggests that many (presumably academic) readers did not understand the careful limits Miller claims for himself: "This essay . . . has been unhappily construed by many readers . . . as meaning that in some mystical pretension I argue for a direct line of intellectual descent as though Edwards were a Hollinshed to Emerson's Shakespeare." On the contrary, he insists that "there is no organic evolution of ideas from Edwards to Emerson."[64] Miller thus specifically eschews the sort of descent that Chase and Pearce often seem to rely on. He nevertheless wants to claim that "certain basic continuities persist in a culture . . . which underlie the successive articulation of 'ideas' " (184–85). He calls New England a "confined . . . laboratory" of ideas, thus making the possibility of continuity more plausible (184). Furthermore, Miller never argues that either Edwards or Emerson represent America. Nevertheless, there are nationalist questions that seem to motivate the essay: "Where did Emerson, Alcott, Thoreau, and Margaret Fuller find this pantheism which they preached in varying degrees . . . ? Was New England transcendentalism wholly Germanic or Hindu in origin?" (187). Even if Miller's focus is on New England, there is nothing to prevent us from making the usual assumption that New England and America are identical for literary purposes. Moreover, this assumption is reinforced by Miller's foregrounding of Emerson, who is then used as a synecdoche for an entire cultural era. He thus becomes more than a representative man, more than "the Central Man"—he becomes the man who takes the place of all of his contemporaries.

Statements that ascribe to Emerson a preeminent position in the American tradition usually use one of three metaphors. Two of them are allusions to Emerson's own work: "representativeness" and "centrality." Although these metaphors are by no means identical, both imply Eliot's conception of a literary tradition as an organic whole. As we have seen, claims for Emerson's centrality are not characteristic of earlier histories such as Parrington's, but become commonplace only later under the influence of Eliot's notion of tradition. The shift from the literary-historical model to that of Matthiessen, Smith, Lewis, and Marx now rendered American literature not an inert mass of documents, but a living thing. As such, it could be, perhaps needed to be, described in spatial terms, so that history becomes flattened out into something like a two-dimensional rendering of the solar system, with the different authors orbiting nearer or farther from Emerson. Where Parrington was chastised for leaving out Poe and James because they did not contribute to the "main currents," the new model is in fact even more restrictive. It in effect establishes a single main current that, though it often is an alternating current of contradictions, separates the truly American from everything else merely written in the United States. If Emerson is "representative," only those who look like him are represented.

The other metaphor by which Emerson has been described is "fatherhood." This metaphor in no way contradicts the other two, since fathers in our culture are typically taken to be representative and central to their families, but it does suggest several other dimensions of the discursive regularity of literary studies. The first should, today, be obvious to everyone: the founder could not be a mother. The tradition needed to be patrilineal. The odd daughter might be included, but a woman could not be the founder. None of the histories of American poetry trace its founding to Emily Dickinson, for example, even though her writing has as much in common with twentieth-century American poetry as does that of either Emerson or Whitman.[65] Second, the metaphor of fatherhood suggests the need for an authority that would justify the aesthetics of American literature. Here I do not mean the authority of Emerson's aesthetic arguments, although the fact that he offered such arguments doubtless made him an impressive candidate. The father of a tradition serves the same function as the father of a child: his name confers legitimacy. Without a father, American literature is the bastard of British literature. It is derivative rather than original. Emerson makes "the American difference in literature"[66] in a way he might have appreciated: merely by giving it his name.

There have been other ways that the "American difference in literature" has been claimed. Reising devotes a whole section of his book to "self-reflexive theories of American literature," which include Charles Feidelson's *Symbolism and American Literature* and Richard Poirier's *A World Elsewhere*.[67] Feidelson's book was both controversial and influential during the fifties, and it has had perhaps even more influence in recent years.[68] Self-reflexivity, however, has not been a widely accepted marker of Americanness. Feidelson defines his project against Matthiessen's claim of his writers' "devotion to the possibilities of democracy" (4, quoting Matthiessen). But democracy, the vision of an agricultural paradise, or even the myth of radical innocence all lend themselves more easily to the nationalist project than the proposition that what distinguishes American literature is symbolism and self-reflexivity. Not only do these characteristics fail to resonate with other representations of American culture, they don't even distinguish American literature from other modern European literatures, except in the sense of priority: Feidelson claims Americans invented symbolism before the Europeans. This sort of claim adds to the perception of the aesthetic success of American literature, but it was likely to have made the greatest impression on those other critics who shared Feidelson's investment in the value of symbolism.

The development of a widely accepted sense of the unity and distinctiveness of American civilization expressed in American literature not only encouraged a proliferation of books celebrating newly discovered forms of unity and distinctiveness, but also some that found the Americanness of American literature unworthy of celebration. We have already seen that Trilling and Rahv had proposed such conceptions, but that these tended to mutate over time to become more positive. Fiedler's *Love and Death in the American Novel*, however, is a full-scale attack on the American novel for its failure to reflect psychosexual maturity. Some of Fiedler's critique is the Rahv/Trilling thesis pushed to its limit, so that American fiction no longer merely evades reality but is "a gothic fiction, nonrealistic and negative, sadistic and melodramatic—a literature of darkness and the grotesque in a land of light and affirmation."[69] It is, of course, not mainly epistemology that interests Fiedler, but sexuality understood relative to Freud's model of healthy development, something that American novels don't often exhibit. Like Feidelson's book, *Love and Death in the American Novel* has never been widely understood as definitive, but its focus on sexuality, especially given its publication in 1960, earned it a wide audience. Fiedler's book would not have been possible without there first being a strong sense that there existed a distinctive thing called the American novel. Somewhat marginal studies such as his are evidence of the strength of the center, not its weakness.

Taken together, the various expositions of American civilization do not make a perfectly clear picture. While certain themes do reappear under new guises in different books, one cannot claim that any kind of consensus has been reached about which qualities distinguish American civilization. Nevertheless, the critical studies of the 1950s, most taking off from Matthiessen in one direction or another, do reach a consensus that there is a distinctive American civilization, and it is American literature that provides the evidence for such a civilization. By the 1960s, American literature had become completely redefined from what it had been in the 1930s and 1940s. No longer an object of historical investigation, American literature was now an ideal order of eternal objects reflecting the mind of a whole people. Such a disciplinary object must inevitably carry with it important limitations on the discourse of the discipline. These limitations have, since the late

1960s, been widely explored by social scientists, historians, feminists, leftists, and advocates of multiethnic literature.[70]

Several such limitations are worthy of further mention here. Nina Baym argues that "gender-related restrictions" on literary meaning and value arise "out of critical theories."[71] Those "theories" assume a masculine point of view, and they define Americanness from that perspective. Baym's argument on this point needs to be historically deepened. The "theories" of the 1950s and 1960s with which she is concerned were more or less invented to deal with an already gender restricted conception of American literature. That gender restriction was built on sexism endemic to American society, but as we have seen, also on unarticulated assumptions basic to the formation of American literature as an object of study, for example, that great American writers would be as much as possible like great English writers. These too are restrictive "theories," but by the 1950s they are so embedded in disciplinary practice that they are part of its ideology. Of course, the same restrictions apply to African Americans, Native Americans, and other nondominant ethnic groups.

Baym suggests an even more exclusionary restriction entailed by the new disciplinary object: "The critic has had to insist that some works in America are much more American than others, and he is as busy excluding certain writers as 'un-American' as he is including others" (127). Garry Wills makes a similar point in the context of trying to read the Declaration of Independence as a historical document rather than secular scripture: "If there is an American *idea*, then one must subscribe to it in order to be an American. . . . To be fully American, one must adopt this idea wholeheartedly, proclaim it, prove one's devotion to it."[72] The Americanness of a person or poem will on these grounds be a matter of the degree to which it conforms to the idea. Pearce finds that "the American Idea," as named explicitly by Lowell, "animates the work of . . . Poe, Emerson, and Whitman" (*Continuity*, 193). The other critics may not be as explicit, but each is concerned with some candidate for the role of the "American idea." Even while the "end of ideology" was being proclaimed, we find that ideological limitations on American literature are being covertly built into the core of the subdiscipline.

Reising has argued a third limitation that he sees resulting from the theories he discusses. This is a limitation on politics and on the ability to understand literature in a social context. Again, some historical perspective can help us to understand the meaning of this limitation in the 1950s. Reising takes Parrington and Hicks as if they were typical of American literary study prior to the New Criticism. He ignores entirely academic literary history, which was governed by the ideal of disinterestedness and was thus as politically disengaged as its practitioners could make it. It is not surprising that when criticism became an academic practice it should also claim disinterestedness for itself, as the New Critical theorists explicitly did. Still, literary historians could and did understand literature as a social product. The myths, symbols, and traditions of the critics, however, seem to stand in for the social, as do "civilization" and "culture" as well. Such terms serve to permit American literature to remain an ideal order, and to refuse it the chance to be treated as a social product. But by refusing the relevance of historical social conditions, the new disciplinary model allowed for a covert politics that earlier historical scholarship had prohibited. To put it simply, the entire project of creating American civilization is political. Depicting America as a civilization had the force of negating whatever criticisms of American culture that a Smith, a Fiedler, or a Marx might offer. The effect of the collective work of the discipline of American literature was to celebrate American civilization. Thus American literature was used to reinforce the pervasive political messages of the postwar era that America had achieved a legitimate global supremacy, threatened only by a potential illegitimate supremacy of communism. America in this view was not merely a civilization, but the savior of civilization itself. The existence of a great and unique tradition of American literature helped Americans believe in this vision.

A New Practice

It has been claimed that the "group of works articulating the distinctively American aspect of American literature . . . enabled that literature to assert itself as a separate intellectual discipline in the 1950s" (Brodhead, 9). As I hope I have shown in earlier chapters of this book, that is an overstatement. American literature had been a distinct subdiscipline of English since the 1920s, and it has not yet become entirely separate. Nevertheless, this claim does point to a fundamental change in the subdiscipline of American literature. What happened in the 1950s was the constitution of a new disciplinary object along the lines that Matthiessen had established in *American Renaissance*. That this new object was one the field had long been struggling to conceptualize accounts for the rapid transformation of the field. The books I have just discussed were very quickly recognized as defining the field of American literature, and the older literary historians put up little in the way of a fight. If they had resisted more strongly, these critical works would not have gained such wide acceptance. In 1958, the NCTE published a guide to *Contemporary Literary Scholarship* aimed at teachers.[73] It contained chapters devoted to each major period of English literature and on two periods of American literature. The essay on American literature to 1900 is by Leslie Fiedler, something that in itself suggests the degree to which criticism was already authorized in the academy. Though written before the publication of the major studies of Chase, Marx, and Pearce, as well as his own *Love and Death*, Fiedler's essay presents a conception of the field that would have been nearly current 10 years later. In part this is true because Fiedler is able to pick out essays that will become essential elements of books published later, but mainly it is because Fiedler is simply able to grasp how the new disciplinary object has been constructed: who the major authors are, what questions are important, and what sorts of answers have been proposed.[74] R. W. B. Lewis's chapter on "Contemporary American Literature" is no less sympathetic to criticism, but is not nearly so clear about its subject. It couldn't be because twentieth-century American literature was not yet a well-defined area. In 1964, a collection of papers from an NCTE convention on *The Teacher and American Literature* was prefaced with a list of books such a teacher should acquire. The list includes several works that represent historical scholarship—the *LHUS*, the MLA's bibliography, *Eight American Authors*, and *Articles on American Literature, 1900–1950*—and it includes some works of critical theory, including *Theory of Literature* and *The Anatomy of Criticism*. But dominating the list are works of critical interpretation, including every one of the major critical works considered in the last section, save *The Machine in the Garden*, which was published in the same year.[75]

Of course, it was not just the study of American literature that changed during the 1950s. The shift to criticism affected the study of British and other literatures as well. Though protests by literary historians, such as the famous MLA presidential address by Douglas Bush in 1948, continued into the 1950s and 1960s, criticism was increasingly the normal practice of English departments.[76] Even Bush, as Graff has shown, was already conceding far more to the critics than prewar literary historians had been willing to grant.[77] Criticism, however, did not result in English literature being redefined in the same way as that of America. If we compare Fiedler's chapter in *Contemporary Literary Scholarship* to those on English literature, we find in the latter a much greater reliance on prewar works and much less focus on critical ones. Although F. R. Leavis and other contributors to *Scrutiny* did develop new notions of English literary traditions, there was no need for these traditions to demonstrate the existence of civilization. More significant, perhaps, are the different ways in which nationality was defined in each case. Americans at least since James Russell Lowell have spoken of "the American idea." To be English is not necessarily to subscribe to any particular set of ideas or have a certain sort of experience; there is no "English idea" that literary works might express or reveal. As a result, criticism of English literature was not burdened with the need to coalesce around a unifying myth or theme. English criticism, then, tended to remain focused on individual authors.

Even with regard to American literature it would be a mistake to think of critical practice as typically imitating the projects of a Lewis or a Marx. As is perhaps obvious, most of those coming into the American literature at this time could not be writing large-scale studies defining new kinds of Americanness. Doubtless there were more dissertations of this kind than we now remember, but even so, the standard critical practice had to deal with pieces rather than the whole. The author remained the most important piece of the whole, and critics-in-training were still more likely to write single-author dissertations than any other kind. Biographies remained important, though they were often the work of older, more historically oriented scholars. The critical article was the staple product of the enterprise, and journals proliferated to accommodate the form. But as a result of this proliferation, such publication was less likely to reach even the desired audience of specialists, and very unlikely to be seen by graduate students or college teachers. One of the major innovations in the dissemination of criticism is the collection of critical essays about particular authors or works. Among the most important of these were Prentice-Hall's Twentieth-Century Views series, edited by Maynard Mack of Yale, and Norton's Critical Editions series, both of which originated in the late 1950s.

These compilations of critical essays were more than just a convenient medium, however. Such collections are the repositories of knowledge produced under the hermeneutic paradigm. Where academic journals were, under the positivist model, understood as records of accumulated knowledge, they now became forums for debate. The collection of pieces culled from such journals represents the most important contributions to such debates. Instead of seeking agreement, however, the editor of a collection must seek disagreements. The Prentice-Hall and Norton series thus represent not the accumulation of knowledge about an author or work, but the record of differing readings of them. That record is the achievement of the discipline, which, though it may in principle continue to believe in a single, correct interpretation, in practice accepts its infinite deferral. The statements that the new discipline of literary studies could produce ad infinitum were interpretations. The value of such statements depends to a high degree on the value of the objects interpreted. Where factual statements seem to be valuable by virtue of their presumed truth, interpretive statements, which are not accorded such a presumption, are significant only if the thing interpreted already has significance.

Under these conditions, it was inevitable that the range of texts and authors that Americanists discussed should narrow considerably. Some early volumes of *American Literature* contained more articles on minor authors and texts than major ones, and some of the founders of the subdiscipline felt that not enough work was being done on minor figures. But during the 1950s and 1960s, work on minor figures became very rare indeed. The vast majority of work within the discipline was now devoted to rereading the major works by the major authors. This state of affairs meant that women authors, African Americans, and other minorities would have even less chance for consideration. There was nothing in the current practice that encouraged critics to expand the range of texts they discussed. On the other hand, interpretations of major authors and works continued to be dispersed. They proliferated without direction or goal and led to no further consensus.

If there was any area of expansion, it was toward more contemporary subjects. Graduate students in search of unplowed areas of the field were increasingly likely to turn to contemporary figures who could not be written off as minor because no definitive judgment had been made. This increased attention to "contemporary" writing was, of course, partially a function of the twentieth century getting older, but there was more attention to living writers as well. The movement of criticism into the university accounts for some of this, but the phenomenon is larger than criticism. Already in 1957 it could be observed that

> the contemporary arts are incarnate within our universities and
> schools, in the person of teaching poets and novelists and
> critics and painters and composers; . . . whatever the effect
> upon the academic world, the effect upon the world of litera-
> ture is the paradoxical rebirth of something very traditional and
> European: truly home-grown men of letters—cultivated artists.
> We are not yet so French that we can look up "men of letters"
> in the classified sections of our telephone-books, as one can in
> Paris; but that privilege may not be long delayed.[78]

These "men of letters" were nothing like Howells or Stedman, but neither were they much like Phillips or Rahv. The university nurtured these "new men of letters" and gave them their authority, but it did not enable them to reach a wide audience or have popular influence. Even Trilling, who had the widest influence, was never regarded as a cultural treasure or symbol. The restriction of influence was less the fault of the university than of the relative decline of the literary as a medium. The power to confer literary value was increasingly held by the university, but that power was relatively less significant. What remained of the literary outside of the university came to have less and less cultural capital. Critics for newspapers and magazines who lacked an academic base were mere "book reviewers." While publishers and their editors might garner cultural capital by association with academics, they themselves increasingly appeared as mere businessmen who had abandoned their roles as enlightened judges of literary value. It is ironic that, at a time when something like an intellectual renaissance could be proclaimed in the United States, the cultural importance of the representative intellectual or man of letters was already in steep decline. What the postwar intellectuals and critics saw as a general renewal of interest in intellectual activity was in fact their own passing from the margins to the center of cultural power. This doubtless conferred the illusion that their own light shone brightly across the cultural map, but in fact the intellectuals had mainly a reflected brilliance. It was the power of government and the universities that worked through them.

Epilogue:
A Trailer

If I have told my story well, the reader will be hoping for more. Even if I've not been such a good storyteller, the reader may be frustrated because the story seems to end in the middle. After all, the last major text I've dealt with, *The Machine in the Garden*, was published in 1964. More important, perhaps, than the simple span of time is the widespread perception that literary studies in general and the study of American literature in particular have undergone nearly revolutionary change in that time. The reality of that change is part of the reason the book ends where it does. Too much has happened in the discipline since the late 1960s for those years to be treated adequately in a chapter or two. But it's not just a matter of quantity; it is much harder to determine what is important in so recent a period than it is for more distant eras. It is because the project of creating American civilization reached fruition in the 1950s and 1960s that it can be analyzed as a coherent historical event. Whatever the changes that have occurred since, most commentators seem to agree that they have not come to a climax. Those years require a book of their own. Hence this brief epilogue should be understood as presenting only a few scenes from what might be a sequel.

Any good trailer will make the audience want to see the picture by giving the impression that there is much left to be resolved by the narrative as a whole. I've said that change in the discipline has been real, but the character of that change remains very much in doubt. As a result, not only the plot but the genre of any possible

345

sequel remains unclear. Have the most important changes in the discipline been in its theoretical assumptions? Have they been in the canon? Have they involved a new kind of practice, aimed at fracturing, at least, the representation of American civilization that the old discipline created? Any definitive answers to these questions must wait, but in the very short space I have allowed myself here, I will sketch out several different ones.

Scene One: Revolution

"Play 'The Marseillaise.'"
Victor Lazlo

There can be little doubt that the academy has changed significantly since 1964. The most important change, the growth of college enrollments, was well under way by then, but it would continue unabated for many years. During most of the period covered by this book, college was available mainly to the bourgeoisie and the professional-managerial classes. The small number of people attending college meant that having a college degree was valuable as a cultural distinction. Under these conditions, literary training continued to provide valuable cultural capital. As a larger percentage of the population began to attend college, the markers of distinction such education made available became relatively less valuable, even as the degree became increasingly necessary for economic success. The interest in American literature—especially modern American literature—that undergraduates showed in the 1950s and 1960s was doubtless in part a reflection of their relatively slight experience with English or classical literatures. The first waves of new students, then, buoyed up American literature. But as more and more students attended college, its function changed. The new students and new colleges—either they were literally new or had been converted from technical or teacher-training institutions—were not strongly committed to liberal arts education. Career training came to be more valuable than the cultural capital literature or other humanities could provide. Language and literature requirements disappeared, numbers of majors declined, and an increasing percentage of English professors found themselves teaching service courses. Yet they continued to be trained as disciplinary practitioners and to have expectations of careers as researchers. And as new or transformed institutions sought the prestige and financial rewards that only research can bring, they increasingly demanded publication. The result was an enormous growth in the quantity of publication in all fields of literary study, including American literature.[1]

The large number of new students included more women, more African Americans, and more members of other minorities than ever before. The civil rights movement, the women's movement, and other 1960s left activism created an environment in which these new students could demand an education more suited to their needs. The expanding research market meant that these educational initiatives would lead to research programs, including Afro-American studies and women's studies. But even within English departments, change did occur. The most glaring change would seem to be an opening up of the canon. While few if any of the old figures have been displaced, there is no denying that the discipline has in large measure recognized a new principle of canon formation.[2] The canon, it is now widely held, must reflect the racial, ethnic, gender, and class diversity of the American public. Works by African Americans and women have now come to be regularly included in anthologies, and they have become frequent topics of critical attention. The writing of other ethnic minorities has received less attention, but there is increasing interest. In the past five years or so, a gay and lesbian presence in American literature has begun to be acknowledged. However, although class is almost always mentioned with race and gender, it has yet to become a significant principle of inclusion in the canon.

It's not just that African Americans and women have been added to the canon. A sophisticated critical literature has developed about writing by both groups. As a result of their different positioning in the culture, the place of writing by African Americans and writing by women in American literature has been differently conceived. Though this has been by no means the explicit ambition of all African Americanists, their studies have created a countertradition.[3] There are numerous reasons for this including racism, but two related ones seem most important. Most studies of African-American literature emerged from the Afro-American studies movement, rather than from English departments in general or the subdiscipline of American literature in particular.

As a result, most scholars of African-American literature had no disciplinary stake in maintaining any version of American literature as an object of study. Secondly, Afro-American studies was very much the product of the renewed black nationalism of the 1960s. The continued importance of the black-nationalist perspective among African-American scholars would inevitably lead to the construction of a tradition. Perhaps the most explicit builder of that tradition has been Houston Baker.[4] In "Archaeology, Ideology, and African American Discourse," Baker discusses the theory of tradition-building from a Foucauldian/Marxist perspective, while at the same time outlining a version of the African-American tradition. His conception of African-American literary history is an "archaeology" that "seeks to discover organizing or formative principles of discourses."[5] While eschewing both "vulgar Marxism" and "an idealistically polemical black nationalism," Baker understands such organizing principles to be ideological and insists that they must be related to the economic conditions of literature itself and of its makers. Thus Baker is building a very different sort of tradition than did earlier Americanists, but he remains, like them, a cultural nationalist.

Studies of (mostly white) women writers have tended to construct a different sort of relationship to the established canon. While there certainly have been critics who have discussed a women's tradition in American literature, the more influential approach has been the attempt to modify the existing canon or to obliterate it. Some of the most important feminist criticism has dealt not with women writers, but with male authors and the dominant critical treatments of them. Two important early studies of this kind were Annette Kolodny's *The Lay of the Land* (1975) and Judith Fetterley's *The Resisting Reader* (1979).[6] The prevalence of this approach doubtless resulted in part from the important role played by literary criticism in the women's movement of the late 1960s and early 1970s. Two widely read manifestos of that movement, Kate Millet's *Sexual Politics* and Germaine Greer's *The Female Eunuch*, relied heavily on the analysis of literary works. Even when feminist critics did go on to focus on women's writing, they did not usually constitute it as a separate tradition. For example, Kolodny's *The Land Before Her* (1984) deals with women's writing about the frontier, taking an explicitly male-defined realm and examining the space that women were able to carve out within it.[7] Kolodny's point is that women were part of what had hitherto been represented as an almost exclusively male experience. Thus the writing she examines does not so much form a new tradition as expand the existing one. In *Sensational Designs* (1985) Jane Tompkins goes further than Kolodny in attempting to modify the dominant tradition. Tompkins wants to make a case for canonization of neglected female writers such as Susan Warner, but she also wants to "point out that the literary works that now make up the canon do so because the groups that have an investment in them are culturally the most influential."[8] Rather than rejecting the idea of a canon, Tompkins proposes to remake the American canon on the basis of a new set of interests. To do this, however, Tompkins is careful to place her new works in the context of others that had been canonized, especially Hawthorne's, but also those of Charles Brockden Brown and Cooper. If Tompkins's new literary history were to become dominant, the result would not be a women's tradition, but a feminist conception of an American tradition.

Despite its continued marginality, the work of African Americanists and feminists has produced change in the discipline of American literature. Studies by Baker, Henry Louis Gates, Kolodny, and Tompkins have been among the most influential books in the discipline. At least two primary works have become major texts in the American survey: Frederick Douglass's *Narrative* and Kate Chopin's *The Awakening*. The major anthologies have continued to increase the representation of both African-American and women writers. The representation of Hispanic, Native American, Asian, and other ethnic minority authors has not increased so dramatically, but their presence has begun to be felt. Moreover, the kinds of texts that are considered "American literature" have greatly increased in number. African Americanists have made the blues and other oral or folk forms central to their conception of their tradition. The feminist version of American literary history gives importance to diaries and other documents that were ignored under the old conception of literature. Even works in nonprint media such as film are now sometimes included in American literature. As a result, American literature as an object of study has been enough changed that we can safely say it will never again look the way it did in the 1950s and 1960s. In fact, American literature is now looking more and more as it did in the *Cambridge History*, where it in principle included all writing in America. Even if most practitioners do not accept Tompkins's argument about the historical contingency of the canon, they have come to accept the claims of African Americans and women to be represented in American literary history.

Scene Two: *plus ça change* . . .

"Round up the usual suspects."
Luis Renault

But is there something wrong with this picture? Lurking beneath its presentation of relatively peaceful, progressive change is an uneasiness, a sense that the changes that have been achieved are insignificant, that they are under constant threat of being undone, and that, in general, business goes on as usual. While the recent public controversy over "political correctness" and the attacks by right-wing groups such as the National Association of Scholars have raised fears of a return to the old canon, these "contras" seem at the moment to have failed. The real concern is with current teaching and research practices, including those of many who are sympathetic to the changes I have just described. For one thing, it would be easy to cite the same anthologies and anecdotal evidence of teaching practices to show that the old canon remains dominant. There is evidence that suggests that the authors represented in the survey remain little changed from those typical of such courses in the 1940s.[9] And even when representatives of marginalized groups are included, they are there as minority representatives and not as part of the mainstream that continues to be embodied in Emerson, Hawthorne, Melville, Thoreau, and Whitman.[10] The survey itself continues to be the fundamental course in American literature, even though a real awareness of countertraditions should render it impossible to claim the objective ground from which a survey may be conducted.

Still, one could explain the slow pace of change in the curriculum as an effect of the glacial movement of institutional bureaucracy and the inevitable delay in articulating new knowledge produced in research universities to those other institutions that mediate it to the majority of students. What is much harder to dismiss is the persistence of dominant research practices within leading universities. These practices continue to be central even to the work of many of those scholars who present themselves as remaking the field. Perhaps the most striking evidence of a lack of fundamental change is that the disciplinary object continues to embody many of the same assumptions as it did during the 1950s and before. Peter Carafiol has argued that traditionalists and radicals alike continue to assume the existence of an American ideal and "the exceptional situation of the new world" as constitutive of their field.[11] In Carafiol's view, "Ritual attacks on the fat target of aesthetic formalism, and on racism and sexism, and rueful acknowledgments of past ethnocentrism are the recurrent rhetorical gestures, the passwords, of what amounts to a New Orthodoxy in American Literary Scholarship" (14). Like the right-wing critics of the academy, Carafiol believes in something like a left hegemony, but unlike them he doesn't see the New Orthodoxy as a radical departure from the old orthodoxy: "This New Orthodoxy is constituted not so much by programmatic agreement as by an implicit loyalty to the disciplinary assumptions that define professional scholars in American literature" (173, n. 12).

Carafiol's conception of a New Orthodoxy includes feminists such as Paul Lauter, Tompkins, and Kolodny, and such distinguished scholars of the dominant tradition as Emory Elliot and Sacvan Bercovitch. He recognizes that the feminists have continued to conceive of an American tradition, while his exclusion of African American scholars suggests an implicit recognition that they have not.[12] But Carafiol himself continues an important aspect of the dominant practice that he does not seem to recognize. Among the things that African Americanist and feminist critics of the canon share is a preference for interpreting texts that do not have a long history of professional interpretation. That cannot be said of Carafiol or most of the myriad of other "New Americanists" who are typically preoccupied with rereading "major" authors and works.[13] One of four sections in Carafiol's book on American literary scholarship is devoted to rereading Emerson and Thoreau. Donald Pease, whose special issues of *boundary 2* make him the scholar most identified as a New Americanist, has been concerned in his own criticism with rereading the "major" writers of the American renaissance.[14] The essays in his "New Americanist" issues are overwhelmingly concerned with canonical figures, in spite of Pease's claim that New Americanists seek to establish a "counter-hegemony." The politics of this strategy are by no means easy to assess. Leading American Marxist theorists, including Fredric Jameson and Gayatri Spivak, have long encouraged their students to reread canonical works. Such readings, it is argued, can better disseminate a Marxist or, to return to the New Americanists, a "counter-hegemonic" cultural analysis and more persuasively demonstrate its power. But what such a strategy concedes is precisely the power of the canon. The New Americanists continue to trade on its authority even while they advocate an end to that authority. My point is that the New Americanists tacitly recognize that the canon established over the course of the century will continue to be part of any new disciplinary object that might be constituted.

But the perception of business as usual is not just a matter of critics reinterpreting the *same* books, but also of their *reinterpreting* the same books. The notion that American literature studies have radically changed usually includes as one major piece of evidence the rise of poststructuralist theory within the field. This was widely perceived to be slow in coming. While poststructuralism has never dominated any major literary discipline in America, it was applied to English and French texts before it was to American ones. The broader movement toward theory—of which poststructuralism was only a strand, though perhaps the major one— included a strong "antihermeneutic" tendency. Jonathan Culler, perhaps the leading American proponent of structuralism and poststructuralism, called for literary studies to move "beyond interpretation" to other tasks.[15] But theory in literary studies has chiefly been understood as a source of "new approaches," that is, new methods of interpretation. Thus, in spite of the widespread perception that Theory had moved us beyond the New Criticism, in practice literary studies remains similar to what it has been ever since World War II.[16] Theory became important in the late 1940s, and its brief decline between, say, 1955 and 1965, should be understood as an aberration. What the second wave of theorizing did was to address the epistemological dissonance engendered by hermeneutic practice but generally covered up by postwar theorists. Instead of producing a new practice, Theory made possible the continuation of the old one.[17] Much of the new work on American literature simply substitutes a new set of themes—the body, race, gender, sexuality, and so on—for those invoked in New Critical practice. Pease asserts a shift in what he calls the "field-Imaginary" of American literature studies and illustrates it by noting opposing book titles from before and after: "Smith's *Virgin Land* gives way to Annette Kolodny's *Lay of the Land* and Slotkin's *Fatal Environment*; R. W. B. Lewis's *American Adam* becomes Myra Jehlen's *American Incarnation* . . . "[18] It seems not to have occurred to Pease that what such an easy set of oppositions might signal is the rootedness of both sides in the same episteme and their participation in the same practice.

There is one element of New Americanist practice, however, that must be considered at least newly significant if not unprecedented in the discipline. That is the self-reflexive attention to the discipline itself that is often the focus of the New Americanists' writing.[19] If Emerson, Twain, Hawthorne, Melville, and their ilk remain the figures most frequently mentioned by New Americanists, Parrington, Matthiessen, Trilling, and the like easily come in second. What the New Americanists recognize that the old Americanists largely did not is that American literature is a socially constructed object. Reising's *The Unusable Past*, Michaels's and Pease's collection, *The American Renaissance Reconsidered*, Pease's introductions to his "New Americanist" issues, Carafiol's "Reading the Tradition" of scholarship on transcendentalism, and Tompkins's chapters on the canon in *Sensational Designs* represent some of the most influential and distinctive work done by Americanists in recent years. The relative importance of such studies would suggest that the New Americanists have adopted Paul Bové's conception of the new mission of the humanities: to investigate the social construction of the old.[20] And yet, when the critique of the discipline is presented in the service of the New Americanists' reinterpretation of the canon, the critique remains internalist and Panglossian. How could it not, when, as Crews shrewdly observes, the New Americanists are in the process of taking over the disciplinary apparatus from the old?[21] The New Americanists are precisely internal to the discipline, and once this is recognized we can see

Pease's claim of a radical disjunction between their field and the one represented by Crews to be a product of the New Americanists' need to legitimate their ambitions.

Scene Three: The Future

"It's still a story without an ending."
Rick Blaine

Whatever the current state of the discipline, there is a great deal of discourse devoted to its future, and almost everyone thinks that it will or should be radically different from past or present incarnations. At first glance it would seem that many think that there should be no new Americanists, nor old ones either. William Spengemann would have American literature reintegrated into English: "The history of what we call American literature, in short, is inseparable from the history of literature in English as a whole."[22] In Spengemann's view, the discipline should be focused on works that we call "literature" because they invented "the language that constitutes the modern world" (162). Language then replaces nationality as the central principle by which literary traditions should be understood. Spengemann's antinationalism is typical of many visions of the future, but most would reject language as an alternative principle of identity. Gregory Jay argues for the "end of 'American' literature," and urges instead that "our goal should be to construct a multicultural and dialogical paradigm for the study of writing in the United States."[23] Jay's vision is thus multilinguistic, but remains defined by the history and present existence of a nation-state. Peter Carafiol also forecasts the end of American literature, arguing that "American Literary Scholarship was created (with still less substantial justification than most other academic fields) out of political and professional motives. Now that all but the most narrow professional justifications have pretty much disappeared, the field, in its current form, should disappear as well" (150). Nevertheless his own prescription for a new practice is that we find "a way of making historical texts participate in contemporary conversations," as his reading of Emerson and Thoreau is meant to illustrate (7). Of course, none of these authors is really advocating an end to American literature, though Spengemann's vision might come the closest. Each is in fact arguing for the continuation of American literature under a new paradigm. The object of study in each case would be different from the dominant one, but it would not be altogether new. Spengemann and Carafiol would perpetuate the current canon, while Jay would try to reconstruct a national tradition. All would continue to treat literature hermeneutically.

To seek an end to American literature is probably a futile struggle, but it may also be a strategic error even for those who oppose most of what has been practiced in its name. "American literature" is more now than an object of study, more than a body of knowledge about that object. It is also a source of value and power within English departments, within the academy, and within the public sphere. To think of what it would mean to literally bring American literature to an end, imagine how many fewer faculty members English departments would need or what high schools would teach instead during the junior year or how the *New York Times Book Review* would certify the value of the next "great" novel. And what would happen to the four MLA Divisions on American literature and all of the academic journals that publish articles about it? Why would academics, hungry for tenure and promotion, give up these sources of lines on the *vita?* The future of American literature may not be guaranteed by its current "use value," but its perpetuation seems likely as long as it has such value. There are, of course, other considerations. "Literature" will not forever be the source of cultural capital that it has been since the nineteenth century; indeed, we have already witnessed a substantial decline. The end of American literature would be entailed in the end of literature. To make the same point from a different angle, it is possible that economic considerations could make English an even more utilitarian subject than it has already become. American literature could finally be sacrificed to business and technical writing.

Assuming that a place remains within the university for American literature, it seems likely that the study of American literature will remain disciplinary in form. While some of us have been urging postdisciplinary conceptions of knowledge, the research university has become all the more strongly committed to disciplinary forms. Tough economic conditions have made research an even more valuable practice. More and more institutions have made publication the most important standard by which faculty are judged. American literature will not in the future any more than the past be defined by its curricular mission. Rather, the curriculum will follow—often at some considerable distance—the trends of research. Some of the more radical conceptions of the field may be doomed by this reality. Jay's focus on teaching, for example, seems to neglect the reality of discipline. He urges "courses in which materials are chosen for the ways in which they *actively interfere* with each other's experiences, languages, and values and for their power to expand the horizon of the student's cultural literacy to encompass peoples he or she has scarcely acknowledged as real" (274). This may be the most cogent pedagogical strategy that can be derived from current cultural theory. But what kind of discipline will support such courses instead of surveys?

In his essay, "The Literatures of America—A Comparative Discipline," Paul Lauter offers a conception that might answer this question. Lauter, like Jay, retains national boundaries to define his proposed field, but he is clearer about conceiving of this field as consisting of multiple traditions: "A full literary history of this country requires both parallel and integrated accounts of differing literary traditions and thus of differing (and changing) social realities."[24] What we see here is an eminently disciplinary vision. The goal, "a full literary history," is consistent with the ambitions of disciplinary knowledge production, while the comparativist method gives a structure to the proposed practice. Lauter goes on to illustrate the sorts of comparisons that would be carried out in such a practice. While formal considerations are not neglected, the focus of comparison falls on the "differing social realities" that the literature embodies.[25] Those realities are not chiefly important for the light they shed on literature; in Lauter's conception, literature, rather, is the bearer of those realities that get lost if the literature does not continue to be read and studied. Lauter's conception provides a way of thinking about the relations of a number of different traditions, which might include women's, African-American, Native American, and others, without folding them back into a single, and inevitably hierarchical, canon.

But if Lauter's conception can meet the requirements of disciplinarity, could it fill the other functions that literary study has fulfilled? Lauter, like most of the revisionists mentioned here, assumes that "literature" must be redefined. For example, he insists that if the writing of marginalized groups is to be appreciated, then we can no longer denigrate writing merely because it is utilitarian or didactic (65). We have already seen that Americanists now include film and other nonprint media in their object of study. But the question of expanding the boundaries of literature may be less troubling than questions of value and judgment. Literary study has historically been concerned with a few texts and authors held to be of high value. Those like Jay, whose conception of "writing in the United States" would seem to mean the abolition of all canons, leave us no option but to proclaim the great value of all writing. While such a claim is not absurd, it does fly in the face of most notions of the production of value. Lauter assumes, I think, that his parallel traditions will produce their own evaluations and hierarchies, and it would follow that no cross-traditional evaluations are necessary or even possible. But is "tradition," which historically has been a restrictive conception tied to nationalism, the best way to continue to conceive of literature or literary history? The future of the discipline of American literature may be caught in the double-bind of wanting to destroy "literature" as a politically pernicious construction, and of needing literature in order to justify the continued political critique it now supports.

The future of the discipline also must be understood in terms of social and cultural conditions. While disciplinary research is to some extent isolated from the larger culture, it is finally a part of that culture. As a result, it is unlikely that the university will allow itself to harbor for long genuinely subversive intellectual enterprises. Lauter writes from a clear political orientation, but he argues for his conception of the discipline on grounds of historical and cultural accuracy. Jay and, even more strongly, Pease envision a subversive discipline. The object of New Americanism, according to Pease, is the creation of a "counter-hegemony." In order to achieve this, the discipline must produce "a 'concrete fantasy' whose 'level of reality and attainability' will elicit identification from previously disadvantaged minority groups and will enable the construction of a prevailing alternative interpretation of reality able to turn the pervasive conflict of interpretations to the use of certain groups."[26] Pease thus wants a new American tradition, one that is politically useful to the disenfranchised. We recognize in this Gramscian language the explicit appropriation of nationalist strategies in the service of (at least in Gramsci's formulation) a class politics. As a plan for the discipline of American literature, such a strategy may be at odds not only with the structures of nation, institution, and discipline but also with the aspirations of the previously disadvantaged who may not wish to become part of this newly invented tradition.

So what will American literature look like in the future? Political, economic, and social change will play roles that cannot be even guessed at here. Furthermore, intellectual changes could occur that are literally inconceivable today. While the conversion of literary scholarship to criticism might have been conceivable in the 1920s, it could not have seemed plausible to very many in the academy. In 2021, 100 years from the founding of the American Literature Group, Americanists could be doing things we would barely recognize today. But since such radical changes can't be conceived even though we are aware of their possibility, we can only picture the future as a version of the present. All of the visions of the future I've discussed so far are that. My guess is, however, that none of them is very likely to come about. Rather, I think something like a "business as usual" scenario is most probable. In this version of things, all of the current tendencies continue. The writing of disadvantaged minorities will be increasingly studied, and more minority traditions will be invented. Literature will increasingly look like the work of both men and women. The texts that are studied will include more items that would not have been considered literature in the past. Increasing attention will be paid to historical and social contexts of these texts. But in spite of all of these changes, there will remain a core canon that will include most of the authors who were the focus of the discipline in the 1950s and 1960s. Doubtless there will be some promotions and demotions. T. S. Eliot may fade while Toni Morrison rises to the top; Howard Hawks may replace Hemingway; but there will be a mainstream, and it will mainly reflect the dominant race, gender, and class.[27] Furthermore, it will continue to be understood as revealing the character of American civilization, even though that character will be perceived differently than it has been since the 1950s. American literature will thus continue to serve an ideological function, even if the details of the ideology differ.

American literature may at the moment seem to be "running guns to Ethiopia" or "supporting the loyalists in Spain," but its current radical activities may well become transformed in the future into the marks of its patriotic commitment. Like Rick Blaine, today's counter-hegemonic Americanists are likely to become supporters of tomorrow's national mission. *Casablanca* may be more than a metaphor here. As a national narrative, it has few peers in the history of American culture, and almost none in the literature of the twentieth century. Its narrative of the transformation of a cynical individualist into a committed patriot is the literal reverse of the "literary narrative" common to most canonical literature.[28] And if *Casablanca*'s canonization may not be as secure as *Moby-Dick*'s, it has been progressing apace.[29] *Casablanca* may be an irresistible emblem of American culture in the post-Cold War era because it identifies progressive values with the nation. The future of American literature will likely not exist in writing only, but it will continue to serve the interests of the state.

Notes

The abbreviation JBH refers to the Jay B. Hubbell Center for American Literary Historiography, William R. Perkins Library, Duke University, a manuscript collection containing the records and correspondence of the American Literature Group and of *American Literature*.

Introduction

1. Of course, in practice even geologists are selective. Rocks having economic value are much more often studied than are worthless ones.

2. Michel Foucault, *The Order of Things: An Archaeology of the Human Sciences* (New York: Pantheon, 1970), 129.

3. Donald Pease, "New Americanists: Revisionist Interventions into the Canon," *boundary 2* 17, no. 1 (1990): 3, uses psychoanalytic terms to describe this phenomenon. Yet the notion that internalized norms and assumptions form a "disciplinary unconscious" renders reflexive understanding of such assumptions impossible: one "cannot at once act upon these assumptions and be conscious of them." My view is that normal disciplinary practice disguises the constructedness of its object, but there is no "bar" preventing the scholar from continuing to practice in light of that knowledge.

4. Kermit Vanderbilt, *American Literature and the Academy: The Roots, Growth, and Maturity of a Profession* (Philadelphia: University of Pennsylvania Press, 1986); Gerald Graff, *Professing Literature: An Institutional History* (Chicago: University of Chicago Press, 1987).

5. On the distinction between internal and external approaches to disciplinary history, see Steve Fuller, "Disciplinary Boundaries and the Rhetoric of the Social Sciences," *Poetics Today* 12 (Summer 1991): 302.

6. Michel Foucault, "Nietzsche, Genealogy, History," in *Language, Counter-Memory, Practice*, ed. Donald F. Bouchard, trans. Bouchard and Sherry Simon (Ithaca, N.Y.: Cornell University Press, 1977), 150.

7. There is also the practical difficulty of locating evidence about teaching and

curriculum. A comprehensive study of these would require oral history, questionnaire surveys, and a vast amount of archival research. The result would be another book.

8. For different versions of the pragmatist tradition, see Richard Poirier, *The Renewal of Literature: Emersonian Reflections* (New York: Random House, 1987), and Giles Gunn, *Thinking Across the American Grain: Ideology, Intellect, and the New Pragmatism* (Chicago: University of Chicago Press, 1992).

9. Cornel West, *The American Evasion of Philosophy: A Genealogy of Pragmatism* (Madison: University of Wisconsin Press, 1989).

10. Michel Foucault, *Discipline and Punish: The Birth of the Prison*, trans. Alan Sheridan (New York: Pantheon, 1978). See also David R. Shumway and Ellen Messer-Davidow, "Disciplinarity: An Introduction," *Poetics Today* 12 (1991): 201–25; and Keith W. Hoskin, "Education and the Genesis of Disciplinarity: The Unexpected Reversal," *Knowledges: Historical and Critical Studies in Disciplinarity*, ed. Ellen Messer-Davidow, David R. Shumway, and David J. Sylvan (Charlottesville: University Press of Virginia, 1993), 271–304.

11. Andrew Abbott, *The System of the Professions* (Chicago: University of Chicago Press, 1989), 2.

12. Raymond Williams was probably the first to make the case, especially in *Marxism and Literature* (Oxford: Oxford University Press, 1977), and Terry Eagleton's widely read *Literary Theory: An Introduction* disseminated it to most members of the profession.

13. Barbara Herrnstein Smith, *Contingencies of Value* (Cambridge, Mass.: Harvard University Press, 1988).

14. On Emerson, see my discussion in Chapter 7 below. On Hawthorne, see Jane Tompkins, *Sensational Designs: The Cultural Work of American Fiction 1790–1860* (New York: Oxford University Press, 1985), 196–99.

15. Giles Gunn, *The Culture of Criticism and the Criticism of Culture* (New York: Oxford University Press, 1987), 8–9.

16. On the emergence of the concept of "civilization," and the anthropological definition of culture, see George W. Stocking, *Victorian Anthropology* (New York: Free Press, 1987), 9–45, 302–14.

17. Eric Hobsbawm and Terence Ranger, eds., *The Invention of Tradition* (Cambridge: Cambridge University Press, 1983).

18. Benedict Anderson, *Imagined Communities: Reflections on the Origin and Spread of Nationalism* (London: Verso, 1983), 30.

19. Eric Hobsbawm, *Nations and Nationalism since 1870: Programme, Myth, Reality* (Cambridge: Cambridge University Press, 1990), 18–19.

20. See Hobsbawm, *Nations*, chapters 4 and 5, for an account of nationalism in general during this period.

21. Ernest Gellner, *Nations and Nationalism* (Oxford: Basil Blackwell, 1983), 56. See also Homi K. Bhabha, "DissemiNation: Time, Narrative, and the Margins of the Modern Nation," in *Nation and Narration*, ed. Bhabha (New York: Routledge, 1990), 297.

22. Donald Pease, "National Identities, Postmodern Artifacts, and Postnational Narratives," *boundary 2* 19, no. 1 (1992): 3–4.

23. Jonathan Arac, "Nationalism, Hypercanonization, and *Huckleberry Finn*," *boundary 2* 19, no. 1 (1992): 14–33.

1. The Literary in America, 1890–1920

1. Randolph Bourne, "Trans-national America," *War and the Intellectuals: Selected Essays, 1915–1919*, ed. Carl Resek (New York: Harper, 1964), 115; first published *Atlantic Monthly* 68 (July 1916).

2. E. C. Stedman and E. M. Hutchinson, eds., *Library of American Literature*, 11 vols. (New York: Charles L. Webster, 1881–90); E. C. Stedman, ed., *An American Anthology* (Boston: Houghton Mifflin, 1900).

3. The notion of "cultural capital" is developed in Pierre Bourdieu, *Distinction: A Social Critique of the Judgment of Taste*, trans. Richard Nice (Cambridge, Mass.: Harvard University Press, 1984).

4. Anon., "Certain Dangerous Tendencies in American Life," *Atlantic Monthly* 42 (October 1878), 402.

5. Raymond Williams, *Marxism and Literature* (Oxford: Oxford University Press, 1977), 47.

6. Rolf Engelsing quoted in Robert Darnton, "First Steps Towards a History of Reading," *The Kiss of Lamourette* (New York: Norton, 1990), 165.

7. Ibid., 166–67; see also David Hall, "The Uses of Literacy in New England, 1600–1850," in Williams L. Joyce et al., eds., *Printing and Society in Early America* (Worcester, Mass.: American Antiquarian Society, 1983), 1–47.

8. Thus it should be clear that the "literary" as I use it here always implies a limited sector of society and only a very selective list of writings assigned high value by that sector. Much that was written, even if imaginative and meeting today's standards of aesthetic excellence, would not be considered "literary" in an earlier historical context.

9. On "symbolic capital" see Pierre Bourdieu, *Outline of a Theory of Practice* (Cambridge: Cambridge University Press, 1977).

10. Louis Althusser, *For Marx* (New York: Random House, 1970), 231–33.

11. James Kavanagh, " 'Benito Cereno' and the Liberal Hero," in *Ideology and Classic American Literature*, ed. Sacvan Bercovitch and Myra Jehlen (Cambridge: Cambridge University Press, 1986), 353.

12. William Dean Howells, "Editor's Study," *Harper's Monthly* (December 1887), rpt. in James W. Simpson, ed., *Editor's Study* (Troy, N.Y.: Whitston, 1983), 111–12.

13. William Dean Howells, *A Hazard of New Fortunes* (New York: NAL, 1965 [1890]), 23. Subsequent references noted in the text as *HNF.*

14. William Dean Howells, "Editor's Study," *Harper's Monthly* (November 1891), rpt. in Simpson, ed., 344.

15. Arthur N. Applebee, *Tradition and Reform in the Teaching of English: A History* (Urbana, Ill.: NCTE, 1974), 24. Horace Scudder, "The Place of Literature in Common School Education," *Literature in School* (Boston: Houghton Mifflin, 1888), 10.

16. This argument is more thoroughly developed in Horace Scudder, "American Classics in School," in *Literature in School*, 44–60.

17. Scudder, "Place of Literature," 14.

18. William Morton Payne, "Three Centuries of American Literature," *Atlantic Monthly* 87 (March 1901): 417.

19. E. C. Stedman, *The Nature and Elements of Poetry* (Boston: Houghton Mifflin, 1892), 163.

20. Charles A. Dunsmore, "Dante's Message," *Atlantic Monthly* 85 (June 1900): 825–34.

21. Frederick Lewis Allen, "Fifty Years of Scribner's Magazine," quoted in Theodore Peterson, *Magazines in the Twentieth Century*, rev. ed. (Urbana: University of Illinois Press, 1958), 3.

22. For accounts of working-class disruptions of performances by English actors and singers, see Lawrence Levine, *Highbrow/Lowbrow: The Emergence of Cultural Hierarchy in America* (Cambridge, Mass.: Harvard University Press, 1988), 60–67.

23. Quoted in Bliss Perry, *The American Mind* (Boston: Houghton Mifflin, 1912), 8.

24. Elsa Nettles, *Language, Race and Class in Howells's America* (Lexington: University of Kentucky Press, 1988), 51.

25. Anon., "Contributor's Club," *Atlantic Monthly* 87 (January 1901): 142.

26. Perry, *American Mind*, 45–46.

27. Nina Baym, "Early Histories of American Literature: A Chapter in the Institution of New England," *American Literary History* 1 (1989): 460

28. Eric Hobsbawm, *The Age of Empire 1875–1914* (New York: Pantheon, 1987), 150.

29. Ellen B. Ballou, *The Building of the House: Houghton Mifflin's Formative Years* (Boston: Houghton Mifflin, 1970), 344, 513.

30. This brief account must suffice here to cover what is obviously a much more complex set of events. See Lawrence Buell, *New England Literary Culture: From Revolution through Renaissance* (Cambridge: Cambridge University Press, 1986), 23–83.

31. Howard Mumford Jones, *The Theory of American Literature* (Ithaca: Cornell University Press, 1948), 86.

32. William Dean Howells, *Literary Friends and Acquaintance: A Personal Retrospect of American Authorship* (New York: Harper, 1900), 136. Subsequent references noted in the text as *LFA*.

33. Richard Brodhead, "Literature and Culture," *Columbia Literary History of the United States* (New York: Columbia University Press, 1988), 472–73.

34. William Dean Howells, "American Literary Centres," *Literature and Life* (New York: Harper, 1902), 173.

35. Richard Ohmann, "Writing and Reading, Work and Leisure," *The Politics of Letters* (Middletown, Conn.: Wesleyan University Press, 1987), 31.

36. Christopher P. Wilson, *The Labor of Words: Literary Professionalism in the Progressive Era* (Athens: University of Georgia Press, 1985), 43.

37. The point here is not Michel Foucault's in "What Is an Author?" *Language, Counter-Memory, Practice*, ed. Donald F. Bouchard, trans. Bouchard and Sherry Simon (Ithaca, N.Y.: Cornell University Press, 1977), 113–38, where authorship is treated as a discursive construct. What I am talking about in this chapter is a change in the actual work of the writer. I will have much to say in later chapters about changes in authorship in the Foucauldian sense.

38. See, for example, Gerald Stanley Lee, "Journalism as the Basis for Literature," *The Atlantic* 85 (February 1900): 231–37; Anon., Contributor's Club, "The Conduct of American Magazines," *The Atlantic* 86 (September 1900): 425–27.

39. Hamlin Garland, *Roadside Meetings*, quoted in Wilson, *The Labor of Words*, 45.

40. Wilson, *Labor of Words*, 59.

41. Richard Ruland, *The Rediscovery of American Literature: Premises of Critical Taste, 1900–1940* (Cambridge, Mass.: Harvard University Press, 1967), 2.

42. Henry F. May, *The End of American Innocence: The First Years of Our Own Time, 1912–1917* (New York: Knopf, 1959), 3, 8.

43. Barrett Wendell, *The Privileged Classes* (New York, 1908), 3, quoted in May, *End of American Innocence*, 76.

44. Theodore R. Sizer, *Secondary Schools at the Turn of the Century* (New Haven: Yale University Press, 1964), 35.

45. Russell Jacoby, *The Last Intellectuals: American Culture in the Age of Academe* (New York: Basic, 1987).

46. Antonio Gramsci, *Selections from the Prison Notebooks*, trans. and ed. Quintin Hoare and Geoffrey Nowell Smith (New York: International Publishers, 1971), 3–23. For a discussion of differing contemporary conceptions of the intellectual, see David R. Shumway, "Intellectuals in the University," *Poetics Today* 11 (Fall 1990): 673–88.

47. Zygmunt Bauman, *Legislators and Interpreters: On Modernity, Post-Modernity, and Intellectuals* (Ithaca, N.Y.: Cornell University Press, 1987), 147.

48. Edwin H. Cady, *The Realist at War: The Mature Years, 1885–1920, of William Dean Howells* (Syracuse, N.Y.: Syracuse University Press, 1958), 12.

49. This is argued persuasively in Levine, *Highbrow/Lowbrow*.

50. Randolph Bourne, "The History of a Literary Radical," in *War and the Intellectuals: Selected Essays, 1915–1919*, 190; first published *Yale Review* 8 (1919).

51. Van Wyck Brooks, *America's Coming of Age* (New York: B. W. Huebsch, 1915), 182–83.

52. Randolph Bourne, "Trans-national America," in *War*, 107–23; Randolph Bourne, "Our Cultural Humility," *The History of a Literary Radical* (New York: B. W. Huebsch, 1920), 40.

53. Van Wyck Brooks, "On Creating a Usable Past," *Dial* 64, (April 11, 1918): 337.

54. Irving Babbitt, *Literature and the American College: Essays in Defense of the Humanities* (Boston: Houghton Mifflin, 1908).

55. Stuart Sherman, "Professor Kittredge and the Teaching of English," *The Nation* 97 (September 11, 1913): 229.

56. Gerald Graff, *Professing Literature: An Institutional History* (Chicago: University of Chicago Press, 1987), 110–18.

57. Van Wyck Brooks, *An Autobiography* (New York: Dutton, 1965), 121, 108.

2. Preprofessional History and Criticism

1. Ora Gannett Sedgwick, "A Girl of Sixteen at Brook Farm," *Atlantic Monthly* 85 (March 1900): 394.

2. Barrett Wendell, *A Literary History of America* (New York: Scribner's, 1900). Referred to in text as *LHA*.

3. William Dean Howells, *Literary Friends and Acquaintance: A Personal Retrospect of American Authorship* (New York: Harper, 1900), 117. Subsequent references cited in the text as *LFA*.

4. George E. Woodberry, *America in Literature* (New York: Harper, 1903), 244.

5. W. C. Brownell, *American Prose Masters* (New York: Scribner's, 1909), 133.

6. Thomas F. Gossett, *Race: The History of an Idea in America* (Dallas: Southern Methodist University Press, 1963), 84–122.

7. Barbara Miller Solomon, *Ancestors and Immigrants: A Changing New England Tradition* (Cambridge, Mass.: Harvard University Press, 1956).

8. Benjamin T. Spencer, *The Quest for Nationality* (Syracuse, N.Y.: Syracuse University Press, 1957).

9. Ruth Miller Elson, *Guardians of Tradition: American Schoolbooks of the Nineteenth Century* (Lincoln: University of Nebraska Press, 1964), 114, 123.

10. Fred Lewis Pattee, *A History of American Literature with a View to the Fundamental Principles Underlying Its Development: A Text-Book for Schools and Colleges*, rev. ed. (New York: Silver, Burdett, 1903), 4.

11. Horace Scudder, "American Classics in School," *Literature in School* (Boston: Houghton Mifflin, 1888), 45–46.

12. Barrett Wendell and Chester Noyes Greenough, *A History of Literature in America* (New York: Scribner's, 1904), v.

13. Moses Coit Tyler, *A History of American Literature*, vol. 1 (New York: Putnam, 1878), 5.

14. Moses Coit Tyler, *A Literary History of the American Revolution*, 2 vols. (New York: Putnam, 1897), 1:7. Subsequent references cited in the text as *LHAR*.

15. Nina Baym, "Early Histories of American Literature: A Chapter in the Institution of New England," *American Literary History* 1 (Fall 1989): 464–66.

16. Charles F. Richardson, *American Literature 1607–1885*, vol. 1 (New York: Putnam, 1889), i.

17. Kermit Vanderbilt, *American Literature and the Academy: The Roots, Growth, and Maturity of a Profession* (Philadelphia: University of Pennsylvania Press, 1986), 112–13.

18. The following histories offered as textbooks or study guides are discussed: Henry A. Beers, *Outline Sketch of American Literature* (New York: Chautaqua, 1887); Brander Matthews, *An Introduction to the Study of American Literature* (New York: American, n.d. [1896]); Fred Lewis Pattee, *A History of American Literature* (New York: Silver, Burdett, 1886); rev. ed. (1903); Katherine Lee Bates, *American Literature* (New York: Macmillan, 1897); Henry S. Pancoast, *An Introduction to American Literature*, 1st ed. (New York: Holt, 1898); 2nd ed. (1912); Walter C. Bronson, *A Short History of American Literature* (Boston: Heath, 1900); rev. ed. (1919); Mary Fischer, *A General Survey of American Literature*, 2nd ed. (Chicago: A. C. McClurg, 1901); Richard Burton, *Literary Leaders of America* (New York: Scribner's, 1903); Thomas Wentworth Higginson and Henry Walcott Boynton, *A Reader's History of American Literature* (Boston: Houghton Mifflin, 1903); Wendell and Greenough, *A History of Literature in America*; Rueben Post Halleck, *History of American Literature* (New York: American, 1911); Roy Bennett Pace, *American Literature* (Boston: Allyn and Bacon, 1915).

19. Vanderbilt, *American Literature and the Academy*, 146–47.

20. Henry F. May, *The End of American Innocence: The First Years of Our Own Time, 1912–1917* (New York: Knopf, 1959), 30–51.

21. Stuart Sherman, *Critical Woodcuts* (New York: Scribner's, 1926), 253–55.

22. Van Wyck Brooks, *An Autobiography* (New York: Dutton, 1965), 108.

23. Higginson and Boynton, *A Reader's History of American Literature*, 168.

24. Brander Matthews, *An Introduction to the Study of American Literature*, 13.

25. W. C. Brownell, *American Prose Masters*, 133.

26. Bliss Perry, *The American Mind* (Boston: Houghton Mifflin, 1912); Bliss Perry, *The American Spirit in Literature* (New Haven: Yale University Press, 1918).

27. John Macy, *The Spirit of American Literature* (New York: Doubleday, Page, 1913), 5.

28. Van Wyck Brooks, *The Wine of the Puritans: A Study of Present-Day America* (London: 1908); "On Creating a Usable Past," *Dial* 64 (April 11, 1918): 337–41.

29. Randolph Bourne, "America's Cultural Humility," *The History of a Literary Radical* (New York: B. W. Huebsch, 1920), 40.

30. Randolph Bourne, "Trans-National America," *War and the Intellectuals: Selected Essays, 1915–1919*, ed. Carl Resek (New York: Harper, 1964), 107.

31. William Peterfield Trent, John Erskine, Stuart P. Sherman, and Carl Van Doren, *The Cambridge History of American Literature*, 4 vols. (New York: Putnam, 1917–1921).

32. David Perkins, "Discursive Form Versus the Past in Literary History," *New Literary History* 22 (Spring 1991): 361–64.

33. For an account of late-nineteenth-century exchanges on this point, see Fred Lewis Pattee, "American Literature in the College Curriculum," *Educational Review* 67 (May 1924): 269–70.

34. See Vanderbilt, *American Literature and the Academy*, 179, where he describes Lodge's chapter as the one that "best illustrated how language does in fact operate in literary expression," and suggests that the editors' judgment may have been too harsh. He also notes, however, that the editors made "enormous cuts and changes" in the chapter.

3. English as a Discursive Practice

1. See Phyllis Franklin, "English Studies: The World of Scholarship in 1883," *PMLA* 99 (1983): 356–70.

2. Arthur N. Applebee, *Tradition and Reform in the Teaching of English: A History* (Urbana, Ill.: NCTE, 1974), 27–28.

3. Michel Foucault, *Discipline and Punish: The Birth of the Prison*, trans. Alan Sheridan (New York: Pantheon, 1978), 170–94.

4. See David R. Shumway and Ellen Messer Davidow, "Disciplinarity: An Introduction," *Poetics Today* 12 (Summer 1991): 201–25.

5. Roger L. Geiger, *To Advance Knowledge: The Growth of American Research Universities 1900–1940* (New York: Oxford University Press, 1986), 22, 29.

6. Michel Foucault, "The Discourse on Language," trans. Rupert Swyer, appendix to *The Archaeology of Knowledge* (New York: Pantheon, 1972), 222.

7. William Riley Parker, "Where Do English Departments Come From?" *College English* 28 (1966–67): 339–51.

8. Howard Mumford Jones, "Graduate English Study," *Sewanee Review* 38 (1930): 465–76; and 39 (1931): 69–79, 200–208 (203).

9. Richard Ohmann (with a chapter by Wallace Douglas), *English in America: A Radical View of the Profession* (New York: Oxford University Press, 1976), 97–206; Richard Ohmann, "Writing and Reading, Work and Leisure," *The Politics of Letters* (Middletown, Conn.: Wesleyan University Press, 1987), 26–41; Evan Watkins, *Work*

Time: English Departments and the Circulation of Cultural Value (Stanford, Calif.: Stanford University Press, 1989), 101–8.

10. These three reform programs are described in Laurence R. Veysey, *The Emergence of the American University* (Chicago: University of Chicago Press, 1965), 57–259.

11. Gerald Graff, *Professing Literature: An Institutional History* (Chicago: University of Chicago Press, 1987), 81–144.

12. Stuart Sherman, "Professor Kittredge and the Teaching of English," *The Nation* 97 (Sept. 11, 1913): 230.

13. E.g., John Livingston Lowes, "Chaucer and the Seven Deadly Sins," *PMLA* 30 (1915): 237–371, or 135 pages.

14. R. K. Root, *The Poetry of Chaucer: A Guide to Its Study and Appreciation*, rev. ed. (Gloucester, Mass.: Peter Smith, 1957 [1922]), v.

15. G. L. Kittredge, *Chaucer and His Poetry* (Cambridge, Mass.: Harvard University Press, 1915); John M. Manly, *Some New Light on Chaucer* (New York: Holt, 1926); John L. Lowes, *Geoffrey Chaucer and the Development of His Genius* (Boston: Houghton Mifflin, 1934).

16. Statistics on the first twenty-five and fifty years of *PMLA* are from Richard F. Bauerle, "A Statistical Survey of *PMLA*, its Contributors, and their Institutions," *PMLA* 73 (December 1958): part 2, 76.

17. My sampling procedure involved an analysis of volumes of *PMLA* at five-year intervals between 1900 and 1930. (The contents pages of intervening years were consulted for evidence that might suggest the sample years were atypical. None was found.) Articles were preliminarily classified according to language field, with an additional class consisting of those in theory or method. Articles in English or American literature, including those on comparative topics involving them, were further classified by topic (e.g., metrics, Milton), period, and approach. I don't claim objectivity for this method, but use it rather as an efficient way to present my reading of a large quantity of material.

18. Francis A. March, *Method of Philological Study of the English Language* (New York: Harper, 1875), v.

19. Jones, "Graduate English Study," n. 7, 467–68. Jones categorized dissertations in English produced at Harvard, 1876–1926, and Chicago, 1894–1927.

20. James Morgan Hart, "The College Course in English Literature: How It May Be Improved," *PMLA* 1 (1884–85): 86. Paper was presented at the MLA Convention, 1883.

21. See Jones, "Graduate English Study," and Edwin Greenlaw, *The Province of Literary History* (Baltimore, Md.: Johns Hopkins Press, 1931).

22. René Wellek, *The Rise of English Literary History* (Chapel Hill: University of North Carolina Press, 1941), vi.

23. René Wellek, *The Rise of English Literary History*, rpt. (New York: McGraw-Hill, 1966), v

24. David Daiches, *English Literature* (Englewood Cliffs, N.J.: Prentice-Hall, 1964), 93–94.

25. Theodore W. Hunt, "The Place of English in the College Curriculum," *PMLA* 1 (1884–85): 127.

26. Richard G. Moulton, *Shakespeare as a Dramatic Artist: A Study of Inductive Literary Criticism* (Oxford: Clarendon, 1888), 64.

27. Lowes, *Geoffrey Chaucer*, 3, emphasis in original.

28. André Morize, *Problems and Methods of Literary History* (Boston: Ginn, 1922), 4–10.

29. Charles H. Grandgent, "The Modern Languages," *The Development of Harvard University* (Cambridge, Mass.: Harvard University Press, 1930), 65–105.

30. Charles Edward Whitmore, "Some Comments on Literary Theory," *PMLA* 45 (1930): 581.

31. S. Griswold Morely, "The Detection of Personality in Literature," *PMLA* 20 (1905): 313. Michel Foucault makes a similar point in "What Is an Author?" *Language, Counter-Memory, Practice*, ed. Donald F. Bouchard, trans. Bouchard and Sherry Simon (Ithaca, N.Y.: Cornell University Press, 1977), though for him it is the "functioning of the author's name" that would be modified by such a change (122).

32. George L. Kittredge, "Guillaume de Machaut and *The Book of the Duchess*," *PMLA* 30 (1915): 24.

33. E. C. Knowlton, "The Novelty of Wordsworth's *Michael* as a Pastoral," *PMLA* 35 (1920): 446.

34. Walter Clyde Curry, "Chaucer's Reeve and Miller," *PMLA* 35 (1920): 208–9.

35. Fredrick Tupper, "Chaucer and the Seven Deadly Sins," *PMLA* 29 (1914): 96–97.

36. Lowes, "Chaucer and the Seven Deadly Sins," *PMLA* 30 (1915): 237–371.

37. So, for example, Morize, *Problems and Methods of Literary History*, 225–62, couples success and influence.

38. T. P. Harrison, Jr., "The Relations of Spenser and Sidney," *PMLA* 45 (1930): 712.

39. John Manly, "The President's Address: New Bottles," *PMLA* 36 (1921): xlviii.

40. Ashley H. Thorndike, *A Quarter Century of Learning: 1904–1929* (New York: Columbia University Press, 1931), 182, 198.

4. American Literature as a Discipline: Constituting the Object

1. Claire Sacks, "The *Seven Arts* Critics: A Study of Cultural Nationalism in America 1910–1930" (diss., University of Wisconsin, 1955).

2. For a general theory of the "author function" in discourse, see Michel Foucault, "What Is an Author?" in *Language, Counter-Memory, Practice*, ed. Donald F. Bouchard, trans. Bouchard and Sherry Simon (Ithaca, N.Y.: Cornell University Press, 1977), 113–38.

3. Richard Ruland, *The Rediscovery of American Literature* (Cambridge, Mass.: Harvard University Press, 1967), quoting Walter Lippmann, 133 (quoted in Manchester, *Disturber of the Peace* [1951], 158), 136.

4. Stuart Sherman, "Beautifying American Literature," *The Nation*, 105 (November 29, 1917): 594.

5. On the New Humanists, see chapter 1 in this volume.

6. Harold Stearns, preface, *Civilization in the United States*, ed. Stearns (New York: Harcourt Brace, 1922), vii.

7. Van Wyck Brooks, "The Literary Life," in *Civilization in the United States*, 188.

8. H. L. Mencken, "The Blue-Nose," *A Mencken Chrestomathy* (New York: Knopf, 1949), 470. First published in *Smart Set*, May 1919.

9. Paul Elmer More, *Shelburne Essays, Second Series* (New York: Putnam's, 1905), 187.

10. Stuart Sherman, *The Genius of America* (New York: Scribner's, 1923), 29.

11. Proceedings, *PMLA* 39 (1924), xxxix.

12. Jay B. Hubbell, "*American Literature, 1928–1954*," *South and Southwest: Literary Essays and Reminiscences* (Durham, N.C.: Duke University Press, 1965), 44.

13. Norman Foerster, "Factors in American Literary History," *The Reinterpretation of American Literature*, ed. Foerster (New York: Russell & Russell, 1959; rpt. of Harcourt Brace, 1928), 25.

14. Robert Spiller, "Those Early Days: A Personal Memoir," in *The Oblique Light: Studies in Literary History and Biography* (New York: Macmillan, 1968), 259.

15. Norman Foerster, introduction, *The Reinterpretation of American Literature*, xxi.

16. See Kermit Vanderbilt, *American Literature in the Academy: The Roots, Growth, and Maturity of a Profession* (Philadelphia: University of Pennsylvania Press, 1986), 273–76, for an extended account of these events.

17. Paul Kaufman, "The Romantic Movement," *The Reinterpretation of American Literature*, ed. Foerster (New York: Russell & Russell, 1959; rpt. of Harcourt Brace, 1928), 114, notes the novelty of Foerster's periodization.

18. Jay B. Hubbell to Foerster, Jan. 14, 1926, in JBH.

19. Jay B. Hubbell, "The Frontier," *The Reinterpretation of American Literature*, 60.

20. Howard Mumford Jones, "The European Background," *The Reinterpretation of American Literature*, 77.

21. Kenneth Murdock, "The Puritan Tradition in American Literature," *The Reinterpretation of American Literature*, 108.

22. Harry Hayden Clark, "American Literary History and American Literature," *The Reinterpretation of American Literature*, 193.

23. Anon. "To Our Contributors," *American Literature* 1 (1929): 75.

24. Arthur Schlesinger, "History and Literary History," *The Reinterpretation of American Literature*, 160–61.

25. Henry Seidel Canby, review of *The Reinterpretation of American Literature*, ed. Foerster. *American Literature* 1 (1929): 81.

26. F. O. Matthiessen, "New Standards in American Criticism, 1929," *The Responsibilities of the Critic* (New York: Oxford University Press, 1952), 182.

27. Suggestions Toward a Program for the Doctorate in American Literature, January, 1928, JBH.

28. Norman Foerster, *American Criticism: A Study in Literary Theory from Poe to the Present* (New York: Russell & Russell, 1962, rpt. of 1929), 223–61. Cited in text as *AL*.

29. Hubbell to Clark, Jan. 4, 1929, in JBH.

30. Norman Foerster, *Nature and American Literature* (New York: Russell & Russell, 1958, rpt of 1923), 68.

5. Institutionalizing American Literature

1. Robert Spiller, "Those Early Days: A Personal Memoir," in *The Oblique Light: Studies in Literary History and Biography* (New York: Macmillan, 1968), 259.

2. Jay B. Hubbell, *"American Literature, 1928–1954," South and Southwest: Literary Essays and Reminiscences* (Durham, N.C.: Duke University Press, 1965), 23.

3. Figures on articles and dissertations are derived from Ernest E. Leisy, "Materials for Investigation in American Literature," *Studies in Philology* 23 (January 1926): 90–115.

4. Ferner Nuhn (Ruth Suckow), "Teaching American Literature in American Colleges," *American Mercury* 13 (March 1928): 328–29.

5. Foreword, *American Literature*, vol. 1, no. 1, quoted in Richard Ruland, *The Rediscovery of American Literature* (Cambridge, Mass.: Harvard University Press, 1967), 278.

6. Minutes of 1928 meeting, in JBH.

7. Jones finished his—it was published as *America and French Culture* (1927), but he was told by the University of Chicago to complete more coursework. Jones refused the demand, and, as a result, never received the Ph.D. See Kermit Vanderbilt, *American Literature and the Academy: The Roots, Growth, and Maturity of a Profession* (Philadelphia: University of Pennsylvania Press, 1986), 448–49.

8. Cambell to Hubbell, January 20, 1927, in JBH.

9. Hubbell to Cairns, September 16, 1931, in JBH.

10. Fred Lewis Pattee, Review of *The Life and Works of Francis Hopkinson* by George Everett Hastings, *American Historical Review* 32 (July 1927): 894.

11. Louise Pound, "Graduate Work for Women," *Selected Writings* (Lincoln: University of Nebraska Press, 1949), 293. A paper read at the meeting of the National Association of Deans of Women, Chicago, February 25, 1922.

12. Louise Pound, "The College Woman and Research," *Selected Writings*, 311. A paper read at a meeting of the American Association of Collegiate Alumae, 1920.

13. Published as Ralph Leslie Rusk, *The Literature of the Middle Western Frontier* (New York: Columbia University Press, 1925).

14. Published as Dorothy Dondore, *The Prairie and the Making of Middle America: Four Centuries of Description* (Cedar Rapids, Iowa: Torch, 1926).

15. Lucy Lockwood Hazard, *The Frontier in American Literature* (New York: Crowell, 1927).

16. Frederic L. Paxson, review of *The Literature of the Middle Western Frontier* by Ralph Leslie Rusk, *American Historical Review* 31 (January 1926): 366.

17. Jay B. Hubbell, "The Frontier," *The Reinterpretation of American Literature*, ed. Norman Foerster (New York: Russell & Russell, 1959; rpt. of Harcourt Brace, 1928), 56.

18. Richard Hofstadter, *The Progressive Historians: Turner, Beard, Parrington* (New York: Knopf, 1968), 367.

19. Lucy Lockwood Hazard, Review of *The Rediscovery of the Frontier* by Percy Boynton, *American Literature* 3 (1932): 492.

20. Ernest Marchand, "Emerson and the Frontier," *American Literature* 3 (1932): 149–74.

21. See Lark Hall, "Vernon Louis Parrington, The Genesis and Design of 'Main Currents in American Thought' " (diss., Case Western Reserve University, 1979).

22. Harry Hayden Clark, "American Literary History and American Literature," *The Reinterpretation of American Literature*, 193.

23. Gene Wise, *American Historical Explanations*, 2nd ed. (Minneapolis: University of Minnesota Press, 1980), 250–57.

24. E. H. Eby, "Vernon Louis Parrington," *Main Currents in American Thought*, vol. 3 (New York: Harcourt Brace, 1930), viii.

25. Bernard Smith, "Parrington's *Main Currents in American Thought*," in *Books that Changed Our Minds*, ed. Malcolm Cowley and Smith (New York: Kelmscott, 1939), 179.

26. Robert Spiller, "The Growth of American Literary Scholarship," *Late Harvest: Essays and Addresses in American Literature and Culture* (Westport, Conn.: Greenwood, 1981), 201.

27. Parrington correspondence quoted in Hofstadter, *Progressive Historians*, 361, n. 8.

28. The general consensus of historians today would suggest that they both greatly exaggerated Rousseau's influence in America.

29. Lionel Trilling, "Parrington, Mr. Smith, and Reality," *Partisan Review* 7 (January-February 1940): 24–40. This essay was combined with another, on Dreiser, to form "Reality in America," which, as part of *The Liberal Imagination* (New York: Viking, 1950), became the definitive denunciation of Parrington. See Hofstadter, *Progressive Historians*, 492. For a critique of Trilling's use of Parrington, see chapter 8 in this book.

30. William E. Cain, *F. O. Matthiessen and the Politics of Criticism* (Madison: University of Wisconsin Press, 1988), 144.

31. Hubbell's notes in JBH; see also Hubbell, "*American Literature*, 1928–1954," 29.

32. Hubbell to R. L. Rusk, March 25, 1929, in JBH.

33. Williams to Hubbell, April 11, 1929, in JBH.

34. Jay B. Hubbell, "Cavalier and Indentured Servant in Virginia Fiction," *The South Atlantic Quarterly* 26 (1927): 22–39.

35. Clarence Ghodes, "Some Remarks on Emerson's *Divinity School Address*," *American Literature* 1 (1929): 27.

36. Anon., "To Our Contributors," *American Literature* 1 (1929): 75.

37. Esther E. Burch, "The Sources of New England Democracy: A Controversial Statement in Parrington's *Main Currents in American Thought*," *American Literature* 1 (1930): 115–30.

38. Gregory Paine, "Trends in American Literary Scholarship with Reviews of Some Recent Books," *Studies in Philology* 29 (1932): 631.

39. Anon., "Note," 75; Paine, "Trends," 633.

40. Claire Sacks, "The *Seven Arts* Critics," 227–34.

41. Paine, "Trends," 633.

42. O. W. Riegel, "The Anatomy of Melville's Fame," *American Literature* 3 (1932): 195. The other two are Russell Thomas, "Melville's Use of Some Sources in *The Encantadas*," *American Literature* 3 (1932): 432–56; and William S. Ament, "Bowdler and the Whale: Some Notes on the First English and American Edition of Moby-Dick," *American Literature* 4 (1932): 39–46.

43. Thomas, "Melville's Use of Some Sources," 456.

44. Morris Schappes, "Errors in Mrs. Bianchi's Edition of Emily Dickinson's *Letters*," *American Literature* 4 (1933): 369–84; George F. Whicher, "Emily Dickinson's Earliest Friend," *American Literature* 6 (1934): 1–17; Anna Mary Wells, "Early Criticism of Emily Dickinson," *American Literature* 1 (1930): 243–59.

45. Richard Pettigrew, "Lowell's Criticism of Milton," *American Literature* 3 (1932): 464.

46. Floyd Stovall, "Main Drifts in Whitman's Poetry," *American Literature* 4 (1932): 21.

47. Killis Cambell, "The Evolution of Whitman as Artist," *American Literature* 6 (1935): 257.

48. Richard Pettigrew, "Poe's Rime," *American Literature* 4 (1933): 159.

49. Aubrey Starke, " 'No Names' and 'Round Robbins,' " *American Literature* 6 (1935): 400–412.

50. John Herbert Nelson, review of *The Negro Author in America* by Vernon Loggins, *American Literature* 4 (1933): 322. Nelson had published *The Negro Character in American Fiction* (1926), which seems to have made him the ALG's resident expert on African-American literature.

51. Vernon Loggins, *The Negro Author in America* (New York: Columbia University Press, 1931), vii.

52. Charles Glicksberg, "Walt Whitman in 1862," *American Literature* 6 (1935): 282.

53. Grace Warren Landrum, "Sir Walter Scott and His Literary Rivals in the Old South," *American Literature* 2 (1931): 256–76; Grace Warren Landrum, "Notes on the Reading of the Old South," *American Literature* 3 (1931): 60–71; Jay Hubbell, "A Commencement Address by Sidney Lanier," *American Literature* 2 (1931): 385–404; Hampton Jarrell, "Simms's Visits to the Southwest," *American Literature* 5 (1933): 29–35.

54. It should be added that the reviews are particularly of interest to those such as Vanderbilt and myself who are writing about the history of the discipline. The articles merely reflect a standard practice. The reviews give a much stronger sense of the meaning and context of that practice.

55. Clark to Hubbell, December 19, 1928; Foerster to Hubbell, January 12, 1929; Hubbell to Ralph Rusk, January 14, 1929; Foerster to Hubbell, January 16, 1929; all in JBH. Harry Hayden Clark, review of *American Criticism* by Norman Foerster, *American Literature* 1 (1930): 206–12. See Vanderbilt, 295–97.

56. I am indebted to Vanderbilt for documenting the accuracy of Cargill's charges, 296–98.

57. Harry Hayden Clark, review of *Quaker Militant: John Greenleaf Whittier* by Albert Mordell, *American Literature* 6 (1935): 209.

58. Paine, "Trends," 642–43, 638.

59. Howard Mumford Jones, review of *Classic Americans: A Study of Eminent American Writers from Irving to Whitman, with an Introductory Survey of the Colonial Background of Our National Literature, on the State of American Literary History* by Henry Seidel Canby, *American Literature* 4 (1933): 311–13.

60. V. L. O. Chittick, review of *The Beginnings of Critical Realism in America, 1860–1920* by Vernon Louis Parrington, *American Literature* 2 (1931): 443, 442.

61. Grant Knight, review of *The Liberation of American Literature* by V. F. Calverton, *American Literature* 4 (1933): 409

62. Robert Spiller, review of *The Great Tradition* by Granville Hicks, *American Literature* 6 (1935): 361.

63. Fred B. Millett, review of *The New American Literature 1890–1930: A Survey* by Fred Lewis Pattee, *American Literature* 3 (1932): 323–24.

64. Fred Lewis Pattee, review of *American Literature: An Introduction* by Carl Van Doren, *American Literature* 5 (1934): 379.

6. American Literature in the Curriculum

1. Arthur N. Applebee, *Tradition and Reform in the Teaching of English: A History* (Urbana, Ill.: NCTE, 1974), 36.

2. Fred Lewis Pattee, "Americanism thru American Literature," *Educational Review* 57 (April 1919): 271; "American Literature in the College Curriculum," *Educational Review* 67 (May 1924): 270.

3. Nina Baym, "Early Histories of American Literature: A Chapter in the Institution of New England," *American Literary History* 1 (Fall 1989): 473.

4. American literature was not the only curricular support offered to democracy. In 1919, Columbia University instituted a course as part of its core curriculum entitled "Contemporary Civilization," which was intended to produce students that were safe for democracy.

5. John S. Lewis, "The History of Instruction in American Literature in Colleges and Universities of the United States, 1827–1939" (diss., New York University, 1941), 238–43; John Hite, "Report to the American Literature Group of the Modern Language Association on the Teaching of American Literature," December 1946, 22–23, in JBH.

6. Ferner Nuhn (Ruth Suckow), "Teaching American Literature in American Colleges," *American Mercury* 13 (March 1928): 328–29.

7. John Hite, "Report to the American Literature Group of the Modern Language Association."

8. T. J. Baker, "American Literature in the Colleges," *North American Review* (June 1919): 783; Stuart Sherman, "For Higher Study of American Literature," *Yale Review* 12 (April 1923): 473; Arthur Quinn, "American Literature as a Subject for Graduate Study," *Educational Review* 69 (June 1922): 15.

9. Franklyn Snyder, "What Is American Literature?" *Sewanee Review* 35 (April 1927): 208–9, 214.

10. Foerster published a partial anthology, *Chief American Prose Writers*, in 1916.

11. Fred Lewis Pattee, *Century Readings for a Course in American Literature* (New York: Century, 1919), v.

12. Martin S. Schockley and Charles C. Walcutt, "The American Literature Curriculum at the University of Oklahoma," *College English* 1 (1939–40): 682.

13. Evelyn R. Bibb, "Anthologies of American Literature, 1787–1964" (diss., Columbia University, 1965), 370.

14. Norman Foerster, *American Poetry and Prose: A Book of Readings 1607–1916* (Cambridge, Mass.: Houghton Mifflin, 1925), iii.

15. Bernard Smith, ed., *The Democratic Spirit: A Collection of American Writings from the Earliest Times to the Present Day* (New York: Knopf, 1941). This book does not seem intended mainly for the textbook market.

16. William Rose Benét and Norman Holmes Pearson, *The Oxford Anthology of American Literature* (New York: Oxford University Press, 1938), v.

17. John T. Flanagan, "American Literature in American Colleges," *College English* 1 (1939–40): 513.

18. I owe this insight to John Mowitt.

19. Floyd Stovall, "What Price American Literature?" *Sewanee Review* 49 (1941): 470.

20. Howard Mumford Jones, "American Scholarship and American Literature," *American Literature* 8 (1936): 118.

21. Elizabeth Wilson, "A Short History of a Border War," *Poetics Today* 9 (1988): 711–35.

22. Norman Holmes Pearson, "Surveying American Literature," *College English* 1 (1939–40): 583.

23. *American Literature in the College Curriculum* (Chicago: National Council of Teachers of English, 1948), 26. All of the statistics on the teaching of American literature in this paragraph and the next two come from pages 26–30 of this report. It is cited as *ALCC* in the text henceforward.

24. Kermit Vanderbilt, *American Literature and the Academy* (Philadelphia: University of Pennsylvania Press, 1986), 461. My account of the effect of the war on American literature in the curriculum is indebted to Vanderbilt.

25. Jane Tompkins, *Sensational Designs: The Cultural Work of American Fiction 1790–1860* (New York: Oxford University Press, 1985), 194.

26. Harold H. Kolb, Jr., "Defining the Canon," in *Redefining American Literary History*, ed. A. LaVonne Ruhoff and Jerry W. Ward, Jr. (New York: MLA, 1990), 45–49, provides a useful table comparing the authors included in five editions of *The American Tradition in Literature* and the first edition of the *Norton Anthology of American Literature*, which replaced the former volume on Norton's list in 1979, while Random House picked up *American Tradition* for its fifth edition, 1981.

27. Richard Dorson, *The Birth of American Studies*, inaugural address delivered at the opening of the American Studies Center, Warsaw University, October 5, 1976 (Bloomington: Indiana University, 1976), 1.

28. Robert Spiller, "Unity and Diversity in the Study of American Culture," in *Late Harvest: Essays and Addresses in American Literature and Culture* (Westport, Conn.: Greenwood, 1981), 218–21, argues that other disciplines, including history, political science, economics, and art history continued to treat American culture as an aspect of European culture. While this was perhaps true to some extent in each field—and to a large degree in art history—American historians and social scientists had long ago made America their most important object of inquiry. Part of the appeal of Turner's 1892 paper on the frontier was its making American history a unique phenomenon, rather than a branch of English or German history. By the 1940s, history, economics, or political science did not explicitly define themselves as nationally bounded disciplines, while English did.

29. Spiller, "Unity and Diversity," 222–23; see also Tremaine McDowell, *American Studies* (Minneapolis: University of Minnesota Press, 1948).

30. See Dorson, *Birth of American Studies*, 1; McDowell, *American Studies*, 44; and Gene Wise, *American Historical Explanations: A Strategy for Grounded Inquiry*, 2nd ed. (Minneapolis: University of Minnesota Press, 1980); and "Paradigm Dramas," *American Quarterly* 31 (1979).

31. Murray Murphey, "American Civilization at Pennsylvania," *American Quarterly* 22 (1970): 495–96; See also Murphey, "American Civilization in Retrospect," *American Quarterly* 31 (1979): 405–6; Bruce Kuklick, "Myth and Symbol in American Studies," *American Quarterly* 24 (1972): 435–50.

32. Gerald Graff, *Professing Literature: An Institutional History* (Chicago:

University of Chicago Press, 1987). See especially his comments on the limitations of American literature studies, 224–25.

7. The Triumph of the Aesthetic

1. William Cain, *F. O. Matthiessen and the Politics of Criticism* (Madison: University of Wisconsin Press, 1988), 29.

2. T. S. Kuhn, *The Structure of Scientific Revolutions,* 2nd ed. (Chicago: University of Chicago Press, 1970), 23–24.

3. Jay B. Hubbell, review of *The American Scholar* by Norman Foerster and *Criticism in the Making* by Louis Cazamian, *American Literature* 1 (1930): 461.

4. See Alfred Kazin, *On Native Grounds: An Interpretation of Modern American Prose Literature* (New York: Harcourt Brace, 1942), 400–452.

5. John Fekete, *The Critical Twilight: Explorations in Anglo-American Literary Theory from Eliot to McLuhan* (London: Routledge & Kegan Paul, 1977), 52.

6. John L. Stewart, *The Burden of Time: The Fugitives and Agrarians* (Princeton: Princeton University Press, 1965), 45.

7. John Crowe Ransom, *God Without Thunder: An Unorthodox Defense of Orthodoxy* (Hamden, Conn.: Archon, 1965 [1930]). Stewart argues that "in *God Without Thunder* may be found virtually the whole rationale of Agrarianism" (*Burden of Time*, 140) and that it "holds the central position in Ransom's prose writings" (268). Fekete asserts that it contains "the assumptions of the preceding and subsequent periods" (*Critical Twilight*, 61).

8. Fekete, *Critical Twilight*, 58–59, shows how "the agrarian position is a deep mystification of the Southern past."

9. John Crowe Ransom, "The South—Old and New?" *Sewanee Review* 36 (April 1928): 147.

10. Richard Ruland, *The Rediscovery of American Literature* (Cambridge, Mass.: Harvard University Press, 1967), 206.

11. John Crowe Ransom, "The Mimetic Principle," in *The World's Body* (New York: Scribner's, 1938), 193–211.

12. John Crowe Ransom, "Criticism, Inc.," in *The World's Body*, 328–29.

13. Letter from Ransom to Tate, May 13, 1939, quoted in Stewart, *Burden of Time*, 192.

14. Allen Tate, "Miss Emily and the Bibliographer," *The American Scholar* 9 (Autumn 1940): 456.

15. See, e.g., Maxwell Geismar, *Rebels and Ancestors: The American Novel 1890–1915* (Boston: Houghton Mifflin, 1953). Geismar acknowledges the value of close reading in an essay attacking most contemporary criticism, "Higher and Higher Criticism," *American Moderns: from Rebellion to Conformity* (New York: Hill and Wang, 1958). Geismar, however, was a literary journalist rather than an academic Americanist.

16. John Crowe Ransom, "Criticism as Pure Speculation," in *The Intent of the Critic*, ed. Donald A. Stauffer (Princeton: Princeton University Press, 1941), 101–2.

17. Allen Tate, "The Present Function of Criticism," *The Southern Review* 6 (Autumn 1940): 246.

18. John Crowe Ransom, *The New Criticism* (Norfolk, Conn.: New Directions, 1941), 279–336.

19. See, for example, "The Critic's Business," *Kenyon Review* 11 (1949): 1–30; "My Credo: A Symposium," *Kenyon Review* 13 (1951): 72–110, 207–30, 561–601.

20. F. O. Matthiessen, "The Responsibilities of the Critic," in *The Responsibilities of the Critic* (New York: Oxford University Press, 1952), 4.

21. Cain, *Matthiessen*, 206.

22. Letter from Matthiessen to Spiller, Sept. 15, 1941, quoted in Kermit Vanderbilt, *American Literature and the Academy: The Roots, Growth, and Maturity of a Profession* (Philadelphia: University of Pennsylvania Press, 1986), 475.

23. Roy Harvey Pearce, "Literature, History and Humanism: An Americanist's Dilemma," in *Historicism Once More* (Princeton: Princeton University Press, 1969): 55.

24. Russell Reising, *The Unusable Past: Theory and the Study of American Literature* (New York: Methuen, 1986), 170.

25. Giles Gunn, *F. O. Matthiessen: The Critical Achievement* (Seattle: University of Washington Press, 1975), 20.

26. F. O. Matthiessen, *The Achievement of T. S. Eliot*, 2nd ed. (New York: Oxford University Press, 1947), 3.

27. T. S. Eliot, "Tradition and the Individual Talent," in *Selected Prose of T. S. Eliot*, ed. Frank Kermode (New York: Harcourt, 1975), 37–44.

28. T. S. Eliot, "The Function of Criticism," in *Selected Prose of T. S. Eliot*, 68.

29. T. S. Eliot, *The Use of Poetry and the Use of Criticism: Studies in the Relation of Criticism to Poetry in England* (London: Faber and Faber, 1933), 22.

30. F. O. Matthiessen, *American Renaissance: Art and Expression in the Age of Emerson and Whitman* (New York: Oxford University Press, 1941), xi (cited in text as *AR*).

31. Floyd Stovall, "Emerson," *Eight American Authors: A Review of Research and Criticism* (New York: MLA, 1956), 62.

32. See Lewis Leary, "Thoreau," *Eight American Authors* (New York: MLA, 1956), 201, who notes that it was Matthiessen's *American Renaissance* "which . . . first approached [Thoreau] seriously and sympathetically as an artist."

33. "The everlasting Yea" is, of course, Carlyle's from *Past and Present*. The second quotation is from John Updike: "Praise *Barth*, who told how saving faith can flow / From Terror's oscillating Yes and No"; the lines occur in a passage critical of liberalism in "Midpoint," *The Midpoint and Other Poems* (New York: Knopf, 1969), 38.

34. V. L. Parrington, *Main Currents in American Thought*, vol. 2 (New York: Harcourt Brace, 1927), 442–50; V. F. Calverton, *The Liberation of American Literature* (New York: Scribner's, 1932), 23; Russell Blankenship, *American Literature: As an Expression of the National Mind* (New York: Holt, 1931), 372.

35. Lewis Mumford, *Herman Melville* (New York: Harcourt Brace, 1929), 361.

36. Irving Howe, *The American Newness: Culture and Politics in the Age of Emerson* (Cambridge, Mass.: Harvard University Press, 1986), 26.

37. René Wellek, *A History of Modern Criticism 1750–1950*, vol. 6 (New Haven: Yale University Press, 1986), 84.

38. See Richard Brodhead, *The School of Hawthorne* (New York: Oxford University Press, 1986), for a contemporary instance of this argument pushed to its limit. Since we now recognize that literary traditions are institutional achievements, the

founder of one can now be canonized on those grounds. Brodhead's book secures the tradition by admitting its constructedness and praising the builders.

39. Willard Thorp, "Walt Whitman," *Eight American Authors,* 303.

40. Jonathan Arac, "F. O. Matthiessen: Authorizing an American Renaissance," in *The American Renaissance Reconsidered,* ed. Walter Benn Michaels and Donald E. Pease (Baltimore: Johns Hopkins University Press, 1985), 96–99.

41. See Cain, *Matthiessen,* 155–56, for a persuasive list of qualifications to Arac's claims.

8. Left Criticism and the New York Intellectuals

1. Alan Wald, *The New York Intellectuals: The Rise and Decline of the Anti-Stalinist Left from the 1930s to the 1980s* (Chapel Hill: University of North Carolina Press, 1987), 3–24, discusses what he calls a general "political amnesia" of the New York Intellectuals about their revolutionary communist positions of the 1930s.

2. Russell Jacoby, *The Last Intellectuals: American Culture in the Age of Academe* (New York: Basic, 1987).

3. Lionel Trilling, "Reality in America," *The Liberal Imagination* (New York: Scribner's, 1976 [1950]), 3.

4. Henry Nash Smith, "American Renaissance," *Monthly Review* 2 (1950): 223, argues that during the 1940s Matthiessen's *American Renaissance* had replaced Parrington's *Main Currents* as the dominant conception of the American tradition. We have already seen that Parringtonian scholarship was never typical of the discipline, and during the 1940s Parrington had little influence on criticism in or out of the university. Gene Wise, *American Historical Explanations: A Strategy for Grounded Inquiry,* 2d ed. (Minneapolis: University of Minnesota Press, 1980), marks 1950 as the beginning of the dominance of what he calls the counterprogressive explanation form in American history and cultural analysis. Matthiessen's work is typical of this paradigm, while Parrington's was typical of the earlier "progressive" paradigm. The major works of progressive history—by James and Mary Beard, Carl Becker, Frederick Jackson Turner, and Parrington—were all written before 1940, and most were completed before 1930.

5. Richard Ruland, *The Rediscovery of American Literature* (Cambridge, Mass.: Harvard University Press, 1967), 186.

6. Vincent Leitch, *American Literary Criticism from the 30s to the 80s* (New York: Columbia University Press, 1988), 9–10.

7. V. F. Calverton, *The Liberation of American Literature* (New York: Scribner's, 1932); Granville Hicks, *The Great Tradition: An Interpretation of American Literature since the Civil War,* rev. ed. (New York: Macmillan, 1935 [1933]).

8. Peter Novick, *That Noble Dream: The "Objectivity Question" and the American Historical Profession* (Cambridge: Cambridge University Press, 1988), 249 n. 7, makes the same point about the discipline of history: "Not much Marxist historical work of any kind appeared during the 1930s."

9. V. F. Calverton, *The Bankruptcy of Marriage* (New York: Arno, 1972 [1928]).

10. F. O. Matthiessen, "The Great Tradition: A Counterstatement," *The Responsibilities of the Critic* (New York: Oxford University Press, 1952), 189.

11. The New York Intellectuals have been the subject of a vast amount of writing, including historical works, commentaries and critiques, and their own memoirs. It

should go without saying that I cannot in a single chapter present the group in the complexity or detail of a book. Of the books on the New York Intellectuals, I have found the following three most useful in preparing this chapter: Wald, *The New York Intellectuals*; Alexander Bloom, *Prodigal Sons: The New York Intellectuals and Their World* (New York: Oxford University Press, 1986); and Terry A. Cooney, *The Rise of the New York Intellectuals*: Partisan Review *and its Circle* (Madison: University of Wisconsin Press, 1986).

12. Wallace Phelps [William Phillips] and Philip Rahv, "Problems and Perspectives in Revolutionary Literature," *Partisan Review* 1, no. 3 (June-July 1934): 4.

13. William Phillips, "The Esthetic of the Founding Fathers," *Partisan Review* 4 (March 1938): 12.

14. This view was later articulated in theories such as those of Norman Podhoretz, Daniel Bell, and Alvin Gouldner. See Andrew Ross, "Defenders of the Faith and the New Class," in *Intellectuals: Aesthetics, Politics, Academics*, ed. Bruce Robbins (Minneapolis: University of Minnesota Press, 1990), 118–25. It had already, however, become a part of the New Yorkers' vocabulary. See, for example, Lionel Trilling, "Young in the Thirties," *Commentary* 41, no. 5 (May 1966): 47–48.

15. William Phillips, "The Intellectual's Tradition," *Partisan Review* 8 (1941): 485.

16. "Editorial Statement," *Partisan Review* 4 (December 1937): 4.

17. Wallace Phelps [William Phillips] and Philip Rahv, "Criticism," *Partisan Review* 2 (March-April 1935): 22–23.

18. Lionel Trilling, "Parrington, Mr. Smith and Reality," *Partisan Review* 7 (January-February 1940): 26, quoting Harry Hayden Clark.

19. William M. Chace, *Lionel Trilling: Criticism and Politics* (Stanford, Calif.: Stanford University Press, 1980), 13.

20. "Our Country, Our Culture: A Symposium," *Partisan Review* 19 (1952): 282–326, 420–50, 562–97. Of the three figures on which I have focused in this chapter, only Philip Rahv seemed at all worried by what he called "the *emborgeiosement* of the American intelligentsia," and even he found "a greater degree of identification with American life" to be inevitable: "Our Country, Our Culture," 304, 306. Irving Howe was certainly the first member of the circle to present a full-scale critique of his fellow members' complicity in the *Zeitgeist*: "The Age of Conformity," *Partisan Review* 21 (1954): 7–33. The editors found it necessary to append a note to Howe's essay acknowledging that it would be controversial.

21. Lionel Trilling, "Our Country, Our Culture: A Symposium," 319, 320.

22. Mark Krupnick, *Lionel Trilling and the Fate of Cultural Criticism* (Evanston, Ill.: Northwestern University Press, 1986), 102.

23. See, for example, Irving Howe, *A Margin of Hope* (New York: Harcourt Brace Jovanovich, 1982), 229.

24. Leslie Fiedler, "American Literature," in *Contemporary Literary Scholarship: A Critical Review*, ed. Lewis Leary (New York: Appleton-Century-Crofts, 1958), 170.

25. Chace, for example, describes Trilling's "aversion to the New Criticism" without noting any similarities between his work and it.

26. Lionel Trilling, "The State of American Writing, 1948: A Symposium," *Partisan Review* 15 (1948): 889.

27. I have borrowed this line from Krupnick, who uses it in a less sweeping generalization about what Trilling "was always saying to his fellow liberals," *Lionel Trilling*, 66.

28. Russell Reising, *The Unusable Past: Theory and the Study of American Literature* (New York: Methuen, 1986), 93; Gene Wise, *American Historical Explanations*, 224. See also David H. Hirsch, "Reality, Manners, and Mr. Trilling," *Sewanee Review* 72 (1964): 420–32.

29. Novick, *That Noble Dream*, 332, notes that the dominant tendency of the history written in the late 1940s was counterprogressive and that historians writing in this mode exaggerated the influence of Beard, Becker, and Parrington during the 1930s.

30. Wise's conception does allow for the pairing of Trilling with the New Critics, but it does not in my view explain their similarities.

31. Lionel Trilling, "The Meaning of a Literary Idea," in *The Liberal Imagination*, 292.

32. Lionel Trilling, "Parrington, Mr. Smith and Reality," *Partisan Review* 7 (January-February 1940): 25.

33. William Troy, "The Lawrence Myth," *Partisan Review* 4 (January 1938): 3–13; "Thomas Mann: Myth and Reason," *Partisan Review* 5 (June 1938): 24–32, (July 1938): 51–64; "A Further Note on Myth," *Partisan Review* 6 (Fall 1938): 95–100.

34. William Phillips, "Thomas Mann: Humanism and Exile," *Partisan Review* 4 (May 1938): 3–10; James Burnham, "William Troy's Myths," *Partisan Review* 5 (August-September 1938): 65–68. For an account of this exchange, see Cooney, *Rise*, 153–60.

35. Richard Chase, *Quest for Myth* (Westport, Conn.: Greenwood Press, 1969 [1949]), 104, quoting Trilling, "The Legacy of Sigmund Freud: Literary and Aesthetic," *Kenyon Review* (Spring 1940).

36. Giles Gunn, *The Culture of Criticism and the Criticism of Culture* (New York: Oxford University Press, 1987), 27.

37. René Wellek, *A History of Modern Criticism 1750–1950*, vol. 6 (New Haven: Yale University Press, 1986), 131, argues this specifically about Trilling.

38. Wallace Phelps [William Phillips], "Three Generations," *Partisan Review* 1 (September-October 1934): 50.

39. William Phillips and Philip Rahv, "Literature in a Political Decade," in *New Letters in America*, ed. Horace Gregory and Eleanor Clark (New York: Norton, 1937), 172–80.

40. Lionel Trilling, "On the Teaching of Modern Literature," *Beyond Culture* (New York: Viking, 1965), 30. First published in the *Partisan Review* as "On the Modern Element in Literature," 1961.

41. Krupnick, *Lionel Trilling*, 49–50, quotes Trilling, "Notes for an Autobiographical Lecture," in *The Last Decade* (New York: Harcourt Brace Jovanovich, 1979), 234.

42. Michael Denning, "New York Intellectuals," *Socialist Review* 18, no. 1 (1988): 144.

43. Irving Howe, "The Idea of the Modern," *The Idea of the Modern in Literature and the Arts*, ed. Howe (New York: Horizon, 1967), 11–40.

44. Lionel Trilling, ed., *The Experience of Literature* (Garden City, N.Y.: Doubleday, 1967).

45. Dennis Donoghue, "A Literary Gathering," review of *The Experience of Literature*, *Commentary* 45 (April 1968): 93, quoted in Krupnick, *Lionel Trilling*, 141.

46. Lionel Trilling, "F. Scott Fitzgerald," in *The Liberal Imagination*, 243–54; Irving Howe, *William Faulkner* (New York: Random House, 1952).

47. It is to the point that both of these writers are often considered to be British. The New York Intellectuals speak of Eliot as such, but treat James as an American.

48. Philip Rahv, "Twilight of the Thirties," *Partisan Review* 6 (Summer 1939): 4.

49. Philip Rahv, "Paleface and Redskin," *Kenyon Review* 1 (1939): 253.

50. Philip Rahv, "The Cult of Experience in American Writing," *Partisan Review* 7 (November-December 1940): 414–15.

51. Geraldine Murphy, "Romancing the Center: Cold War Politics and Classic American Literature," *Poetics Today* 9, no. 4 (1988): 737–47.

52. Richard Chase, *The American Novel and Its Tradition* (Baltimore: Johns Hopkins University Press, 1980 [1957]), 13.

53. See Hirsch, "Reality, Manners, and Mr. Trilling," 421–25, for a different analysis of this inconsistency.

54. Lewis's *The American Adam* is as important, but it owes as much to Matthiessen and Perry Miller as it does to the New York Intellectuals.

9. Civilization "Discovered"

1. V. F. Calverton, *The Liberation of American Literature* (New York: Scribner's, 1932), 31.

2. Richard Ruland, *The Rediscovery of American Literature: The Premises of Critical Taste, 1900–1940* (Cambridge, Mass.: Harvard University Press, 1967), 275–87; Robert Spiller et al., eds., *The Literary History of the United States* (New York: Macmillan, 1948), cited hereafter as *LHUS*; Raymond Williams, *Marxism and Literature* (Oxford: Oxford University Press, 1977), 51.

3. Frank Lentricchia, *After the New Criticism* (Chicago: University of Chicago Press, 1980), 3–4.

4. Paul Lauter, "Society and Profession, 1958–1983," *Canons and Contexts* (New York: Oxford University Press, 1991), 20, n. 8.

5. My discussion of the *LHUS* is indebted to Kermit Vanderbilt's detailed account of the planning, composition, and reception of the project in *American Literature in the Academy: The Roots, Growth, and Maturity of a Profession* (Philadelphia: University of Pennsylvania Press, 1986).

6. Robert Spiller, "History of a History: A Study in Cooperative Scholarship," *PMLA* 89 (May 1974): 608.

7. Jones to Spiller, October 25, 1940; Wright to Spiller, October 25, 1940; Hubbell to Members of the Committee on a Co-operative History of American Literature, November 1, 1940; Hubbell to Spiller, November 1, 1940; Jones to Hubbell, November 7, 1940, and November 16, 1940; all in JBH.

8. Harry Hayden Clark, "Suggestions Concerning a History of American Literature," *American Literature* 12 (1940): 288–96.

9. Yvor Winters, "On the Possibility of a Co-operative History of American Literature," *American Literature* 12 (1940): 297–305.

10. Robert Spiller, "The Task of the Historian of American Literature," *The Third Dimension: Studies in Literary History* (New York: Macmillan, 1965), 15–25.

11. Louis B. Wright, "Toward a New History of American Literature," *American Literature* 12 (1940): 287.

12. Spiller, "History of a History," 612, quoting the *LHUS* editors' guidelines for their project.

13. I judge the publication of Emory Elliot, ed., *The Columbia Literary History of the United States* (New York: Columbia University Press, 1988) to mark the beginning of a contest to determine a new definitive history, and thus the fall of the old one.

14. First articulated in 1941 in a lecture delivered at Fordham University: Robert Spiller, "Blueprint for American Literary History," in *The Third Dimension*, 26–36. It was given full, separate articulation in *The Cycle of American Literature* (New York: New American Library, 1955).

15. Vivian C. Hopkins, "Emerson and Cudworth: Plastic Nature and Transcendental Art," *American Literature* 23 (1951): 80.

16. Sidney E. Lind, "James's 'The Private Life' and Browning," *American Literature* 23 (1951): 315–22.

17. Marie P. Harris, "Henry James, Lecturer," *American Literature* 23 (1951): 302–14.

18. Anon., "To Our Contributors." *American Literature* 1 (1929): 75.

19. Jones to Gohdes, April 29, 1951, in JBH, emphasis added.

20. Hubbell to Members of the Advisory Board of *American Literature*, November 16, 1951, in JBH.

21. Hubbell to Members of the Editorial and Advisory Boards of *American Literature*, January 18, 1952, in JBH.

22. Charvat to Gohdes, December 13, 1954, in JBH.

23. That the contest between criticism and literary history remained very much alive in 1969 when Turner was appointed is suggested by the comment in the *PMLA* announcement of that event that "conservatives" were hoping that the new editor would keep the journal devoted to literary history, while liberals hoped for more criticism. "For Members Only," *PMLA* 84 (1969), 150.

24. Mary E. Dichmann, "Hawthorne's 'Prophetic Pictures,' " *American Literature* 23 (1952): 188–89.

25. Robert Spiller, *Late Harvest: Essays and Addresses in American Literature and Culture* (Westport, Conn.: Greenwood, 1981), 217. It is also worth noting that Spiller had been successful in obtaining foundation support for the project, something which seems fairly unusual in American literary studies up to that point.

26. Sigmund Diamond, "The American Studies Program at Yale: *Lux, Veritas, et Pecunia*," *Prospects* 16 (1991): 44–46.

27. See Gene Wise, "Paradigm Dramas," *American Quarterly* 31 (1979): 308–9.

28. Ralph H. Gabriel, review of *Characteristically American* by Ralph Barton Perry, *American Literature* 23 (1951): 139.

29. Anon., *American Quarterly* 1 (1949): 2.

30. Anon., *American Quarterly* 1 (1949): 145.

31. See Carl Bode, "The Start of the ASA," *American Quarterly*, 31 (1979): 352.

32. Ray B. Browne, *Against Academia: The History of the Popular Culture Association / American Culture Association and Popular Culture Movement 1967–1988* (Bowling Green, Ohio: Bowling Green State University Popular Press, 1989). The elitist/populist split between the two groups has become increasingly wide in the intervening years even though both groups now deal with the objects of high culture and popular culture. Rather, the ASA represents academic hierarchy, its convention and journal typically being dominated by scholars from major research institutions,

while the PCA and the *Journal of Popular Culture* have been more the province of faculty employed by teaching institutions. The PCA Convention's "democratic" program policies—all papers proposed are accepted—is perhaps the ultimate rejection of invidious academic distinctions.

33. Hubbell to Advisory Board, November 16, 1951, in JBH.

34. For a discussion of this conception of the intellectual see Paul Bové, *Intellectuals in Power: A Genealogy of Critical Humanism* (New York: Columbia University Press, 1986).

35. Donald Weeks, "Two Uses of *Moby Dick*," *American Quarterly* 2 (1950): 155.

36. One of the things that the articles by Dichmann and Weeks share is the influence of Matthiessen, who is cited no less than five times by Dichmann and who first argued that there were significant parallels between *King Lear* and *Moby Dick*.

37. Leo Marx, "The Pilot and the Passenger: Landscape Conventions and the Style of *Huckleberry Finn*," *American Literature* 28 (May 1956): 129–46.

38. Russell Reising, *The Unusable Past: Theory and the Study of American Literature* (New York: Methuen, 1986). The idea clearly goes back to the 1920s, when theories of American literature were regarded with suspicion by most Americanists. Howard Mumford Jones may have been the first to give the conception of competing theories extended treatment in *The Theory of American Literature* (Ithaca, N.Y.: Cornell University Press, 1965 [1948]). There is also an anthology based on this premise: Donald M. Kartiganer and Malcolm A. Griffith, eds., *Theories of American Literature* (New York: Macmillan, 1972).

39. Donald Pease, "National Identities, Postmodern Artifacts, and Postnational Narratives," *boundary 2* 19, no. 1 (1992): 3–4.

40. Ironically, perhaps, Pease may be performing the same work on Lewis, Smith, and Miller that Lewis performed with Cooper, Bird, and Brown: creating a unified narrative out of disparate stories.

41. As Peter Novick, *That Noble Dream: The "Objectivity Question" and the American Historical Profession* (Cambridge: Cambridge University Press, 1988), 332–48 shows, "consensus" was the 1950s historians' term for their own work, but he also demonstrates the increasingly conservative politics of these historians. The term was far less significant among literary critics, though it has been applied retrospectively to them at least since the early 1970s. For what seems a fundamental misunderstanding of consensus and American literary scholarship, see Sacvan Bercovitch, "The Problem of Ideology in American Literary History," *Critical Inquiry* 12 (Summer 1986): 631–53, where Parrington is called a consensus historian and the postwar period is defined by "the achievement of Matthiessen and Spiller to consolidate a powerful literary-historical consensus" (633). It is my argument that no agreement between literary critics and literary historians was achieved.

42. A stronger case can be made for the conflict/consensus narrative if one takes literary criticism as one's subject. In becoming increasingly institutionalized in the academy, criticism doubtless became more monolithic. I would attribute this to the effects of disciplinarity rather than to a new model of culture.

43. D. H. Lawrence, *Studies in Classic American Literature* (New York: Viking, 1923), 2.

44. R. W. B. Lewis, *The American Adam* (Chicago: University of Chicago Press, 1955), 104, quoting Lawrence, 62–63 (emphasis added by Lewis). Lewis's ellipses

cover several paragraphs, and omit Lawrence's description of the American as "a killer," a characterization at odds with Lewis's version of the innocent American.

45. Leo Marx, *The Machine in the Garden* (New York: Oxford University Press, 1964), 145, quoting Lawrence.

46. Perry Miller, preface to the Beacon Press edition, *Orthodoxy in Massachusetts 1630–1650* (Boston: Beacon, 1959 [1933]), xviii.

47. For a bibliography of discussions of Miller by historians, see John C. Crowell, "Perry Miller as Historian: A Bibliography of Evaluations," *Bulletin of Bibliography and Magazine Notes* 34 (1977): 77–85. Some of the more important discussions include: Robert Skotheim, *American Intellectual Histories and Historians* (Princeton: Princeton University Press, 1966), 186–212; Robert Middlekauff, "Perry Miller," in *Pastmasters: Some Essays on American Historians*, ed. Marcus Cunliffe and Robin Winks (New York: Harper, 1969), 167–90; Gene Wise, *American Historical Explanations*, 2nd ed. (Minneapolis: University of Minnesota Press, 1980), esp. 315–43; "James Hoopes on Perry Miller's *The New England Mind*: A Symposium," *American Quarterly* 34 (Spring 1982): 3–48.

48. I am suggesting that Miller is something of a sport in the history of the study of American literature. He was more the historian than most practitioners of literary history, but he was also more the interpreter.

49. Miller's mastery obviously must have discouraged some potential competitors from taking up the Puritans. Hoopes points out in "James Hoopes on Perry Miller" that no historian has yet presented an alternative thesis comprehensive enough to equal the breadth of Miller's primary interpretations (3 n. 3). But again, many historians have tried to improve on Miller, while relatively few literary critics have bothered.

50. Henry Nash Smith, *Virgin Land: The American West as Symbol and Myth* (Cambridge, Mass.: Harvard University Press, 1950), 123.

51. Smith, *Virgin Land*, 251, quotes Turner, "The Significance of the Frontier in American History," *Early Writings*, 187.

52. Henry Nash Smith, "Symbol and Idea in *Virgin Land*," *Ideology and Classic American Literature*, ed. Sacvan Bercovitch and Myra Jehlen (Cambridge: Cambridge University Press, 1986), 28.

53. Smith, "Symbol and Idea," 23, confirms this reading of his intentions: "The structure of the book is basically a conflict between an assumed historical reality and the ideology, myths, and symbols generated in American culture."

54. On Lewis's implicit restriction of his claims, see Wise, *American Historical Explanations*, 308–12.

55. Robert Spiller, review of *The American Novel and Its Tradition*, *American Literature* 31 (1959): 82–83.

56. Leo Marx, "Pastoralism in America," *Ideology and Classic American Literature*, ed. Sacvan Bercovitch and Myra Jehlen (Cambridge: Cambridge University Press, 1986), 43.

57. Marx, *The Machine in the Garden*, 8–9, makes specific reference to Freud's conception of the problem in *Civilization and its Discontents*.

58. Richard Chase, *The American Novel and Its Tradition* (Baltimore: Johns Hopkins University Press, 1957), 11.

59. Roy Harvey Pearce, *The Continuity of American Poetry* (Princeton: Princeton University Press, 1961), 41.

60. Richard Brodhead, *The School of Hawthorne* (New York: Oxford University Press, 1986), 9. Brodhead himself argues for Hawthorne's centrality to the American tradition in fiction, albeit on more rigorously historical terms than Chase.

61. Spiller et al., eds., *LHUS*, vol. 1, 358.

62. Hyatt Waggoner, *American Poets: From the Puritans to the Present* (Boston: Houghton Mifflin, 1968), xii.

63. Leslie Fiedler, *Waiting for the End* (New York: Stein and Day, 1964), 209.

64. Perry Miller, *Errand into the Wilderness* (Cambridge, Mass.: Harvard University Press, 1956), 184.

65. Of course, there is another explanation for Dickinson's not being accorded the status of founder: since her poetry was largely suppressed until the twentieth century, she could not have been an actual historical influence on the poets of the early part of this century. The fiction of actual historical influence, on the other hand, helps support the claims for Emerson's paternity. But given the slender threads by which this influence hangs, including such devices as "the Emersonian spirit," which can preexist the man himself, arguments for Dickinson as founder could have been offered. No one read Taylor's poetry until the twentieth century, 300 years after it had been written.

66. The phrase is from Harold Bloom, "Mr. America," *The New York Review of Books* (November 22, 1984): 23.

67. Reising, *Unusable Past*, 163–217; Charles Feidelson, Jr., *Symbolism and American Literature* (Chicago: University of Chicago Press, 1953); Richard Poirier, *A World Elsewhere: The Place of Style in American Literature* (New York: Oxford University Press, 1966).

68. See Barbara Foley, "From New Criticism to Deconstruction: The Example of Charles Feidelson's *Symbolism and American Literature*," *American Quarterly* 36 (Spring 1984): 43–64.

69. Leslie Fiedler, *Love and Death in the American Novel*, rev. ed. (New York: Stein and Day, 1966 [1960]), 29.

70. For criticisms from within American Studies, see Wise, *Paradigm Dramas*, and *American Historical Explanations*; Bruce Kuklick, "Myth and Symbol in American Studies," *American Quarterly* 24 (1972): 438–50; Robert Berkhofer, "Clio and the Culture Concept," in *The Idea of Culture in the Social Sciences* (Cambridge: Cambridge University Press, 1973), 77–100; R. Gordon Kelly, "Literature and the Historian," *American Quarterly* 26 (1974): 143–59; Fred Mathews, "The Myth and Value Approach to American Studies," *Canadian Review of American Studies* 3 (1972): 112–21; Cecil Tate, *Search for a Method in American Studies* (Minneapolis: University of Minnesota Press, 1973); Thomas Krueger, "The Historians and the Edenic Myth," *Canadian Review of American Studies* 4 (1973): 3–18; Luther Luedtke, "Not So Common Ground," in *The Study of American Culture: Contemporary Conflicts*, ed. Luedtke (New York: Everett Edwards, 1977), 323–67. For left, feminist, and multiculturalist critiques, see the Epilogue, "A Trailer."

71. Nina Baym, "Melodramas of Beset Manhood: How Theories of American Literature Exclude Women Authors," *American Quarterly* 33 (Summer 1981): 125.

72. Garry Wills, *Inventing America* (New York: Doubleday, 1979), xxii, emphasis in original.

73. Lewis Leary, ed., *Contemporary Literary Scholarship: A Critical Review* (New York: Appleton-Century-Crofts, 1958).

74. Leslie Fiedler, "American Literature," in Leary, *Contemporary Literary Scholarship*, 157–85.

75. Lewis Leary, ed., *The Teacher and American Literature* (Champaign, Ill.: NCTE, 1964), viii.

76. Douglas Bush, "The New Criticism: Some Old-Fashioned Queries," *PMLA* 64, suppl., part 2, (March 1949): 13–21.

77. Gerald Graff, *Professing Literature: An Institutional History* (Chicago: University of Chicago Press, 1987), 185–88.

78. R. W. B. Lewis, "Contemporary American Literature," in Leary, *Contemporary Literary Scholarship*, 201–2.

Epilogue: A Trailer

1. See Paul Lauter, "Society and Profession, 1958–1983," *Canons and Contexts* (New York: Oxford University Press, 1991), 3–21, for an extended discussion of these changes.

2. As evidence for the acceptance of this new principle I cite changes in the major anthologies, *The American Tradition in Literature* and *The Norton Anthology of American Literature*. For a quick overview of the changes, see Harold H. Kolb, "Defining the Canon," *Redefining American Literary History*, ed. A. LaVonne Brown Ruoff and Jerry W. Ward (New York: MLA, 1990), 45–49. The publication and success of *The Heath Anthology of American Literature* are significant in a different way, since this volume was designed by canon reformers to represent a new vision of American literature. The publication of the Ruoff and Ward collection by the Modern Language Association signals the imprimatur of that organization on the new conception of the canon, though it was not the work of the American Literature Section. Finally, even those on the intellectual right are beginning to accept the representational model: see Diane Ravitch, "Multiculturalism: E Pluribus Plures," *Debating P.C.: The Controversy Over Political Correctness on College Campuses*, ed. Paul Berman (New York: Dell, 1992), 271–76.

3. I cannot begin to survey that literature here. The bibliography of "African American Literature" in *Redefining American Literary History* lists 121 general studies, all but 5 published in the last thirty years.

4. Houston Baker's first book, *Long Black Song: Essays in Black American Literature and Culture* (Charlottesville: University Press of Virginia, 1972), is already at work on this project, though no overall conception is offered. *Blues, Ideology, and Afro-American Literature: A Vernacular Theory* (Chicago: University of Chicago Press, 1984) does provide such a conception. *Modernism and the Harlem Renaissance* (Chicago: University of Chicago Press, 1987) concerns the construction of a literary period within the tradition. Henry Louis Gates has attempted to found an African-American tradition in theory by locating and identifying "how the 'black tradition' had theorized about itself," *The Signifying Monkey: A Theory of Afro-American Literary Criticism* (New York: Oxford University Press, 1988), ix. For a treatment of a black female literary tradition, see Barbara Christian, *Black Women Novelists: The Development of a Tradition, 1892–1976* (Westport, Conn.: Greenwood, 1980). For a historical and theoretical analysis of the emergence of an African-American tradition, see Ronald A. T. Judy, *(Dis)Forming the American Canon: African-Arabic Slave Narratives and the Vernacular* (Minneapolis: University of Minnesota Press, 1993), 1–21.

Some African-American literary history does seem to move beyond tradition-building. For example, Hazel Carby, *Reconstructing Womanhood: The Emergence of the Afro-American Woman Novelist* (New York: Oxford University Press, 1987), treats such novelists as part of a particular social history. Her book is more a reading of that history than of their work.

5. Houston Baker, "Archaeology, Ideology, and African American Discourse," *Redefining American Literary History*, ed. A. LaVonne Brown Ruoff and Jerry W. Ward (New York: MLA, 1990), 164.

6. Annette Kolodny, *The Lay of the Land* (Chapel Hill: University of North Carolina Press, 1975); Judith Fetterley, *The Resisting Reader: A Feminist Approach to American Fiction* (Bloomington: Indiana University Press, 1979).

7. Annette Kolodny, *The Land Before Her: Fantasy and Experience of the American Frontier, 1630–1860* (Chapel Hill: University of North Carolina Press, 1984).

8. Jane Tompkins, *Sensational Designs: The Cultural Work of American Fiction 1790–1860* (New York: Oxford University Press, 1985), 5.

9. Paul Lauter, "Reconstructing American Literature: Curricular Issues," *Canons and Contexts*, 98–99.

10. For a critique of the conception of the canon implied in the notion of a "mainstream," see Paul Lauter, "The Literatures of America—A Comparative Discipline," in *Canons and Contexts*, 48–53.

11. Peter Carafiol, *The American Ideal: Literary History as a Worldly Activity* (New York: Oxford University Press, 1991), 11–12, quoting Myra Jehlen, "Introduction: Beyond Transcendence," *Ideology and Classic American Literature*, ed. Sacvan Bercovitch and Jehlen (Cambridge: Cambridge University Press, 1986), 14.

12. No major African Americanist is mentioned by Carafiol.

13. The label "New Americanists" was coined by Frederick Crews in a highly critical review of new work in American literature, "Whose American Renaissance," *New York Review of Books* (October 27, 1988): 68–81. It was picked up by Donald Pease to name two special issues of *boundary 2*: vol. 17, no. 1 (1990), and vol. 19, no. 1 (1992). The New Americanists do include some feminists, and the term does not necessarily exclude African Americanists or students of other countertraditions, but those most closely identified with the "movement" have focused on the established tradition. Among those often associated with it besides Pease are Jonathan Arac, Sacvan Bercovitch (though Pease apparently would contest this), Philip Fisher, Myra Jehlen, Steven Mailloux, Walter Benn Michaels, Daniel O' Hara, and Carolyn Porter. It should go without saying that these critics disagree a great deal with each other and that not all of them would welcome being mentioned in this company.

14. Donald Pease, *Visionary Compacts: American Renaissance Writings in Cultural Context* (Madison: University of Wisconsin Press, 1987).

15. Jonathan Culler, *The Pursuit of Signs: Semiotics, Literature, Deconstruction* (Ithaca: Cornell University Press, 1981), 3–17.

16. See William E. Cain, *The Crisis in Criticism: Theory, Literature, and Reform in English Studies* (Baltimore: Johns Hopkins University Press, 1984), 104, who argues that "the New Criticism is alive and well." Also, Paul Lauter, "The Two Criticisms—or, Structure, Lingo, and Power in the Discourse of Academic Humanists," in *Canons and Contexts*, 133–53, who holds that Theory remains formalist.

17. There is a sense in which Theory itself was a "new" practice, for even though

theory was practiced in the 1950s and before, it was not generally recognized as a disciplinary specialty. The continued prominence of one book, René Wellek and Austin Warren, *Theory of Literature* (New York: Harcourt Brace, 1949), suggests the relative insignificance of theory as a practice during the 1950s and 1960s. By the late 1970s, theory had become an important disciplinary specialty, but writing about theory never came to rival interpreting literature as the dominant practice.

18. Donald Pease, "New Americanists: Revisionist Interventions into the Canon," *boundary 2* 17, no. 1 (1990): 32.

19. That, of course, would seem to make me a New Americanist, although I do not feel much loyalty to this "granfalloon."

20. Paul Bové, "The Political and Critical Need for Collective Research in the Humanities," *The GRIP Report*, Vol. 2, n.p., n.d. It is not a coincidence that Bové is editor of *boundary 2*, and that New Americanists Arac, Pease, and Daniel O'Hara are members of its editorial collective.

21. Crews concludes his review: "The truth is that for any works written before the last seventy years or so, the most influential academics get to decide who's in and who's out. And the New Americanists themselves seem destined to become the next establishment in their field. They will be right about the most important books and the most fruitful ways of studying them because, as they always knew in their leaner days, those who hold power are right by definition" (81). This analysis is more strictly genealogical than any offered by the New Americanists.

22. William C. Spengemann, *A Mirror for Americanists* (Hanover, N.H.: The University Press of New England, 1989), 161.

23. Gregory S. Jay, "The End of 'American' Literature: Toward a Multicultural Practice," *College English* 53 (March 1991): 264. Jay's article shows remarkable awareness of the problems of reconstituting American literature given the assumptions of the current academic left and the history of the discipline. Below I express several reservations about Jay's project, but on the whole I find this article is the most compelling revision of the field. Alas, I do not find it the most likely to succeed.

24. Paul Lauter, "The Literatures of America—A Comparative Discipline," *Canons and Contexts*, 53.

25. Lauter differs from Jay mainly in rejecting Theory as a basis for the new discipline he proposes. Lauter, for example, is perfectly happy to name social realities represented in literary works "themes." On epistemological grounds Jay refuses both social "realities" and "themes" and insists instead on "problematics," which are "made up simultaneously of material conditions and conceptual forms" and which indicate "how and where the struggle for *meaning* takes place" (my emphasis). Unlike "themes," "problematics" are not "structures of consciousness" (277). Jay's epistemology leads to a distinction without a difference in the practice of interpretation, since meanings are always structures of consciousness. Only in a new, nonhermeneutic practice could the need for themes and meanings be displaced.

26. Pease, "New Americanists," 30, quoting Antonio Gramsci, "The Modern Prince."

27. Kolb, "Defining the Canon," 41, presents what I see as a version of the "business as usual" canon. He pictures a hierarchy that includes a "first level" of Hawthorne, Emerson, Thoreau, Melville, Whitman, Dickinson, Twain, Henry James, T. S. Eliot, Richard Wright, Faulkner, and a "second level" of Franklin, Irving, Cooper, Poe, Douglass, Howells, Stephen Crane, Henry Adams, Dreiser, Cather, Chopin, Frost,

Fitzgerald, Hemingway, Jewett, O'Neill, Pound, Stevens, Ellison, William Carlos Williams, James Baldwin, and Momaday. His "third level" would include numerous figures, some older and others "massed like the Boston Marathon runners at Hopkinton, in the race but with endurance yet to be tested." Only here does Kolb's canon really open up, yet he acknowledges that an educated American would be expected only to know some of these writers. In practice, of course, we know that most college graduates will know few of them, since they will be lucky to read beyond level one.

28. The distinction between "national" and "literary" narratives is made by Jonathan Arac, "Nationalism, Hypercanonization, and *Huckleberry Finn*," *boundary 2* 19, no. 1 (1992): 14–33. Arac finds the literary narrative typified by *Huckleberry Finn*, while national narrative is represented by Cooper and *Uncle Tom's Cabin*.

29. Film scholars intent on exposing the ideology of *Casablanca* contribute as much to this process as do those who celebrate the film. As we have seen, when it comes to canonization, the fact of discussion is far more important than the specific judgment.

Index

Compiled by Eileen Quam and Theresa Wolner

Index

Index

Brooks, Cleanth, 237, 240, 242; and *Partisan Review*, 279; (with Warren) *Understanding Poetry*, 205, 221, 231, 233

Brooks, Van Wyck: on Harvard, 58–59; *Life of Emerson*, 187; as literary radical, 53, 54, 56–57, 58, 59, 85–86, 129, 131; *Makers and Finders*, 86, 131; on nationalism, 131; on professors of American literature, 56–57, 58; *Sketches in Criticism*, 187; on usable past, 54, 56–57, 85, 86, 131, 133; *The Wine of the Puritans*, 131

Brown, Charles Brockden, 161, 295, 326, 331, 349

Brown University: American civilization courses in, 215; and ALG, 153, 172–73

Brownell, W. C., 62, 63, 83

Bryant, William Cullen, 76, 94, 139, 161, 180; in anthologies, 26, 200; in curriculum, 205; as standard author, 26, 74

Burke, Kenneth, 236

Burton, Richard, 74

Butler, Samuel, 131

Cabell, James Branch, 130

Cain, William: on Matthiessen, 238–39, 254–55; on New Criticism, 222

Calverton, V. F.: *The Liberation of American Literature*, 187–88, 264–69

Cambell, Killis: and ALG, 152

Cambridge History of American Literature, The (CHAL), 57, 60, 66, 87–95, 124, 151, 156–57, 162, 189, 319, 350; bias in, 91, 196, 300–301; as collaboration, 66, 87; on concept of literature, 221; contributors, 89; criticism of, 88, 149; editors, 129, 157, 163; as encyclopedic history, 88; ideology of, 91; inclusiveness of, 89, 91; as product of literary researchers, 60; as racist, 91; selection in, 196; as sexist, 91

Canby, Henry Seidel, 139; *Classic Americans*, 187; on literature and history, 140, 141; and *LHUS*, 302, 305; review of *Reinterpretation of American Literature*, 140, 141, 184

Canon: and concept of literature, 62; vs. contemporary practice, 25; and English as discipline, 117; historical contingency of, 14–15; self-perpetuation of, 15; vs. standard authors, 25, 59; and time, 62

Canon, American: and *Cambridge History of American Literature*, 94; criteria for, 183, 190; emergence of, 126, 179–80, 188–90, 195–200, 206–7; and Emerson, 62, 94, 160, 244; vs. history, 176–77, 260; Kolb's, 388–89n; Matthiessen and, 239, 241, 243–44; modernists in, 200, 293; narrowing of, 206–7, 211–12; and national narratives, 20; New Critics and, 236; New Humanism and, 145; opening of, 346–50; power and persistence of, 350–52

Canon, English, 62, 96–97, 108–9, 125–26; as model for American canon, 126, 212

Canon, modernist: and American canon, 292–93; New York Intellectuals and, 262, 275, 287–93

Capitalism: industrial, 29

Carafiol, Peter, 351, 353, 354–55

Career training, 346

Cargill, Oscar: *American Literature*, 199–200

Casablanca (film), 359, 389n

Cather, Willa, 48, 161, 206–7

Century: and literary ideals, 45; on social conflicts, 34; and taste, 37

CHAL. See Cambridge History of American Literature

Chase, Richard: *The American Novel and Its Tradition*, 210, 286, 296, 298, 332; as critic, 278; on novel, 261; *Quest for Myth*, 286

Chaucer, Geoffrey, 108, 112, 114,

Index

125; books on, 104–5, 113; *The Canterbury Tales*, 115; use of physiognomy, 115

Chicago, University of, 106, 153

Child, Francis, 96

Chopin, Kate: *The Awakening*, 349

CIA, 276

Citizenship: English language as requirement, 39

Civilization: vs. barbarism, 16, 40; character of, 60; creation of, 6, 20; definition and usage, 16–18, 362n; discovery of, 299–344; existence of, 318–39; in graduate education, 214–18; literary defense of, 293–98; and rationality, 16. *See also* Culture

Clark, Harry Hayden, 137, 139–40, 141, 184–85

Class: conflict, 34; and education, 36; and literary, 36; and literature as restricted, 13–15, 29, 32; professional-managerial, 34, 36; unity, 36. *See also* Aristocracy; Elitism; Lower class; Working class

Class bias: of American literature, 124; of disciplines, 9; of literary histories, 71, 72; of society, 14. *See also* Elitism

Class struggle: in fiction, 33–34

Classics: and patriotism, 39

Close reading: and literary theory, 235; and New Criticism, 222, 239–40

Cold War, 209, 299, 313, 321

Coleridge, Samuel Taylor, 112, 251

Colonial literature: in anthologies, 198; and cultural inferiority, 265

Comprehensive histories. *See* Literary histories

Concord, Mass., 42

Consensus history, 320, 383n

Cooper, James Fenimore, 76, 94, 180, 295, 326, 329, 331, 349, 350; American history in, 20; in curriculum, 206; Leatherstocking novels of, 322; as standard author, 74

Cosmopolitan, 31

Coursework. *See* Curriculum, American literature

Cowley, Malcolm, 11, 129

Crane, Hart, 200

Crane, Stephen, 33, 48, 139, 206, 331, 350; *Maggie*, 34

Crews, Frederick, 353–54, 387n, 388n

Critical histories. *See* Literary histories

Criticism, literary: and competition, 11, 28; development of, 13, 28, 341–42; division in, 227; in English departments, 223–24; histories of, 3–4, 11, 108; vs. history, 107, 222–23; and literary values, 15; and marginal groups, 227; modern practice of, 11; in 1920s, 128–32; nonacademic, 11; and past/present, 241; professionalizing, 230–31; repression of, 224, 226, 307; and revolutionary literature, 275; and study of literature, 341–42, 382n; and theory, 234, 294. *See also* Feminist criticism; Left criticism; Marxist criticism; New Criticism; New York Intellectuals

Cuddlesworth, Ralph: *True Intellectual System of the Universe*, 307

Culler, Jonathan, 352

Cultural capital, 363n; literary as, 27, 30–31; of literature, 14, 26, 40

Cultural history, 243

Cultural relativism. *See* Relativism

Culture: as alternative to religion, 27; aristocracy of, 190; and communism, 300; defense of, 293–98; definition and usage, 16–17, 362n; and disciplines, 6; dissemination of, 300; diversity in, 319; as elitist, 17, 28; and European civilization, 37, 375n; and industrialism, 139; and romanticism, 16. *See also* Civilization; Nationalism

Curriculum, American literature, 25, 191–218; and aesthetics, 221; and English curriculum, 192; expan-

Index

Index

Fuller, Steve, 5, 361n

Garland, Hamlin, 48, 139, 161, 206, 268, 271
Gates, Henry Louis, 349, 386n
Geiger, Roger, 98
Geismar, Maxwell, 233, 376n
Gender bias. *See* Sexism
Genealogy, 6–7, 10–11, 123
Genteel tradition, 36, 131
Geology, 2, 361n
George Washington University, 213
Graduate education: and American studies, 212–18, 343; and mental discipline, 110. *See also* Curriculum, American literature
Graff, Gerald, 218; *Professing Literature*, xii, 4–5
Gramsci, Antonio, 52
Greenough, Chester Noyes: (with Wendell) *A History of Literature in America*, 65
Greenough, Horatio, 241–42
Greer, Germaine: *The Female Eunuch*, 348
GRIP Project, xi

Harlem renaissance, 9
Harper's Monthly: audience for, 52; circulation, 46; critic for, 50; and knowledge production, 98; as literary, 45, 48, 129; and taste, 37
Harte, Bret, 161
Harvard University: American civilization program in, 151, 209, 215–16; first professor of English at, 96; and graduate training, 213; and literary culture, 42, 58–59, 79; literary research at, 106, 112; and modernism, 59; social influence of, 42
Hawthorne, Nathaniel: academic Americanists on, 139, 154; canonical status of, 180, 241, 350; in curriculum, 205, 206; as feminist, 160–61; *The House of the Seven Gables*, 197; Matthiessen on, 243, 244, 249–52, 258, 297; New Criti-

cal readings of, 310–11; nonacademic criticism of, 130; and paucity of materials, 257; Parrington on, 164; preprofessional evaluation of, 61, 72, 77, 84, 94; "Prophetic Pictures," 310–11; and religion, 42; as romancer, 295; as standard author, 25, 74; and tradition of American fiction, 295, 329, 331, 333, 377n, 385n
Haymarket anarchists, 51, 52, 128
Hazard, Lucy Lockwood, 149; *The Frontier in American Literature*, 156, 159–61
Hemingway, Ernest, 206, 225, 293
Herder, Johann Gottfried, 16
Hergesheimer, Joseph, 130
Hermeneutics: development of, 235; and New Criticism, 234, 262, 299; and New York Intellectuals, 262; and positivism, 223, 234, 283
Hicks, Granville, 270, 282; *The Great Tradition*, 188, 264, 267–69
Higginson, Thomas Wentworth, 49, 82
History: and criticism, 258; vs. literature, 67
Hobsbawm, Eric: on education, 39; on nationhood, 19
Holmes, Oliver Wendell, 61
Hook, Sidney, 261
Houghton Mifflin, 43
Hound and Horn (journal), 231
Howe, Irving, 291–92, 293, 379n
Howells, William Dean: and American tradition, 331; in anthology, 197; as critic, 50, 52; criticism of, 84, 94, 181–82, 268, 271; in curriculum, 205, 206; as custodian of culture, 76; as editor, 31, 50; *A Hazard of New Fortunes*, 33–34, 41, 59; on history of American literature, 49; influence of, 49, 50, 225, 277; *Literary Friends and Acquaintance*, 43, 44, 59, 61; on literary tradition, 62; on literature defined, 41; on men of letters, 37; on New England, 45; Parrington

on, 139, 169, 171; on poets, 62; and prewar literary culture, 128; on realism, 33–34, 51, 52, 55; as socialist, 52; as symbol, 51; on Wendell, 79

Hubbell, Jay B.: and *AL*, 173–76, 184–85, 302–3; and ALG, 88, 133, 150; *American Life in Literature*, 209; on criticism, 224; on frontier, 136, 138; and *LHUS*, 302–3; on nationalism, 134, 209

Hubbell Center for American Literary Historiography. *See* Jay B. Hubbell Center for American Literary Historiography

Hudson Review (journal), 231

Humanism: and American literature, 144–47; and literary study, 8; as system of ideas, 8. *See also* New Humanism

Humanities: histories of, 3; understanding of, 7

Idealists, 33–37; and ethnocentrism, 37; and imperialism, 37; vs. realism, 33, 34. *See also* Romanticism

Ideology: definition and usage, 32

I'll Take My Stand, 227, 228, 229

Imaginative writing: literature as, 12, 13; reading of, 29

Immigrants: Americanization of, 19, 38, 39

Imperialism: and democracy, 53, 81–82; and idealism, 37; reaction to, 18

Industrialism: dominance of, 18; and standardization of culture, 139

Influence, 115–17

Intellectuals: vs. academy, 56; as critics, 53; and men of letters, 31, 52; oppositional, 53–54. *See also* specific type

Interpretation: and *American Literature*, 140, 174–76, 178, 179, 181; in American Studies, 216–17; as disciplinary practice, 339–44, 352–53; Hazard and, 161; in literary historical practice, 108–10,

117, 179, 251; Matthiessen and, 141, 243, 251, 258; and New Criticism, 205–6, 234–35, 285; Parrington and, 139, 170, 284; in *Reinterpretation of American Literature* (Foerster, ed.), 135, 139; and teaching, 201, 205–6, 301; Trilling and, 284–85. *See also* Hermeneutics

Irving, Washington, 76, 90, 154, 180, 331; in curriculum, 205, 206; as standard author, 74

Jacoby, Russell, 262

James, Henry: *American Literature* on, 307; in anthology, 197; canonical status of, 90; criticism of, 84, 130, 268; in curriculum, 206; Matthiessen on, 241, 251, 257; and mode of literary production, 48; New Critics on, 236, 331; New York Intellectuals on, 293, 295, 297, 331; Parrington on, 139, 162, 164, 171; and tradition of American fiction, 329, 331

James, William, 84, 87, 138, 211

Jameson, Fredric, 352

Jay, Gregory, 354, 355, 356, 357, 388n

Jay B. Hubbell Center for American Literary Historiography, 361n

Jehlen, Myra: *American Incarnation*, 353

Jewett, Sarah Orne, 92, 169, 196

Jews: as Other of academic disciplines, 9

John Reed Clubs, 270

Johns Hopkins University, 98

Johnson, Thomas H., 305

Jones, Howard: and ALG, 152, 154, 203, 307–8; on European background, 136, 139, 143; on freshman English, 101; and graduate English study, 111–12, 152, 371n; *Major Writers of America*, 200; on teaching American literature, 202–3

Journalism: criticism of, 53; as liter-

Index

Manly, John M.: on literary studies, 118; and MLA, 118–19, 149; *Some New Light on Chaucer*, 104, 113

March, Francis A.: as first chair in English, 96; on philological studies, 106

Marx, Leo, 330–31; *The Machine in the Garden*, 323, 330, 345

Marxist criticism (1930s), 227, 262, 263–69, 280–81; development of, 263; influence of, 264; types of, 264

Masculinism, 95

Mass culture, 59

Materialism: dominance of, 18; literature as alternative to, 35

Matthews, Brander: on Americanism, 82, 83; as man of letters, 49

Matthiessen, F. O.: *The Achievement of T. S. Eliot*, 241; on aestheticism, 141; *American Renaissance*, 12, 196, 216, 237–60 *passim*, 263, 318; and close reading, 239; on cultural history, 243; importance of, 238–39, 264; influences on, 237, 240; as literary historian, 251; and New Criticism, 236–60; personal life of, 237; "The Responsibilities of the Critic," 239; and romanticism, 249–50

May, Henry, 76

Media: and the literary, 225–26; and marginal groups, 226–27

Medieval literature: research in, 106

Melville, Herman: as American Shakespeare, 317; canonical status of, 94, 180–81, 189, 241; in curriculum, 205, 206; *The Encantadas*, 180; Matthiessen on, 241, 249–53, 257, 297; *Moby-Dick*, 1, 197, 205, 250, 252–53, 258, 317, 359; *Pierre*, 252; as romancer, 295; and tradition of American fiction, 329

Men of letters, 49–53, 54–60 *passim*; authority of, 25, 26, 31, 43, 48, 99, 120, 129; and bourgeoisie, 52; as critics, 53; and institutional power, 43; and intellectuals, 31, 52; and national literature, 44, 50; Puritanism of, 58; vs. scholars, 49–50; within universities, 25; as unspecialized, 51; Victorian, 37, 51

Mencken, H. L.: on civilization and culture, 128, 130, 131–32; and naturalism, 128; and postwar literary culture, 128, 130

Miller, Perry: on Emerson, 334–35; on European influences, 143; as historian, 384n; *Major Writers of America*, 211; *The New England Mind*, 216, 324; *Orthodoxy in Massachusetts 1630–1650*, 324

Millet, Kate: *Sexual Politics*, 348

Milton, John, 108, 113, 125

Mimesis, 230

Minnesota, University of, 216, 312, 313

Mitchell, Margaret: *Gone With the Wind*, 225–26

Mitford, Mary Russell, 158

MLA. *See* Modern Language Association

Modern Language Association (MLA): and American literary tradition, 133; and English/literature as academic field, 125, 148; meetings, 58; membership, 69; presidents, 105, 118, 149; publications, 90, 94; researchers in, 103; specialized research groups, 119, 149, 150. *See also* American Literature Group; *PMLA*

Modern Language Notes (journal), 103

Modern Philology (journal), 103, 173, 174, 231

Modernism: at Harvard, 59; invention of, 262, 275, 287–93

Moral realism, 281

Mordell, Albert: *Quaker Militant*, 186

More, Paul Elmer, 54, 56, 60; on Emerson, 94–95

Morize, André, 109–10, 112

Mumford, Lewis, 251

Index

Munsey, Frank, 46

Murdock, Kenneth, 136, 139, 143, 152, 153, 215

Murfree, Mary Noailles, 196

Murphy, Geraldine, 296

Myth, 253, 257–60, 322–23; and symbol, 21, 285–88, 320, 327–32, 339

Narrative of the Life of Frederick Douglass, 349

Nation: definition and usage, 18, 19

Nation (magazine), 129, 278

National Council of Teachers of English (NCTE): on teaching of American literature, 173, 206–7, 340, 375n

Nationalism: and American coursework, 192–94, 208, 212; cultural, 16, 30, 299; deployment of, 39; dominance of, 19; and ethnicity, 19; and identification with past, 18–19; impact of, 19–20; literary, 6, 15–16, 18–21, 44, 64, 65, 93–94, 120, 132, 242, 389n; and non-elite, 19; and print medium, 18; vs. regionalism, 79, 82; and ruling class, 20; and sovereignty, 70; and world wars, 18, 20, 133. *See also* Literary tradition

Native Americans: literature of, 69, 92; as other, 17, 69

NCTE. *See* National Council of Teachers of English

New Americanists, 351–52, 387n

New Criticism, 140, 190, 221–60, 299; and academic practice, 221–36, 301; and *American Literature*, 308–11; and American Studies, 217, 302, 316–17; as discipline, 231–32; and history of literary studies, 301; and intellectual right, 230, 321; journals of, 231; and literary theory, 234–35; and New Humanism, 230; vs. New York Intellectuals, 279–87; politics in, 232–33; vs. romanticism, 236; and specialization, 314; and the survey course, 204–5,

206, 210; teaching methods of, 209–10, 233; as a theoretical shift, 222, 234, 261

New England: emphasis on in anthologies, 196–97; and institutional power, 41–43; literary culture in, 41, 42, 45, 68; literature as substitute for religion in, 42; and national literature, 44; regionalism, 79; renaissance, 75, 76, 77, 78, 198; and seriousness of literature, 76; in 17th century, 216, 324; social rigidity of, 80; and unification, 39

New Humanism, 144–47; and Agrarianism, 229; as antimodern, 55–56; and aristocracy, 55; and classical tradition, 55, 56; and conservatism, 124; critical judgment of, 26; and New Criticism, 230; as reactionary, 55–56; and reason, 55; as right wing, 54; vs. university, 56–58. *See also* Literary radicals

New Masses (journal), 270

New Republic, 129, 176

New York City: as literary center, 30, 45

New York Intellectuals, 270–98; vs. Agrarians, 279; on American civilization, 293–98; as antipopulist, 272; vs. Communist writing, 270, 272, 274, 290; development of, 272; and historical sense, 276, 280; and left criticism, 86, 261–98; and literary radicals, 86; and modernism, 262, 287–93; vs. New Critics, 279–87; on theory, 280, 294

News: and national culture, 225

Newspapers: as literary, 41; as literature, 41; and nationalism, 18. *See also* Journalism

Nietzsche, Friedrich Wilhelm, 6

Norris, Frank, 33, 48, 139, 206, 268, 331; *The Octopus*, 34

North American Review, 42, 45, 184

Novels: and nationalism, 18

Index

Oppositional intellectuals. *See under* Intellectuals

Orators, 198

Pancoast, Henry S.: school history by, 74

Parker, Theodore, 258

Parrington, Vernon Louis, 85, 135, 149, 282; on culture, 281–82; *Main Currents of American Thought*, 20, 90, 147, 162–72, 221, 263–64, 187; as positivist, 283; on realism, 136–37, 139, 281–82; Trilling on, 164, 263, 281–87

Partisan Review (journal), 235, 270–80 *passim*, 282, 285–87

Pastoral myth, 21

Patriotism: and American coursework, 192–93; and classics, 39

Pattee, Fred Lewis: and ALG, 152; on American literary independence, 64, 127, 133, 193; *Century Readings in American Literature*, 195–98, 200; on histories, 137; *The New American Literature 1890–1930*, 188; as populist, 197; school history by, 74–75; on Wendell, 79

Pearce, Roy Harvey: *Continuity of American Poetry*, 332, 333; on Matthiessen's criticism, 238

Pearson, Norman Holmes: *The Oxford Anthology of American Literature*, 200

Pease, Donald, 320, 351, 353, 361n

Pennsylvania, Universitiy of, 153, 312, 313

Periods, literary, 76

Perry, Bliss, 38; *The American Mind*, 83–84; *The American Spirit in Literature*, 83, 84

Perry, Ralph Barton: *Characteristically American*, 313

Phelps, William Lyon, 54

Phillips, William, 261, 270, 271–72, 280; on modernist literature, 287–89

Philology, 106; and hermeneutics, 235; and literary history, 112, 284; and nationalism, 19

PMLA (journal), 100, 103–6 *passim*, 109, 112, 118, 119, 148, 150, 173, 175, 176, 180, 184, 309, 368n; and English as discipline, 100, 148; as English studies journal, 105; and New Criticism, 231; on 19th-century literature, 207; philological studies in, 106; as professional venue, 103; as representative, 103

Pochmann, Henry, 152, 154

Poe, Edgar Allan, 130, 154, 164, 172, 181; in anthologies, 197–99; as a critic, 145, 195; in curriculum, 205, 206; men of letters on, 37; in preprofessional histories, 74, 76, 84, 90

Poetry: and *American Literature*, 182; in anthologies, 199; as criticism of life, 28; definition and usage, 13–14; marginalization of, 227; as synonymous with literature, 109

Poirier, Richard: *A World Elsewhere*, 336

Popular Front, 270–71, 272

Positivism, 9; and the canon, 183; and criticism, 224, 235; and hermeneutics, 223, 234, 283; and literary history, 96–120, 180, 304, 307; and the survey course, 201

Pound, Ezra, 243

Printing: and decreased value of writing, 27; and increased literacy, 28–29

Professionalism, 11

Proletarian literature, 85, 267, 268, 270, 288–89

Publishers: and advertising, 46; editorial control by, 26; institutional power of, 43, 45; and literary control, 31; literary occupation of, 40 and symbolic capital, 41

Puritanism: criticism of, 86; and liter-

Index

Index

Scholars: vs. men of letters, 49–50

School histories. *See under* Literary histories

Science: and American society, 170; Foerster on, 135, 146; history of, 3; literary study as, 108–10, 117, 135, 232, 284; vs. literature, 13, 28, 36, 327; New Criticism and, 224, 229, 232; and the New Humanists, 55, 57, 229; New York Intellectuals and, 275, 284, 285; and truth, 28

Scribner's, 37, 45

Scudder, Horace: on culture, 17; on teaching literature and patriotism, 27, 34–35, 39, 65, 192–93

Self-reflexivity, 336

Sewanee Review (journal), 173, 176

Sexism: of American literature studies, 124, 126, 338; of disciplines, 9; of the literary, 32; of literary histories, 72, 75, 91; in society, 14

Shakespeare, William, 108, 113, 125

Sherman, Stuart, 129–30; on academic literary history, 104; and criticism of historical figures, 60; on Mencken, 128; as moralist, 129; on nationalism, 132; as New Humanist, 54, 56, 57, 129

Sidney, Philip: and Spenser, 116–17

Simms, William Gilmore, 183

Sinclair, Upton, 48

Slavery, 81

Slotkin, Richard: *Fatal Environment*, 353

Smart Set (magazine), 277, 278

Smith, Adam, 166

Smith, Barbara Hernstein, 14–15

Smith, Bernard, 199, 282, 284

Smith, Henry Nash, 217; *Virgin Land*, 158, 326–27, 353

Smith, J. Allen, 163

Snow, C. P., 28

Social sciences: vs. literature, 28, 203–4

Songs: in anthology, 197

Source studies: defined, 115

South Atlantic Quarterly, 173, 174, 176

Southern Review (journal), 231

Southwest Review, 184

Spencer, Herbert, 19

Spengemann, William, 354–55

Spenser, Edmund, 108, 112, 125; and Sidney, 116–17

Spiller, Robert: and ALG, 86, 133, 150, 152, 153; and *American Literature*, 184, 309; and American Studies, 215, 312–13, 314; on *CHAL*, 88, 149; on Chase, 329–30; *Cycle of American Literature*, 331; on Emerson, 334; on Foerster, 134–35; on Hubbell, 150; and *LHUS*, 302–6; on nationalism, 133, 134, 306; on Parrington, 168; reader for *PMLA*, 309

Stalinism, 265, 272, 274, 281, 282, 294

Statesmen: in anthologies, 198

Stearns, Harold, 133; *Civilization in the United States*, 131

Stedman, E. C., 35, 37, 49, 50, 76; *An American Anthology*, 26

Steffens, Lincoln, 48

Stein, Gertrude, 9, 200, 204, 288

Stevens, Wallace, 200

Stoddard, Richard, 51

Stowe, Harriet Beecher, 85, 91, 161

Studies in Philology (journal), 103

Survey courses. *See under* Curriculum, American literature

Surveys: of American literature in curriculum, 193–94, 206–7

Symbol, 21, 285–86, 320, 327–32, 336, 339

Symbolic capital, 363n; the literary as, 29–30; nationalism as, 29–30; publishers' use of, 41

Symbolism, 288, 336

Taine, Hippolyte: on history of English literature, 111, 127, 137

Tarbell, Ida, 48

Taste: class-defined value of, 13, 14, 29, 36, 40; and education, 36; and sensibility, 13, 15

Index

ture, 76; ethnocentrism of, 80–81; *The France of Today*, 79; (with Greenough) *A History of Literature in America*, 65; *A Literary History of America*, 65, 75–82; on society and language, 283–84

West, Cornel, 8

Wharton, Edith, 206–7

Wheatley, Phillis, 72, 92

Whig party: and American history, 42; and democracy, 193; and response to ethnic diversity, 39

Whipple, T. K., 302

Whitman, Walt: and American Idea, 338; and American poetic tradition, 333, 336; in anthologies, 195, 197–98; canonical status of, 180, 181, 183, 202, 241, 350; in curriculum, 205, 206; Foerster on, 146–47; and frontier, 138; Hicks on, 268; and homosexuality, 183; *Leaves of Grass*, 253–54; Matthiessen on, 241, 243, 244, 247, 250, 253–54, 256–57; men of letters on, 37; Mencken on, 130; and New Humanism, 146–47; Popular Front on, 271; in preprofessional histories, 74, 76, 84, 87, 90; Rahv on, 295

Whittier, John Greenleaf: in anthologies, 196, 200; biography of, 186; canonical status of, 94, 180; criticism of, 85, 90–91; as standard author, 26, 39, 74

Williams, Raymond, 54; on reading, 12; on term "literature," 13, 15, 26, 27, 40, 109; on terms "civilization" and "culture," 16

Williams, Stanley, 174, 175, 215, 301; *The American Mind*, 199, 221

Wilson, Christopher: on editorial elite of magazines, 48; on publishing industry and authorship, 47

Wilson, Edmund, 236; *Axel's Castle*, 288; as nonacademic critic, 11, 129

Wilson, Elizabeth, 203

Wilson, Woodrow, 20, 194, 199, 255

Winters, Yvor, 236–37

Wise, Gene: on American Studies, 216; on Parrington, 163–64, 170; on Trilling, 282, 283

Wollstonecraft, Mary, 168

Women: in the academy, 155–56; on ALG boards, 155; in *American Literature*, 182; in anthologies, 196; frontier writing by, 156–62; as Other of academic disciplines, 9; in survey courses, 206; writing by, 347–50

Woodberry, George: on history of American literature, 49; on literary tradition, 62; on literature and race, 55

Woolson, Constance Fenimore, 196

Wordsworth, William: *Michael*, 114

Working class: control of, 34; cultural distinction of, 37; Mattiessen on, 255; as oppositional force, 34, 364n. *See also* Labor movement; Lower class

World War I: and nationalism, 20, 133

World War II: and American literature in the curriculum, 208–9; and American Studies, 208–9; and "discovery" of American civilization, 299; and nationalism, 208, 299, 306

Wright, Louis B., 302–5

Writing: commodification of, 40; distinctions among, 27; and literature, 7, 15, 25, 27; as sacred, 27; value of, 27

Yale Review, 141

Yale University, 153; and American Studies, 151, 208, 213, 312; survey course at, 301

David Shumway is associate professor of literary and cultural studies at Carnegie-Mellon University. He is the author of *Michel Foucault* (1989) and of several articles on disciplinarity, cultural practices, gender, and popular culture.